Dedication

To my wife, Edith; my older daughter, Chinelo; my first son, Uchechukwu;
my second daughter, Ifeoma; and my younger son, Kenechukwu.

Contents

Chapter 4. Tourism and Political Geography in Southern Africa   52
David B. Weaver

Chapter 5. Tourism Policy Formulation in the
Southern African Region   62
Carson L. Jenkins

Part II: The Case Studies of Selected African Countries

Chapter 6. Planning Sustainable Tourism in Ghana   77
Edward Inskeep

Chapter 7. Planning Tourism in a Reconstructing Economy:
The Case of Eritrea   98
Peter M. Burns

Part IV: Future Perspectives

List of Figures

List of Tables

Foreword

Africa. Mention the name and it raises a multitude of thoughts regarding the continent and its enormous diversity of geography and people. It is a continent rich in opportunity but, at the same time, seriously handicapped and hampered by a host of problems. Many of the problems are of its own making; others were inherited—the legacy of colonial times. Africa lies like the giant Gulliver in the kindergarten story, who was tied down on his back with thousands of little stings by the thumb-sized people of Lilliput.

Will the giant be able to lift itself up and begin to fulfill its great promise? It is possible. Many positive and greatly encouraging developments have taken place in Africa during the last years of this century. There is talk, but also real signs, of an African Renaissance. The beginning of the new millennium might just be the beginning of Africa's rebirth.

Three of the most immediate and urgent problems that African leaders will have to address are first, to establish peace, security, and stability; second, to deal with poverty and create jobs; and third, to preserve the environment. It is important to note that tourism is directly linked to all three of these major challenges.

The need for peace, security, and stability speaks for itself. It is only in such a climate that the confidence that is a prerequisite for growth and development will establish itself and strengthen. Tourism can contribute to such a climate. It has the potential to create a better understanding between peoples of different cultures, values, traditions, and customs. It contributes to mutual tolerance and respect. Tourism is a powerful tool for peace.

The link between tourism and poverty lies in the fact that tourism has become the world's largest creator of jobs. These jobs are filled by millions of small entrepreneurs and large numbers of people with no training and few skills. These jobs are in the cities but also spread across the country, in small towns and rural areas. For many developing countries tourism has become the only, or one of the very few, immediate opportunities for generating more jobs and combating poverty.

The importance of tourism as an engine of economic growth and job creation is widely recognized. As a result of greater disposable income and more free time in the developed countries, the industry continues to expand at a rate higher than that of average world economic growth. A recent report by the World Tourism Organization (Tourism: 2020 Vision) forecasts that by the year 2020 there will be 1.6 billion international tourist arrivals, compared to the 625 million in 1998. It is inevitable that growth of this size will have a major impact on the natural, as well as the cultural and social, environment.

The impact on the life-supporting systems that nature provides us with—those ecological processes that form the climate, clean the air and water, regulate water flows, recycle essential elements such as nitrogen and oxygen, create and regenerate soil, and generally keep the planet fit for life—will have to be monitored and managed. Careful and responsible planning and management of the tourism trade will be required.

The natural environment is undoubtedly one of Africa's greatest assets. Its natural heritage, if properly protected and developed sustainably, could prove to be a source of unlimited wealth for African countries. Environment-related tourism (often referred to as ecotourism) is attracting more tourists than any other single activity. Herein lies the great challenge that must be taken up with determination if the 21st century is to become the century of Africa's revival.

It is against the above scenario that the significance of this volume, edited by Dr. Peter Dieke, will be appreciated. First, the publication is the first to link international tourism to Africa's long-term development. Second, it provides a wealth of insights into and information on the theoretical and technical aspects of tourism development in Africa. Third, it gathers contributions offering a wide variety of interdisciplinary perspectives, including practical experiences from a number of destinations. The editor and contributors are to be commended for their useful insights into—in the words of the editor—"a region that, judged by any comparative standards, is underresearched in the tourism development literature."

As the Deputy Secretary-General of the World Tourism Organization (WTO), I warmly welcome *The Political Economy of Tourism Development in Africa*. It will make a valuable contribution to charting the way ahead for Africa's tourism development in the 21st century. It can also be profitably used by tourism students and researchers, government policy-makers, and planners of tourism, and others who are interested in the tourism development process, not only in Africa but also in the wider developed and developing economies. Perhaps, above all, it will complement the work of the WTO in this region of the world.

Dr. Dawid J. de Villiers
Deputy Secretary-General
World Tourism Organization
Madrid, Spain

Acknowledgments

I would like to offer thanks to the many authors who kindly gave up their valuable time to contribute to this volume. Special recognition is given to Professor Carson L. Jenkins who, as my teacher and now an academic colleague, has in many ways been a constant source of inspiration. I am also indebted to Dr. Lee Jolliffe for her useful comments on two of the chapters, coming at a time when I was overwhelmed with the volume of work. Leslie Mitchell was also helpful in converting a number of difficult files. I thank Robert Miranda, the publisher, for covering part of my hotel expenses in New York. All have my gratitude.

Chapter 1

The Nature and Scope of the Political Economy of Tourism Development in Africa

Peter U. C. Dieke

Summary

The purpose of this chapter is threefold: to provide the theoretical orientations for understanding of the political economy of tourism development; to review, within the context of Africa, the relevance of the approach to tourism study; and to identify the region's place in the international tourism marketplace. By reference to differences within and between Africa's subregions with respect to their political economies, the chapter explains variations in performances. Finally, the chapter concludes by presenting an outline of the book structure, focusing on the underlying factors that influence the development of tourism in the region. Perhaps the most important of these is a clear understanding that tourism development in Africa and indeed in developing countries generally cannot meaningfully be analyzed in isolation from other components of society, history, economics, and polity. For example, in the process of decision-making with respect to tourism development, it is necessary to formulate policies based on an analysis of the market and also within the perspective of certain institutions and their modus operandi while taking into account the resources available in the countries and also the vested interests and opinions of various pressure groups. It is also evident from the various chapters that the implementation of tourism policies depends on the responses of private or public institutions and individuals to those policies and the institutions through which these policies are to be implemented. Institutions are thus important in defining tourism issues (e.g., distributional issues, environmental problems and concerns, and cultural matters), in mobilizing resources, in mediating interests, and in implementing tourism policy.

Key words: Implementation barometer; Tourism policy; Policy formulation; Political economy; Tourism development; Africa; Institutional structure; Tourism strategies

Introduction

Africa, as defined in the World Tourism Organization (WTO) classification of countries and regions, refers to the Islamic countries of the northern subregion (excluding Egypt) as well as sub-Saharan Africa (i.e., the central, eastern, southern, and western subregions) and the Indian Ocean Africa islands (Figure 1.1). The continent presently comprises 53 countries with a population of about 800 million people (see Economic Commission for Africa [ECA], 1999a) but is varied in its resources, culture, historical legacies, and economic, social, and political structures. However, the diversity of the countries and subregions should not disguise the common development challenges and travails confronting them, witnessed since the 1960s' political independence era, culminating in the 1980s' "lost decade." The

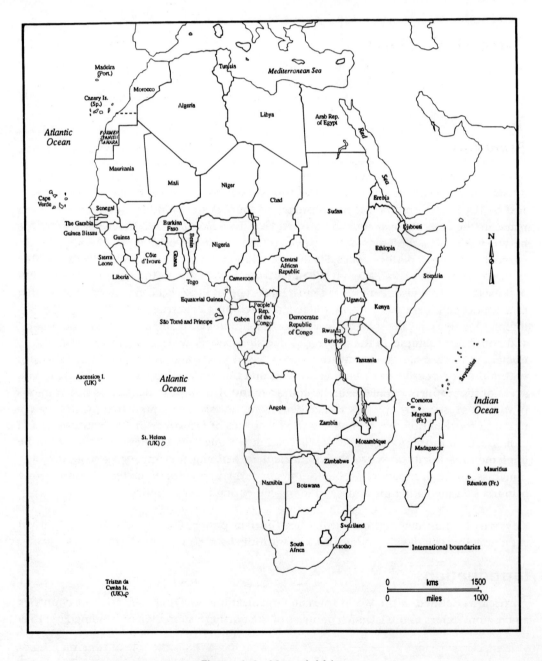

Figure 1.1. Map of Africa.

differences and constraints do have important repercussions for tourism with respect to the level and types of tourism development found in the region and also manifested in the policies, institutional arrangements, and strategies devised for the tourism sector.

First, there are considerable variations in the scale of tourism development in Africa, from the dominant (i.e., most developed) in theoretical tourism development continuum to the Johnny-come-lately (i.e., least developed or late starters). Some countries in the region, for example, Kenya in the east, Mauritius and The Seychelles in the Indian Ocean, Morocco and Tunisia in the north, South Africa and Zimbabwe in the south, and Côte d'Ivoire and Senegal in the west, are well-established, "successful" tourism destinations. There are others, like Nigeria, Cameroon, Eritrea, Sierra Leone, Angola, and Zambia, which, for a number of reasons, have limited tourism development but considerable potential. Second, there is clearly a wide variety of different types of tourism available in the continent—from safari tourism (wildlife, desert), beach tourism, "roots" tourism, to marine tourism. Some others include cultural/heritage and archaeological tourism, ethnic tourism, "overland" tourism (or desert, as noted), and, perhaps to a lesser degree, sex tourism.

This spectrum of contextual "mixes" is perhaps better presented in a multidisciplinary schema that can incorporate a plurality of general situations. Hence, the central theme for this book requires insights and perspectives from history, politics, society, and economy— a political economy—for a number of reasons. One relates to the need to point not only to the differences in the scale and level of tourism but also to the fact that the countries share certain policy planning and strategy orientations. Also, the theoretical and research debate is that

> Discussion of tourism is typically divorced from the historical and political processes that determine development. Debate on the advantages and disadvantages of tourism is conducted without regard to those theories of political economy concerned with persistent poverty and the causes of increasing inequality between and within nations. (S. G. Britton, 1982, p. 332; see also de Kadt, 1979)

In the framework of this book, the argument is that it is important to appreciate the wide range of political, economic, and other internal and external forces and factors influencing tourism development policy in Africa—a region that, judged by any comparative standard, is underresearched in the tourism development literature (see Hyman, Ojo, & Wall, 1980; Lea, 1981). As will be argued shortly, without relating tourism in Africa to such broader perspectives within which tourism development occurs, any analysis of the industry would merely be cosmetic and is perhaps unlikely to advance intellectual debate on tourism and development issues in the region.

Thus, the purpose of this book is to examine four aspects of the dynamics of the political economy of tourism development, particularly in the context of Africa. First, to consider the way tourism has developed in the region and the nature of tourism activities there. Such examinations will include the economic, sociocultural, historical, political geography, and policy frameworks of the development process. Second, by way of some selected country studies, to use the synthesis to appreciate the role of policy for, and planning of, tourism in this context. Third, with relevance to the background analysis, to identify institutional structures and strategic parameters and draw lessons. Finally, to offer perspectives on tourism's implications for long-term economic development dynamics of Africa.

As an introduction, this chapter focuses on the general issues that are of concern in the book and, as a starter, by providing the theoretical orientations of the political economy of tourism development. Then the chapter moves on to consider the role of tourism in economic development, reviews Africa's place in the international tourism market place, and, by reference to differences within and between Africa's subregions with respect to their political economies, explains variations in performances. The chapter ends with an outline of the book's structure.

Conceptualizing the Political Economy of Tourism Development

Definitional Issues

The term "political economy of tourism" (PET) focuses attention on all forms of tourism development, primarily in a developing society. In particular, PET considers the interconnections between politics and economics and their role in economic decision-making and implementation of tourism development programs. The whole purpose here is to underscore the need for a scholarly approach to tourism development somewhat broader than that usually adopted by economists (see Wilkinson, 1997, pp. 11-24). As Todaro (1986, 1996) has acknowledged:

> Political economy goes beyond traditional or simple economics[1] to study, among other things, the social and institutional processes through which certain groups of [mainly] economic and political elites . . . and other interest groups both within and outside these societies . . . influence the allocation of scarce productive resources now and in the future, either exclusively for their own benefit . . . often at the expense of the larger population as well. (p. 10, p. 8)

From the above statement, the following observations relevant to the problematic nature of this volume can be made. First, tourism is an *economic* activity, but, for reasons that will become clear later on, it is important that the analysis of the process of tourism development also be viewed in its political context. This is to take account of the important influence of "power," both economic and political, in the real world of economic decisions and choices in developed and developing countries. Furthermore, tourism development is linked with *policy*, implying action that is conscious in intent and collective in nature (see Edgell, 1990; Hall, 1994; Jenkins, 1991). The argument suggests that "Tourism is a chosen policy. It is not a policy forced upon a reluctant regime by political pressures. . . ." (Richter, 1989, p. 14). The policy choice may stem from several considerations, not least being a lack of viable, alternative development possibilities open to a country. Thus, for many developing countries that are characterized by a shortage of development resources (e.g., finance, human resources, etc.), the positive economic argument of tourism to contribute to development justifies their involvement in the tourism sector.

There is another dimension to the policy question relating to economics that needs stating. Economists are concerned with what policy decisions regarding tourism as a development strategy are appropriate in a given economic situation. These decisions might pertain to attainment of national development objectives such as economic surplus to stimulate development or full employment and therefore increased income. Whatever the situation, there are economic and other consequences for the country and its people that flow from it.

Of course, the converse is that tourism policies are not made just on the basis of economic analysis but are also under the influences of noneconomic, social, historical, and political factors. Moreover, policy decision regarding tourism development, especially in a developing economy, must be put into practice in a society that somehow must accommodate itself to the vested interests of various pressure or special interest groups (SIGs) existing in the internal and external environment of the tourist-receiving host country. In relation to the latter, for example, the influence of international corporations in economic development generally (see Cypher & Dietz, 1997; Meier, 1996) and tourism in particular (see Dunning & McQueen, 1982a) seems to be more important, or at least less transparent and nonsystematic, in developing countries than in the developed countries. Given, therefore, the technical, marketing, purchasing, financial, and managerial economies of scale advantages associated with such foreign interests in the tourism sector, it is not surprising that tourism policies in the tourist-receiving countries will reflect these interests, as epitomized in the metaphor of the "piper."

The third, and related, perspective on the definitional clarification necessary for understanding the complexity of the political economy of tourism development centers on the mechanics of decision taking with administrative processes in the context of *institutions*. This subject has been expounded in greater detail elsewhere (see S. G. Britton, 1982). It will suffice here to say that the institutions, be they local or foreign, public or private, are those related to tourism policy formulation and planning, including the execution and implementation of those policies. Moreover, the operational parameters of the institutions will, to a large extent, be guided by the pulse rate of the SIGs already described. In essence, three key questions are relevant here. First, who participates in the decision-making? Second, how much freedom is allowed in decision-making? Third, what about implementation? These questions are addressed in the section on processes below.

Short Historical Framework

Interest in political economy as a separate sphere of scholarly inquiry is not of recent origin. It emerged in the post-Industrial Revolution era of transition from feudalism to capitalism that occurred in mid-18th century England (see Maddison, 1982). In the formative stages of the field during this period in focus, the influence of some Scottish moralists, notably Hume in his *Essays on Commerce* (1772), Adam Smith in the *Wealth of Nations* (1776), among others, ensured that political economy had a recognized place in the analysis of economic development. Thus, in the words of Cypher and Dietz (1997),

> These classical political economists attempted not only to explain the reasons for the rapid expansion of total economic wealth that accompanied industrialization, but also the enigma of extremes of wealth and poverty that attended this process and the lack of authentic development affecting a large segment of the population. (p. 106)

Within tourism, S. G. Britton (1982) pioneered the analytical study on the political economy of tourism development in developing countries, and with other writers (e.g., de Kadt, 1979; Erbes, 1973; C. L. Jenkins, 1982; Pleumarom, 1994; Truong, 1990) helped shape the nature of tourism research in such societies to this day. This approach was therefore innovative, relative to the earlier analytical studies on tourism that were based on a stand-alone discipline, as C. L. Jenkins (1997a, pp. 55–56) has noted.

About 40 years ago, when scholars embarked on research on tourism, they did so either from an economic perspective, which was concerned with the economic impacts of tourism, or, as sociologists (e.g., de Kadt, 1979) in the mid-1970s, they were concerned with the social impacts arising from tourism development. Only rarely were these issues related to each other. Although tourism writers are still concerned with these issues (Ioannides & Debbage, 1998; C. L. Jenkins, 1997b), the perspectives and context have changed. For instance, from about the early 1980s, especially with the Madrid Conference (see World Tourism Organization/United Nations Environmental Program [WTO/UNEP], 1982), events moved on to incorporate environmental issues in tourism.

Related to Africa, what is also significant (of which more will be discussed later) is the form that tourism research takes today. The situation in the 1990s is that some researchers have begun to analyze tourism from the point of view of regional cooperation and integration (see Dieke, 1998; ECA, 1996a; Teye, 1991) because of the changes closely related to global body politics. In Africa, this process has been given impetus or, as it were, institutional expression, by the 1991 Abuja Treaty (which became operational in 1994) as the nucleus of Africa's development strategy. This treaty led to the setting up of Regional Economic Communities (RECs), which would form the foundation for a Pan African Common Market (see Organization of African Unity [OAU], 1991, 1996, 1998).

The importance of these initiatives for the purposes of our subject is to highlight the influence of economic change on politics and of politics on economic development. The founding fathers of the Abuja Treaty have acknowledged that the power of global change is mediated by local structure with wide-ranging consequences for tourism development in Africa. Given these brief historical points, the questions to answer are: (1) why is it so important to understand tourism development in its political economy context? and (2) what explanations can be advanced for this?

Significance of PET

Reference was made above to policy decisions to encourage tourism development in a country on the basis of tourism's economic potential to contribute to development. It is argued here that such a policy will have implications at different levels, resulting in a situation whereby there are winners and losers. The winners might be those individuals and organizations who welcome the economic and other benefits accruing from tourism; the losers are concerned that, in the words of Richter (1989), "the politics of tourism are not played according to 'the rules' " (p. 2).

The importance that PET has therefore assumed in recent years has been in part a reflection of the changing geopolitical landscape (e.g., the integration of markets in many regions of the world), in part the dynamic scope or nature of tourism, and in part the changing role of government not just in tourism (see C. L. Jenkins, 1994) but also in other economic sectors of global significance (see World Bank, 1997). The approach pursued here adds a further level of explanation. It argues that it is in many ways in the interest of government leaders responsible for tourism and their supporters to pursue a type of development strategy that conforms to the interest group analysis.

At one level (internally) there are the politicians in power and at another (externally) there are also the various pressure groups. In both instances, there is the potential to introduce corruption[2] (see Chalker, 1999; see also "How Corruption is Killing Africa," 1999, pp. 15–41), one of the central features of economic life in many countries, into the explanation of strategy choice for the tourism sector, because of its influence on the structure of the tourism industry, and on the relationship of the individual to the institutional arrangements for the tourism sector. While it is not possible to detail the many economic and political dimensions of tourism in this section with respect to these factors, some general points, many interrelated, can be made.

First, a political economy approach to tourism development differs in many ways from other explanations. As a problem of policy formulation and implementation, it is related to the opportunities created in response to the evolving changes in the global economic networking. The political economy approach may therefore be highly relevant for analyzing these developments. Second, the approach focuses "attention on the formative politi-

cal, economic, social, and institutional processes that influence societal organization . . . (including) a consideration of institutions, notably those related to tourism policy
and planning" (Wilkinson, 1997, pp. 22–23).

Third, as an economic activity, tourism development has both positive and negative
consequences for other aspects of life and society, as noted above. However, an economist
cannot exempt himself/herself from problems of the industry (e.g., bureaucracy, the imbalance in benefits sharing marked by winner-takes-all imperative, the relationship between the private and public sectors of the tourism sector, both in terms of their sizes and
the influence exercised from each sector on the other) when in fact the problems are
inseparable from a structure of the industry determined by his/her policy for tourism
development. Perhaps, finally, the existence of an environment in which interest groups
become the conduit for individuals to belong to patronage networks is an area of concern.
This is because this situation has the potential to stimulate corruption, as noted above, a
vice believed to be a main influence on strategy choice. Thus, to appreciate the importance of the foregoing and subsequent comments in terms of a common thread in all the
chapters in this book, it is important to review the subject in the context of an approach
format.

Processes of PET

In this section it is important to identify and analyze the broad principles involved in
the political economy of tourism development. The sole purpose here is to offer additional conceptual insights into the thread linking the various chapters and also to complement previous analyses above. In this respect, the political economy of tourism development can be further conceptualized or studied as a three-stage process: situation analysis,
decision-making, and implementation. It needs to be emphasized that the issues to examine differ from stage to stage, each offering examples of the processes of the political
economy of tourism in developing countries, taking into account the differing contexts
within which tourism development takes place, as discussed below.

Situation Analysis

By "situation analysis" is meant an analysis of the structure of the tourism market, the
interdependent relations among the various activities and entities that constitute the tourism industry, and the consequent problems arising from these relationships. This interdependence includes both international and domestic relations, involving private and public
sector interests in the development of the tourism sector. In addition to an awareness of
interdependent relations, there are several interrelated factors that need to be considered
in such an analysis.

The first is the question of the development stage of a country because of its bearing on
the stage of tourism development in the country. This is a subject that has evoked some
debate in the tourism literature in recent times, in relation to the meaning and significance of the concept (Sinclair, 1998). Further exposition seems unnecessary, save to say
that from the perspective of developing countries, the "level of development" controversy
highlights several interrelated issues pertinent to this book. These include the extent of
the impact of tourism on a country that, in itself, will determine how the host culture and
society can cope with the values and roles needed to operate a successful tourism sector.
Another issue is the nature of tourism: the suggestion is that the nature of tourism development covers a wide spectrum, such as the type of visitors the country wants to attract;
what facilities and ancillary services to provide or are indeed available; what organizations or institutions should influence the tourism system; and how the trigger market
might induce demand (Dieke, 1989).

A second important aspect of the analysis is the relative role of the public sector vis-à-vis the private sector in tourism development. The evidence suggests that, both for reasons of equity and on grounds of economic efficiency, in most developing countries the influence of the public sector in policy formulation and planning in the tourism sector is considerable (C. L. Jenkins & Henry, 1982). Although this situation has not changed much in several years, it needs to be stated that the relative weight of government in each country varies on the basis of the country's history, economic policy, and political orientation (see S. G. Britton, 1982). In recent years, however, in many developing countries, privatization has become fashionable because of the inefficiency associated with government-owned and -operated tourism enterprises. The message is, quite simply, that "government should not do what the private sector is able and willing to do" (C. L. Jenkins, 1994, p. 8).

Just as the analysis acknowledges the changing role of government in tourism in the context of trend changes in the global economy, so too is the need to recognize existence of the different scales of tourism. The lesson from all this is that tourism development policy measures are chosen out of an array of instruments available, including those that, although potential, have not been used but could be deployed in the future. The difficulty, as ever, is that the experience of less developed countries seems to be rarely used when policies are developed elsewhere (Dieke, 1993a), possibly because their experience of tourism is somehow limited.

Fourth, what is also important in tourism development is an understanding of the institutional or regulatory framework, recognizing that the structure is not immutable. The implication must be that there is nothing in the tourism structure that is written on tablets of stone, considering that policy priorities change over a development period (see Jafari, 1986), as was the case in The Gambia relatively recently (Dieke, 1993b). For instance, institutional changes might permit ownership of assets (e.g., allowing foreign investors to buy land rather than lease it), or perhaps joint ventures and possibly the privatization of government-owned tourism enterprises. Such changes in ownership and power of acquisition of land becomes significant where tourism is used to open up more remote areas of the country, where perhaps local investors may be unwilling to invest. Another may pertain to where a foreign investor is allowed to build and locate in an area not specifically designated for tourism, given the need to attract entrepreneurs with capital to the sector. In the latter case there is transparency in liberalizations of certain restrictions that have been imposed by the government or its agencies responsible for the tourism sector.

A fifth political economy issue associated with tourist development is the setting of clear objectives for the tourism sector, as possible prerequisites for future policy and strategy development. This is because the effectiveness of tourism vis-à-vis the wider economic sectors to contribute to development needs to be appraised in the light of these objectives. Therefore, the purpose of tourism development may be defined in terms of maximizing or minimizing economic, political, and social objective functions, which are usually articulated in national development plans. Economic objectives might be related to using tourism, for instance, to diversify the economic base of a country, to enhance per capita gross national product (GNP) or gross domestic product (GDP) while simultaneously seeking to minimize leakages because of imports of materials to support tourism activity.

Political objectives center on maintaining friendly international relations between countries, as Richter (1989) has argued; or to unify a people who by default, historically, have been separated from their indigenous homelands and are now dispersed in many parts of the globe. The Jews (because of the Holocaust) and black Africans (through slavery and the slave trade) are examples of the Diaspora phenomenon. The role of economists in all this is to clarify the costs and benefits of pursuing such political objects. Social welfare function of tourism might be the provision of health facilities to benefit not just foreign tourists but the host community as well.

Sixth, further to the economic and political objectives, three caveats can be made. First, for reasons noted below, it is reasonable to segregate the objectives with reference to a time horizon: for example, short-term (within 5 years), medium-term (between 5 and 7 years), and long-term (beyond 10 years) objectives. Analytically, these time horizons correspond to Schumpeter's (1965) concept of three business cycles or waves. Schumpeter's thesis is important for tourism development because it focuses not only on the choice of policy objectives, but perhaps also on the extent to which the objectives are implemented. Just as businesses cannot be run in isolation of global economic trends, so too is the development of tourism influenced by fluctuating fortunes of the tourist-generating countries and therefore very dependent on the tourist "trigger" markets to achieve the stated objectives.

In considering the political economy of tourism development, it is one thing to identify the officially stated objectives in their time horizons and quite another to realize the objectives. This is the second caveat to be made. In order, therefore, to justify the inclusion of particular objectives it is important to examine the extent to which the gaps between stated and achieved objectives might be bridged. More fundamentally, also, there are mutual relations among the short-, medium-, and long-term objectives, each reinforcing the other. For instance, in the same way that short-term objectives are important to help achieve the medium-term objectives, so also are the medium-term targets a prerequisite for attaining long-term tourism development objectives. In terms of length of period, the linchpin of all the objectives is the degree of political implications—the longer the time frame, the more political the implications of the objectives. It is also useful to set the objectives to reflect the international realities and, as previously discussed, also the stage of development.

The third caveat regarding tourism development objectives is the question of how the three levels of objectives (i.e., the time frames) interact among themselves. It is usual to find that different objectives (e.g., foreign exchange earnings) may contradict the objective of maintaining strict religious observance in the face of mass tourism. One possible explanation for this inconsistency in objective is the problem of coordination, in part because different objectives are maintained for the same period or because of failure to prioritize the objectives of the three periods as well as those in the same period. This situation is relevant in cases involving, for example, noneconomic international relations. Therefore, the political economy issue to consider is not so much how a country can reconcile such contradictions or trade-offs among the various objectives as it is perhaps what policy measures are taken to resolve them.

Seventh, in analyzing the environment within which tourism development occurs, attention should also focus not only on the likely effects of objective policy construct but on how quickly these effects are realized. Put differently, it means that the speed with which the affected individuals are able to adjust themselves to the economic, political, and other impacts arising from tourism development objectives is critical. On this basis, one might therefore argue that tourism policies need to reflect long-term objectives rather than the short- and medium-term objectives if a final choice of tourism as a development strategy has to be made. Additionally, such a decision ought to be based also on a careful analysis of the interrelations between various policy measures and the three levels of objectives. In the final analysis, the structure of the tourism market should be a reflection of both the characteristics of the sector and its international linkages.

The Process of Decision-Making

The preceding section detailed the environment within which tourism development takes place. It is expected that this analysis of the tourism market will help to identify the potential for future development and, as a consequence, set out broad parameters on development. These matters are the major concern of this and subsequent sections: to consider the nature of, and the need for, development strategies for the tourism sector.

The use of the word "strategies" connotes that countries differ in the nature and scale of the problems, current and future, facing them in developing tourism. Although strategy development embraces both policy formulation and implementation (C. L. Jenkins, 1991), in this study, however, a third dimension will be added, which is to examine not only the processes involved in both counts but also to examine the constraints on their realization. This is because of the need to situate the issues within a political economy context relevant to tourism development in the less developed world. This section therefore concentrates on policy formulation, while the next deals with the tourism policy implementation processes.

The formulation of policies is hardly an easy task, especially in such a diverse sector as tourism. This exercise will obviously involve the question of how tourism interacts with other sectors of the economy (previously discussed). Policies are formulated through careful consideration of alternative possibilities. Judgements involve political, economic, social, and environmental considerations—the key inputs to tourism development. This brief background to the nature of tourism policy formulation has prompted C. L. Jenkins (1991) to pose two questions: "why is such a policy necessary? and who should formulate the tourism policy?" (p. 62).

The Lomé IV Convention ("Lomé IV Convention," 1996) has strongly emphasized the need for policies related to the tourism sector: "Specific tourism development measures shall aim at the definition, adaptation and development of appropriate policies at national, regional, sub-regional and international level . . ." (p. 36). Lickorish and Jenkins (1997) have also sought to exemplify the importance of developing a tourism policy by raising a number of questions in the following way: "What type of product can be supplied? What type of tourism product should be supplied? How should tourism be marketed? Which type of tourists might be attracted? What are the likely impacts arising from policy choices?" (pp. 172–174).

There are no simple answers to these questions. However, the main issues arising from the questions that pertain to policy guidelines for the tourism sector might be usefully summarized as follows. Tourism provides opportunities to contribute to economic development in terms of foreign exchange earnings, employment, and income generation, as well as contribution to government revenues, and as a development catalyst. However, there are important social, cultural, environmental, and economic implications stemming from its development. For this reason, it is necessary to manage the growth of the tourism sector and to have clear guidelines to ensure that growth is compatible with national and sectoral objectives. A tourism policy provides the required guidelines and the reference point against which any future development in the sector should be evaluated.

With respect to the second question (i.e., who should formulate the tourism policy?), a number of suggestions have been proffered, ranging from the government sector to the private sector to a combination of both. Again, the Lomé IV Convention, with respect to the African, Caribbean, and Pacific (ACP) countries, for example, is explicit. The Convention clearly indicates a role for the private sector:

> The aim should be to support the ACP States' efforts to derive maximum benefit from national, regional and international tourism in view of tourism's impact on economic

development and to stimulate private financial flows from the Community and other sources into the development of tourism in the ACP States. Particular attention shall be given to the need to integrate tourism into the social, cultural and economic life of the people. ("Lomé IV Convention, 1996, p. 36).

There is another suggestion that, at a more fundamental level, there is in developing countries a place for the government sector in three areas: developmental, planning, and investment roles (C. L. Jenkins, 1997a). In exercising its developmental role, government acts as an entrepreneur investing in and operating hotels for tourists, occasioned by the need to provide basic facilities to kick-start tourism in developing countries, without which the sector's material objectives cannot be achieved. In the planning process, government, as custodian of the nation, makes allocative resource decisions based on a rational and prioritized basis, especially in the expectation of future benefits. In its investment function government provides the facilitating infrastructure that is needed to permit subsequent developments in the tourism sector to materialize (e.g., the provision of access facilities to the country, etc.).

However, in recent years the traditional role of government has been changing. To a large extent this might be a consequence of the move towards the free-market liberalism—a trend that is global and is also supported by several international donor agencies. There are many reasons for this, not least being the imperfections that typically have characterized or dubbed government-run enterprises, including tourism, not just in the developing world but also in many parts of the developed countries (C. L. Jenkins, 1994; World Bank, 1997). In particular, the consensus now is that "government does not have the market-based understanding or flexibility to react to market signals" (C. L. Jenkins, 1994, p. 8).

The foregoing idea should not be interpreted to mean that the state is not relevant in tourism development in less developed countries; quite the contrary. Rather, it merely relaunches or redefines the state in a new focus within the tourism sector. If anything, government has ultimate control over the sector—in what is more usually described as an "enabling" or facilitating role, reflecting the view which has been expressed that "Tourism development cannot be left to market forces alone if national benefits are to be secured. . . . For success there must be a public–private sector partnership" (Lickorish & Jenkins, 1997, p. 183). In policy formulation for the tourism sector, government should also liaise with the private sector to create a tourism identity or image that is projected for the country, and should also be proactive by setting relevant policy guidelines, including, as necessary, monitoring the sector's trends and development growth.

From the above analysis, it is obvious that in the processes of tourism policy formation in developing countries prime emphasis is given to two key questions: one is explicit and the other implicit. The explicit question is: who participates in decision-making? The implicit question is: how much freedom is allowed in decision-making (i.e., how are decisions made)? These are the kinds of questions that need answering and they are taken up in the rest of this section. Sufficient to say at the onset that, in the main, the processes of tourism policy formation are chosen within the framework of certain institutions and their modus operandi while taking into account the vested interests and opinions of various pressure groups.

Broadly speaking, tourism-making processes in developing countries have many participants, including, as seen, the government and private sectors. Reference was also made to the existence of domestic and international pressure groups or SIGs as a credible force in this process—an area of study on which the literature on tourism development has remained silent to date. However, in this section only a "package tour" of SIGs is examined and, as will be argued, SIGs offer one possible explanation for the particular choice of tourism policy pursued in developing countries. By their nature, SIGs exhibit a number of institutional characteristics (e.g., corruption is endemic, state autonomy tends to be low) that promote a type of inward-looking development strategy that is doomed to failure (see Kruer, 1996). In consequence, SIGs will be less concerned with policy formulation and more with particular administrative decisions.

Needless to say, SIGs are not necessarily big business groups only. They also include representatives of the specific interests of a certain social group (e.g., professional associations, trade associations, informal group, etc.) who lobby the government on behalf of their members. How much influence these pressure groups have on choice of policies will, to a greater or lesser degree, depend not just on their characteristics but also their positions in the country. For instance, in many developing countries, government enterprises and their managers are important pressure groups. Government officials, the army, or even bureaucrats in ministries whose various activities impinge on tourism exercise considerable influence on tourism policy matters. Hence, government bureaucrats participate in decision-making on policies: first, as tourism "experts" or representatives of governmental interest, and second, as representatives, though not exclusively, of their own ministerial interests.

The success of the SIGs in terms of market and political power will further depend on a range of factors related to the organization (e.g., internal cohesion, convergence of objectives, and ethnic homogeneity of members) and circumstances surrounding SIGs (e.g., degree of competition, social mobility and the class structure, international mobility of labor and capital, ethnic and occupation composition of the country, and international competition in trade relations). These factors will be dissimilar and disproportional between countries but no doubt will progress or impede the process of decision-making on tourism policy formation, including policy implementation as examined below.

The Process of Implementation

Once policies have been determined to provide guidelines for the future development of the tourism sector in developing countries, the next logical step in developing tourism is to implement the policies. Managing the implementation process has four aspects: resource allocation, personnel provision, and delineating the roles of the public and private sectors. As will be discussed below, the adopted policies are often further modified in the implementation process in light of these constraints. These four factors are each considered in turn below, together with an assessment of the difficulties associated with each implementation barometer and perhaps possible ways to overcome these issues and concerns.

The importance of an adequate *budget* provision for the tourism sector cannot be overemphasized (see World Tourism Organization [WTO], 1996a), as arguably the level of funding allocation will make or break the tourism policy implementation process. The word "adequate" is relative. First, the amount of budget considered appropriate is determined by the state of a country's development stage and available resources, and the significance of the tourism sector within the overall national economy. The budget should be also assessed in relation to a country's future tourism targets (e.g., in visitor arrival numbers). Second, it is often too easy to simply ask government for a higher budget for tourism: government has many demands on its available resources, given the deteriorating economic and financial position of most developing countries.

At any rate, a sufficient budget is needed for a variety of reasons, which include inter alia the need to: upgrade service standards in the tourism sector; diversify products and markets; provide training and perhaps recruitment of new workers to the sector; secure the physical facilities and infrastructure to support future expansion of tourism development; improve the sector's performance particularly, as noted, in the areas of market research, promotion, and product development; and permit future sustained development of the tourism sector. In all of these cases the rationale is understandable:

> In a highly competitive market [a developing country] needs to protect its market share, should attempt to diversify its markets and launch new products. This costs money. To do nothing is simply to be the servant of market forces without any attempt at proactive management of external forces. (C. L. Jenkins, 1990, p. 8)

These are factual statements and the phrase "to protect its market share" is important: for countries to be competitive in the international tourism market they must provide internationally acceptable facilities and should develop destination distinctiveness to protect against substitution possibilities.

Conversely, adequate budget allocation is one thing, and the kind of uses to which the budget is put and how much of it is actually spent in implementation quite another. These are arguments that might point to the efficiency of government tourism policy programs and the potential of a "hidden hand" at work. The conclusion from all this must be that, in practice, things do not always work as planned and so the thorny issue of adequate budget may never be realized. For one thing, budget is an important item in the development plan of many developing countries. In these countries, one finds that the government in power retains discretionary power to reallocate any budget, described in civil service jargon as the "process of viament." This process allows the government of the day ultimate power to reallocate any budget item, including tourism, to another place for some other, perhaps unexplained, purpose. We also find that SIGs, for whatever reasons, may try to prevent the policies from being implemented. Still, there may be cases of misallocation or misuse of the estimated allocations, which often occurs in the process of implementation.

What the above situation demonstrates is that without realistic budget and the political support to see the implementation process through, the National Tourist Organization (NTO) will be unable to stimulate the development of the tourism sector, as its authority will be undermined or ineffective and in consequence tourism policies as envisaged will not be achieved, as a recent study on the subject has shown (WTO, 1996).

A second prerequisite for tourism policy implementation is the availability of well-managed organizations of qualified *personnel* to undertake, manage, and deliver the implementation process. The personnel may be government and private business or organizations and individuals, with the latter category being usually described as "the trades" (Lickorish & Jenkins, 1997). Without question, cooperation or the extent of relationship between and among the various agencies is one litmus test in the success of policy implementation. This is particularly relevant in a situation in developing countries where government resources are limited. Another success factor may be the capacity and discipline of government officials entrusted with tourism activities to play the part expected of them, and the timing and speed to realize the policies.

To minimize, if not completely overcome, the absence of implementing expertise, governments of developing countries face two options: either to use international sources to supply technical assistance (e.g., support from the European Union, United Nations Development Program, and WTO) or, as Lickorish and Jenkins (1997) have suggested, "to use a counterpart training initiative" (p. 179). Either way, there are good and bad aspects to the matter. First, the use of foreign support has the advantage of bringing an element of objectivity to the implementing exercise, but there is the cost incurred particularly related to the leakage of the foreign exchange component of the process. As regards the apprenticeship scheme, apart from the gestation period involved, Lickorish and Jenkins (1997) have also suggested the possibility that "the local person will gather sufficient knowledge and expertise to continue the implementation process after the specialist consultant has left" (p. 179).

The reality is that, in developing countries, once the foreign consultant leaves, it is not surprising that the implementation process is discontinuous or that "the counterpart is transferred to other duties or that he has not acquired sufficient expertise or skills" (Lickorish & Jenkins, 1997, p. 179). To these difficulties will be added others, including a change of government, either through a military coup d'état (Africa is taken as a case in point) or a democratic process with implications for continuity. In the latter case, possibly the local counterpart may be a political appointee who then steps aside once his political master is no longer holding a political office. Such changes of government might also result in the dissolution of statutory bodies or boards, including those responsible for tourism.

A third crucial factor that may determine the implementation of tourism policies is *organizational* (i.e., what government offices are responsible for this task). On this perspective, it can be argued that the more bureaucratic the organizational structure, the more difficult it will be for the system to function effectively and efficiently, particularly related to the speed of implementing the policies. One study has shown, though in a different context, that the bureaucratic pyramid tends to be smaller in less developed countries (Ichimura, 1983). This means a clear division of responsibility to the extent that no individual unit head has too many persons reporting to him.

To some degree, this characterization is also true in a multifaceted economic activity like tourism, which is regulated from more than one government ministry or parastatal. As such, one finds that different activities in the tourism sector (e.g., infrastructure provision, transport, statistics, health, etc.) fall under the ambit or umbrella of different organizations. A consequence of this diversity and varying inputs might be that coordination of action takes time, if not difficult and ineffective, with wider implications for control over operational standards in the tourism sector. Amidst this morass one also finds that what policies exist for the tourism sector are difficult to implement, at least without a struggle, not only because, as already noted, of a lack of qualified human resources, but the difficulty of coordinating the various ministries, parastatals, and other organizations and agencies whose respective role in this regulatory function impinges on building a strong tourism development profile. But then what is the role of the private sector in all this?

Finally, the aspect of the *responses of the private sector* to tourism policies will be one main determinant of the future success of the policies in developing countries. For instance, the private sector operators, being closest to the market, will be best placed to guide capital investment in the tourism sector. Such an investment is usually centered on the provision of revenue-earning or -generating amenities (e.g., accommodation, transportation services, shopping, etc.). Without such profit potential and the provision of the amenities, it is doubtful whether private sector involvement in the sector will be secured or guaranteed, let alone seeing tourism as a viable development option.

Apart from expectation of profit, another key consideration in private sector support for tourism policies is related to business confidence, defined as a complex combination of objective "(dis)incentive" factors and subjective "confidence" factors (see International Finance Corporation [IFC], 1980, p. 12), which collectively can stimulate or constrain the implementation of tourism policies. A number of examples can be given to illustrate this idea.

A lack of business confidence in any given country is related to "objective" conditions: for example, political instability; government or its agencies' pronouncements accusing investors of exploitation and profiteering; the public service bureaucracy is unhelpful, obstructive, or even hostile to investors, resulting in unnecessary delays in obtaining various types of clearances. Subjective conditions might arise in a situation whereby the business community has fears that government policies and practices may change for the worse in the future. In these instances, the foreign tourism investors may feel vulnerable, exposed, and their response may be one or all of the following possibilities: take their investment elsewhere; collude with the locals to encourage corrupt practices; where the economy is not fully monetized, tacitly promote "black market" practices.

Investor confidence also requires certain other conditions (e.g., incentive schemes) to be met or in place as a basis for that support. Notable among these schemes are the following. First, capital reduction incentives aimed at reducing the capital cost of building the tourism asset (e.g., waiving duties on imported construction material, or offering development finance at below market rates of interest). Second, there is the operating cost reduction incentive, which essentially focuses on reducing the cost of operating the facility (e.g., offering working capital at subsidized interest rates vis-à-vis other loan sources available in the open market; giving training grants). Third, government can provide capital mobility protection package by giving investors guarantees relating to, for example, repatriation of capital or repatriation of profits. These "bread-and-butter" issues are equally critical in securing private sector support for government tourism policy programs.

Before returning to a discussion of how these conceptual issues apply to Africa, it is pertinent to examine and consider the place of tourism in the global, national, and regional economic development efforts.

The *Prima Facie* Case: Tourism in Economic Development

In the last 30 years tourism has developed to become one of the major world economic activities. Three global economic indicators help to underscore the expansion and significance of international tourism, including inter alia, GNP, merchandise exports, and trade in services. For instance, the latest statistics from the World Tourism Organization (WTO, 1998a) show that in 1997 international tourism accounted for approximately 1.5% of world GNP, 8% of world merchandise exports by value, and 35% of the world exports of services. This growth pattern in international tourism has consequent impact on employment.

One area of the positive impact of international tourism is in the hotel subsector, which created close to 11.3 million jobs globally in 1997 (WTO, 1998a). If historical trends are to be believed, the forecast is that international tourism will continue to expand in volume (arrivals) and value (receipts) terms, for the following reasons (WTO, 1998b). It is estimated that 613 million tourists traveled worldwide in 1997, a growth rate of 3.1% in comparison with 1996 and 5.5% in 1996 over 1995, and by the year 2020 arrivals will rise to about 1.6 billion. It is further estimated that US$444 billion was generated in international tourism in 1997 (2.2% higher than 1996) and similarly earnings in international tourism will increase to US$2 trillion in 2020.

An important aspect of international tourism demand is the flow patterns and the relative shares by regions and countries in total movement. There is a heavy concentration of tourist movement and therefore tourists in the traditional tourism regions (e.g., Europe and North America). However, there are other emerging regions, the newly industrializing countries of the developing world, which have increased their share of the market at the expense of the traditional generating countries. This global redistribution in the foci of tourism activities, spurred by economic growth in the emerging countries, has created not only an awareness of new destinations but has also led to travel flows on a geographic basis (i.e., intraregional travel). The situation in East Asia and the Pacific region in 1997 is instructive.

During this period, the region recorded about 15% on international tourist arrivals and also as much as 19% of tourist earnings, a respective increase of 11.2% and 14.6% in 1990 (WTO, 1998a). In the same vein, following market liberalization in some countries of Eastern Europe (e.g., the Czech Republic, Poland, Hungary), tourism's significance to the local economies of these countries should not be underestimated.

Further to the foregoing point about intraregional tourism, one finds that 82% of global tourism in 1997 was dominated by this trend (e.g., in the African region where 30% of the total movement in 1997 was intraregional travel) (WTO, 1998c). Among the many factors making this kind of travel possible, the following should be recognized (United Nations Conference on Trade and Development [UNCTAD], 1998a): geographic closeness to the major source markets; reduction in air travel cost for long-haul destinations, thereby enhancing further reductions in tour packages (although international transport is a major source of tourism-induced revenue; air fare's significance in relation to broader tourism expenditure is marginal); and perhaps, above all the fact that the emerging economies, as seen, tend to target what Bryden (1973) has described as "low volume of high spending tourists," as reflected in the high quality of product they offer (e.g., accommodation, transport, and food). In the African context the success of South Africa, Kenya, and Zimbabwe attests to this idea.

In the area of world trade in services, developing countries have faired better than the rest of the world. In fact, between 1980 and 1996 the developing countries registered a positive balance in the travel account, rising from US$4.6 billion in 1980 to US$69.9 billion in 1996, a dramatic increase attributed to increased inbound tourism mainly to Asia and the Pacific Rim countries, and in Africa (UNCTAD, 1998b). While the expansion has benefited developing regions, this has been on an unequal basis and thus highlights a heavy concentration of both tourist arrivals and tourism receipts within and between developing countries (see WTO, 1998a, 1998c). Within the Asia–Pacific Rim, Singapore and Hong Kong (China) received more tourists and also earned more from tourism than the combined performance of Indonesia, South Asia, and Thailand in 1997. For Africa, the region's tourist arrivals tripled those of Singapore in 1997, but tourism contributed about 8% more than Singapore. On the surface, these figures are impressive; however, a recent UNCTAD study (1998a) concludes that developing countries accounted for less than 30% of tourism receipts in 1996.

Until now, discussion of tourism has focused on international tourism, leaving domestic tourism from any consideration in relation to scale, characteristics, or even significance. A distinction has to be made between the two markets and their importance in development explained. The basic distinction between domestic and international tourism by definition is whether or not the trip (for recreation or business reasons) is taken within or outside national boundaries. While domestic tourism is a trip taken within the frontiers of a country, international tourism, on the other hand, implies the crossing of a national frontier. Whatever the dichotomy, both markets are important for several reasons (see Lickorish & Jenkins, 1997, pp. 52–53). Although domestic tourism accounts for about 80% of all tourism activity, governments of most developing countries would rather promote international instead of domestic tourism. The reasons are simple.

As noted previously, foreign visitors create foreign exchange earning possibilities for developing destinations that are lacking in development resources (e.g., finance). Foreign exchange earning potential is a national tourism development priority objective. While domestic tourism does not provide such opportunities, it does of course lead mainly to a distribution of national income. Another important area is that the domestic tourist has lower per visit spending, but also has greater sympathy for local cultural norms than the international tourist. Both domestic and international tourists "generate employment, income, contribute to regional development" (Lickorish & Jenkins, 1997, p. 53). These issues are examined further below.

In addition to the generation of foreign exchange, there are other economic stimuli that enhanced tourism activity can generate. Such add-on (or multiplier and spillover) benefits to the developing countries are, as stated, in the jobs created and therefore incomes earned. Many of the jobs, especially at the threshold level, are of either unskilled or semiskilled nature. The basic question to consider is not whether tourism jobs have these characteristics but whether the unemployed in developing countries are better off without any jobs at all. Considering rapidly growing populations and high levels of unemployment among the youths in many developing countries, a prime consideration must be to get these people into work.

Therefore, given these benefits from tourism, it is not surprising to observe that increasingly tourism is having a major impact on the economic development efforts in many developing countries. In consequence, in these countries, the traditional economies (e.g., subsistence agricultural production) are now giving way to tourism, thereby making some countries in the Caribbean more reliant on the tourism sector as a viable mode of economic diversification. However, the downside is that tourism as a development option is not without some criticisms, particularly of leakages of foreign exchange on which the UNCTAD (1998b) has shed more light:

> Leakages of foreign exchange earnings are a major obstacle to the positive contribution of tourism to development. Leakage is the process whereby part of the foreign exchange earnings generated by tourism, rather than being retained by tourist-receiving countries, is either retained by tourist-generating countries or remitted back to them. It takes the form of profit, income and royalty remittances; payments for the import of equipment, materials and capital and consumer goods to cater for the needs of international tourists; the payment of foreign loans; various mechanisms for tax evasion; and overseas promotional expenditures. (p. 6)

Another criticism of tourism-led development strategy points to weak backward linkages between tourism and other sectors of the economy (i.e., intersectoral linkages) with consequent impact on low employment and income multipliers in part because of increased imports. Furthermore, as a risky, "candyfloss industry," tourism is not immune from natural disasters or even economic downturns in the source markets. If anything demand is income elastic.

In addition, tourism does not thrive in an environment in which foreign visitors are insensitive to social and cultural norms of host communities. As C. L. Jenkins (1997b) puts it, perhaps for some unexplained reasons, "international tourists do not so much *integrate* with local communities but rather *confront* them" (p. 4). In this situation, two reactions are inevitable: the locals may reject foreign tourist behavior patterns or they may accept or adopt them. Either way, tourism is known to stir up a number of effects, encapsulated in such buzz words: "social demonstration effect," "IRRIDEX," and other similar catchphrases. The economic, social, and cultural fallout from tourism development raises questions about the development impacts of tourism in developing countries.

The analyses described have highlighted a number of policy challenges of an economic, political, social, and even environmental nature that are relevant at the levels of the tourism trade itself, the governments, and the international community. These matters are the subject of a detailed examination in the concluding chapter. For the moment, however, prime emphasis is on examining how the general principles of "political economy" as described are applicable to the development of tourism in Africa and these are taken up in the following section.

PET and Its Relevance to Africa

Within the scope of our subject, the pattern of tourism development in African countries can be appreciated by examining the countries' decision-making styles in terms of political liberty and economic activity. Political liberty because of the rather centralized and consequent restrictive nature of political processes in some of these countries, and economic activity given the importance of the market in tourism development. In both counts, the message is that a permissive environment of civil society and economic stability is fundamental to the development of tourism. Otherwise, an analogy of pursuing "*perestroika* without *glasnost*" (Dieke, 1995, p. 91) might be a relevant conclusion. At any event, two questions will be central to the analysis: first, who participates in the tourism decision-making activity? and second, how much influence does each participant exert on the process? But in order to contextualize the issues, a review of the African tourism market situation seems necessary.

Market Analysis

The extent and impact of international tourism, as with Africa's market shares in the total movement and receipts in 1998, have been noted. Within the African region, the dispersion of tourism arrivals and revenues by subregional groupings in 1998 is shown in Table 1.1. North Africa had the highest share of traffic (34.6%) and revenue (33%), followed by southern Africa (30.8%, 30.9%) and eastern Africa (23.1%, 25.4%), with western Africa (9.5%, 9.6%) and middle Africa (1.9%, 0.9%) trailing behind.

In terms of tourist source regions (see WTO, 1999, p. 36-37), almost 40% of all visits in 1998 originated within the region (i.e., intraregional tourism), with Europe accounting for

Table 1.1. Tourism Trends by Subregions: 1995-1998

Subregions	Tourist Arrivals (000s)	% Change Over	Market Share of Total Africa (%)		Tourist Receipts (US$m)	% Change Over	Market Share of Total Africa (%)	
	1998	1997	1995	1998	1998	1997	1995	1998
Eastern	5,761	7.7	21.7	23.1	2,426	5.75	23.4	25.4
Middle	483	7.81	1.4	1.9	82	5.13	1.7	0.9
Northern	8,623	7.79	38.7	34.6	3,176	9.90	38.1	33.3
Southern	7,671	7.94	29.9	30.8	2,950	2.54	28.1	30.9
Western	2,365	4.97	8.3	9.5	917	4.23	8.5	9.6
Total Africa	24,903	7.5	100.0	100.0	9,551	5.9	100.0	100.0

Eastern: Burundi, The Comoros, Djibouti, Ethiopia, Kenya, Madagascar, Malawi, Mauritius, Mozambique, Réunion, Seychelles, Somalia, Uganda, Tanzania, Zambia, Zimbabwe.
Middle: Angola, Cameroon, Central Africa Republic, Chad, Congo (Brazzaville), Equitorial Guinea, Gabon, Sao Tomé & Principé, Democratic Republic of Congo (Kinshasa).
Northern: Algeria, Morocco, Sudan, Tunisia.
Southern: Botswana, Lesotho, Namibia, South Africa, Swaziland.
Western: Bénin, Burkina Faso, Cape Verde, Côte d'Ivoire, The Gambia, Ghana, Guinea, Guinea Bissau, Liberia, Mauritania, Niger, Nigeria, Sénégal, Sierra Leone, Togo.
Source: World Tourism Organization (1999, pp. 14-29).

Table 1.2. Top Five Destinations in Africa: 1998

Rank	Country	Tourist Arrivals (000s)	% Change Over 1977	Market Share of Total Africa (%)
1	South Africa	5,981	10.0	24.0
2	Tunisia	4,718	10.7	18.9
3	Morocco	3,243	5.6	13.0
4	Zimbabwe	1,600	7.0	6.4
5	Kenya	951	–5.0	4.3

Source: World Tourism Organization (1999, p. 31).

about 36% of the total arrivals market. The remaining flows were, in descending order of importance, from the Americas (3.6%), Middle East (3.3%), and Asia/Pacific (2.8%). Share of total European arrivals by subregional groupings in 1998 was: northern Africa (53%), eastern Africa (22%), southern Africa (13%), western Africa (10%), and middle Africa (1.5%).

The leading five destinations and earners from tourism in 1998 are shown in Tables 1.2 and 1.3. South Africa took a very high proportion of total arrivals (24%), followed by the two northern countries Tunisia (18%) and Morocco (13.0%) and the two eastern countries Zimbabwe (6.4%) and Kenya (4.3%). In receipt terms, again South Africa (24.8%) topped the list, with Tunisia (losing share) and Morocco (gaining dominance) alternating with each other. Mauritius and Tanzania, another two eastern countries in order of importance, replaced Zimbabwe and Kenya.

In summary, although these broad trends disguise many factors (as will be argued below), some brief, general observations can be made, particularly pertaining to the scope and impact of tourism in Africa. One, there are variations in traffic and earnings between the continent's subregions and countries. Bryden's (1973) description of a "tourism country" on the basis of gross tourism receipts as a portion of revenue from exports of goods is instructive, modified here to underline the relative importance of tourism to the regional, subregional, and national economies. While some subregions (e.g., northern, southern) and countries (e.g., South Africa, Morocco, Tunisia) are highly reliant on tourism as a contributor to their economies, other countries (e.g., Somalia, Central African Republic) regard the sector as peripheral to their economic development strategies. Second, the success of the "tourism countries" does not mask the fact that, by any comparative standard, the tourism sector in Africa is overall a low-volume industry very reliant on regional markets, mainly from neighboring countries and the implications that go with it. The uneven-

Table 1.3. Top Five Earners in Africa: 1998

Rank	Country	Tourist Receipts (US$m)	% Change Over 1997	Market Share of total Africa (%)
1	South Africa	2,366	3.0	24.8
2	Morocco	1,600	10.9	16.8
3	Tunisia	1,550	8.9	16.2
4	Mauritius	503	3.7	5.3
5	Tanzania	431	9.9	4.5

Source: World Tourism Organization (1999, p. 33).

ness and variations in relative importance and performance of the tourism sector in African subregions and countries might raise one simple question: why?

The Metaphor of the "Iceberg"

The answer to the question posed above is to be found in the metaphor of the "iceberg." It is a useful metaphor used here mainly to pinpoint and illustrate the range of influences on African tourism development experiences. There are at least two explanations for this. First, it attempts to set the African situation in the tourism sector against a background of the "behind-the-scene" problems and issues underpinning tourism planning, policy, and implementation strategies. It could be argued that some of these matters are a legacy of the colonial past, while others are of somewhat recent origin. Second, in terms of size and scope of the sector, the metaphor identifies and distinguishes the factors that inhibit and facilitate tourism development. In this way, it helps to underscore the differences between and within the African subregions and countries in the development of the tourism sector.

For analytical purposes, three ranges of the iceberg, namely the top, the middle, and the bottom, can be discerned. *At the top of the iceberg* are the standard explanations regarding the structural deficiencies of Africa, which are of an economic and political nature, about which so much has been written (see Conable, 1990, 1991; ECA, 1989; Rodney, 1989). These are in themselves barriers to tourism development. A detailed examination of these matters is beyond the scope of this chapter, but a short description cannot be ignored. It needs to be stated at the outset that, to a large degree, Africa's problems and difficulties are a consequence of international market pressures and demands, although one might conversely argue that the problems are self-inflicted.

Whatever the view, there is no doubting that the late 1970s and early 1980s were a period of major economic decline in Africa, both internally and externally. The hiatus came in the mid-1980s when the International Monetary Fund- and the World Bank-inspired Structural Adjustment Programs (SAPs) were introduced in most countries in (mainly sub-Saharan) Africa. For many people, justification was hardly required but far from justifiable in the manner of SAPs' application and implementation. For example, it is recognized that the Northern subregion countries were not part of the "scorchearth" economic policy of the Bretton Woods Institutions. However, the SAPs were perhaps merely reflecting Achebe's (1958) view four decades ago: the African (economic) world had fallen apart; Africa needed to return to a "proper" economic development path and thus to become a viable member of the "global village."

The economic malaise was also exacerbated by political instability that had hitherto gripped the region, through military coups d'état resulting in rhythmic changes of government (see Teye, 1988). Without question, these developments should have adverse ramifications for tourism development in the continent, as Ankomah and Crompton (1990) have sought to portray. In addition to an unstable political environment, the authors' view is that four major sets of factors can be ascribed to Africa's poor performance, including a negative public image in the market regions; foreign exchange constraints that hinder the implementation of services and infrastructure necessary to sustain tourism; a lack of skilled labor (which fosters a reliance on expatriate workers in critical technical and managerial positions); and weak institutional framework for tourism planning (Ankomah & Crompton, 1990). The logical outcome of this reality is the widening of tourism development gap in the African region.

Below the waterline where the iceberg is not visible is the question of the dominance of some subregions. For instance, one strand of the argument is that the northern dominance is due to the subregion's proximity to the major European source markets, as encapsulated in the suggestion back in 1972: the subregion is "simply a natural extension of European resorts, in the path of the inevitable southern push towards the sun and, initially at least, towards less crowded beaches" (Hutchinson, 1972, p. 45). However, the proximity theory cannot be wholly responsible for the significance of tourism in other countries in the region (e.g., South Africa, Kenya). The answer lies in two other considerations.

The first is that through colonialism, arguably, these countries had put to better effect their longstanding economic and political links with their erstwhile "mother country." The second is that the geographical climate had perhaps permitted the settlement in these countries of vigorous expatriate communities. The settlers in turn had sought to advance their commercial interests and, through hunting expeditions for wildlife tourism purposes, provided pioneer facilities to advance the cause of tourism: "where foreign enterprises were present in a country's tourist industry they would be the most successful" (S. G. Britton, 1982, p. 340). In order to appreciate fully the significance of this, a short economic history of Africa relating to aspects of colonial policy in Africa seems necessary.

Deep below the waterline of the iceberg lies, straddling the spectrum just described, the legacy of colonial policy in Africa. As expected, the policy tended to differ from one subregion to another depending on local circumstances but had profound implications for the size and scope of the differences in tourism that were to develop in the respective subregions. It is well known (see Kennedy, 1988) that for centuries prior to the colonial era, long-distance trade caravans traversed the African Sahelian belt and the main grassland areas and were carried along inland waterways. The cities of Dar-es-Salaam (Tanzania), Kano (Nigeria), Timbuktu (The Sudan), and Port Sudan (The Sudan) as trading ports, among others, owed their existence and prosperity to this trade trend. In terms of tourism, one could argue that, tourism, as generally defined to include business, was well developed in some parts of Africa in the precolonial times.

The 18th and 19th centuries ushered in the presence in Africa of Europeans and other nationalities almost everywhere (e.g., Levantines in West Africa, Asians in East Africa, Turks, Syrians, and others from the Arabian peninsula in North Africa). These immigrants, by participating in trade, investment, and business in Africa, thus altered the precolonial trade patterns and systems. But it was the Berlin Conference of 1884 and 1885, which carved up Africa into colonies and protectorates among the colonial overlords (e.g., the British, French, Portuguese, Dutch, etc.), that further reinforced and consolidated the change patterns. The "spheres of influence," generally described as Anglophone, Francophone, and Lusophone, enabled the colonizers to control the leading economic sectors, including tourism, thereby highlighting significant differences between the western, eastern, southern, and the northern African subregions. The main features of colonial policy and the measures devised to realize the policy have been described by many historians of Africa (see Afigbo, Ayandele, Gavin, Omer-Cooper, & Palmer, 1992).

In West Africa, colonial policy focused on the promotion of peasant cash crop production, and the "warrant chief" system (see Afigbo, 1972) ensured that the local chiefs threw their weight behind the colonial agenda. In East and southern Africa, the main thrust of colonialism was on settlers' ownership of commercial agriculture, mining, and factories. This policy was achieved through a variety of measures including land alienation, taxation, the imposition of restrictions on the range of economic activities open to the native population, and also the securing of a male migrant labor force for settlers' agricultural estates. The situation in the northern subregion was very different because, as stated, people, capital, and goods had always moved throughout the area, thereby allowing a substantial accumulation of indigenous capital. In addition, the area had a well-developed, indigenous civil service and therefore colonial policy took the form of suzerainty: the northern states remained internally autonomous but a protectorate was imposed.

This short description only serves to confirm a number of points in a context of tourism development: by the time "modern" tourism began in the 1950s and 1960s, the seeds of variations in African tourism development experience were already sown; the development of the sector was marginal in West Africa, minimal in eastern and southern Africa, and fairly substantial in northern subregions. Much of all this has to do with the colonial phase when Europeans and other nonindigenous groups exercised considerable control over economic opportunities offered by colonialism. Accordingly, the focus shifts to examine the main elements of the African political economy of tourism development.

The Development of Strategies

As previously suggested, strategy development involves the processes of policy formulation and policy implementation. Thus, the analysis that follows of the situations in African countries with respect to the tourism sector will concentrate on both perspectives. But to exemplify the processes, attention will be directed toward technocrats and business interest groups whose decision-making styles will be assessed in terms of political liberty and economic activity, for reasons already advanced. In this connection, Chapter 5 by Jenkins on 14 Southern Africa Development Community (SADC) countries is both very revealing and informative in strategy development terms. The chapter also clearly illustrates, however, the problems that are associated with such an analysis considering, in the words of the author, "the very diverse characteristics of the countries, their relative stages of development and the importance of tourism within the individual economies." This remark may well be reflective of the situation with respect to the SADC countries, but it also has general relevance to a majority of the countries in the Africa continent.

Policy Formulation Process

In regard to policy formulation in the tourism sector in Africa, a number of approaches to and levels of the process can be identified. The process might be described as *participative* or *liberal* to allow diversified views and so to enrich process outcomes, or *authoritative* to stifle and alienate grassroots opinions—reminiscent of the past "command economy" approach to development planning. Within such generalities, it is possible to divide the participants into two groups—technocrats and business interest groups—and observe their process styles and levels within the confines of political and economic circumstances and considerations.

Namibia, South Africa, and Zambia probably represent an example of the "best practice" in the participative model. In these countries, perhaps because of the existence of political liberties of the press, expression, and association, or for some other reasons, there is transparency in the policy formulation process. Everything is openly aired and openly debated to garner inputs to the process from as wide a spectrum of government/industry representatives as possible. As Jenkins has argued, there are three reasons for this: a need to empower the people in the formation process; a need to give them a sense of ownership, especially on completion of the policy document; and the need to stimulate a dialogue and cooperation between government and private sector bodies. In this sense, everyone is seen to be "singing from the same hymn sheet" with all equally sharing in any corresponding consequences arising from this collective responsibility and partnership.

Conversely, the examples from other countries like Botswana, Lesotho, Swaziland, and Tanzania present a different scenario. Jenkins' statement that in these countries "there is no indication of how the policies were formulated," could induce one to surmise that the countries might well meet the authoritarian criterion relating to the formulation process.

Perhaps this characterization, harsh as it may seem, has more to do with their past political orientations and philosophies than any other factor. Given, therefore, the current global dispensation, politically and economically, it is only fair to suggest that their positions are now changing. Nonetheless, the biblical idea of "the evil that men do lives after them" is insightful in this respect and cannot very easily be swept aside.

In comparison, some clear picture emerges from all this, especially relating to technocrats (or the public sector and its agents) and private sector operators and their respective levels of participation in the tourism policy formation process. First, the participative model in Namibia, South Africa, and Zambia shows an equal balance between the public sector and the private sector. In Botswana, Lesotho, Swaziland, and Tanzania, the situation is somewhat different because of the rather unclear, if not secret, way the process follows. Government participation here is as pervasive as in Namibia, South Africa, and Zambia but the private sector is much less so. It could therefore be argued that major decisions in Botswana, Lesotho, Swaziland, and Tanzania on tourism policies are almost always initiated by the government sector interests, with little or no input from the private sector.

Second, although participation in policy-making by the private sector in Namibia, South Africa, and Zambia is recognized, clearly this suggests that business groups in these countries exert great influence and pressure on national economic policies, including tourism. On the latter case, Jenkins again makes the point that "the private sector will not necessarily support national as opposed to sectoral development objectives through investment without being participants in the policy formulation process; it has to have a degree of ownership of the policy."

Third, further contrasts can be made in the political and economic spheres. As expected, the participative model countries exhibit liberal tendencies. This is opposite to Botswana, Lesotho, Swaziland, and Tanzania, for example, where, as noted, the political environment of the press, free speech, etc., is restrictive and centralized. Also, the importance of the market for tourism policy formulation has been recognized. Again, with respect to the two models discussed, it needs stating that the characteristics of their economies are indeed a reflection of the countries' political leanings. Hence, in the "command economy" model countries their economy is much more oligopolistic than in the "participative" model countries. One feature common to both models, though, is the very large state tourism enterprises—to the extent that the market may not really be as liberal as first thought.

That said, the political and economic walls are now coming down, changes are taking place, almost without exception, everywhere in Africa (e.g., democratization, liberalization, privatization) (see White & Bhatia, 1998). These changes seem irreversible and certainly will affect the pattern of tourism development in Africa and perhaps further widen the differences from one country and subregion to another in the near future. The key to managing the changes lies in the development of effective implementation strategies (see Laws, Faulkner, & Moscardo, 1998).

Policy Implementation Strategies

This chapter has offered detailed perspectives on the need for tourism policy implementation and the difficulties associated with the process, while noting that existence of policies is no guarantee of their implementation. As also noted, the success or failure of the implementation process depends to a lesser or greater degree on the availability of implementing budget, expertise, organizational structure, or even a strong (or a lack of a strong) support of private sector's response to the policies. There are, of course, other considerations, including, as Jenkins has explained, "the particular circumstances of a country, how tourism is organized and administered and how important it is in the economy."

The situation in African countries in these respects varies from country and subregion to the next, given the diversity of the region. Nonetheless, there is a consensus on three areas. The first of these is the recognition of the importance of the considerable political and economic changes currently taking place not only in Africa but also in the wider global community in influencing the process of implementation. Second, in other countries in Africa, which are perhaps impervious to a radical change or indeed where change is slow to catch on, policy implementation has focused on the existing institutions and structures.

Third, recently across the continent no less than 12 new subregionally based organizations have been created, as provided for in the Abuja Treaty briefly referred to above. Some major ones are: Common Market for Eastern and Southern Africa (COMESA), Economic Community of Central African States (ECCAS), and Economic Community of West African States (ECOWAS). Others include SADC, Arab Maghreb Union (UMA), and, for tourism per se, Regional Tourism Organization of Southern Africa (RETOSA). These formations have been spurred by developments elsewhere in the world (e.g., the intensification of competition, etc.).

As was also envisaged in the Treaty, these institutions should serve as vehicles to translate national, subregional, and sectoral tourism and other economic policy initiatives into actuality (see Dieke, 1998). The problem in Africa is not as much a lack of guidelines for tourism development as with improving and building a consensus from all concerned, both public and private, on future directions. Therefore, the need for cooperation and integration or coordination of various tourism activities is paramount. This is because, considering the differing stages of tourism development in Africa, some countries in the region might be tempted to pursue national rather than subregional or even continent-wide interests and aspirations.

Plan of the Book

The chapters in this book focus on tourism development in Africa mainly within the nexus of the political and economic processes of development. The contents of the volume have been arranged to highlight the different approaches to tourism development, by offering case studies and topical foci, together with an examination of key theoretical debates and salient issues that have emerged over the years and that are significant in the region. This is reflected in the organization of the book into four parts, successively containing broad conceptual overviews and analytical frameworks, a small selection of country experiences with tourism development, institutional and strategy scenarios, and conclusions and prospects.

However, these are linked by several unifying themes running through the volume, reflecting conceptual issues raised in this chapter. Perhaps the most important is a clear understanding that tourism development in Africa and indeed in developing countries generally cannot meaningfully be analyzed in isolation from other components of society, history, economics, and polity. For example, in the process of decision-making with respect to tourism development, it is necessary to formulate policies based on an analysis of the market and also within the perspective of certain institutions and their modus operandi while taking into account the resources available in the countries and also the vested interests and opinions of various pressure groups. It is also evident from the various chapters that the implementation of tourism policies depends on the responses of private or public institutions and individuals to those policies and the institutions through which these policies are to be implemented. Institutions are thus important in defining tourism issues (e.g., distributional issues, environmental problems and concerns, and cultural matters), in mobilizing resources, in mediating interests, and in implementing tourism policy.

Notes

[1]According to Todaro (1994, p. 8) traditional neoclassical economics deals with an advanced capitalist world of perfect markets; consumer sovereignty; automatic price adjustments; decisions made on the basis of marginal, private profit, and utility calculations; equilibrium outcomes in all product and resource markets. It assumes economic "rationality" and a purely materialistic, individualistic, self-interested orientation toward economic decision-making.

[2]The practice of corruption can be delineated into two strains. First, there is *petty corruption*, which is national in character and typically involves public servants being bribed to dispense services that they are already being paid to provide free of charge. Second, there is *grand corruption*, which is international, an example being the practice of bribing high-ranking government official by the global companies in order to be awarded multimillion dollar projects (see "How Corruption Is Killing Africa," 1999, p. 18).

Editor and Publisher Note

The views expressed in this book are those of the particular contributors and are not necessarily shared by the editor or publisher. It is also clear that there are many opposing and conflicting opinions and conclusions. Contributors have not had the opportunity to read and discuss each other's work. Therefore, each chapter should be seen as separate and independent. There is a great diversity of approaches rather than any single and consistent message. It is perhaps this that most characterizes contemporary African tourism.

PART I

THEORETICAL AND COMPARATIVE PRISMS

Chapter 2

Tourism in the African Economic Milieu: A Future of Mixed Blessings

Robert A. Poirier

Summary

Research on tourism in the context of the political economy of Africa has been sparse, particularly as it relates to the question of tourism's impact in alleviating Africa's deepening economic woes. This chapter focuses its discussion on the vast potential of tourism as a major earner of foreign exchange but within the context of international and internal political economy. The role of International Monetary Fund (IMF) structural adjustment programs as a major engine driving tourism projects is examined, providing the international dimension of the chapter. The interaction of these external forces with the dynamics of intracontinental and African domestic politics provides the African political context.

It is argued that tourism adoption has shown both positive and negative results in Africa, making a consensus for tourism as a policy tool difficult to achieve. The examination of these counter views traces the manner in which countries have grappled with the potential for economic gain on the one hand and the social and environmental cost on the other hand.

This chapter demonstrates that, with constrained resources available to African countries and uneven attractions for tourists, it will be impossible for the whole of the African continent to embark on a major expansion of tourism. Further limitations will come about as a result of structural adjustment pressures, political crises, and unstable democratization directions. Nevertheless, given the prospects of comparative advantage, privatization strategies, and integrated markets, it may well be feasible for many African countries to pursue tourism.

Key words: Structural adjustment programs; Euro-dependency; Sustainability; Development; Political stability; Intraregional

Introduction

It is commonly understood that African economies are seriously deficient and that the continent's marginalization raises challenges to decision-makers in government and multilateral agencies and makes effective strategies to counter these problems difficult to conceive and implement. Development for most of Africa, however defined, appears more unreachable now than at any time since political independence in the 1960s. This chapter explores one proposed "remedy" used by a growing number of African countries to earn foreign exchange, namely tourism.

It is difficult to understand why tourism has not been given more attention as a potential money earner for a number of countries on the continent, especially since its importance to many countries such as Tunisia, The Gambia, and Kenya is well known. This may be partly because the current debate on structural adjustment has been framed with an emphasis on economic rationalization, diversification, self-sustainability, and the issues of privatization and debt. In addition, there is a widespread belief that tourism does not provide positive development, and that the social, cultural, and environmental costs outweigh any potential economic benefits (de Kadt, 1979; Lea, 1988; Mathieson & Wall, 1982).

This chapter attempts to briefly address some of the important developmental issues related to the expansion of organized "mass" tourism in Africa; to consider whether economic benefits do, in fact, accrue from tourism; to place this strategy within the wider context of the debate on structural adjustment and the arguments concerning potential economic strategies for African states; and to increase awareness of the issues surrounding tourism in Africa.

Importance of Tourism

Today tourism is second only to oil as the world's leading export commodity, accounting for global earnings of more than $300 billion, or nearly 25% of total world GNP. Over the last two decades, tourism has proved to be the world's fastest growing economic sector, with average growth per year of 7.1% in arrivals and 12.5% in receipts. World Tourism Organization projections up to the year 2020 predict global earnings will reach US$2 trillion. Continental Africa, however, accounts for only about 3% of global receipts and is not expected to exceed 5% of that total by the end of the second decade of the 21st century (WTO, 1997e).

While the international division of labor marginalizes Africa at the periphery of the world's economy, the international division of leisure (Turner, 1976) relegates Africa to what Turner and Ash (1975) called the "pleasure periphery" of world tourism. More than two thirds of Africa's tourists emanate from the predominantly "white" Europe and North America, and only 37.5% of tourists are intracontinental. However, intracontinental tourism in North Africa is extensive along the Mediterranean littoral because of the relative ease of travel. Tourists from Maghribi countries, in fact, accounted for a large share of Tunisian tourism in recent years, about 32% in 1996. The share of European arrivals in Tunisia has conversely fallen from a high of 82% in 1987 to 64% in 1996 (Office National du Tourisme Tunisien [ONTT], 1996).

Tourism's Euro-Dependency

Despite this, tourism in Africa is Euro-dependent, which has many political, economic, and social implications. In addition, the difficulties in promoting intra-African tourism because of financial, cultural, and infrastructural problems hinder prospects of developing an indigenous and self-sustaining African tourist industry less susceptible to the vagaries of the international political economy.

The relative importance and performance of tourist industries in Africa differ markedly from country to country and from region to region. Many small states lack the infrastructure and resources (such as luxury hotels, transportation, game parks, etc.) to attract large numbers of tourists, although the relative successes of The Gambia, Tunisia, and Seychelles in promoting beach vacations show that small size alone should not be the sole determinant (E. Carter, 1987; Green, 1979). As a whole, the continent's tourism receipts are 9.6% of total export receipts, although North Africa (14.8%) and East Africa (11.4%) are above this average. Southern Africa (5.2%), West Africa (3.5%), and Central Africa (2.6%) fall below the average ("Dossier: Tourism," 1990). Individual countries, such as Kenya, Tunisia, The Gambia, and South Africa, earn much more from tourism in both relative and absolute terms than others such as Gabon or Malawi. The potential for expansion of tourism is quite high and, in 1996, for example, earnings from tourism improved for Morocco (US$1.3 billion) and Tunisia (US$1.4 billion) (WTO, 1998c).

Tourism and Development

At a continental level, 1991 was designated as the *Year for African Tourism* in recognition of the important economic contribution tourism makes to many countries. But this activity belies the fact that little general dialogue is being articulated concerning the benefits and potential pitfalls of promoting tourism. Unlike many other economic policies, tourism programs have to be consciously selected and implemented by governments. In other words, this appears to be one of few real policy choices left open to African decision-makers (C. L. Jenkins & Henry, 1982). In addition, there are powerful clusters of interest groups in the policy-making process favorably disposed to tourism, while there is little organized opposition (Matthews, 1978). Likewise, tourism can be used as a political tool to shore up regimes lacking sufficient political capital, thus opening up the possibility that the "new governmental function of tourism promotion will be a potential source for expanding power" (Richter, 1980, p. 257). For example, Tunisia recently developed a tourism complex in Tabarka in a high unemployment region near the Algerian border as a buffer to stave off Islamic fundamentalist from Algeria. Over the last 2 years, countries such as Algeria (Economist Intelligence Unit, 1990), Sierra Leone (Akasah-Sarpong, 1990), Ghana and Senegal (Forrester, 1989) have specifically indicated a change in attitude towards tourism and are attempting, in cooperation with Western business interests, to develop infrastructures to attract tourists.

Tourism Risks

The strategy, however, is risky because tourism operates as an "elastic" commodity that can shrink rapidly under political pressures and economic constraints often outside of the government's control (Sinclair & Tsegaye, 1990). Unlike other commodities, tourism can be affected by events in the overseas country rather than the host country, such as a recession, or perhaps the fluctuating price of oil or terrorism threats as have occurred relatively recently with the Gulf War (see WTO, 1991). Tourism is also adversely affected by political instability within the host country, so again bringing pressure to bear on political authorities to maintain domestic stability. Tourism in Egypt was adversely impacted by Islamic fundamentalist attacks against tourists in 1993–94, although entries did rebound later. However, a more recent attack (November 1997) killed nearly 60 tourists at a popular site in Luxor. Preceding this attack (September 1997) 10 foreigners were killed in their bus outside the Egyptian Museum in Cairo. The impact of these attacks was quick and devastating to the economy. Officials estimated that the revenue loss for 1998 was as much as $2 billion. One month after the Luxor attack, tourism officials in Egypt were reporting occupancy rates of 18% nationwide and 10% in Luxor ("Attack Devastates Industry," 1997).

Another issue is that the tourism industry in Africa has traditionally been dominated by transnational corporations (TNCs), primarily Western, making this a questionable and controversial area of economic development (S. G. Britton, 1982; Dunning & McQueen, 1982b).

Transport of tourists to Africa is preponderantly carried out by Western airlines; accommodation is often provided in hotel chains owned and managed by TNCs (though generally in joint ventures with indigenous partners); senior management of tourist facilities tends to be expatriate; the level of net to gross earnings is relatively low because of "leakage" of revenue out of the country; and food consumed by tourists is often imported specifically for them, especially in the West Africa region.

Benefit or Liability?

These factors raise the obvious question: how much do African states really gain from tourism? Such an extroverted economic sector depends on "trickle down" for development to occur in auxiliary jobs, such as waiters, crafts people, etc., while the larger share of earnings is repatriated overseas. Green (1979, p. 84) has calculated that slightly more than one job per hotel bed is created by tourism, at an average cost of $10,000 per job. Both Farver (1984) and Summary (1987), in surveys of The Gambia and Kenya, respectively, found that tourism provided less employment than many had anticipated. The situation for Tunisia, however, has been more positive, but this may well be because the government has emphasized privatization and local entrepreneurship reducing the TNC hold on the industry (Poirier, 1995).

Though jobs may well be created and the burgeoning informal sector may provide a step up from poverty, such labor reinforces the low self-esteem that many Africans have been historically forced to contend with by placing them into a "service" mentality vis-à-vis Europeans. Tourism's impact also affects the sexual division of labor. There has been little scholarly research on the specific employment role of women in tourism (Grown & Sebstad, 1989). General findings on the inequality of salaries between genders holds true for the tourism sector, with men generally taking managerial positions. Attempts to increase the productivity of the domestic agricultural sector to provide food supplies to tourists (rather than continue to import supplies) impacts on women's central role in agriculture. However, tourism could also distort the agricultural sector and undermine current agricultural patterns. Large-scale mechanization of agriculture to meet high tourism-related food demands could further marginalize rural women producers on the continent.

Another concern is that tourism is an industry that requires expert marketing and the careful cultivation of potentially fickle customers. Marketing strategies in the West for African tourist destinations often display blatant and crude symbolism equated with "cultural imperialism," depicting Africa as a virgin pleasure park to explore without in any way dealing with the realities of the African condition. Charles Geshekter (1987) quotes this Kuoni advertisement:

> Visit Kenya's sun-drenched Coast with idyllic beaches lapped by the clear enticing waters of the Indian Ocean; dream-filled days of sun flickering through palm leaves, cocktails by the pool to cool the inner man. . . . Even if you never set foot outside the hotel grounds you will have experienced something of the real atmosphere, the timelessness, and serenity of a [traditional] African town . . . where the pulsating rhythm of tribal drums and dances can still mystify and thrill; unbelievably, besides this scene from a Tarzan epic the glorious golden beaches shimmer in the sun. (p. 58)

Such marketing may be inevitable given the demands of the "consumer," but does not mesh easily with Africans' own perception of themselves and their continent, and so provides a potential justification for the rejection of tourism on cultural grounds.

Structural Adjustment Programs

Structural adjustment programs (SAPs) have been implemented in about half of Africa's states, with differing levels of commitment and varying levels of pressure exerted on those countries by the International Monetary Fund (IMF) and World Bank. The debate on SAP effectiveness has raged for several years, with some believing that a minimal state role and a strong diversification program will bring a revival to these troubled economies. Others question the validity of these programs and their impact on social sectors, and prefer indigenous plans and self-sustainable programs. The diverse range of opinions was epitomized in 1989 by the bitter debate between the World Bank and the United Nations' Economic Commission for Africa (ECA). The World Bank supports a neo-modernization program, rolling back the interventionist state, diversifying exports, and freeing up the private sector and prompting major foreign investment into Africa's troubled economies. Tunisia, for example, has taken major steps towards privatization through the usual techniques of reducing state monopolies, selling state assets to private firms, and generally liberalizing the economy to allow for more foreign investments, which would, of course, include tourism-oriented enterprises (Poirier, 1995).

Given the fact that the majority of tourists traveling to Africa emanate from Western Europe, it is not surprising that agreements have been made between the European Union (EU) states and Africa over tourism policy. However, no mention of tourism was made in the first two Lomé conventions between the African, Caribbean, and Pacific (ACP) countries, and this sector received scant attention in Lomé III. One has to look hard within the 1990 Lomé IV convention to find the vague, general clauses concerning cooperation over tourism. In Title IX, Chapter 3, Article 121, the convention states:

> The aim shall be to support the ACP States' efforts to derive maximum benefit from national, regional and international tourism in view of tourism's impact on economic development and to stimulate private financial flows from the Community and other sources into the development of tourism in the ACP States. Particular attention shall be given to the need to integrate tourism into the social, cultural and economic life of the people. ("Dossier: Tourism," 1990)

Four areas of policy are to be emphasized: human resources, product development, market development, and research and development. The EC has given increasing amounts of aid to the ACP countries to promote tourist infrastructure, rising from ECU 3.45 billion in Lomé I to ECU 12 billion, which was earmarked for the 1990–95 period (Lee, 1990). However, it is difficult to see how this partnership will work. No detail is given on how tourism will be "integrated into the social, cultural, and economic life" of Africa. And furthermore, given the chronic condition of African economies, it appears likely that African states will be more dependent upon European finance and investment, technology, and tourists.

United Nations Goals

The UN's Economic Commission for Africa (ECA) had a strong motivation to promote tourism under African rather than expatriate control. The ECA stressed its main goals as: development of intra-African tourism; increase in technical training for indigenous staff; the creation of interstate (or intraregional) tourist circuits; and cooperation at a continental level to extract the maximum from Africa's tourist potential (Sako, 1990).

These goals may appear to be modest, but they run counter to the prevailing pattern of tourism that exists in Africa. Generally tourists on organized vacation programs are flown to single locations (beach, town, or safari locations) by foreign airlines, where they remain in tourist "enclaves" until they are ready to leave. Club Méditerranée is perhaps the best known, but by far not the only, example of this enclave tourism. Hotels are generally pre-paid in foreign exchange at departure (not arrival) and interstate travel, where it exists, provides little tangible benefit to indigenous providers.

The ECA's strategies fit well with its overall desire to strengthen and deepen African control over productivity, but in terms of tourism the "commodity"—namely the tourist— is not something easily controlled, and can select other non-African destinations if she/he senses a problem with the destination. Intra-African tourist development remains a problem due to the relative lack of indigenous African tourists. Economic hardships across the continent have bitten deep into African middle classes, who possess little or no surplus capital for leisure. Those that do have surplus capital tend to retain vertical allegiances with Europe rather than risk the potential hazards of visiting their neighboring African countries. Infrastructural bottlenecks, poor intraregional transport, and simmering political difficulties also hamper intraregional tourism.

Despite some of the above constraints, it is evident that the ECA will encourage African governments embarking on major tourism programs to attempt self-sustainable and self-reliant policies. Unfortunately, the short-term prospects for such programs appear bleak, as has been shown in Tanzania (S. Curry, 1990). It is important to note that tourism in a number of countries is already well entrenched and locked into a vertical relationship with Western TNCs. Challenging the status quo may be difficult in political and economic terms, and serious clashes would only serve to frighten off the very tourists that African countries wish to attract.

Promoting intra-African tourism is also a difficult task in the absence of convertible African currencies and the shortage of foreign exchange. A financial mechanism to promote intraregional tourism would be needed, such as the common currency base used by the East African Community members prior to the break-up of the Community in 1977, or with the CFA franc in West Africa. This requires political concessions on sovereign issues, and most governments do not appear ready to make those concessions. It also implies that there is the political goodwill to cooperate in tourism projects, which may not be the case. As the potential earnings from tourism rise, states may well compete for these scarce resources (i.e., tourists), rather than agree to share them. Kenya's manipulation of the Tanzanian tourist market in the 1970s is a good example of competitive strategies. Notwithstanding the Maghreb Union, Tunisia and Morocco compete for the same tourist clients.

Intraregional Tourism

Another interesting issue concerns the potential compatibility of European tourism and intraregional tourism. No real studies have been undertaken concerning whether each group of tourists requires the same or different leisure facilities. European tourism is at the top end of the spectrum in terms of long-haul, luxury vacations, and this perhaps does not equate with the aspirations and budgets of African tourists. It would be imprudent to expect that countries serving as current destinations for Western tourists would suddenly switch to intraregional tourism only, nor does it seem feasible for countries now embarking on tourism programs to plan deliberately to exclude Western tourists. Thus, however one looks at this issue, African tourist programs will be reliant upon Western consumers for the foreseeable future with all the potential problems that such reliance entails. Ironically, the rapid democratization in Eastern Europe, combined with the troubled economic situation in Western Europe and continuing tensions in the Middle East, can lead us to speculate that Eastern Europe will be the boom tourism destination for the next decade, further marginalizing Africa on the tourism periphery. Tunisia, however, has begun to counter the trend by marketing intensely in East Europe and showing impressive gains for the effort.

Tourism's Cost

Tourist infrastructure requires significant capital outlay—for hotels, transport, water supplies, sewage, telecommunications, etc. Traditionally TNCs have attempted to avoid major financial exposure, preferring host countries to provide basic infrastructural facilities (Poirier, 1997). Expansion of tourism raises the obvious and simple question (i.e., from where will the new finance materialize?). Africa's chronic economic situation is well documented, with sub-Sahara Africa's total debt being $135 billion, roughly equal to its GNP and 350% of export earnings on 1990 figures (Conable, 1990). Indigenous financing is difficult to raise because of limited domestic savings, and spending scarce resources on "luxury" hotels (rather than on basic housing) puts an inordinate strain on political authorities in the face of domestic discontent.

Tourism also depends on the expansion of airline services, an expensive yet selective area of spending. Given the marginal financial stability of many African carriers, it appears unlikely that African airlines can expand to meet potential traffic demands. Currently, African states are turning to European airlines such as Lufthansa and Condor to provide increased services to the continent. European airlines invest $5 billion annually to upgrade their fleets, a figure that cannot be matched by Africa (Eser, 1989). It appears as though the most feasible strategy here would be to attract foreign investment, based on World Bank exhortations, and accept the political risks that such a strategy generates.

The fragility of African economies must be seen in the wider context of the fragility of political structures within the continent. The SAPs initially attempted to reform existing political economies without attempting to democratize and challenge entrenched political elite. Structural adjustment has had the effect of shoring up the position of political elite by attempting to repair existing economies rather than radically reforming them. The apparent retreat of the state (and confusion over its future role) has had the effect of encouraging the development of civil organizations in many countries recently, so prompting embryonic democratization processes across the continent. This has led to a flurry of debate as to what the eventual outcome of these processes will be, but few scholars or decision-makers have any firm idea of what will happen. Conventional wisdom stated that economic change required nondemocratic political structures to be achieved, but that appears to have been reversed to conclude that democratic structures are essential for economic restructuring (Bienen, 1990; Duignan, 1990; Herbst, 1990). It is perhaps safe to assume that transitions that occur may not be wholly peaceful, and may usher in periods of extreme instability. There is already considerable evidence to show that instability is anathema to tourism: the collapse of tourism in Uganda in the 1970s or the inability of Zambia to create tourist growth because of potential South African violence are just two examples of the impact of political upheaval on tourism (Teye, 1986, 1988).

Conclusion

This chapter has attempted to initiate discussion on issues rarely touched upon in the current debate on African political economy: namely, the role to be played by tourism. Adoption of tourism programs has both positive and negative results, and there is not (nor may ever be) a consensus on their utility. The balance between economic gain on the one hand and social/environmental costs on the other is difficult to gauge, although implementing more sensitive tourism strategies may diminish the latter problem. Unfortunately, there is the likelihood that even if African governments opt for expansion of tourism programs, the rapidly changing geopolitical and economic climates in the global system may leave African tourist markets underdeveloped.

Given the extreme economic hardship currently within the African continent, and the potential benefits that tourism offers, it is expected that governments will attempt to expand tourism opportunities in an effort to boost revenue. Current scenarios suggest that the majority of these programs will be dependent upon Western investment and visitors, and so could further undermine attempts to promote self-reliant development in Africa.

Chapter 3

Tourism in Africa:
The Social and Cultural Framework

David Harrison

Summary

During the last decades of the 19th century and for much of the 20th century, tourism throughout Africa, especially where there were relatively large settler populations, was developed by colonialists for colonialists. In general, black Africans possessed neither the financial nor the cultural capital to compete with Europeans. Later, when mass tourism on an international scale developed, settler capital was joined by international capital, and this structure was one of the bequests of colonialism. The association of tourism in Africa with white colonialism led some Africans to oppose the tourism industry as another form of "underdevelopment." Another bequest of colonialism was the formation of several contradictory images of Africa, as the habitat of noble yet dangerous people, of noble yet dangerous animals, and similarly as a series of beautiful but untamed landscapes. Such contradictions are reinforced in the West by current mass media coverage of Africa, which tends to portray the continent as prone to disease, poverty, and war, and tourism development is likely to be hampered as long as such images continue to dominate.

Key words: Africa; Capitalism; Culture; Colonialism; Globalization; History; Racial stereotypes; Social structure; Tourism

Introduction

As other chapters in this book indicate, there is no single "African experience," and to lump together societies that differ so widely, internally and externally, in their demography, economies, social structures, cultures, and geography can be immensely misleading. In what ways, then, is it possible to refer sensibly to a "social and cultural framework" of tourism development in Africa, especially when (relative to other, more developed tourism destinations) so little research on tourism has been carried out in the region? The response adopted here, albeit with a degree of speculation, is to link current tourism development to the historical process of colonialism, and to argue that insofar as African countries are successful in attracting tourists, their success has been conditioned, but not determined, by the prior and specific history of colonialism in the region. It was this background, either of "development" or neglect, that—along with more recent international and intranational events—has helped frame the context of modern Africa and its tourism.

The Historical Background

It has been argued elsewhere (D. Harrison, 1995) that the development of tourism in Swaziland, a small kingdom in southern Africa, has always been in non-African hands. In the 19th century, very basic accommodation was provided for individuals seeking mineral rights and for big game hunters but, when these natural resources were exhausted, the hotels catered almost exclusively for business visitors to industrial or administrative centers. It was much later, in the 1960s, that efforts were made by the colonial government and then, after independence, by the Swazi authorities, to attract foreign tourists, primarily with casinos, which were banned in the Republic of South Africa, and (according to some commentators) by encouraging an early variant of "sex tourism" across the color line, an assertion that has more recently been questioned (Crush & Wellings, 1987; D. Harrison, 1994). In this more recent tourism development, the lead was taken by transnational capital based in South Africa, in conjunction with capital provided by the Swazi monarchy.

The Swazi contribution to African tourism is hardly significant. Indeed, its limited success as a destination area has been crucially influenced by its position as a periphery of the Republic of South Africa, to which its currency is tied, with which the bulk of its trade is carried out, and from which two thirds of its tourist arrivals emanate (D. Harrison, 1995). However, the development of tourism in this small kingdom does provide clues as to how tourism in other parts of Africa may be approached, and there is some evidence that the pattern of development of Swazi tourism is not unique.

In her study of the evolution of tourism in Kenya, Uganda, and Tanzania, Rajotte confirms similarities with the Swazi case. In these countries, too, tourism was first introduced by Europeans for the benefit of Europeans.

> The 1920s saw the beginning of economic recovery in East Africa, as elsewhere, but as yet there was no significant flow of tourists into an area which remained remote, expensive to reach, and somewhat hazardous to visit. . . .
> All foreign arrivals from outside Africa came by sea, a time-consuming and expensive undertaking, and what publicity there was . . . was guaranteed to repel rather than attract. Beach holidays on the Kenyan and Tanganyikan coasts primarily served the white settlers and administrators of East Africa and Southern Rhodesia (Zimbabwe), and the facilities, owned exclusively by white colonists and later by a few Asians, consisted of small family-operated hotels and beach cottages. (Rajotte, 1981, p. 6)

As Rajotte goes on to point out, subsequent tourism development in East Africa was much influenced by events in Europe (which restricted the financial ability of British nationals to travel anywhere overseas, let alone to sub-Saharan Africa) and, later, by divergent policies followed in Kenya, Uganda, and Tanzania. In Kenyatta's Kenya, transnational capital was much encouraged, in Obote's Uganda the state took a leading role in the hotel subsector, only to see the tourism industry effectively disappear under Amin's tyranny from 1971 to 1979, and in Nyerere's Tanzania there was an uneasy liaison of state and private capital (Rajotte, 1981, pp. 27–39).

Evidence of a different kind comes from accounts of travelers in Africa. There are hundreds of these, but one such case is provided by Perham (1974), an historian of Africa, in her diary of a journey made in late 1929 and early 1930 through southern Africa. When read in the 1990s, the diary seems a mixture of acute analysis, paternalism, and prejudice, and records 5 months of encounters with the great, the good, and as many representatives of southern African society as this intrepid young woman could reasonably accost. Governor Generals and their wives, District Officers and village headmen, and a selection of train passengers and fellow guests are all there in a rapidly changing social kaleidoscope where Boer and English compete for power in the recently established Union of South Africa, over and above indigenous Africans already restless for independence. And every now and then, in passing, she refers (too briefly) to the hotels.

After changing trains at East London, a "dapper little port" with "clean hotels," Perham (1974) journeys to Umtata, in the Transkei, and en route experiences a less than wholesome comfort stop, which she mentions in an aside:

> Perhaps I should explain that the train having stopped at a small European settlement, I got out, when I was instantly accosted by a gross-looking white with a coloured servant who insisted that I should come and have lunch at his place. The guard, clearly an accomplice, said it was a good idea and cheerfully promised to keep the train waiting until I returned. I was put in a ramshackle car and run half a mile out to the "Hotel." Here I sat down alone at a table set for thirty, while mine host stood over me, drinking and a native servant brought me disgusting food, which, under the eye of the hotelier, I had at least to nibble. Meanwhile he blasted the niggers, which did not improve my appetite. I was then run back, and the waiting train went on. (p. 70)

Arriving at Umtata, still suffering food poisoning from the previous episode, her trials continue:

> The hotel was horrible: the bed was a board with a deep hole in the middle; the servants were speechless black women who ran like hares from my desperate gesticulations. Clearly no one of importance or affluence can ever visit this centre of the most important of the native territories. (Perham, 1974, p. 72)

Other hotel visits are mentioned: the local hotel at Maseru, in Basutoland (now Lesotho), which "was not at all attractive" (p. 87) and "a vile hotel" in Johannesburg (p. 130), a city she loathed and found "beastly" (p. 141). In Pretoria, which she found more congenial, her luck apparently changed and she booked in at "*The Residentia*, a Dutch Hotel" (p. 157) where, as night fell, "the coloured man—always coloured bed-makers—brought in my blankets and pillows, made the bed and collected the very reasonable 3s fee" (p. 164).

In Durban, a clue is given as to why the bed-makers were always "coloured." Intimate contact of white women with black men was taboo. Perham is introduced to Champion, the "arch agitator" of the militant (native) Industrial and Commercial Union (ICU):

> Champion is a big Zulu. He greeted us with some ceremony, more especially directed to me and made a little speech. When I held out my hand he put his behind him on the grounds that I was breaking the rule of the whites in offering mine to a black man. (p. 193)

While in Durban, Perham was taken by Champion, initially against her better judgement, to a native meeting, a brave decision on her part but nevertheless an experience she much enjoyed, possibly even to the point of being sexually aroused by the dancing (pp. 199–200). While waiting for him to collect her, the "white" nature of hotels is again made clear by a fellow guest:

> A woman who heard I was interested in natives came up and sat beside me, and proceeded to blackguard them and, by inference, me, in the most outrageous manner.

She was a handsome, white-haired woman, in a beautiful evening dress, and loaded with jewels. I really felt quite sick as I listened to the usual flow of words—spoiled—lazy—animals—keep them down. She knew nothing—nothing. She boasted a lifetime in the country and she knew not the first fact of the situation. And the unprovoked vindictiveness with which she attacked me for daring to study the question! . . . Argument was useless, and I did not want a scene on the *stoep*, especially as Champion would shortly arrive and run the gauntlet. (pp. 195–196)

Similar contrasts arise at other stages of her journey. When visiting the Belgian Congo, for example, she is entertained at the guesthouse of Union Minière, "a very fine house, in beautiful order, but, apparently, with no servants. All happens by magic" (p. 222). The scene was different in Southern Rhodesia. At a hotel in Bulawayo she "watched hearty Rhodesians treating each other to whisky and soda, served by 'boys' who are under a prohibition law" (pp. 247–248).

Several characteristics of hotels in southern Africa (and to a lesser extent the Belgian Congo) emerge from Perham's diary. They were generally situated at ports and junctions, and in industrial, administrative, or agricultural centers, and they were operated by whites for whites, although not necessarily efficiently or comfortably. As in Swaziland, where the earliest hotels were considered to be little better than beer houses or "liquor canteens" (D. Harrison, 1995, p. 140), the worst were distinctly rough and ready, but—however bad—they were not for black Africans. Indeed, as Perham (1974) notes, there was a feeling that such people should be neither seen nor heard:

I saw the advertisement of a little watering place near East London—whose location I visited—saying—"Come to bright, clean X. All white area. No native locations." I wonder how long that will last and whether the workers live underground. (p. 152)

There was, in effect, a colonial mode of tourism development. Whereas many tourist facilities in developed countries were initially funded with local capital (R. Butler, 1980), those in sub-Saharan Africa and other less developed regions were initially provided and funded by expatriate settlers, usually European but sometimes of Asian origin. For most of the colonial period, indigenous Africans possessed neither the finance nor the cultural capital to invest in tourism, which, from its inception, was operated for Europeans for the benefit of other Europeans, local and from overseas. On the rare occasion that indigenous Africans did possess the material means and the incentive to involve themselves in the hotel industry, colonial governments discouraged them from doing so (Jommo, 1987, pp. 13–14), and even after political independence, in Kenya, at least, black African involvement in tourism was felt to threaten "standards" of hospitality (Jommo, 1987, p. 76).

The Infrastructural Inheritance

Patterns of colonial settlement, most pronounced where natural resources were plentiful, prompted the development of roads, railways, and the infrastructure of travel that enabled traders, hunters, soldiers, administrators, missionaries, and adventurers to move with variable degrees of comfort across sub-Saharan Africa.[1] They set the pattern for future tourism development.

Comfortable facilities and a developed infrastructure are equally important to the traveler in the late 20th century. This can be gauged from even a cursory examination of any modern travel book and is particularly apparent in travel advisories issued on a regular basis by the U.S. State Department.[2] There, almost at a glance, is the world summarized in terms of its accessibility and safety for the U.S. citizen and any other interested reader. The advisories may not always be entirely politically neutral but they do provide a rating of tourist destination areas in terms of the availability of tourist and health facilities, crime rates, political stability, and the difficulties of local travel, and the picture they give largely reinforces the impression that, in sub-Saharan Africa, few destination areas are considered safe enough for the average tourist.[3]

At the end of May 1998, advisories on 46 African countries were available. Of these, only 18 were considered unequivocally to be politically stable and the U.S. State Department discouraged travel to no less than 13 on the grounds that warfare or terrorism would endanger tourists' lives. Fourteen others were said to be dangerous because of unpaved roads and undisciplined driving, and crime in 32 was reportedly of a serious nature. Tourist facilities were said to be extensive in only 13 countries, and in 24 health provision was inadequate, with limited health services in most of the others. The 13 given relatively good ratings—Botswana, Egypt, Kenya, Madagascar, Mauritius, Morocco, Namibia, Senegal, South Africa, Swaziland, Tanzania, Tunisia, and Zimbabwe—included 8 of the top 10 tourism earners (indicated in Table 3.1) and, as no advisory was issued for Réunion, omitted only Ghana.

An examination of those countries in Africa[4] that earn most from tourism (nearly 85% of the continent's tourism earnings), as shown in Table 3.1, indicates that among them are societies that were most settled by Europeans and are most accessible. Details of the extent (and contrasting views) of white settlement in tropical Africa can be found elsewhere (Gann & Duignan, 1962; Grenfell Price, 1939; Legassick & de Clerq, 1984), but South Africa, for instance, currently the recipient of more than a quarter of Africa's receipts from tourism, was first settled (in the Cape) in 1806 and has the largest of all white settler populations in Africa—which may help explain why domestic tourists in that country account for seven times more overnight stays than international arrivals (WTO, 1995, p. 22). Namibia and Zimbabwe, too, were developed as settler societies, whereas Tunisia and Morocco, although colonized later (1883 and 1912, respectively), were easily accessible to tourists from Europe and, at least in the case of Tunisia, accommodated a considerable settler population. In East Africa, Kenya, first colonized in 1890, was soon to become the focus of numerous schemes for European settlement, and Mauritius was primarily developed as a plantation economy with sugar as the main crop. Réunion, first colonized by the French in the 17th century and a *département* of France to this day, was subject to considerable

Table 3.1. Top Ten Tourism Earners in Africa: 1997

Rank			Country	Receipts: $US (million)	% change: 1997/96	% of total: 1997
1985	1990	1997				
3	2	1	S. Africa	2,297	15.1	26.3
2	3	2	Tunisia	1,540	6.1	17.6
1	1	3	Morocco	1,200	−13.1	13.7
9	5	4	Mauritius	504	0.0	5.8
4	4	5	Kenya	502	5.9	5.7
21	11	6	Tanzania	360	11.8	4.1
—	—	7	Réunion	273	5.8	3.1
17	10	8	Ghana	266	6.8	3.0
15	13	9	Zimbabwe	250	14.2	2.9
—	9	10	Namibia	210	1.0	2.4
			Total 1–10	7,402		84.6
			Total Africa	8,742		100.0

Source: WTO (1998c, p. 33).

white settlement and now has a largely ethnically mixed population (as does the Seychelles, which also relies considerably on tourism for its foreign exchange). Finally, Ghana was first settled by Europeans in the 15th century and, after changing colonial hands on a regular basis, was finally confirmed as a British possession in 1874.

Africa differs from other WTO regions in that it is the only one where travelers on business outnumber holidaymakers (WTO, 1990, p. 5). However, an examination of tourism in selected African countries again indicates considerable differences, and these, too, may be explained by reference to different colonial experiences. In fact, with the possible exception of Morocco, the top 10 earners clearly rely on holidaymakers,[5] as indicated in Table 3.2, as do some small, coastal countries and island states (e.g., The Gambia, Réunion, Madagascar, and Senegal), whose lack of other natural resources and accessible coastlines encourage a reliance on tourism. Indeed, only 13 African countries rely on holidaymakers for more than half their international arrivals.

Table 3.2. Selected African Countries Ranked in Terms of Importance of Holidaymaking and Leisure Tourism, and in Terms of Their Tourism Earnings and GNP

Country	Rank in Tourism Earnings (1997)	Holidaymakers as % of All Visitors[a]	Rank	GNP per Capita: 1995	Rank	Tourism Receipts as % of Exports[b]	Rank
South Africa	1	67.4	8	3160	5	5.9	15
Tunisia	2	90.0 (est.)	3	1820	8	28.4	5
Morocco	3	30.5	18	1110	11	31.5	4
Mauritius	4	91.7	2	3380	4	26.9	7
Kenya	5	78.7	4	280	28	27.7	6
Tanzania	6	68.7	7	120	41	42.1	3
Réunion	7	54.4	14	9386[c]	1	—	—
Ghana	8	64.0	10	390	22	19.6	10
Zimbabwe	9	75.3	6	540	18	7.5	14
Namibia	10	65.3	9	2000	7	12.1	13
Botswana	11	11.9	25	3020	6	1.8	19
Senegal	12	—	—	600	16	26.2	8
Seychelles	13	77.5	5	6620	2	223.1	1
Uganda	14	58.8	12	240	33	15.2	11
Côte d'Ivoire	15	58.6	13	660	14	1.1	20
Madagascar	17	32.2	17	230	34	20.7	9
Zambia	18	36.6	15	400	21	4.7	17
Gambia	—	100	1	320	26	77.1	2
Swaziland	—	63.9	11	1170	10	—	—
Niger	—	36.4	16	260	29	5.1	16
Gabon	—	—		3490	3	0.2	23
Algeria	—	—		1600	9	0.6	21
Lesotho	—	4.7	27	770	12	13.2	12
Congo	—	—		680	13	0.5	22
Cameroon	—	—		650	15	3.3	18

Source: WTO (1996b, 1998c); International Bank of Reconstruction and Development (the World Bank) (1997, pp. 6–9).
[a]1994 unless otherwise stated. This includes those not staying overnight.
[b]Latest available figures.
[c]Estimate for 1996.

Admittedly, such figures are not decisive, but they reinforce the notion that African countries most colonized by white settlers are the most incorporated into the world tourism industry. By contrast, those least colonized (or most neglected) by the colonial powers have a relatively minor share in international arrivals.

Images of Africa

If one result of colonialism was to bequeath to some former colonies the rudiments of a hospitality industry, of equal significance were the images of Africa transmitted, over generations, to residents of metropolitan societies. In this context, a detailed analysis of white images of black Africa is not possible. However, whereas the South Sea islands, for example, have frequently been portrayed as "paradise," whether lost or found, as in Grimshaw (1907), Howarth (1983), Spate (1988), or recent tourism brochures, and their inhabitants regularly described as "friendly and hospitable," such epithets have rarely, if ever, been applied to sub-Saharan Africa. Rather, travelers have more often looked upon the region and its peoples with a mixture of awe, fear, and apprehension, a perspective remarkably similar to Shakespeare's picture of Othello, who is portrayed negatively as "thick lips," an "old black ram," a "barbary horse," and a "lascivious Moor." By contrast, he is also "the valiant Moor," a "noble and valiant general," a virtuous man, "more fair than black," and said to be "of a constant, loving, noble nature." Such ambivalence, which is at the heart of Shakespeare's play, was undoubtedly recognized and shared by the groundlings at the Tudor playhouse, and there is ample evidence that such images of the African have lasted well into the 20th century, reinforced by more than 200 years of administrators' accounts, reports from scientific expeditions, popular plays and novels, and travel writing, a genre that itself has become a proper subject of analysis (cf. Blunt, 1994; M. L. Pratt, 1992).

Once more, Perham provides a good example. Writing her diaries 70 years ago, a liberal young woman on her first visit to southern Africa (later to write several well-received books on Africa), she talked to people and visited places conservative white settlers in the region preferred to avoid. It is clear from her account that most white people she met, English or Boer, regarded any notion of equality with "the native" as unthinkable, and when confronted with crude and cruel racial stereotypes she bristled with indignation. However, her own position was ambivalent. Although she had already traveled widely, including to the U.S., the South Pacific, and Somaliland, on arriving at Durban she is (almost literally) stunned:

> These men were dressed almost entirely in black coal sacks. . . . Beneath the coal-blackened jute, legs and arms sometimes flashed with copper wire; ears were weighed with lumps of wood and tin; some woolly heads were shaved to strange designs. . . . They looked up at us impudently, their faces nearly fell apart with their continuous laughter, and every now and then they hurled themselves into a battling whirl of limbs over some small largesse from the decks. The people on the boat laughed and commented: "Look at the niggers!" "Aren't they priceless?" "Throw them a penny and see them fight for it."
> I went below after a bit and sat in my cabin. I felt faint but the cause was mental rather than physical. Whether my mind had become softened with three weeks of isolation from the puzzling world, I don't know. But the sight of the Kaffirs on the docks was like a stunning blow. I seemed to feel the immensity of the problem they represented and the absurdity of my attempting to understand it. How could any humane relationship be established between the people on the wharf and ourselves, the people on the decks? (Perham, 1974, p. 30).

Later, when meeting educated Africans, she emphasizes their need to understand the fear whites felt for blacks (p. 50), and is shocked at the contrast between white housing and the "stench" and "pathetic attempts at decency" she found in the native location where the servants lived (p. 66). At Tsolo, in the Transkei, she visits women in a "heathen 'red' kraal":

> Their eyes met us, wild, shy and uncomprehending. Their huts were black as night inside, windowless and soaked with smoke. They had no furniture, only cooking pots. One woman offered us a tin of the muddy beer. I smelt it; a heady whiff struck my nostrils. She grimaced at our bad taste, drank half herself, and poured the rest down the throat of her small naked baby. Miserable cats and lame dogs cringed round the kraal. The men were obviously away at a beer-drink. (p. 82)

On visiting the mines, another aspect emerges:

> Perhaps what most impresses is the beauty of the men. In the afternoon, Saturday, they were lying around resting, many dressed only in their blankets. Most of them could be called primitive tribesmen with the peculiar beauty and fascination of their kind. It is hard to describe this beauty: it is partly in the carriage of the body, generally a fine body, and carried unselfconsciously, with the grace of an animal, which a very little sophistication can destroy. There is the expression of the eyes which, whether defiant, sad or happy, seem to express a different system of thought from ours. Then there are all the trappings of savagery, fantastic earrings, wrists and ankles loaded with metal, hair flowing long or cut into weird patterns on the scalp. (p. 147).

Again, when watching Zulu dancers in Durban:

> The impressiveness became almost overwhelming. I was surrounded by these flashing brown bodies with muscles running up and down skins glossy with sweat. Yet it was beautiful, this living frieze of dark bronze bodies. (p. 199).

However "liberal" Perham professed to be, she wrote at a time when relations between black and white in Africa were strictly circumscribed. Although varying from colony to colony in their manifestation and local implementation, race relations throughout sub-Saharan Africa were governed by what Kuper (1947) termed the uniform of color, "a uniform that individuals are not permitted to discard" (p. 52). This "uniform" was especially prominent in colonies where there was an established white settlement, most notably where there was a high proportion of white women (Gann & Duignan, 1962, p. 72; Henriques, 1974, pp. 119–123). In the late 17th century, legislation was enacted in Cape Province outlawing marriage between white men and slave women and more legislation in the 20th century, notably 1902, 1927, and 1957, simply reinforced previous attempts to outlaw what, in any case, was supposed to be "unnatural" (Henriques, 1974, p. 131). Similar laws were enacted in Swaziland (D. Harrison, 1994, p. 430) and Southern Rhodesia (Gann & Duignan, 1962, p. 72).

Such draconian restrictions on interpersonal relations between ethnic groups must be seen in the wider context of policies of segregation throughout sub-Saharan Africa, sometimes *de jure* (as in the Union of South Africa, especially after the Nationalist victory in 1948) and Rhodesia (e.g., in the 1913 Natives Land Act in Southern Rhodesia) and de facto elsewhere. In turn, they reflect a distinct pattern of colonial settlement and capitalism in which, as Perham and many others have recognized, white settlers relied on black labor for their prosperity. Long after her diaries were written, Perham (1974) felt that "our colonial rule was, on balance, an immense and essential service to Africa" (p. 28). Others, of course, have been less positive, and Legassick and de Clercq (1984) suggest that "the fate and lives of the working people of South Africa have been subjected to a movement between home and work dependent on the dynamic of accumulation, rather than the satisfaction of their needs" (p. 165).

How relevant to the study of tourism today are the images of Africa that emerge from Perham's diaries and other travel writing of the period? It has to be recognized, first, that her diaries were published more than 200 years after the earliest travel books on Africa were written by Europeans (and almost 50 years after they were written). She was thus at the end of a long line of European writers whose changing perspectives, "scientific" or otherwise, influenced European opinion (and thus future travel writers) on the "dark continent." Like her predecessors, she was helping to *produce* the European image of Africa (M. L. Pratt, 1992, p. 5).

Second, white images of Africa are important because Europe is already an important source of tourists to Africa, and is seen by many National Tourism Organizations (NTOs) as a market with considerable potential. In 1994, one third of all tourist arrivals were from Europe (WTO, 1995, p. 47) but, again, marked differences emerge when countries are examined in more detail (WTO, 1996b). European visitors were vital to Tunisia, Morocco, and the island destinations of Mauritius and Réunion, and constitute more than half of Kenya's visitors. By contrast, destination countries in southern Africa rely primarily on arrivals from within the region, and relatively little (normally around 10%) on visitors from the European region.

Clearly, accessibility is a key factor in choosing a holiday destination, and it takes many more hours to travel by air from Europe to southern Africa than to northern Africa. That said, such destination areas as Réunion, Mauritius, Kenya, Tanzania, and the Seychelles (where 82% of the visitors are from Europe) and, in another region, Sri Lanka, can hardly be described as short-haul destinations, and rely considerably on European visitors (WTO, 1996b). Accessibility, then, is not the only factor, and there are good reasons to assume, at the outset, that the prior image held of a destination area is a major factor in holiday choice.

How far such images are reproduced in modern tourism brochures is a question those interested in the sociology of knowledge could legitimately explore. In fact, although much has been written on the promotion of tourism destinations generally (cf. Dann, 1996; D. Harrison, 1997a), there is relatively little on the relationship of European stereotypes of Africa to tourism promotion. Referring to promotional literature of the Third World, R. Britton (1979, p. 322) points to its distorted focus on escape to exotic, untouched, unspoiled, and sensuous paradises, along with the emphasis that some familiar elements, for example, language, cuisine, and European management, are retained to avoid the threat of the "exotic" becoming too foreign. Similar distortions are noted by Mohamed (1988) in his analysis of the way Morocco was promoted as a destination area in France, with natives always represented as friendly and hospitable, as servants, as attractions, but never as real people.

Analyses of promotional material on sub-Saharan Africa are uncommon. However, Tresse (as cited in Dann, 1996) notes the tendency in photographs of African destination areas to depict "Africans as naked, with peculiar hairstyles and exotic bodily adornments" (p. 209), and a similar focus has also been noted for Swaziland and, more generally, for southern Africa (D. Harrison, 1992c, pp. 158–160). An examination of four recent brochures on Africa at the time of writing[6] confirms the continued importance of such themes. There is, first, an overwhelming concentration on animals and their landscape. Second, where people are shown, they are most often tourists in the company of other tourists, and, third, where Africans are depicted (which is quite rare), they are either in colorful "traditional" dress or guiding tourists on their safaris.

Insofar as the stereotyped images held by whites of sub-Saharan Africa are repeated and reinforced in tourism brochures, they are also supplemented by other sources, some of which may counter messages designed to promote Africa as a tourism destination. On the one hand, such feature films as *Out of Africa* promote a positive image of Africa or, at least, of the African landscape. On the other hand, along with information provided by governments (as in the U.S. advisories), television news coverage of Africa, especially sub-Saharan Africa, regularly portrays it as a region of poverty, famine, wars, suffering, and cruelty, with graphic and heart-rending images that must act as a powerful counter to the messages of the brochures. Famine in Ethiopia, genocide in Uganda and Rwanda, street crime and political unrest in Nairobi, the prevalence of AIDS in East Africa, wars in Sierra Leone and the Sudan—the list is almost endless. Right or wrong, the image of Africa as a platform for war, violence, and brutality—the savage side of the "noble savage"—is thus reinforced, which means, as Lundberg and Lundberg (1993) recognize, that tourism in Africa "is not likely to become a large factor for at least one or two decades" (p. 324). Irrespective of the causes of such instability, which may still be linked to the continued problems of decolonization (Teye, 1986, 1988), it is nevertheless an inheritance that operates against the development of tourism.[7]

The Development of Global Tourism

It has been recognized elsewhere that tourism is an important feature and spur of globalization (Go & Pine, 1995; D. Harrison, 1997b), and transnational corporations (TNCs) are key players in this process. Their role in Africa is discussed by other contributors to this book, but several points relevant to the overall thesis of this chapter should be made. First, TNCs involved in the hospitality industry normally cater for tourists (on business or holiday) on a large scale and, as a consequence, their hotels are nearly always either near urban centers or, in the case of beach tourism, are designed to accommodate guests on one site in relatively large numbers. For this reason, although there are exceptions (e.g., Nairobi National Park), they are unlikely to be situated in or close to national parks and game reserves, unless they are provided with specific government support, as seems to have occurred in Kenya (Jommo, 1987, pp. 57–58).

Second, while only one of the world's top 50 hotel chains—Sun International, based in Johannesburg (Go, 1988, p. 32) and with extensive properties throughout southern Africa—has its headquarters in Africa, other TNCs are well represented in the hospitality industry. Of 50 African countries listed in 1996 (Walden Publishers, 1996), they are present in all but 10, and eight of these, notably Chad, Equatorial Guinea, Eritrea, Malawi, Mali, Mozambique, Rwanda, and Somalia, are among the poorest countries of the continent and are little visited by tourists, even though they may have considerable tourism potential. Of the two remaining, Zambia and Namibia, the former is relatively poor, and is marketed as a place for "travellers, not for tourists, [who] want to get away from big hotels" (Adventure World, 1996/97, p. 48) while Namibia, by contrast, is relatively wealthy (as indicated in Table 3.2) but, like Zambia, also concentrates very much on safari tourism.

Third, there are marked differences in the degree of TNC involvement in African countries that earn most from tourism, arising at least in part from the extent of urbanization (itself a measure of colonial influence) and the nature of a country's tourism industry. In southern Africa, Namibia's tourism industry, which is focused on safari tourism, seems to be financed largely by local (but probably white) capital, whereas TNCs are heavily involved in tourism in the urban centers of South Africa (especially Holiday Inn and Southern Sun) and Zimbabwe (Southern Sun and Best Western). TNCs also have a high profile in North Africa, especially Egypt and Morocco. They are less in evidence in Tunisia where, during the 1960s, the state itself led the growth in tourism and restricted the role of private capital, especially overseas capital (Poirier, 1995, p. 158). When these restrictions

were eased and then removed, the trajectory of tourism development in Tuni.
ready set and it is likely that the focus on European package tourists, along with
ingness of the Tunisian middle class to invest in hotels, reduced the opportunities f.. TNC
involvement.

In East Africa, the importance of TNCs varies. Those operating in Kenya seem to have
played an important role, as suggested by Jommo (1987, pp. 33–62) and Bachmann (1988a),
a situation that seems to have changed but little over the last decade:

> The overwhelming part of the tourist industry is run by the private sector, and a
> substantial part of it is owned by foreign companies. As the Malindi example showed,
> about half the capital issued for hotel investment is foreign owned, while the remain-
> ing capital mostly stems from Europeans residing in Kenya. This ownership structure
> is probably similar in other tourist areas. Actually, there are very few African promot-
> ers in the tourism business, and most of these are Nairobi businessmen taking minor-
> ity equity shares. (Bachmann, 1988a, p. 302)

TNCs are less important in Tanzania, perhaps because of the former's more socialist-ori-
ented policies since independence. It is noteworthy, however, that the colonial government
of Tanganyika was less successful than Kenya in attracting white settlers, and that its tourism
focus is more specifically on safari tourism than Kenya, which started making special efforts
to promote beach tourism in the 1970s and 1980s (Bachmann, 1988a, p. 142).

In the rest of Africa, holidaymakers are less frequent and the pattern is for one or two
TNC hotels to be situated in major administrative or industrial cities, primarily for the
benefit of business tourists. This explains, for example, why ACCOR, the leading French
TNC in the hospitality business, is found throughout cities in sub-Saharan Africa, especially in former French colonies. Similarly, Méridien, a hotel chain owned or managed by
Air France, can be found in (formerly Belgian) Congo, Gabon, and the Sudan. The extent to
which ownership and operation of hotels in former British colonies has "followed the
flag" is more difficult to ascertain, as in recent years there have been numerous takeovers,[8]
but—as other chapters in this book indicate—British capital continues to have extensive
hotel interests in Africa. By contrast, U.S. capital is less in evidence, and tends to be concentrated in North and South Africa, notably Egypt, Morocco, South Africa, and Zimbabwe
(Walden Publishers, 1996).

The involvement of transnational corporations in African tourism must be seen in its
historical context. Insofar as tourism was developed by the colonial powers, it was by
whites for whites. Africans were rarely willing or able to provide tourist facilities, and
their nonparticipation in the tourism industry was reinforced by insistence that all members of society continue to wear their "uniform of color." After World War II, when modern
tourism developed in the region, and especially when the bulk transportation of passengers by air became possible, those countries that already possessed a developed infrastructure were at an advantage and, along with the established settler class, transnational
companies soon started to meet the needs of the tourist market. Even much later, when
black Africans did start to become involved in tourism, as in Kenya, they were most likely
to run smaller guesthouses to accommodate other black African travelers (Bachmann, 1988a,
p. 220). In effect, transnational companies involved in the hospitality industry in Africa are
the successors of the early settlers.

White Tourism and a Black Backlash

The major role played by white settlers and, later, European and North American
transnational corporations, in African tourism did not meet universal approval. The rela-

tive luxury of tourist facilities and the apparent wealth of the tourists contrasted starkly with the material deprivation encountered on a daily basis by many Africans. In addition, resentment against what some saw as the continuation of colonial relations was exacerbated by evidence that young people were falling victim to what are now known as "demonstration effects" and were showing too unhealthy an interest in the tourist dollar, pound, franc, or deutschmark (D. Harrison, 1992b, p. 30). At the academic level, too, the enthusiastic adoption of underdevelopment theory in the 1970s and early 1980s, and its application to international tourism (which was also linked to Third World nationalism), prompted many to criticize the industry for failing to deliver "development" to most members of host populations (D. Harrison, 1988, pp. 62–148; 1992a, pp. 8–10). The combined result of these trends was that tourism in Africa, as in other less developed regions, was subjected to considerable criticism.

As an example of local hostility to tourism in Kenya, Migot-Adholla (as quoted in Bachmann, 1988a) feels able to state:

> It is now generally acknowledged that tourism in the Third World is helping the spread of prostitution, alcoholism and crime, and it also demoralises the local people. (p. 270)

And despite findings that people in Malindi, Kenya, generally expressed very positive sentiments about tourism, Bachmann (1988a) suggests that

> well-informed and concerned Kenyans are often much more critical towards tourism. Thus, a hotel manager asked about the negative effects of tourism for the Malindi population enumerates: the almost legal, widespread prostitution, the omnipresent "beach boys" and male prostitutes, drug consumption and uncontrolled shell collection; in sum: "all this definitely ruins and plunders the cultural and natural heritage of our people." . . . Thus, the host–tourist relationship is perceived by the coast people as good and friendly, though a better knowledge of tourism is likely to increase the negative statements about tourism and tourists. (pp. 271–272)

Similar "well-informed" opposition to tourism in Africa was articulated by others, including contributors to *The Standard*, a daily newspaper in Tanzania, most of whom regarded luxury tourism as inimical to socialist development (Shivji, 1975) and those involved in the Africa Network of the Ecumenical Coalition on Third World Tourism (Amoa, 1986). Academics, too, weighed into the debate, suggesting that tourists and Africans were increasingly being isolated from one another:

> The gap between the two grows ever wider. The tourist gets little authenticity for his money, and the local people get little of the tourist's money. It is an exploitative situation in which only the large-scale investors stand to gain any substantial profit. (Rajotte, 1987, p. 89)

While not suggesting that tourism has no ill effects, it is worth noting—as Bachmann (1988a, p. 272) himself points out—that at the time of his research hotel managers were concerned about increased competition, a factor that may well have colored their assessments of the situation. The personal experience of Migot-Adholla, too, recounted to Bachmann (1988a), must surely (and understandably) have influenced his view of Kenyan tourism:

> Even during day time Africans are interrogated by the hotel staff about their whereabouts when they enter a hotel complex. In the evening, there are usually security controls at the hotel entrance. It is therefore not surprising that a black Kenyan hav-

ing his evening walk along the hotel-owned beach strip was arrested by the hotel security people. Although the African insisted he was a hotel guest having spent a night in that hotel, the security man didn't believe him. Only after the intervention of the hotel manager was the Kenyan professor released. (p. 299)

It seems that, even in the 1980s, international hotels in Kenya were still considered to be only for guests who were white.[9]

Objections to the role of settler and transnational dominance of the upper end of the tourism industry in Africa, a continuation of structures and cultures inherited from the colonial past, are linked to another bequest from colonialism: the tendency of colonial governments to allocate the best agricultural land to white settlers, and to actively debar their African subjects from cultivating export crops. As Gann and Duignan (1962) remark, "territorial segregation became the order of the day in Kenya as it did in Rhodesia and South Africa" (p. 63). As a result of such policies, black Africans were further marginalized, both physically, in terms of the land they were able to occupy, and socially, in that their occupational status was correspondingly confirmed as being at the lower levels of the colonial hierarchy.

As other contributors to this book discuss in more detail, native Africans were further marginalized when colonial powers also allocated land to animals. Ironically, in parts of southern Africa this was deemed necessary because of the indiscriminate behavior of *European* hunters who, by the early 1900s, had wiped out huge populations of elephant and other wildlife (D. Harrison, 1995, p. 141; Sugg & Kreuter, 1994, pp. 22–25). In Uganda in 1958, Africans were displaced when the Kidepo National Park was established (Sugg & Kreuter, 1994, p. 24) and in East Africa, too, as early as 1900, the British were planning to reserve land for wild animals (Bachmann, 1988b), while the Akagera National Park was created in Rwanda in 1934 (Shackley, 1995, p. 63). Indeed, towards the end of the colonial period, inequalities in access to land over vast swathes of Africa were exacerbated by the allocation of wide areas as national parks (Bachmann, 1988b, p. 52; Sugg & Kreuter, 1994, p. 23).

Postcolonial independent governments have tended to continue colonial policies in efforts to protect local fauna, partly for reasons of conservation and partly to encourage safari tourism. Indeed, as indicated earlier, wild animals figure prominently in Western images of Africa, even in brochures of Uganda, "somewhat misleadingly given that most of them were killed during the civil war" (Borzello, 1994, p. 12). As a result, in many parts of Africa there are clear conflicts over the rights of animals, the rights of humans to hunt them for food (seen by the authorities as "poaching"), and the rights of the governments and tour operators to keep them alive. It is a debate in which tourism is central (cf. Berger, 1996; Boonzaier, 1996; Gibson & Marks, 1995; Keefe, 1995; Mitchell, 1998; Potts, Goodwin, & Walpole, 1996; Rajotte, 1987; Shah, 1995; Wheat, 1997).

Conclusion

In this chapter, it has been suggested that tourism throughout Africa was developed primarily by colonialists for the benefit of other colonialists. During most of the colonial period, Africans possessed neither the financial nor the cultural capital to compete with European domination of the nascent tourism industry, which was most advanced in those African countries with a relatively large settler population. Even towards the end of formal colonialism, those few Africans who did attempt to enter the hospitality "industry" were discouraged from doing so. With the introduction of mass tourism that came with advances in aircraft technology, settler capital was generally joined by transnational capital, sometimes in competition (as in Kenya) and sometimes in cooperation, as (possibly) in South Africa. This structure of the tourism industry, with whites at the top and black Africans, if involved at all, at the bottom, was a major bequest of colonialism.

Another colonial bequest, and one of long standing, was a series of ambivalent images of Africa that portrayed the black African, especially the black male, on the one hand as dangerous and threatening and, on the other, as noble and childlike. Africa was also seen as the habitat of wild animals, even though many had actually been indiscriminately slaughtered by professional white hunters, and as a series of landscapes. Such varying and conflicting images, it is suggested, continue to be presented in the pictures and texts of tourist brochures, and in regular media reports of political and civil unrest, wars and rumors of wars, and famine and poverty.

Such problems will continue to condition the development of tourism in Africa. For those who oppose tourism, they might be considered to carry out a protective function. For those wishing to see tourism further developed, they present barriers that need to be overcome. In general, though, one fact is clear: like the colonialists who preceded them, tourists prefer to visit places that are already at least partly "developed." They do not wish to see emaciated children and war-ravaged landscapes, and war zones or inadequate medical services hold no attraction for them. However, at the same time, they do not hanker after too much development. In this respect, at least, modern tourists have much in common with some of tourism's harshest critics: the natives must be "traditional," wear colorful and exotic clothes, and, of course, shows signs of being friendly and hospitable. Ironically, modern tourists and their critics may also have inherited another characteristic from the colonial past: an inability to imagine or concede that local people in tourist destination areas may simply aspire to possess the consumer durables carried by tourists—and even to be given the same choices that people in more "developed" societies take for granted.

Notes

[1] Further north, in the Sudan in the late 19th century, steam ships and railways constructed for military and (secondarily) commercial purposes were also used to carry tourists, including big game hunters, and "made the Sudan fashionable and for some a welcome change from the routine rounds of the European spas" (Hill, 1965, p. 66). Indeed, until the early 1900s, senior personnel (British and Egyptian) were drawn from the armed services. The first hotel was opened in Khartoum in 1900 and in 1902 another was opened by a mining company, as a condition for receiving mineral rights. It later became the Grand Hotel. It is clear from Hill's account that relations among the British, Egyptians, and Sudanese were far more egalitarian than those found in sub-Saharan Africa, possibly because from 1898 until 1956 Britain and Egypt governed the Sudan jointly (Hill, 1965, pp. 51–53, 66, 152–155).

[2] A similar service is carried out in the United Kingdom by the Foreign and Commonwealth Office (FCO) Travel Advice Unit.

[3] Data in this section are taken from the U.S. travel advisories available on the World Wide Web on May 26, 1998.

[4] The World Tourism Organization includes Egypt in the Middle East category, and it is not much discussed in this chapter. If treated as African, it would rank in the continent's top five for international arrivals and earnings from tourism and, like Morocco and Tunisia, which also rely to a large extent on European tourists, should be regarded as part of the European tourist "periphery" (WTO, 1996b, p. 56).

[5] The "purpose of visit" of 35% of all international arrivals to Morocco is classified as

"other," about the same proportion as those classified as arriving for "leisure, recreation, or holidays," and more than 25% of arrivals are consistently unaccounted for (WTO, 1996b, p. 117).

[6]Brochures examined were Suntravel's 1996/7 and 1998 *Africa,* Adventure World's 1996/ 7 *Africa from the Cape to Cairo* (all issued in Auckland) and Adventure World's *Africa: Safaris and Expeditions* (which was published in Sydney).

[7]In support of this view, a recent survey suggests that both guide books and travelers view Africa as a region of social instability and consider the health of visitors there to be more at risk than in any other region (S. Carter 1998, pp. 354–355). The perception of Africa as generally unsafe, for U.S. tourists especially, was undoubtedly reinforced by the bombings of U.S. embassies in Nairobi and Dar es Salaam in August 1998.

[8]In 1987, for example, Labrokes purchased Hilton International from Trans-World Air- lines, and in March 1998, Bass plc, a British TNC already owning 2400 Holiday Inns in 60 countries, including several in Africa, purchased Inter-Continental Hotels, which operates hotels in Europe, the Middle East, and Africa, from a Japanese company (Adel, 1998, p. 123).

[9]It should also be noted that throughout sub-Saharan Africa, especially in urban centers, hotels catering primarily for African clients are often strongly associated with prostitution and other less-formal sexual liaisons. In many, it is not uncommon to rent rooms by the hour or half-hour.

Chapter 4

Tourism and Political Geography in Southern Africa

David B. Weaver

Summary

The functional approach in political geography maintains that state power structures must constantly impose and reinforce a variety of "centripetal" (or state-enhancing) forces to offset the existence of various "centrifugal" (or state-eroding) forces. This chapter applies the functional approach to the tourism sector of southern Africa, emphasizing the central role of the Republic of South Africa. During the Apartheid era, tourism was deliberately if tacitly employed as a centripetal tactic to generate revenue, attract potential immigrants, and, most importantly, to legitimize the "homelands" while providing a convenient outlet for tourism products then illegal within South Africa itself. Concurrently, neighboring "casino states" such as Swaziland and Lesotho also attempted to capitalize on the demand for these activities. Tourism is also used as a centripetal force in post-Apartheid South Africa to assist in regional development and wealth redistribution strategies, and to promote the iconography of the new dominant ideology. However, tourism is also seen by some neighboring states as a potential centrifugal force that promotes regional integration (and hence the weakening of state power) and facilitates the expansion of the South African sphere of influence.

Key words: Political geography; Centripetal and centrifugal forces; South Africa; Bantustans

Introduction

This chapter applies a political geography perspective to the tourism sector of southern Africa, and demonstrates how this underutilized approach, and the functional theory in particular, can contribute to an understanding of tourism as a deliberate state-reinforcing mechanism. The Republic of South Africa is the focal point of this analysis, by merit of its relatively large and complex tourism industry, data availability, and, in particular, the presence of an active geopolitical environment that implicates all of southern Africa and can be conveniently divided into two vastly dissimilar eras (i.e., Apartheid and post-Apartheid). The first section of this chapter considers the nature of political geography and the functional approach, and shows in a generic sense how this is relevant to tourism. Subsequently, the political geography of South Africa over the past 40 years is outlined in order to provide a context for the consideration of tourism. The remaining two sections examine tourism, first from the perspective of the Apartheid era and then from the post-Apartheid perspective.

The Nature of Political Geography

The field of political geography is highly diverse, and unconstrained by any single universally adopted definitions or paradigms (Glassner, 1996). However, the interplay between space and politics that is implied by the term is central to virtually all interpretations. According to Pacione (1985), political geography is

> concerned with the geographical consequences of political decisions and actions, the geographical factors which were considered during the making of any decisions, and the role of any geographical factors which influenced the outcome of political actions. (p. 1)

For most political geographers, the critical analytical frame of reference is the state, given that such units are theoretically vested with the greatest amount of power in the modern political system, relative to other types of political–spatial structures (P. Taylor, 1994). Those who govern states, according to the functional theory of Hartshorne (as cited in Glassner, 1996), attempt to maintain and enhance the state by minimizing the *centrifugal forces* that destabilize the state, and maximizing the *centripetal forces*, or cohesive forces, that engender stability (Getis, Getis, & Fellman, 1996). Implicit within the functional approach is the view that states, however ostensibly altruistic their actions, are fundamentally occupied with their own self-interest. When classifying centripetal and centrifugal forces, a distinction can be made between those that are internal and those that are external. Four categories of force result, as depicted with examples in Table 4.1. It should be noted that a particular situation may serve as both a centripetal and centrifugal force, depending on the circumstances. For example, the granting of regional autonomy can either defuse or encourage the separatist agitations of a dissatisfied national minority, while a border dispute can either threaten the integrity of the state or unite a disputatious

Table 4.1. Centrifugal and Centripetal Forces

Force	Centrifugal	Centripetal
Internal	• Ethnic minority concentrations (e.g., more than one nation) • Strong subunits (e.g., Provinces) and weak central govts. • Spatial disparities in resources, wealth • Internal geographic barriers • Unusual shape (e.g., linear, enclaves) • Poorly developed transport networks	• National cohesion • Strong raison d'etre (or reason for being) • Strong iconography (unifying symbols of statehood) • Strong central government • Lack of internal geographical barriers • Integrative transportation networks • Regional development strategies • Relocation of capital city
External	• External dependence • Hostile neighboring states • Formation of strong blocs • Pan-nationalism • Irregular or contested boundaries	• Alliances • Trade surpluses • Common external threats (including boundary disputes)

population against a common external threat. Trade blocs can act centripetally by strengthening national economies, but also centrifugally by conceding sovereign powers to the supranational power structure.

As reflected in Table 4.1, few if any explicit references to tourism as either a centrifugal or centripetal force have been made, although the element of cross-border travel in international tourism is essentially both a political and geographical act. In any case, clear linkages can be cited for both possibilities. Regarding the former, a very overt example involved the destabilizing actions of Iranian pilgrims in Mecca during the 1987 Hajj. The use of tourism as a vehicle for asserting sovereignty in Antarctica, by claimants such as Chile and Argentina, is another direct example (Hall & Wouters, 1995). As well, tourism can provide an economic rationale for the would-be secession of regions already dissatisfied with the central government, as in some peripheral islands in Caribbean archipelagic states (Weaver, 1998a). More indirectly, uncontrolled tourism development is frequently associated with increased local hostility as sociocultural and environmental carrying capacities are exceeded, a development that can translate into hostility toward the national government that condones or contributes to such stresses. From a centripetal perspective, tourism may contribute to political stability through the generation of wealth for peripheral or other regions, and may be used as a propaganda tool. For example, inbound tourism in China, at least in its earlier phases, was used by the government to showcase its alleged achievements, and to confer international legitimacy. Bhutan has also issued tourist passports as a means of reinforcing its sovereign prerogatives in the face of perceived threats of Indian expansionism (Richter, 1989).

Since its inception as a subfield in the mid-1800s, political geography has experienced many turns in fortune, but has always resurfaced and thrived during eras of large-scale geopolitical change (Glassner, 1996). During such times, cumulative centrifugal forces appear to overwhelm centripetal forces across a broad geographic front, often initiating the dissolution or emasculation of existing states, and the formation of new states in their stead. Moreover, as argued by Wallerstein (1979) in the context of world systems theory, the reverberations of these forces are felt across the globe. For example, the collapse of the Soviet Union, which represented the culmination of the most recent period of large-scale change (P. Taylor, 1994), may be identified as a critical factor in the subsequent reconfiguration of the state system in Africa, as considered in the following section.

Political Geography and Southern Africa

Over the past 50 years, the political geography of sub-Saharan Africa has been dominated by a relentless north-to-south process of decolonization, and subsequent attempts by the newly independent African states to acquire enough centripetal capacity to offset a multitude of serious centrifugal factors (e.g., poverty, tribalism, irrational boundaries, unintegrated transportation systems). If these processes have any particular geographical frame of reference, then this role must surely belong to South Africa, given its great economic and military clout, entrenched history of white rule, and active interference in the affairs of neighboring states as it attempted to maintain a *cordon sanitaire* of client buffer states.

With the gradual erosion of this buffer zone, the main internal geopolitical response of the South African government between 1959 and 1991 involved the creation of bantustans or "homelands" for specific ethnic groups. Insofar as these bantustans were intended to become independent (thereby reducing South Africa's territory), they may technically be considered a centrifugal force. However, by disenfranchising virtually the entire African population of South Africa, they would act as a centripetal force by leaving in their wake a

South African state with a majority of white citizens. Of course, this entire strategy of "Grand Apartheid" was subverted by the political developments of the early 1990s, which, as suggested, were inextricably linked to events in the Soviet Union. As long as the African National Congress (ANC) maintained a Soviet-backed Socialist stance, the Apartheid regime could present itself as a strategically vital bulwark against the expansion of the Soviet orbit, and one that the West was willing to tolerate despite its blatantly racialist policies. The Soviet collapse, however, forced both the ANC and the white regime to move toward the political center, and a transition to majority rule was the logical outcome of this fundamental change in the global geopolitical equation (Beinart, 1997).

While the end of minority rule in South Africa may be seen as the culmination of the sub-Saharan decolonization process, this by no means implies the geopolitical stabilization of the region. The attainment of majority rule in South Africa was clearly a welcomed development, but the initial euphoria attending this transition has been replaced by ambivalence as new geopolitical realities become apparent, and as existing and often latent issues now acquire a higher profile. For example, the termination of the decolonization process has deprived the region's states of their most potent external centripetal force (i.e., South Africa, the common enemy). In addition, the transition to majority rule has in no significant way reduced South Africa's status as the region's economic and military powerhouse, its GNP being four times larger than all of its South African Development Community (SADC) (see Chapter 10) partners combined ("South Africa Dreams of Unity," 1995). Accordingly, the rhetoric of post-Apartheid regional cooperation and integration, espoused through the SADC, is tempered by concerns among weaker states, such as Mozambique ("South Africans Return to Mozambique," 1996) and Zimbabwe (Dhliwayo, 1997), over the unrestricted expansion of South Africa's economic and political orbit, and the subsequent emergence of a new self-interested "imperial" South Africa. In 1995–96, South African companies invested an estimated US$5 billion in Africa, and announced further investments of US$10 billion (Nevin, 1997; Timewell, 1997). Exacerbating such fears are ongoing border-centered problems of illegal immigration, poaching, drug trafficking, and gun running, which are generating stress in the bilateral relations between South Africa and its nearest neighbors ("Neighborhood Watch in Southern Africa," 1994). Nevertheless, tangible physical evidence of regional integration is emerging through such multilateral initiatives as the Walvis Bay–Botswana–Gauteng–Maputo development corridor (Ndivanga, 1998).

Internal geopolitical uncertainties are also apparent. Tribalism remains a potent centrifugal force within South Africa, particularly as the bantustan system served to reinforce the territorial identity of each main indigenous ethnic group, and reinforce the spatial dichotomy between a rural black "Third World" and an urban white "First World." In addition, there is a growing sense of bifurcation between the African-dominated east, symbolized by Johannesburg, and the white/colored-dominated west, symbolized by Cape Town (Beinart, 1997). Centripetal strategies clearly intended to counteract these tendencies have included the establishment of a federal structure providing a high degree of autonomy to nine constituent provinces, the formulation of strategies designed to facilitate both national reconciliation and the redistribution of wealth, and the introduction of a flag that effectively combines the iconography of black and white South Africa.

Tourism and Political Geography in South Africa

Tourism has played a variety of roles in the political geography of South Africa throughout the period discussed above. The following subsections examine these roles in the context of Apartheid era and post-Apartheid era southern Africa, respectively.

Tourism in South Africa: Apartheid Era

During the Apartheid period, a great deal of energy was expended by government to attain a number of concurrent centripetal objectives. These included the strengthening of the national economy (to offset and override international sanctions), attaining recognition as a legitimate member of the world community, and increasing the white population while simultaneously reducing both the *de jure* and *de facto* black population (Rhoodie, 1972). In all of these strategies, a contributory though rarely acknowledged role was played by the tourism sector. Regarding the strengthening of the national economy, tourism was long recognized as a regionally significant vehicle for economic development and diversification, which could contribute to the reduction of spatial disparities in wealth. With respect to international legitimacy, the presence of tourists from other countries augments this objective in at least three ways. First, the very presence of international tourists may be interpreted as a sanctioning of the state's legitimacy, as acknowledged by the occasional call for tourist boycotts to effect the alienation and isolation of states (as in the case of Burma). It was therefore in South Africa's interests, wholly aside from the positive economic impacts, to attract as numerous and diverse a body of international tourists as possible. Second, the admittance of international tourists involves actions (e.g., the stamping of passports, the negotiation of landing rights) that affirm and give substance to the sovereign prerogatives of the state. Third, by attracting tourists to the more prosperous neighborhoods of Soweto or neat "model" villages inhabited by contented natives, tourism functioned as a propaganda tool for disseminating the best possible image of South Africa to the international forum. This was effectively the motive underlying South Africa's promotion of "fact-finding tours" during the 1970s and 1980s. Finally, tourism had long been employed by the South African government as a vehicle for encouraging white immigration from Europe and other regions, on the assumption that at least some of these tourists would augment the white population by returning as settlers (personal communication with former tourism officials, 1979). The strategy of perceiving tourists as potential immigrants was not unique to South Africa, but was also attempted (albeit not very successfully) in other colonial situations such as Fiji (D. Harrison & Brandt, 1997).

The use of tourism as a centripetal legitimization strategy was extended to the bantustans in the 1970s as part of the attempt to gain their acceptance in the international community. However, there were several crucial differences between the motives and outcomes pursued by South Africa for these bantustans as opposed to South Africa itself. For example, while South Africa at least maintained diplomatic relations with a number of legitimate countries, the "independent" bantustans (i.e., Transkei, Bophuthatswana, Ciskei, and Venda) were full-fledged pariahs, with recognition being accorded only by South Africa and the other independent bantustans. Unable to force other countries to confer diplomatic recognition, bantustan governments could insist that visitors obtain the necessary visas for entering their territory. This therefore constituted a form of quasi-recognition, or "recognition by stealth," which it was hoped would serve as a stepping stone toward conventional diplomatic relations. (A similar effect was obtained whenever franked letters bearing the postage stamps of Transkei or Bophuthatswana successfully reached addressees outside of South Africa or the bantustans.)

The question of tourism as a tool for regional development also acquired special significance in the context of the bantustans. By any reasonable measure, these entities were spectacularly undeveloped, accounting cumulatively for only 2.7% of the South African GNP in 1973 (South Africa Department of Information, 1976). Few viable options were available to stimulate economic development in these entities and thereby give further credibility to their establishment as independent states. However, tourism was soon recognized as one sector that could prosper, while simultaneously fulfilling other geopolitical objectives. Specifically, the effort since the late 1970s was focused upon the establishment of gaming-oriented resorts controlled and operated by South African corporations. Such forms of tourism apparently provided an almost perfect vehicle for weaning the impoverished bantustans away from their revenue dependency on South Africa. According to Crush and Wellings (1987),

> In (the hotel industry) the South African state has found a perfect foil for its grand strategy for the bantustans. For the state this "alliance" has had the advantage of giving considerable weight to its attempts to legitimise bantustan independence in the international forum and has also allowed it to replace a considerable portion of the costs of subsidising the bantustan strategy with private capital. Tourism capital has, for its part, discovered in the bantustans a highly profitable arena for investment. (p. 107)

Essentially, the demand for gaming in the bantustans was underpinned by the illegality of such activities within the Republic itself, and by the proximity of some bantustans (and especially Bophuthatswana) to major metropolitan areas such as Johannesburg. In a different country, "sinful" but profitable activities such as gambling and interracial sex could thus be conveniently accommodated without contradicting or undermining the fundamental precepts of the white-ruled state, while preempting demands for reform within South Africa itself (Crush & Wellings, 1987). The casino option came to be symbolized by the notorious Sun City and Lost City mega-resorts in Bophuthatswana, which involved such facilities as an artificial rain forest and ocean/beach complex (Koch, 1994). For those bantustan governments less willing to move toward independence, the possibility of similar revenue-generating casinos was held out as a lucrative incentive to encourage such an evolution (Crush & Wellings, 1987).

The establishment of large-scale gaming ventures in the bantustans should also be discussed in the context of earlier tourism-related developments in the bona fide black states bordering South Africa. In the 1960s, in a way similar to the bantustans, outgoing colonial governments encouraged the establishment of casinos as a way of facilitating economic development by capitalizing on the proximity of the then-colonies to the South African market. After independence, the continuation of this policy clearly served to tie Lesotho and Swaziland in particular into the South African sphere of influence, despite official policies promoting disengagement. During the 1970s, the proportion of inbound tourists originating in South Africa varied from 75% to 90% for both countries (Crush & Wellings, 1987; Stern, 1987; Wellings & Crush, 1983). The highly skewed pattern of tourism development in these "casino states," characterized by the establishment of gaming resorts in the capital city or in rural areas along the border, can be interpreted as a consequence of regional geopolitics involving spheres of influence, core–periphery relationships, and other factors similar to those at play in the bantustans (see above). By facilitating economic development, the casinos were centripetal from the Lesotho/Swaziland perspective; but by fostering further dependency on South Africa, the effect was centrifugal, although the counter-rationale is that such dependency was inevitable in any instance.

From a South African perspective, the casino states provided a convenient safety valve and source of revenue generation for the private sector, at least until the bantustans emerged as an even more compliant and accessible venue. Perhaps the main characteristic of the casino states that differs from all examples discussed so far was the relative lack of control exercised by the South African state, although the latter could have theoretically destroyed the sector had it chosen at any time to prevent its citizens (e.g., as with the U.S. vis-à-vis Cuba) from traveling to those countries. Surprisingly, there is little evidence, aside from a few isolated murders and attacks on tourists by radical members of the Pan Africanist Congress (Koch, 1994), of tourism being targeted for centrifugal purposes by the resistance movement.

Tourism in South Africa: Post-Apartheid Era

All of the motivations and strategies described above were rendered obsolete during the transition period toward majority rule between 1990 and 1994, although this is not to say that tourism has relinquished its role as a significant factor in the political geography of South Africa and its neighbors. The following discussion examines, respectively, the internal and external dimensions of this relationship.

In the domestic arena, the ANC-dominated government of Nelson Mandela has assiduously espoused policies of "national reconciliation" and redistribution of wealth in order to placate the seemingly contradictory demands of all major population segments, and thereby avoid balkanizing centrifugal outcomes. There are several ways in which tourism has been mobilized in order to attain these objectives. First, as with the Apartheid regime, tourism is intended to provide a tangible indicator of international affirmation. A recent advertising campaign uses the symbolism of an awakening lion to convey the emergence or dawning of a new South Africa (Hannaford, 1997). Accompanying this iconography is text that emphasizes the link between visitation and eyewitness support for the new state of affairs:

> There's a new spirit in the land. A new nation has been born. It's a dynamic, historic time—with many people of goodwill working together towards the future. Experience this land where the ecology is part of the culture. A land of huge vistas, exotic peoples, amazing fauna and flora. Now's the time to show your commitment—to see this magnificent country. And, in years to come, you'll be able to say, "I was there." (Hannaford, 1997, p. 19)

Quite clearly, tourists are meant to convey their profound experiences to others in their home countries, thereby disseminating a positive image of South Africa, and stimulating further visitation by other would-be witnesses. Reinforcing this strategy is the promotion of new tourist attractions, such as the Sharpeville massacre site and Robben Island, that capitalize on and reaffirm the heroism of the resistance movement, while simultaneously demonizing the Apartheid regime. Not incidentally, with Robben Island alone accommodating 100,000 visitors in its first year of operations as an attraction (personal communication with the Director of Robben Island Museum, 1998), tourism also provides a source of funding for the maintenance of these national shrines. A particularly illustrative example of tourism as a propaganda tool is found in the Cape Town bid for the 2004 Olympic Games, which was heralded in some quarters as one of the most significant events to potentially be held in the country. The Olympics were meant, among other goals, to symbolize the reemergence of an internationally condoned and economically developed South Africa (i.e., capable of hosting the games), although the internal competition also highlighted the rivalry between Cape Town and Johannesburg. As well, the use of a torch in the shape of Africa was intended as a symbol of pan-Africanism and of South Africa's reintegration into Africa, specifically. The rejection of the Cape Town bid, accordingly, was widely perceived as a major national disaster and humiliation. The use of tourism as a centripetal mechanism is not restricted in the region to South Africa. Swaziland, in its advertising campaigns of the early 1990s, utilized "the Royal Experience" as a slogan to affirm the country's traditional power structure (D. Harrison, 1995).

The use of tourist attractions as iconography is not restricted to international visitors. If anything, their purveyance as domestic icons is far more significant as a way of achieving a sense of shared nationhood. The new government has therefore identified the development of domestic tourism, especially among the African population, as a priority policy issue in the tourism sector. This impulse, furthermore, relates to the elimination of internal travel restrictions, the desire to foster a positive tourism trade balance, and the desire to have residents of different regions and ethnic groups come into greater contact with one another.

A second way in which tourism centripetally supports new national policy is through the fostering of sustainable tourism and ecotourism as mechanisms for the redistribution of wealth, especially within rural areas. Fundamentally, this effort capitalizes on the surge of market interest in these "postindustrial" modes of environmentally and socially responsible tourist experience (Poon, 1993). Fortuitously, such modes of production adhere almost perfectly to the government rhetoric of redistribution and community participation. Reflecting the utilization of ecotourism as a deliberate tool for achieving rural reconstruction, the Industrial Development Corporation has committed US$171 million to related projects (Koch, 1994). The South African Tourist Board, for its part, has produced a policy document recommending that public funding for lodges be provided only if community participation in the venture is guaranteed, the assumption being that economic development for local communities is the ultimate goal of ecotourism (Koch, 1994). Thus, the extensive community involvement demonstrated by many of South Africa's private ecotourism-type businesses, such as Wilderness Safaris, the Mabula Game Lodge, the Inyati Game Lodge, and the Sabi Sabi Private Game Reserve (South African Tourism Update [SATU], 1997), may derive more from political expediency than from any profound commitment to the principles invoked. In any case, the South African government has clearly identified ecotourism as an activity that can facilitate economic development in peripheral areas, and especially in areas adjacent to major protected areas such as Kruger National Park (which interestingly still retains its Afrikaaner identity in its name).

In the external context, tourism is assuming a significant role in the proliferating attempts to foster the regional integration of southern Africa. For example, the development of accommodations and attractions is an explicit component of several bilateral and multilateral Spatial Development Initiatives (SDIs). Specifically, the Maputo Development Corridor (from Maputo to Witbank) is expected to receive US$42 million in tourism-related investment, including (ironically, given their association with the Apartheid regime) three casino complexes. Comprehensive tourism strategies are also being formulated for the Platinum Toll Road (involving South Africa's Gauteng province, Botswana, and Namibia), and a US$39 million 156-km highway connecting the coastal regions of South Africa and Mozambique (SATU, 1997). Interest is also being expressed in an "Ivory Route" to extend from KwaZulu Natal province in South Africa to Botswana and Zimbabwe, involving lodges, tented camps, and 4×4 trails (SATU, 1998). Special Development Areas (SDAs) are also being designated to facilitate the multilateral management of cross-border resources in areas such as the Kalahari Desert (South African Development Community, 1996). Organizationally, the Regional Tourism Organisation of Southern Africa (RETOSA) was established in 1996 to promote the integration of the regional tourism product. In order to encourage the development of multicountry itineraries, RETOSA will apparently support projects that involve at least three regional countries (Foottit, 1998).

Consideration is also being given to the establishment of cross-border protected areas. Ironically, entities such as Kruger National Park and certain game reserves in Natal were both tacitly and overtly utilized during the Apartheid era as buffer zones helping to shield the built-up areas of South Africa against incursions from Mozambique-based guerrillas (Koch, 1994). Today, the geopolitical emphasis has shifted dramatically to include proposals for the creation of a southern African "peace park" incorporating Kruger National Park and adjacent protected areas in Mozambique and Zimbabwe ("Good and Bad at Game," 1996). The logic underlying such initiatives, already being implemented in Central America and other regions (Weaver, 1998b), is multifarious. On one hand, they provide a tangible symbol of international cooperation. According to Nelson Mandela, a single park, as described above, "would be . . . a concrete symbol of regional unity and a spur to development" (as cited in Pons, 1998). The development component is represented primarily by tourism, on the assumption that such units would constitute a highly attractive product by merit of their large size, biodiversity, and range of facilities. However, concerns have also been expressed that such "de-fenced" border areas could compromise national security by exacerbating rather than reducing the existing problems of illegal immigration, poaching, and smuggling (Pons, 1998).

South Africa's neighbors harbor some ambivalence regarding the trend toward regional tourism integration. As in other sectors, the attainment of relative stability and the ability to capitalize on proximity to South Africa's infrastructure and tourist market are obviously welcomed by these weaker states. However, some of the likely consequences of integration, including the reinforcement of dependent core–periphery relationships and the incremental cession of national powers to regional bodies, could ultimately prove more centrifugal in their effects than the circumstances of the Apartheid era. Namibia, for example, remains extremely dependent on South African tourist markets (62% of 1993 inbound traffic), investment capital (i.e., ownership of major Windhoek hotels), and imported goods consumed by tourists (90% supplied by South Africa) (Weaver & Elliott, 1996).

Conclusions

During the Apartheid era, the self-interest of the minority government of South Africa was overtly expressed through a spectrum of centripetal strategies that occasionally involved the tourism sector. Tourists were attractive as revenue generators, potential immi-

Table 4.2. Tourism-Related Centrifugal and Centripetal Forces

Force	Centrifugal	Centripetal
Internal	• Opposition movements target tourists & tourism industry • Regional competition for tourist market share & mega-events	• Tourists as potential immigrants • Tourism entry formalities as a form of quasi-recognition • Tourism as a source of revenues and economic diversification • Tourism as a tool of regional development • Tourism as promotion for national iconography
External	• International tourists as a destabilizing force • Tourism as a factor in regional integration (= dependency, erosion of state prerogatives)	• Tourists as disseminators of positive images • Tourism as a factor in regional integration (= economic development, improved relations) • "Safety valve" effect • Promotion of national iconography internationally

grants, and vehicles for the dissemination of positive images. As part of the Grand Apartheid strategy, tourism was to assist in the legitimization of the "independent" bantustans by providing a viable source of revenue, while simultaneously reducing the internal demand for activities that threatened the principles of the white-ruled state. Motives similar to the latter were also evident with respect to the "casino states" of Lesotho and Swaziland. In many ways, the post-Apartheid situation is far more complicated. Internally, tourism is still being mobilized as a propaganda tool (though not as an immigration stimulant), but has additionally assumed great significance as a vehicle for the redistribution of wealth in rural areas, and through domestic tourism, as a device to dissuade regionalism. Externally, the line between self-interest and altruism is blurred, as regional integration through tourism facilitates economic development as well as increased dependencies on South Africa. Euphoria in the region over the emergence of a new South Africa is therefore tempered by concerns over the unfettered expansion of that country's still white-dominated but now politically acceptable corporate interests.

This case study of southern Africa demonstrates the continuity and relevance of political geography, and the functional approach in particular, as a useful framework for analyzing and interpreting the tourism sector as a vehicle for state enhancement. At its core is the belief that states are primarily concerned with their own self-interest, and that tourism will be utilized to the greatest possible extent by those in power as a deliberate centripetal mechanism that contributes to the perpetuation of the state. The findings in this chapter allow for a reconfiguration of Table 4.1, taking into account, in a generic way, tourism-related phenomena only (Table 4.2). Empirical investigations of other case studies are now warranted to extend theoretical developments in this area.

Chapter 5

Tourism Policy Formulation in the Southern African Region

Carson L. Jenkins

Summary

Most of the countries comprising the Southern African Development Community (SADC) have attempted to formulate policies to guide the future development of the tourism sector. The approaches adopted have been very different, with some countries making an explicit policy statement while others have incorporated policy intentions within broader tourism planning exercises. In most of the countries, with the exception of Angola, tourism is an important sector in the respective economies and is recognized as having potential to contribute to general development objectives. A new feature of the policy formulation approach in the southern African countries is the participation of the private sector into this process, and the key role that the private sector will have in financing and in implementing future development.

The change in the formulation process has been in the respective roles of government and the private sector, leading to the development of a partnership initiative. The contents of the various policy statements have areas of common concern (e.g., product development, marketing, funding, human resources). There is an explicit preference to develop tourism within the existing sociocultural traditions and with consideration of environmental quality standards. Implementation of policy is largely reliant upon the existing institutional structures and with the extant legislation. Without appropriate changes in inadequate institutional structures and human resource capacity building, implementation strategies will be frustrated.

Key words: Tourism policy; Formulation process; Policy content; Implementation; Southern Africa

Introduction

In this chapter an attempt is made to present the role of policy in tourism development and to examine this process by reference to selected southern African countries. The southern African countries comprising the Southern African Development Community (SADC) are Angola, Botswana, Democratic Republic of Congo, Lesotho, Malawi, Mauritius, Mozambique, Namibia, Seychelles, South Africa, Swaziland, Tanzania, Zambia, and Zimbabwe. Policy formulation is deliberately described as a process rather than an action to emphasize its continuous nature. It rarely comprises a single action other than as a response to ad hoc situations, but is rather a series of decisions, actions, and implementation. In tourism, which is particularly a multisectoral activity with ramifications that are economic, social, cultural, environmental, and often political, a tourism policy will be an amalgamation of many subpolicies pertinent to different areas.

A policy is defined by the *Oxford English Dictionary* as being:"prudent conduct" and a "course of general plans of action." A policy is essentially a strategic declaration of intent within which tourism is expected to develop. It provides a reference framework to guide tourism development actions. For example, in Indonesia (1992), the current 25-year Long-Term Development Plan is the strategic parameter for the Five-Year Development Plans (*Repelitas*). In this country one of the national long-term development goals (also relevant to the tourism sector) is to encourage development in eastern Indonesia. Detailed tourism development planning has concentrated on provinces within this region. Without such strategic direction, market forces would probably continue to invest resources in western Indonesia, particularly in Java and Sumatra, thereby frustrating the attainment of national economic objectives. Market forces can be channeled and directed but cannot be ignored by government. In tourism, particularly where demand is often mainly international in character, government has to work closely with the private sector in a partnership to facilitate development. Tourism development planning is now more a product of cooperation rather than prescription, necessitating a fundamental change in the approach to policy formulation, which is discussed below.

Tourism policy is not always explicit. In many developed countries, such as the U.S., U.K., and Sweden, for example, there is no written policy for tourism. Support for tourism is given by politicians and governments implicitly, but such support is not verifiable by the existence of a document or written statement. In the U.S., Belgium, and Sweden there are no National Tourist Organizations. In these examples governments have chosen to let future tourism development be motivated by initiatives of the private sector. This is not the situation in most developing countries, where development planning is a central feature of government activity.

One of the most important aspects of tourism policy formulation—and one of the most ignored—relates to the institutional arrangements for implementation of the policy and the legal framework necessary to support implementation. These considerations, together with those noted above, will be discussed generally and then in the context of the southern African countries.

As a multisectoral and multifaceted activity, tourism development is subjected to many considerations and pressure groups, and the formulation of policy is not always a straightforward process. The plethora of government ministries and agencies, nongovernmental organizations, and the private sector, all of which have legitimate interests in tourism, can make policy formulation difficult. Some of these difficulties are discussed below.

Aspects of Policy Formulation

Changes in Approaches

The conventional approach to tourism policy formulation in developing countries has been for government to state what the policy is and to direct or expect the private sector to support it. It was unusual for governments to involve the private sector in this process. At the early stages of development in the tourism sector government provided not only the required infrastructure but also acted as an entrepreneur, investing in a range of facilities such as hotels, airlines, travel and tour operations, shopping facilities, etc. In African countries with a generally strong tradition of central planning and state investment (e.g., Zimbabwe, Zambia, Kenya), this tendency was particularly pronounced. There was limited cooperation between the public and private sectors in tourism development, and in some countries a situation of mutual suspicion of each other's intentions prevailed.

The primacy of government's role in development planning was a feature in most developing countries and certainly in southern African countries. This situation was to remain unchanged until the cataclysmic collapse of the Soviet Union in 1991. This historic event has been, indirectly, a major change agent in the nature of the support given for *political purposes* by developed to developing countries. No longer is there a need to defend Cold War policies or to seek the votes of many developing countries in the United Nations forum. Aid and trade policies became more developmental and humanitarian rather than being primarily political. This shift in emphasis, accompanied in the case of some donor countries by considerations of human rights practices in recipient countries, was supported by a recognition of the poor record of many governments in managing their development investments. Where direct comparison permits, government-owned enterprises' performance vis-à-vis private ownership was generally poor. With so many demands on the resources of government, questions were beginning to be asked as to why governments were operating services normally provided by the private sector in the developed countries?

In part, the answer to these questions lies in the nature of the development process. In many developing countries the private sector was either unable or unwilling to provide tourism investment and services. Government had to do so in order to initiate development in the sector. The existence of Tourism Development Corporations in many countries (e.g., Zimbabwe, Zambia, Ghana) testifies to governments' perceived need to kick-start the tourism sector. Without such initiatives, the embryo of tourism development would not have been formed or would only have taken place at a much later stage. The long-term cost of such initiatives is a history of accumulated financial losses, often poor standards of amenities and quality of service, and failure to generate sufficient profit to maintain and improve tourism amenities and facilities.

As a result of this inefficient and general poor performance, institutional lenders and particularly major lenders, such as the World Bank, the European Community, and the International Monetary Fund through its role in Structural Adjustment Programs, began to insist on a greater role for the private sector as a condition of loan. Governments' role was defined as providing an "enabling environment" within which private sector enterprises could flourish. Provision of such an "enabling environment" did not exclude government from management or participation in the tourism sector but rather discouraged it from taking an operational role in providing tourist services (e.g., in hotels, transport, travel agencies). In essence, government was being encouraged to provide only those services that the private sector was unable or unwilling to provide.

This privatization process has been noticeable in the southern African countries only in the 1990s. It is an uneven process, but one affecting most state-run enterprises in all economic sectors. In some countries (e.g., Zambia) there has been a rapid move towards privatization (e.g., the long-term leasing of tourism facilities in the national parks to domestic and international investors). In Namibia, government has preferred to retain control of the national park-based tourist resorts and camps but has devolved management to an autonomous subsidiary of government, Namibia Wildlife Resorts. In Zimbabwe the Tourism Development Corporation has been abolished. In another African country, Ghana, the State Hotel Corporation has been dissolved and its assets sold to the private sector (Government of Ghana, 1996). This privatization process has been rapid in the southern African region and is likely to be irreversible. This does not, of course, mean that government has no role to play in the future development of the tourism sector. There are many areas of policy and action where only government has the power to act; for example, bilateral air transport agreements, visa regulations, work permits, and investment incentives, all areas that affect tourism development (Lickorish & Jenkins, 1997, pp. 182–207). As tourism is multisectoral it is inevitable that in creating an "enabling environment" government will have to take into account the needs and problems of the private sector and, increasingly, bring the private sector into the policy formulation process.

Some Problem Areas

Policy formulation requires consideration of a wide range of issues of direct and indirect relevance to tourism. The very breadth of these issues can inhibit the policy formulation process, particularly where important decision-making authority (e.g., civil aviation policy) is outside the responsibility of the National Tourism Organization, which may or may not be a Ministry of Tourism. In the following section, some of the main problems relating to tourism policy formulation and implementation are identified.

The Nature of Tourism as an Activity

As previously noted, tourism is a multisectoral activity that requires inputs of an economic, social, cultural, and environmental nature. Likewise, its impacts can affect each of these areas to a greater or lesser extent. It is usual that inputs to the tourism sector fall under the responsibility of different ministries; for example, land use in the Ministry of Land; human resources under the Ministry of Labor and/or Ministry of Education; data collection under the Ministry of Foreign Affairs/Immigration; budgetary allocation under the Ministry of Finance. The difficulty for tourism policy-makers is that all these areas are necessary inputs to a policy but fall outside the normal remit of a Ministry of Tourism. This means that although subpolicies (e.g., on tourism training and education, on zoning of tourism development areas) may be made, they will require the cooperation and goodwill of other government ministries and agencies to implement. This then raises the issues of institutional structure and interministerial cooperation.

Institutional Structure

Although it may formulate a policy for the tourism sector, any single Ministry of Tourism is unlikely, for reasons given above, to have control over its implementation. First, it will depend on the cooperation and support of other ministries, which may or may not be forthcoming. For example, in road construction and maintenance what may be a priority road for tourism access may have a low priority in the ranking given to it by the appropriate ministry. Similarly, the immigration authorities may give low priority to classifying and processing tourist-related data. In most countries attempts to improve coordination often rely on interministerial committees, which are not always well attended or effective. Decisions, once made, will take time to filter down to those charged with implementation.

Second, institutions within the tourism sector may not have clearly demarcated responsibilities. In some countries there is a Ministry of Tourism, a Tourism Board, and a Tourism Development Corporation. The roles of each need to be specific and, wherever possible, duplication of responsibility avoided. This is not always the case. Without a clear division of responsibilities and effective coordination, policy is difficult to implement.

Third, as the private sector is expected and encouraged to become involved in the policy process, the question invariably arises: who represents the private sector?

In most of the southern African countries there are usually hotel and other trade associations to represent tour operators and travel agents, safari operators, and car hire, etc.

These trade associations usually include the bigger companies and operators but are not necessarily representative of the tourist sector, which includes many small businesses. To create representative voices for most, if not all, subsectors in tourism, attempts have been successfully made in countries to form representative and democratically elected organizations properly constituted and usually legally incorporated. These organizations, such as the Zimbabwe Tourism Council, provide conduits for discussion between the private sector and government. Increasingly, these representative and legally constituted trade associations are becoming involved in the formulation of tourism policy. At a regional level a similar forum is represented by the Regional Tourism Organisation of Southern Africa (RETOSA), a combination of 14 countries including participants from government and private sectors from each country.

Although such organizations do not necessarily represent all trades and services in the tourism sector, it is a first step in seeking to provide a platform for representative sector views.

Legal Framework

The disparate and multisectoral nature of tourism means that as an activity it is subject to much legislation (e.g., town and country planning legislation, immigration regulations, health and safety at work, etc.). Much of the legislation can be outdated and yet some areas are commonly neglected (e.g., consumer protection). The wide range of legislation that can apply to tourism is often difficult to identify and may have been written in an era when tourism was barely developed. For countries involved in international tourism, which all of the southern African countries are, international laws and conventions may apply. The region depends very heavily on tourists from the European Community countries. Those who travel on package tours are covered by the Community's Package Tour Directive (European Union [EU], 1993), which has major commercial implications for operators in the tourist-receiving countries.

Tourism policy is difficult to implement without a supportive and appropriate legal framework. Much of the legislation affects tourism policy (e.g., land use regulation, investment incentives, employment of foreign nationals) but may not have been specifically prepared for the tourism sector. In southern African countries tourism is dependent on wildlife and what is generally described as ecotourism. Major efforts have been and are being made to ensure that the environment is properly managed in the interest of sustainability. However, much of the legislation supporting management objectives is specific to environmental concerns and does not always consider the use of the environment by, for example, tourism development. The symbiosis between environmental management and tourism development is often not recognized either in the prevailing legislative framework or the institutional structures available. Wherever possible and appropriate, tourism-relevant legislation can be consolidated into a Tourism Act. In both Namibia and Zambia this action has been initiated. To achieve a successful outcome will require the support of many ministries. For example, in Zambia the incorporation of tourism-specific investment incentives in the draft Tourism and Hospitality Bill required the agreement of the Ministry of Finance and the Zambia Investment Centre, which is responsible for the implementation of investment incentives.

The Scope of Tourism Policy

There is no consensus on what should be included within a tourism policy. It may involve a simple statement of intent ("to maximize the benefits from tourism while minimizing its disadvantages") or be incorporated into more detailed documents, such as those seen in Namibia, Botswana, and the Republic of South Africa. To a certain extent the existence of a specific tourism policy document will be a reflection of the importance of the sector. Although the scope of a policy may be broad, it is likely to contain what might be regarded as essential features. Some of these features are discussed below.

Commitment by Government to the Tourism Sector. The most important feature of a tourism policy is that it should include a commitment by government to support the development of the sector. This commitment is usually accompanied by proposals on how the government intends to offer support (e.g., by offering specific investment incentives or perhaps by devising promotional strategies). The commitment is essential because it sends a signal to potential investors both domestic and international. However, statements of commitment need to be accompanied by appropriate actions. In Ghana for example, although Cabinet has declared tourism to be a priority sector, the Ministry of Finance has not yet officially included tourism in this category, thereby excluding it from various incentives support and from government guarantees on foreign debt (Ghana Ministry of Local Government, 1996).

Clear Statement of Development Objectives. The policy should include a clear statement of government's development objectives. Such objectives can be both national and subnational, focusing on specific areas of the country or even on specific activities in tourism.

Although in developing countries the main feature of government's support for tourism is centered on economic and financial benefits (e.g., generation of foreign exchange earnings), it is unusual not to relate these to social and political objectives. For example, in the southern African countries much tourism development has been based on the existence of high-quality environmental attractions, including wildlife. Most tourism policy statements would include explicit objectives to protect and carefully utilize environmental and other natural assets. On Namibia's Skeleton Coast, for example, there are strict limits on visitor access and government licenses only one tour operator to take visitors into the area.

The policy statement should indicate *how* tourism will contribute to the attainment of national objectives. In the southern African countries sustainability has become a major goal. The United Nations Commission on World Development defined sustainable development as "the development that meets the needs of the present without compromising the ability of future generations to meet their own needs" (World Commission on Environment and Development, 1987, p. 43).

Sustainability is not just an environmental concern but has social, cultural, political, and even economic implications. In countries where incomes are low and many people live on the margins of subsistence, it is difficult to educate them to the concept of long-term planning. They seek immediate benefit to improve their conditions of living and may only be encouraged to develop sustainable practices if they directly benefit from them. The success of the CAMPFIRE project in Zimbabwe and ADMADE project in Zambia are both examples of local participation in antipoaching activities directly linked to financial rewards and employment opportunities. Such schemes contribute to governments' national objectives of improving the conditions of people living in rural areas, enhancing employment, and in creating entrepreneurial and income-earning opportunities.

How Will Objectives Be Achieved? For each objective there should be a proposed action. For example, to ensure that tourism initiatives meet environmental standards it can be stipulated that any proposed development will require an environmental audit to ascertain its likely impact on a particular site and surrounding location. Development planning now incorporates environmental safeguards into its remit. However, as governments are motivated mainly by economic considerations, it does not follow that negative environmental and social indicators will prevent development. Long-term political will and development vision are often the most important of developmental attributes.

Tourism development is essentially a long-term, incremental process that requires careful planning. Its needed inputs of social, cultural, and environmental assets make it a difficult development process to manage. It is further complicated by the diverse nature of tourism activity and where it takes place. The government's responsibility to create an enabling environment for tourism must take into account the needs and opinions of all stakeholders and not only the investors in tourism.

How Will Policies Be Implemented? One of the weaknesses of tourism development planning has been the limited implementation of the completed plans. This can be attributed to a number of reasons. First, that the scale and cost of the plan is too large to be resourced. Second, that in the planning process the question of implementation has been considered as an end product of the plan and not considered at the outset of planning. This makes difficult the management of the implementation process, particularly where the plan has been formulated by foreign experts and its implementation becomes a domestic responsibility. Third, in all cases, to ensure effective implementation, a careful assessment of implementation capacity is needed that should include both institutional and human capacity.

Over the period of planning it is necessary to consider not only how the plan will be implemented but by whom. Most planning teams will operate a system of counterparts training where an expert is linked to a national employee who works with the expert. The idea is that counterpart relationships will be the conduit for transferring expertise and imparting an element of training. In practice, this system does not always work, with breakdowns in the process occurring for many reasons, not the least being the incompatibility of the counterparts.

Institutional arrangements are much more difficult to change as they reflect the particular organizational structure of governments. A current problem in many developing countries is how to accommodate the increasing participation of the private sector in the policy formulation process. This is a particular difficulty where there is no or limited experience of private sector participation. For this reason institutional development in the tourism sector has to include both government and private sector considerations.

In the southern African region RETOSA not only includes government and private sector representation from 14 countries, but is also an example of a supranational organization that was conceived as a private sector-dominated (and financed) entity that would seek to promote tourism in the region. The structure of the organization perhaps reflects at a regional level one of the most successful integrations of private sector representative bodies into an area of policy and action previously dominated by governments.

Management of Policy. Government must retain the ultimate responsibility for development of the tourism sector. It may delegate to designated bodies certain responsibilities (e.g., physical and economic planning, marketing and promotion, development of tourism quality standards), but it is still the final arbitrator of major development decisions. The type, scale, and location of tourism development will not only require public sector inputs—which have alternative uses—but also generate impacts of a sociocultural, environmental, and political nature. In some southern African countries an example is the enclosing of vast areas of land for game parks and the consequent relocation of local people. Another example is the creation of a tourism sector that has traditionally been run by foreigners for foreigners with little regard being paid to the needs of and opportunities for local people to participate in tourism. These are very complicated issues that can only be addressed on an individual country basis. However, these issues should not be ignored, and many tourism policy statements now specifically include reference to the domestic market.

Although tourism policy is the means to guide development it is inevitable that circumstances change which may require reconsideration of policy. An example is the recent killing of tourists in Uganda, which has caused the Uganda Tourist Board to change its promotional message to emphasize the additional security measures being taken to ensure the safety of tourists. The widespread reporting of violence in South Africa is another example. As tourism is a rapidly changing activity driven by market forces externally and influenced by domestic circumstances, it does require monitoring.

Monitoring of tourism should not be narrowly construed to counting the number of tourist arrivals or the amount of receipts. It should also include the monitoring of its effects on the society, culture, environment, and locations. Monitoring of these areas will permit the identification of problems of concern and lead to appropriate actions and, possibly, to changes in policy. Many of these remedial measures can only be taken by governments (e.g., legislation to prohibit antisocial actions).

Tourism in the Southern Africa Region

In the early discussions of African economic development both in Monrovia in 1979 (Organization of African Unity [OAU], 1979) and Lagos in 1980 (OAU, 1980) tourism was not identified as a development sector. The first specific reference to the significance of tourism as a regional development option was in the Treaty Establishing the African Economic Community (OAU, 1991). The main points of the Treaty applicable to tourism were:

(i)   strengthen intra-African cooperation in tourism particularly through:
- (a) promotion of intra-African tourism;
- (b) harmonization and coordination of tourism development policies, plans and programs; and
- (c) joint promotion of tourism products representing Africa's natural and sociocultural values.

(ii) promote the establishment of efficient tourism enterprises adapted to the needs of the African people and attractive to foreign tourists, through:
- (a) the adoption of measures designed to promote investment in tourism with the view to the establishment of competitive African tourist enterprises;
- (b) the adoption of measures designed to develop and utilize human resources for tourism in Africa; and
- (c) strengthening or establishment of high-level tourism training institutions where necessary.

The Treaty concluded the intentions towards the Protocol on Transport, Communications and Tourism by stating:

> Member States should adopt all requisite measures for the development of African tourism that takes due account of the human and natural environment and the well-being of the African peoples and which contributes effectively to the implementation of the continent's political and socioeconomic integration and development. (OAU, 1991, p. 64)

The OAU scheduled a meeting in May 1999 to further discuss these issues.

The Treaty was signed by 51 Heads of State. Although the Treaty recognized the potential of tourism as an input to general development strategy, there was no specific recommendation as to how such development could be progressed. It did recognize that Africa naturally divided into development zones (e.g., North, East, South, and West), and recommended the establishment of Regional Economic Communities (RECs) [e.g., ECOWAS (Economic Community of West African States)].

In southern Africa, the Heads of State or Governments Declaration in Lusaka in April 1980 committed themselves to pursuing policies aimed at economic liberalization and integrated development. This commitment and Declaration gave rise to the establishment of the Southern African Development Coordination Conference (SADCC). Further development of regional cooperation led to the setting up of the SADC in 1992. In Chapter 7, under Areas of Cooperation, no specific mention is made of tourism. This is perhaps not surprising as the major tourism destination in the region—the Republic of South Africa— was dominated by a minority government that was increasingly coming under international and regional sanctions. South Africa had also the best developed general and tourism infrastructure and perhaps the greatest market presence. It would obviously become not just the major regional power after a change of government but also the main tourism destination in the region.

Although Angola is a member of SADC it has no tourism development because of its long civil war and the continuing fighting. Mozambique is now enjoying a postwar peace, allowing it to begin rebuilding of its infrastructure to support rapid development of its tourism potential. The regional tourism product is primarily based on wildlife and culture, with beach tourism being an option in Mozambique, South Africa, Tanzania, and to a lesser extent in Namibia. The homogeneity of these products is to some extent differentiated by location and culture factors. But they are connected closely to the concepts of ecotourism and environmental management, and active policies are essential to the sustainability of the tourism sector in the region.

Tourism Policies in Southern Africa

A major problem found in analyzing tourism policies in the 14 SADC countries relates to the very diverse characteristics of the countries, their relative stages of development, and the importance of tourism within the individual economies. In some cases there are explicit statements of tourism policy (e.g., Zambia, Namibia, and the Republic of South Africa). In other countries (e.g., Malawi and Swaziland) government commitment to tourism policies is implied rather than explicit. For purposes of analysis, seven tourism policy documents were examined from Botswana, Lesotho, Namibia, South Africa, Swaziland, Tanzania, and Zambia. The analysis focused on three questions: What was the process of formulating tourism policy? What was the content of the policies? What were the recommended implementation strategies?

The Formulation

Only three policy documents—those of Namibia, South Africa, and Zambia—described *how* the policy was formulated. In two cases, Namibia and South Africa, the formulation process was guided by either a Steering Committee (Namibia) or by the Interim Tourism Task Team (South Africa). In Zambia, the formulation was an integral part of the Medium-Term Tourism Development Strategy, which was guided by the Ministry of Tourism. In these three countries policy issues were identified from published documentation and surveys of the current industry situation. This information was refined into logical segments, in the case of Namibia by using the SWOT (Strengths, Weaknesses, Opportunities, and Threats) framework, and then these were discussed with the Steering Committees. A series of options was identified for each issue, and action was agreed. The Steering Committees were constituted from tourism industry representative organizations and government members. A series of workshops was held to present policy recommendations to the wider industry, debate issues, and make any modifications appropriate and necessary.

In following this approach the three countries had each taken steps to involve as wide a range of tourism representatives as possible. This was done for two reasons. First, to *empower* the representatives by giving them active roles in the formulation process, and second, to provide a sense of *ownership* to the industry when the policy was eventually finalized. The process also had another advantage of bringing together in a partnership environment government and the private sector. In southern Africa this was a major shift in emphasis from the traditions of central planning, command economies, and the exclusion of the private sector from the policy process. This change in approach was essential as all three countries recognized that the future development and, to a large part, funding of tourism development would become the responsibility of the private sector.

In the three countries the consultative process was as transparent as possible and involved the private sector as an equal partner with government. This does not mean that there was unanimity of view on all issues, but the process did provide a forum for discussion and ultimately a policy document for delivery to government.

The experience of these three countries suggests that the tourism formulation process has a number of aspects. First, government has to realize and accept that a policy for tourism is a prerequisite for managed development of the sector. Second, that in the 1990s there has been a growing tendency to see development initiatives as being based on government–private sector partnerships. Third, as governments increasingly withdraw from operational and commercial participation in tourism (e.g., management of hotels and airlines) it will increasingly rely on the private sector for both investment and management expertise. Fourth, the private sector will not necessarily support national as opposed to sectoral development objectives through investment without being participants in the policy formulation process; it has to have a degree of ownership of the policy. Fifth, as tourism is essentially market driven, product development, quality, and service delivery are private sector functions. Governments should provide the enabling environment that will support the private sector in these areas. Sixth, without a continuing consultative process between government and the private sector, initiatives may not be sustained and embryonic partnerships put under strain.

The policy statements from Botswana, Lesotho, Swaziland, and Tanzania are quite explicit but there is no indication of how the policies were formulated. Although each sets out the roles of government and the private sector, the tone of the statements seem to reflect the old "command economy" approach rather than the more participative model used in Namibia, South Africa, and Zambia.

Content of the Tourism Policies

Within the confines of this chapter it is not possible to review the content of all the policy documents in detail. However, there were common areas of coverage that indicate what the basis of a tourism policy might be. These main areas are discussed briefly below.

Commitment of Government to the Tourism Sector

As may be implied from the production of the policy documents, each contained a commitment by government to support the future development of the tourism sector.

Statement of Tourism Development Objectives

Some countries (e.g., South Africa) set out indicative growth targets for the tourism sector related to contribution to gross domestic product and visitor arrival numbers over a period of time. Other countries left such specificity to follow-up Tourism Development

Plans (e.g., Zambia, Namibia, and Botswana). All the policy statements reviewed contained three main development principles. First, that the growth of tourism should respect the heritage, culture, and traditions of the country. Second, that tourism was recognized as having sustainable potential to contribute to development provided it was achieved without detriment to sociocultural and environmental parameters. Third, that the benefits expected to accrue from tourism would contribute to national development objectives and, wherever possible, benefit all classes and groups within the country. The need to integrate tourism within the national development framework was noted in all cases.

Action Areas

The policy documents were very similar in the areas that they included. The general areas are identified as the following.

Product Development. Each country noted the need to improve and, where possible, expand its product base. There seemed to be recognition of the highly competitive nature of tourism within the region and in the wider international market. It was also noted that product development would be limited unless continuous attention was given to sourcing capital for tourism and improving skills and, subsequently, service levels.

Capital. Most of the documents accepted that it was not possible for government to completely finance the development of the tourism sector and specifically gave to the private sector the predominant role for product development. Governments, as part of creating an enabling environment, would provide whenever possible the appropriate infrastructure and, through the availability of investment incentives, encourage both domestic and foreign investors into the sector.

Human Resource Development. All the regional countries intended to stimulate the development of human resources. Without this initiative it would be difficult, if not impossible, in most countries to provide the quality of service that tourists expected. In some policy statements (e.g., Zambia, South Africa, Botswana, and Namibia) human resource development initiatives were linked with the need to indigenize the ownership of the tourism sector by encouraging entrepreneurial skills and attitudes. This was recognized as being a long-term development objective but one that was crucial to the future success—and acceptance—of tourism. In some cases these intentions were linked to institutional-strengthening measures.

Marketing. In an internationally—and regionally—competitive industry like tourism, appropriate marketing is an essential action. In the period before the mid-1990s the majority of international marketing was done by governments through their Ministries of Tourism, National Tourism Organizations, or designated agencies. For most regional countries, limited marketing budgets were a major constraint on promotional efforts, and it was financial assistance, particularly from the European Union, that enabled the regional countries to participate in the major tourism fairs such as the World Travel Market in London and ITB in Berlin. There was limited cooperation between government(s) and the private sector with the latter unwilling to contribute towards the financing of what was sometimes described as "government junketing." The new approach to tourism development, with the private sector more involved in policies and actions, should help to mitigate this problem.

It was also noted in the policy documents that marketing should not be confined to attracting international tourists. It was recognized that, for historic reasons, domestic tourism needs had received scant attention and also measures needed to be taken to encourage more domestic and intraregional participation.

Institutional Framework. The policy documents tended to view the implementation of tourism policy as being possible within the existing institutional structures. Only in Namibia and South Africa was particular attention given to the need of changing the existing administrative and institutional frameworks. These changes are not easy to obtain as they essentially dislocated what is often a long-standing governmental structure. Most policy documents avoided this major issue by allocating "roles" to specific agencies or ministries, and also between the public and private sector. Again, as a policy statement this position may be justified if the issue is addressed in a subsequent tourism planning exercise.

Legislative Framework. As a multisectoral activity, tourism planning and development is surrounded by a plethora of legislation. It is often difficult to identify tourism-specific legislation; much of what exists is often out of date. Although most of the policy documents made reference to the need for supportive legislation, the policy intention was not always clear.

Management of the Sector. This was primarily seen as a function of government, with an effective discharge of responsibilities being attained by closer cooperation with the private sector. Little or no mention was made of the possibility of self-regulation by the industry trade associations, particularly through the setting and monitoring of standards. No mention was made of the need for consumer protection, arguably one of the main features of a tourism quality program.

Implementation Strategies

Each country recognized the need for an effective implementation strategy. In the case of South Africa it was not included in the White Paper but proposed as a separate document needed to reflect the great changes in that country, many of these arising from the Reconstruction and Development Programme. In the other countries implementation strategies tended to be based on the existing structures, but in Namibia two new organizations—Namibia Wildlife Resorts and Namibia Tourist Board—were recommended and created to facilitate tourism policy implementation.

The question of implementation is perhaps one of the most neglected areas of tourism development. Without an appropriate and effective strategy much of the policy recommendations and actions will not take place. What is an appropriate strategy will depend on the particular circumstances of a country, how tourism is organized and administered, and how important it is in the economy. Coordination and centralization of legislation related to tourism is desirable. However, this is unlikely to happen where tourism is concerned because it infringes on the responsibility of other government ministries and departments. The best that may be hoped for is to improve interministerial coordination and cooperation and, by working more closely with the private sector, to obtain a consensus on priority actions.

Conclusion

The analysis of tourism policy in the southern African countries has given some points to consider. First, that the formulation of tourism policy is a continuous process and not a single action, and is a process that should involve all stakeholders. Second, there is now a trend towards including representatives of the private sector in the process. Third, that the implementation process is usually focused on the existing institutional structures. Fourth, that most policy statements cover common areas of interest and concern, including marketing, product development, funding, human resource development, environment, culture, and legislative support. Fifth, there is recognition of the dominant role of the private sector as the main catalyst for future tourism development.

Although policy in this analysis has been treated as a single entity, it is inextricably linked to development planning for which it provides a framework. Without a tourism policy it is difficult to take consistent development decisions that lead to the attainment of designated objectives. From this premise it can be suggested that a tourism policy is a necessary precursor to development planning. It should be the agreed framework that informs and guides such exercises. It is probable that, in the course of development planning, certain policy objectives may be viewed as being unrealistic, such as development of certain market segments or, perhaps, the development of tourism in certain locations. These examples are not failures of policy, but demonstrate that policy has to be flexible, can be modified, and is inextricably linked with the planning process.

PART II

THE CASE STUDIES OF
SELECTED AFRICAN COUNTRIES

Chapter 6

Planning Sustainable Tourism in Ghana

Edward Inskeep

Summary

Concepts of sustainable tourism have been refined in recent years and are now commonly applied to all types of tourism development. The Integrated Tourism Development Programme (ITDP) for Ghana represents a comprehensive planning approach to achieve the sustainable development of international and domestic tourism, applying contemporary approaches to planning for sustainable tourism. Financed by the United Nations Development Programme and Government of Ghana and executed by the World Tourism Organization, the ITDP was implemented by the Ghana Ministry of Tourism utilizing a team of international and national consultants working closely with ministry counterparts. The ITDP included national and regional planning, development programming, marketing, financial planning, project analysis, establishing a tourism information system, and other institutional improvements. The tourism policies and plans were formulated within the framework of overall national development policy and planning. Emphasis in the ITDP was given to developing a wide range of types of tourism based on the tourism resources available; spreading the benefits of tourism widely throughout the country; consideration of economic, environmental, and sociocultural factors; involvement of all stakeholders in the tourism planning process; developing community-based tourism projects; and specifying implementation techniques. Achieving environmental protection and historic and cultural heritage conservation objectives through tourism was a major theme of the ITDP. Considerable effort was directed to facilitating financing of public and private development projects. Training was an important element of the program in order to enhance capabilities in both the public and private sectors of tourism. Providing the institutional basis for effective development implementation and continuous tourism management was an essential aspect of the ITDP. Many of the approaches used in this program are applicable to other countries in Africa.

Key words: Ghana; Tourism policy; Tourism planning; Tourism development; Tourism resources; Tourism management; Sustainable tourism; Environmental protection; Historic and cultural heritage; Conservation of resources; Integrated development; Comprehensive planning; Institutional framework

Introduction

This chapter first examines the concepts of planning for sustainable tourism that have evolved during the past several years and that have been adopted by the World Tourism Organization and other international agencies. These concepts are then related to the planning of tourism in Ghana. The chapter draw conclusions from the Ghana planning program that have application in planning other areas in Sub-Saharan Africa.

The planning efforts in Ghana were carried out under the umbrella of the Integrated Tourism Development Programme (ITDP) for Ghana, which was financed by the United Nations Development Programme (UNDP) and Government of Ghana with the World Tourism Organization (WTO) as the executing agency and the Ghana Ministry of Tourism as the implementing agency. As a politically stable country offering a variety of natural, historic, cultural, and other resources for tourism, and with the comprehensive program framework provided by the ITDP, Ghana therefore offers a good case study of applying contemporary tourism planning principles for sustainable development.

The ITDP represents the current approach of the WTO and UNDP to preparing tourism plans in developing countries and providing the foundation for implementation of the plans and continuing management of the tourism sector. The ITDP particularly reflects application of principles for developing tourism on a sustainable basis, which has the objective of balancing generation and distribution of economic benefits with protection of the environmental, historical, and cultural heritage of the country. The ITDP also demonstrates the importance of promoting institution building as the essential basis for achieving sustainable tourism development, and the emphasis that must be given to involving all concerned parties in the planning process so that they understand and support the recommendations.

Planning for Sustainable Tourism Development

The World Conservation Strategy, issued by the International Union for the Conservation of Nature and Natural Resources (IUCN) in 1980, first introduced the concept of sustainability on a global basis. Sustainable development was further articulated and popularized with publication of *Our Common Future*, the 1987 report prepared by the World Commission on Environment and Development (the Brundtland Commission) for the United Nations General Assembly. That report defines sustainability as development that "meets the needs of the present without compromising the ability of future generations to meet their own needs" (World Commission on Environment and Development, 1987, p. 8). At the United Nations Conference on Environment and Development, popularly known as the Earth Summit and held in Rio de Janeiro in 1992, the sustainable development approach was further elaborated and expressed in Agenda 21, which was adopted by the conference. Based on that statement, the WTO, in cooperation with the World Travel and Tourism Council and The Earth Council, prepared and adopted Agenda 21 for the Travel and Tourism Industry, which specifies priority areas for action by governments and the industry and includes a priority area on planning for sustainable tourism development. The WTO defines sustainable tourism as follows:

> Sustainable tourism development meets the needs of present tourists and host regions while protecting and enhancing opportunity for the future. It is envisaged as leading to management of all resources in such a way that economic, social and aesthetic needs can be fulfilled while maintaining cultural integrity, essential ecological processes, biological diversity and life support systems. (World Tourism Organization, World Travel and Tourism Council, The Earth Council, 1995, p. 30)

The WTO has taken the position that all types of tourism development, both larger and smaller scale, should be sustainable and that emphasis must be placed on applying practical approaches to achieving sustainable tourism. This principle has been elaborated in the general tourism planning literature (e.g., Inskeep, 1991) and by the WTO in its planning publications (WTO, 1994, 1998d), as well as applied in planning projects such as the one for Ghana, which is described in this chapter. The importance of using practical approaches to achieving sustainable tourism development was expressed in the initial issue of the *Journal of Sustainable Tourism* in 1993 as:

> Sustainable tourism is a positive approach intended to reduce the tensions and friction created by the complex interactions between the tourism industry, visitors, the environment and the communities which are host to holidaymakers. It is an approach which involves working for the long-term viability and quality of both natural and human resources. It is not anti-growth, but it acknowledges that there are limits to growth. Those limits will vary considerably from place to place, and according to management practices. It recognizes that for many areas tourism was, is and will be an important form of development. It seeks to ensure that tourism developments are sustainable in the long term and wherever possible help in turn to sustain the areas in which they operate. And, for good measure, sustainable tourism also aims to increase visitor satisfaction. (Bramwell & Lane, 1993, p. 2).

Sustainable tourism planning approaches have been further refined to include important institutional factors, for example, the interdependence of all stakeholders—the public and private sectors, the host communities, and the natural environment—which must closely collaborate to achieve sustainability and manage tourism issues on an interactive basis, instead of taking adversarial positions (Getz & Jamal, 1994). The commonly, though not universally, accepted policy on planning for sustainable tourism has been stated as one of ". . . convergence. This position represents the latest understanding of sustainable tourism as a goal that all tourism, regardless of scale, must strive to achieve. . . ." (Clarke, 1997, p. 229). This definition is one adopted by international agencies and many developing country governments. This concept of sustainable tourism now provides a policy framework for planning tourism in any area, realizing that application of the policy must be adapted to each local situation, and techniques are still far from perfect. As a case study, further specification of the principles of sustainability and their application are examined here in the approach to carrying out the tourism program for Ghana.

Overview of Ghana

Planning for tourism in Ghana can best be understood within the context of the country's geography, history, culture, economy, and political and administrative structure. This information has been summarized from the National Tourism Development Plan for Ghana (Republic of Ghana/UNDP/WTO, 1996b).

Physical Setting

Ghana lies on the Gulf of Guinea in West Africa about 5–11 degrees north of the equator. The Greenwich Meridian passes through the country. With an area of about 238,540 km^2, Ghana is medium size compared to other West African countries and is similar in size to the U.K. The country is comprised of plains, dissected plateaus, escarpments, hills, and mountains with the highest mountain rising to 872 m near the eastern border. Scenic bays, headlands, intermittent beaches, and river estuaries characterize the coastline. Some of the beaches along the eastern coastline are eroding. The major river is the Volta River, the lower part of which has been dammed to form the Volta Lake, one of the larger man-made lakes in Africa. This dam and lake provide hydroelectric power for most of the county with some power being exported to neighboring countries, although this power source is now being supplemented by thermal power generation.

Ghana has a tropical wet climate with considerable variation of rainfall throughout the country. Rainforest predominates in the southwest, coastal savannah in the southeast, deciduous and mixed forest in the south-central area, Guinea Savannah (wooded grassland) in the north central area, and Sudan Savannah (mostly grassland) in the far north. There are 15 designated national parks and reserves in Ghana, which occupy about 5.2% of the country. In addition, considerable lagoonal areas along the coast have been designated as Ramsar sites, wetlands of international significance that attract many resident and migratory birds and provide nesting areas for marine turtles. Also, about 10% of the country is designated as forest reserves. A great variety of wildlife, including large mammals such as forest and savannah elephants, lions, leopards, hippopotamus, bongos, buffalo, and several species of antelopes and primates, as well as various species of amphibians and many species of birds, can be found, especially in the national parks and reserves.

Culture and History

Ghana is a polyethnic society of which the Akan people are the most widespread, but other groups including the Ewe, Ga-Adangbe, Gonja, Dagomba, Dagaba, Konkomba, Mamprussi, Sisala, and several others are also important. Related to the ethnic groups, various linguistic groups are represented in the country, although English is the national language. Outside urban areas, the ethnic groups have largely retained their separate identities. Traditional religious beliefs and practices prevail in many areas while Christianity and Islam also have large numbers of adherents. Traditional medical treatments utilizing natural medicines are well developed in Ghana and widely practiced. Some of these medicines have proved to be efficacious by the standards of modern medicine. The traditional chieftaincy system, and its hierarchy, is important and recognized by the government.

West Africa, including Ghana, has a long history of occupation and migration. West Africa established trading in gold and other items with North Africa, which in turn traded these goods with Europe, many centuries before European discovery and settlement in West Africa. Europeans first arrived in the late 15th century and a permanent trading center was established by the Portuguese with the construction of St. George's Castle at Elmina on the coast in 1482. Several other European countries established trading posts along the coast during the 16th to 18th centuries and by the mid-19th century there were more than 40 coastal trading forts, castles, and lodges developed in what is present-day Ghana. About 25 of these remain, most of which are intact and being used for various functions, although some are ruins.

The coastal trading initially involved gold and other goods but by the early 16th century included slaves, mostly destined for the Americas, and slaves soon dominated the trade. The British eventually consolidated their control of the coast and established the Crown Colony of the Gold Coast. By the early 19th century, the Ashanti Kingdom based in Kumasi had become a powerful state and controlled much of the interior of the country. In a series of hard-fought wars the Ashanti were eventually defeated by the British in 1900 and incorporated into the Colony of the Gold Coast. Under the leadership of Dr. Kwame Nkrumah, the Gold Coast was granted independence in 1957 and its name was changed to Ghana. Much development, including some large hotels, was carried out during the early years of independence. During the 1970s and early 1980s the country experienced political and economic problems, but political stability was achieved and economic recovery commenced in the 1980s.

Economic, Political, and Administrative Structure

With the introduction of the Economic Recovery Programme and Structural Adjustment Programme in 1983, the country has experienced an average annual growth rate in the gross domestic product (GDP) of about 5%. Per capita income in 1993 was estimated at about US$430. In 1993, the sectoral contributions to the economy, as a percentage of GDP, were: 41% for agriculture (crops and livestock, cocoa, forestry/logging, and fisheries); 15% for industry (mining/quarrying, manufacturing, construction, electricity, and water); and 44% (transport, communications, trade, hotels/restaurants, financial, and other services). During the decade prior to 1993, agriculture had a rather slow average annual growth of 1.8%, while the industrial sector grew at an average annual rate of 7.4% and the trade and hotels/restaurants subsector of services grew at an average annual rate of more than 10%. The major commodity exports are gold, cocoa, and timber with tourism being the fourth largest earner of foreign exchange.

The population of Ghana was estimated to be 16.5 million in 1994 and is projected to be 20 million by the year 2000. With an annual growth rate of about 3%, there is a high ratio of dependents to working population. About 33% of the population live in urban places and the remainder in village and rural areas. Accra, with some 1.5 million residents, is by far the largest city and Kumasi, Sekondi-Takoradi, and Tamale are the next largest urban locations. Major seaports are located at Tema near Accra and Takoradi. Kotoka International Airport is situated near Accra.

The county is divided into 10 administrative regions, each with a regional capital. The regions are divided into administrative districts. The regional and some district boundaries correspond fairly closely to areas of different ethnic groups.

National development objectives and policies are set forth in *Ghana—Vision 2020* (Republic of Ghana, National Planning Commission, 1995). This plan takes both the long-term 25-year (1996–2020) and medium-term 5-year (1996–2000) perspective. A major target is that Ghana will have a balanced economy and become a middle-income country by 2020. Tourism is identified as one of the sectors to be further developed. The plan recognizes the importance of protecting the environment and achieving equity in distribution of the benefits of development. By government policy, all development planning, including tourism, must fit into the framework of *Vision 2020*.

Organization of the Tourism Program

The ITDP was commenced in mid-1994 and the planning and most other elements were completed by mid-1996. However, some activities continued to mid-1998.

Terms of Reference

The overall development objective in the terms of reference (TOR) of the program was stated (Republic of Ghana/UNDP/WTO, 1994a) as:

> expand tourism on a sustainable basis. For international tourism, expansion is intended to increase the economic benefits of income, contribution to the gross domestic product, employment, foreign exchange earnings and government revenues. International tourism will also provide greater exposure to the world of Ghana's cultural, historical and environmental heritage. For domestic tourism, expansion will provide more recreational opportunities to Ghanaians, expose them to their national

heritage and geographically spread economic benefits, especially from urban to rural areas. (p. 10)

The three immediate objectives and several outputs were specified in the TOR as follows:

- **Planning guidance for the development of tourism.** Preparation of a 15-year national tourism development policy and structure plan, 5-year action program and a financial plan, a regional tourism plan for each of the ten administrative regions, and prefeasibilty studies for a priority tourism development project in each of the 10 regions. The planning outputs included a tourism marketing strategy and promotion program, tourist facility development and design standards, environmental, sociocultural, and economic analysis, a public awareness program on tourism, a tourist behavior code, various institutional elements including manpower development, organizational structures, and techniques of implementation. Planning was for international, regional African, and domestic tourism.
- **Enhancement of capabilities in tourism management.** Conducting a tourist survey and establishing a tourism information management system, in-country and out-of-country training for tourism officials, counterparting of officials with project team members, improvement of hotel and restaurant standards, and providing advice to the Ministry of Tourism by the planning team on a continuous basis. Some training courses were provided for the private sector tour and travel operations personnel and managers.
- **Improvement of the government Hotel, Catering, and Tourism Training Center.** Improvement of training knowledge, skills, and techniques of the faculty, preparation of a feasibility study for development of a new campus and expansion of the center, and assistance on upgrading training of present hotel, catering, and tour operations personnel including mobile training in the tourism areas.

As can be seen in the TOR, emphasis was on a comprehensive approach involving virtually all aspects of tourism with much consideration given to achieving sustainable development, applying an integrated approach based on a hierarchy of planning from macro- to micro-level, giving much weight to enhancing tourism management capabilities, institutionalizing human resource development, and incorporating implementation techniques into the program.

Project Team and Activities

A large team of seven international and ten national consultants in various areas of specialization, under the direction of the Chief Technical Adviser (CTA—UNDP terminology for Team Leader/Tourism Development Planner) was employed during the course of the project. Emphasis was on maximizing use of national consultants in fields where local capabilities exist because of their knowledge of Ghana and to give them experience in tourism analysis and planning. Based on their experience with the project, the national consultants can carry out future tourism studies in the country.

The consultants were each assigned a counterpart from the staff of the Ministry of Tourism, Ghana Tourist Board, or training center with one from the Ministry of Environment. Counterparts are expected to work closely with their assigned project team members, including attending meetings, going on field trips, and assisting in the work output. The concept of counterparting is to transfer knowledge to local staff and for them to understand the reasons that recommendations are made so that they can better help implement the plans. In addition to this one-on-one approach to training, all the counterparts as well as other staff participated in the formal training program of training courses, study tours, and on-the-job attachments in other countries.

Field trips were made by the relevant consultants and their counterparts to all parts of the country to inspect tourist attractions, facilities, services, and infrastructure. Field trip analysis included evaluation of the environmental and social carrying capacities for tourism development and visitor use, in keeping with the sustainable development approach. Visits by the CTA and his counterpart were also made to neighboring countries to review their tourism development and potential, to provide the basis for regional cooperation on tourism. The Marketing Specialist visited or otherwise contacted the major tourist market countries to obtain the views of international tour operators on the potential of Ghana to attract tourists.

An international tourist survey, which is an ongoing activity, obtained information on tourist characteristics, their expenditure patterns, and attitudes toward Ghana's attractions, facilities, and services. Other special surveys were conducted, including on the sociocultural impacts of tourism and tourist perceptions of the quality of infrastructure. Meetings were held by the project team with all relevant government agencies, the private tourism sector, nongovernmental organizations (NGOs) involved in tourism, community leaders, and traditional chiefs. It was important to involve traditional leaders because of their influence on decision-making at the local level and, through the Councils of Chiefs, at the regional and national levels. Close coordination was maintained with other projects related to tourism.

Plan Review Procedures

Emphasis was placed on review of project findings and recommendations by the government, private sector, and other interested parties, so that local knowledge and ideas were incorporated into the plans and stakeholders were educated about the recommendations so that they would understand and support them. A Project Steering Committee was organized to guide project activities and especially to review and comment on the draft reports and recommendations. This committee comprised representatives of all the involved government agencies, the private sector, and other interested bodies. The reports were also reviewed by Ministry of Tourism officials, the UNDP, and WTO.

After preparation of the draft report of the national tourism plan, a 2-day high-level National Tourism Seminar was organized for specific review of the plan by all major stakeholders in tourism. More than 250 persons attended the seminar, which was considered very successful and resulted in some improvements to the plan. Just as importantly, the seminar provided a forum for stakeholders to learn more about tourism and the recommendations for expanding this sector in the country. The seminar received wide publicity in the local media, which gave the tourism plan some general public exposure.

Each regional tourism plan was reviewed at regional seminars held in the 10 administrative regions. These seminars included the district administrations and traditional leaders so the local government and traditional chiefs were involved in the review process. The regional seminars also served to educate persons about tourism and the plan recommendations. Much interest was expressed by regional and community representatives in developing tourism in their respective areas.

Applying Concepts of Sustainability in Ghana

The approaches used to carry out the Ghana ITDP were aimed at meeting national objectives of rapid economic growth and distribution of the benefits of development widely throughout the country, while still striving to achieve sustainable and integrated tourism development. The concept of sustainable tourism development applied in the ITDP was that many types of tourism, including urban, resort, nature and ecotourism, cultural, health, special interest, village, and other types, should be and can be sustainable. However, some kinds of tourism are not considered appropriate for Ghana based on other considerations, especially those that would be incompatible with local cultural values. Additionally, concepts of sustainability were applied to the implementation and management of tourism and to political support for this sector.

Sustainable tourism development in the ITDP for Ghana is based on the following major considerations:

- **The natural, historic, cultural, and other resources for tourism are conserved and where necessary enhanced for continuous use in the future, while still bringing benefits to the present society.** In the case of Ghana, many of the resources require enhancement so that they are more useful for both present and future use. Particularly important is improved conservation of natural areas, historic places, arts, crafts, traditional architecture, and some cultural traditions. Tourism can help achieve these conservation objectives.

- **Tourism development is planned, developed, and managed so that it does not generate serious environmental or sociocultural problems.** Environmental planning approaches and carrying capacity analysis, based on limits of acceptable change, are viewed as important techniques in planning for tourism development.

- **The overall environmental quality of the tourism areas is maintained and improved where needed.** There are several types of environmental quality problems in Ghana, and improvement of environmental quality is considered essential both for the benefit of residents' well-being and for tourism.

- **The socioeconomic benefits of tourism are spread widely throughout the country and society.** By spreading the benefits of tourism, this sector will bring many needed benefits throughout the country and engender popular support for it. Development of various types of tourism in different parts of the country, depending on the local resources, encouraging community-based tourism programs, and establishing stronger economic cross-sectoral linkages are viewed as important means of spreading economic benefits.

- **A good quality level of tourism is developed and maintained.** Quality tourism is defined as tourism development that generates substantial economic benefits per tourist, attracts the types of tourists who respect the environment and social values and customs, and is based on good standard facilities and services that are environmentally well designed. Quality tourism also offers "good value for money," which helps sustain the tourist markets and keeps the destination competitive. Ghana does not want to become a low-cost mass-market tourist destination.

- **A high level of tourist satisfaction is maintained so that the country retains its marketability and popularity.** Sustaining the tourist markets is an inherent aspect of sustainable tourism. Maintaining the quality level of the tourism product as set forth above, as well as constant enrichment of the tourism product, is key to achieving a high level of tourist satisfaction and successfully competing with other destinations. At the same time, regional cooperation with other African countries on joint tour programming, product development, and marketing is mutually beneficial to all the countries concerned.

- **Tourism planning and development are integrated into overall national development planning and patterns.** Tourism is more likely to be successful and sustainable if it is integrated into overall national and regional development policy and planning.

The tourism plans were prepared within the framework of *Vision 2020*, the national development policy and plan.

- **Tourism development is based on the political realities of the area.** The recommendations of the plans were designed to be politically acceptable without compromising sound development principles. Political realities related particularly to geographic distribution of tourism and staging of development so that all major jurisdictions and ethnic groups will receive some benefits of tourism. Even though the level of tourism development varies greatly among the areas, depending on availability of local tourism resources, each area should receive some benefits so that it can participate in the development process.

Tourism Policy and Plan Formulation

The national tourism development policy and plan were formulated based on survey and analysis of the tourism resources (which are reviewed in a subsequent section), market analysis, existing tourist facilities and services, transportation, and other relevant factors.

Tourism Development Policy

Tourism policy was formulated within the framework of the national development policy; it included elements of previous tourism policy and incorporated the concepts of sustainability described previously. Policy is elaborated under the categories of policy goals, policy framework, and policy guidelines and differentiates policies where appropriate for international, regional African, and domestic tourism. The tourism policy goal is "to develop tourism as a leading socioeconomic sector of the country and a good quality, internationally competitive tourist destination, within the framework of maintaining its permanent sustainability." A basic policy framework statement is that "Tourism must be developed in a manner that helps achieve conservation of the country's cultural, historical and environmental heritage." An important policy guideline is that "Holiday tourism is to be based primarily on the inherent attractions and heritage of the country including its historical sites, cultural traditions and events and the natural environment, especially nature parks and beaches. In addition to holiday tourist markets, business, conference and incentive tourism will be developed" (Republic of Ghana/UNDP/WTO, 1996b, pp. 44–46).

Market Analysis

Market targets for international and regional African tourist arrivals were established for the three major categories of: business travelers, visiting friends and relatives (VFR) by Ghanaians living overseas (of which there are many), and holiday tourists. Tourist arrivals are targeted to increase from an estimated 286,000 in 1995 to slightly more that 1 million in 2010 with about one half of these being holiday tourists (Republic of Ghana/UNDP/WTO, 1995d). Also a target is increasing the average length of stay from the present 9 days to 10.5 days. The market analysis identifies major market countries and groups. One of the important special interest markets is African-Americans seeking their ancestral "roots" in Ghana. Already some African-American tour groups are visiting the country. Targets were not established for domestic tourists, but recommendations are made to encourage domestic tourism including youth, student, worker, and church groups as well as family trips and local business travel, and make it affordable to larger segments of the population. Domestic travel is already important to attend festivals and funerals, which are important affairs in Ghana, as well as for business and government purposes.

Based on the market targets, accommodation needs for two-star and higher levels were determined in total and by region. These are the levels of facilities that would be utilized by most of the international and regional tourists. In addition, there is already much budget accommodation available in the country, which is used mostly by domestic tourists. The amount of accommodation projected is all well below the carrying capacity of each region, which will allow for expansion of tourism beyond 2010.

Tourism Structure Plan

The national tourism structure plan, illustrated in Figure 6.1, contains the following elements (Republic of Ghana/UNDP/WTO, 1996b):

- *Tourist gateways* into the country, which include both air access and land border crossings. Most long-haul tourists arrive by air but there is considerable land travel between Ghana and neighboring countries by African tourists for holiday, VFR, and business purposes, and by budget international tourists traveling overland in West Africa. International cruise ship tourism is recommended to be developed and the two seaports will then also become entry points.
- *Tourism development zones*, which are focused on several major attraction features and comprise integrated geographic units. Based on their tourism resources, some zones will have considerable tourism development while others will have limited development. Each administrative region has a development zone based on its particular attractions, which will gain political support of tourism in all the regions.
- *Tourism centers*, one in each zone, which contain a concentration of tourist facilities and services and serve as a base for local tours. The tourism centers are the regional capitals because they are already developed with some tourist facilities and are transportation hubs of their regions. Some tourism centers also possess major tourist attractions, which form the basis for urban tourism.
- *Tourist stopovers*, about 75 in total, which are major attraction features and provide tourist facilities and services. These include national parks and reserves, other scenic features, major historic features, craft villages, and beach, lake, and mountain resorts.
- *Excursion roads* that connect the gateways, tourism centers, and tourist stopovers. Many of these roads provide scenic views. Virtually all the designated excursion roads are existing but will be improved where needed to serve tourism as well as general needs.
- *Excursion railway*, which, when the current railway rehabilitation program is completed, can provide transportation for tourists to some tourism centers and stopovers and offer interesting scenic views. Special tourist coaches have already been obtained.
- *Tourist boat cruises* on Volta Lake and the major rivers. A short tourist boat excursion on Volta Lake is already available and this can be extended, and various riverboat cruises can be organized.

In order to encourage near-term development of tourism throughout the country and spread the benefits of tourism, staging of development was not indicated by development zones. All the zones can proceed with some tourism development simultaneously, but tourism should be staged within each zone so that there is no overdevelopment of facilities at any particularly time. The rapid improvement of the transportation network in Ghana will permit this approach.

Recommendations on Other Plan Elements

Recommendations are made on infrastructure required for tourism with emphasis on provision of proper access to tourist attraction and facility areas, and of adequate water supply, waste management, electric power, and telecommunications in tourism areas. Development standards are recommended for resorts and other tourist facilities, including

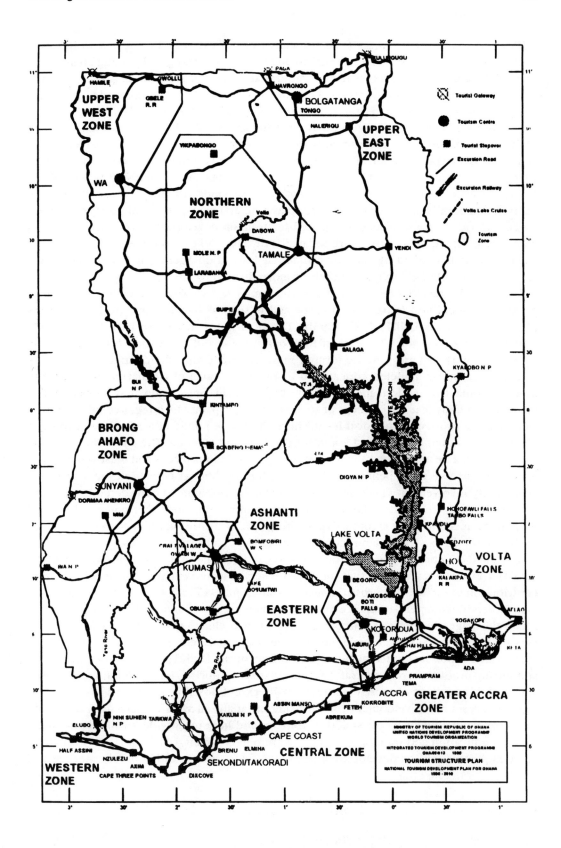

Figure 6.1. Tourism structure plan for Ghana.

sufficient setbacks of buildings from the coastline, providing public access to beaches, controlling building heights, and providing adequate landscaping and parking areas. Architectural design guidelines stress use of traditional styles and local building materials and relating building design to the tropical climate. Recommendations were made on improving quality standards of hotels and restaurants (Republic of Ghana/UNDP/WTO, 1994b).

The plan deals specifically with environmental and sociocultural considerations. Environmentally, the focus of recommendations is on improving environmental cleanliness and waste management, controlling water pollution, and reducing depletion of forest resources, threats to wildlife, and loss of biodiversity (Republic of Ghana/UNDP/WTO, 1996b). The problems of beach erosion and degradation of wetlands in some places are addressed. Environmental guidelines are set forth for planning and management of protected nature areas, historic sites, and places designated for tourism development. The environmental impact assessment (EIA) procedure for major development projects is now required in Ghana and administered by the Environmental Protection Agency, and the plan recommends that the EIA be applied to hotels of more than 20 rooms.

Based on the results of social surveys, tourism is not viewed as creating any serious negative sociocultural impacts at present and is seen as having some positive impacts (Republic of Ghana/UNDP/WTO, 1995b). The plan notes that there have been outside influences in Ghana for 500 years in the coastal areas and more than 100 years in the central and northern areas, in the form of European trade and administration, missionary activities, European-modeled educational institutions, travel of Ghanaians overseas, and now the impact of modern media of newspapers, magazines, radio, and television. The plan recommends that the concept of social carrying capacity be integrated into the tourism planning process at the local level. There should be public education about tourism and tourists should be informed about local values and customs. The authenticity of arts and crafts must be maintained. Visitors must respect religious places and must wear proper dress and observe good behavior when attending traditional ceremonies and festivals. Community involvement in all aspects of tourism development is considered essential to prevent or mitigate negative impacts, and the plan recommends that community-based tourism projects be implemented. Crime, drugs, and prostitution are not major problems in Ghana but do exist; the plan recommends controls on these activities.

A detailed economic analysis of tourism was prepared (Republic of Ghana/UNDP/WTO, 1996a). The analysis indicated that the tourism sector would expand from making a gross contribution of 3.5% to the gross domestic product in 1995 to 7.4% in 2010 based on the plan targets. Recommendations are made on enhancing the economic benefits of tourism. Sectoral linkages, however, are already good and the foreign exchange leakage factor is not very high. Many locally produced food items, for example, are used in tourism enterprises, most construction materials for hotels and other tourist facilities are available in Ghana, and locally produced arts and crafts are popular with tourists. Encouraging local ownership and management of tourist facilities, to the extent possible, is stressed.

Human resource development for tourism was analyzed with respect to determining future personnel needs in all aspects of tourism and how to provide qualified personnel through education and training programs (Republic of Ghana/UNDP/WTO, 1995a). Especially important will be developing a new campus for an expanded hotel, catering, and tourism training institute.

Conservation and Development of Tourism Resources

The sustainable development approach is reflected in the plan's recommendations on conservation and development of the country's natural, historic, and cultural heritage (Republic of Ghana/UNDP/WTO, 1996b). Emphasis is placed on conservation and interpretation of specific features both to preserve the heritage and be interesting attractions for tourists, with tourism helping pay for conservation.

Natural Environment

The many protected areas, under the administration of the Ghana Wildlife Department, and other scenic places such as waterfalls provide the basis for development of nature and ecotourism. Although a great variety of wildlife species exist in Ghana (and West Africa), wildlife is not as abundant nor as easily viewed (because of the greater amount of vegetation) as in eastern and southern Africa. Therefore, imaginative approaches and giving emphasis to vegetation as well as wildlife need to be taken in Ghana for visitors to appreciate its natural environment. However, bird life of both resident and migratory species is abundant and bird-watching has much potential for development.

Only two of the 15 protected areas have appreciable visitor facility development, although all of them have some staff engaged in conservation activities. The largest park, Mole National Park, occupies a savannah area in northern Ghana and the existing visitor facilities are proposed for upgrading. Kakum National Park, a moist evergreen forest located in the south, is receiving international assistance and has developed a visitor center complex, nature trails, and a canopy walk. The canopy walk, the first in Africa, comprises a series of suspended walkways at the canopy level of the forest, which offers views of the upper forest ecology. Kakum has become very popular with both domestic and international tourists. Management plans have been prepared for most of the other parks and reserves, and all these plans propose improved conservation and eventual development of visitor facilities. Scenic areas not designated as protected areas are also shown on the plan for conservation and development of visitor facilities. Numerous sacred groves of trees associated with traditional religious beliefs are protected by local communities and visitors are allowed if they show due respect for the groves.

Poaching of wildlife and encroachment by farmers are problems in several of the protected areas, and corrective measures are being taken by the Wildlife Department but its budget and staff are limited. The tourism plan recommends that community-based conservation programs be organized. These programs would provide alternative sources of employment and income, including from tourism, to villagers to lessen their need to misuse the protected areas, combined with education of villagers about the importance of conservation. More generally, there is growing concern in the country about the depletion of the forests on both public (forest reserves) and private lands for commercial lumbering operations, making of charcoal, and clearing for agriculture. The government is attempting to apply measures to control deforestation and achieve sustainable forestry management.

Beaches, lakes, and mountains provide the basis for development of various types and sizes of resorts and public recreation areas. Because of erosion problems and dangerous offshore currents affecting some beaches, beach resort locations must be carefully selected. Resorts are recommended to be developed as integrated units, with densities based on carrying capacity analysis and planning and design derived from environmental and cultural factors.

Historic Sites

The many forts and castles along the coast, historic buildings, and urban districts associated with missionary and colonial activities, some chiefs' palaces, and religious shrines offer excellent resources for historic heritage tourism. Many of these sites have been designated as national monuments by the Museums and Monuments Board and other sites warrant preservation.

The castles at Elmina (Figure 6.2) and Cape Coast and Fort St. Jago at Elmina have been designated by United Nations Educational, Scientific and Cultural Organization (UNESCO) as World Heritage Sites. With international assistance, these places have been restored and developed with visitor facilities including museums in each of the castles. Both castles are open to the public, offer tours, and are now receiving many domestic and international visitors. The other intact forts along the coast are recommended in the tourism plan to be restored with consideration given to using them for good-quality tourist accommodation and restaurants similar to the paradors in Spain. The revenues from commercial operations will help pay for restoration and maintenance of the forts and development of museums and visitor facilities.

Historic district preservation programs are recommended for now-deteriorating historic urban areas in several cities and towns and of early missionary buildings in several places, with tourism helping defray the cost of preservation. Ancient Sudanic-style mosques in northern Ghana are particularly interesting and recommended for restoration and development with visitor facilities. Some chiefs' palaces have been or are planned for restoration and development with museums. Ghana has some important archaeological sites that are shown on the tourism plan but recommended not to have improved access nor be developed with visitor facilities until they have been properly excavated and strict security measures applied. This approach is essential to prevent further theft of artifacts, which are already being removed and smuggled out of the country for sale.

Figure 6.2. St. George's Castle at Elmina, built in 1482, has been restored and is designated as a World Heritage Site. The castle is a popular attraction for both domestic and international tourists.

Closely related to the historic heritage of Ghana is the recently organized Slave Route Project sponsored by UNESCO, WTO, and various national governments. A Slave Route Conference, held in Ghana in 1995, resulted in the Accra Declaration on the Cultural Tourism Slave Route project, which states the commitment:

> to rehabilitate, restore and promote the tangible and intangible heritage handed down by the slave trade for the purposes of cultural tourism, thereby throwing into relief the common nature of the slave trade in terms of Africa, Europe, the Americas and the Caribbean. (Republic of Ghana/UNDP/WTO, 1996b, p. 85)

Pursuant to the conference, an action plan has been prepared for implementation of this project. The tourism plan of Ghana incorporates the Slave Route Project, showing a map of the slave routes and markets in the country and designating, in addition to the forts and castles, several of important slave market sites, remains of village defense walls (built to repel slave raiders), and other places associated with the slave trade to be developed with memorials and visitor facilities as tourist stopovers.

Cultural Heritage

The rich cultural heritage of Ghana, both traditional and contemporary forms, offers many opportunities for tourism. Crafts of hand-made textiles, including the internationally known "kente" cloth, Ashanti stools, and other carved wood items, brassware, ceramics and pottery, jewelrey, leather work, and woven fiber items are already well developed. Certain villages specialize in production of specific crafts. The plan recommends that, in addition to redevelopment of the main craft market in Accra and improvement of craft markets in other cities and towns, craft centers be developed in the major craft villages. These community-owned centers would include exhibits and demonstrations of craft production as well as sales outlets and other visitor facilities. Accommodation would be developed by the villagers for tourists who wish to stay for some time to learn craft-making.

Contemporary art of paintings, ceramics, and sculpture are also well developed and available in art galleries and hotel exhibits. Fashion designer clothing using local textiles is being produced and is popular with tourists.

Numerous festivals, often including durbars (meetings) of chiefs, are held in many places throughout the year and are of much interest to tourists. The main adaptation to tourism is the need to plan and announce the dates of festivals sufficiently in advance for tour operators and tourists to schedule their itineraries to include the festivals. A major new festival is PANAFEST (Pan African historical and cultural festival), held biannually, that attracts many domestic and international guests (Figure 6.3). A national arts festival is organized annually.

Traditional music and dance are interesting, although not much organized for tourists to view. The plan recommends that more performances be organized for both international and local audiences, so that these traditional skills do not wither away. A national theater and national cultural center in Accra provide venues for art exhibits and performances, and some regions have cultural centers. Contemporary "pop" music, including the uniquely Ghanaian Highlife music, is popular and appeals to some tourists.

Traditional village architecture and activities can be of much interest to cultural tourists. In addition to village tours, the plan recommends development of village tourism projects such as shown in Figure 6.4, which is designed for northern Ghana based on the local architectural style. These projects would involve development of accommodation in the local style, located near the villages, with the facilities owned and operated by villagers. Guests would eat local cuisine and learn about village life, culture, and economic activities. Profits from the projects would be used to improve village infrastructure and

Figure 6.3. Durbar of chiefs at the Pan African Festival (PANAFEST), which is held biannually in Ghana. The festival attracts many Ghanaian and international participants and tourists.

community facilities such as schools and medical clinics. To expose both urban Ghanaians and tourists to the different traditional architectural styles and village activities of the country, a Ghana Folk Village is proposed to be developed near Accra.

Various types of tours are recommended in the plan to expose tourists to traditional natural medicines and how they are prepared. Recommendations are made on tourist visits to traditional fetish shrines and tours of mines, factories, timber mills, rubber and palm plantations, and cocoa farms. Agrotourism development is proposed for some of the plantations. The national museums in Accra are recommended to be improved, and regional museums in the regional capitals to be improved or new ones developed where needed. A new railway and harbor museum, housed in an historic building, is proposed in Sekondi. Sports facilities and beach parks should be improved. The plan encourages that there be more use of Ghanaian cuisine in restaurants. International exchange and home visit programs, already existing in Ghana, should be expanded to provide more direct and noncommercial contact between Ghanaians and tourists.

International, regional, and domestic conference and meeting tourism should be promoted, including making better use of the relatively new Accra International Conference Centre. Urban hotels and beach, lake, and mountain resorts should include meeting facilities.

Plan Implementation and Tourism Management

Implementation of tourism plans is always problematical, especially in developing countries with limited financial resources, weak public institutional structures and technical/

Figure 6.4. Village tourism accommodation in the northern savannah.

managerial capabilities, and often an inexperienced private sector. Also essential is effective continuous management of the tourism sector. Therefore, increasing emphasis is being given in tourism planning to identifying mechanisms for plan implementation and to strengthening the institutional framework and capabilities for effective tourism management, as essential aspects of achieving sustainable tourism development.

Implementation Approaches

The implementation approaches taken in the Ghana ITDP include the following:

- Considering implementation techniques throughout the planning process and drafting the plan to be financially and politically realistic to achieve without compromising the principles of sustainability.
- Ensuring that there is understanding and acceptance of the plans and active support of them by all the stakeholders in the both the public and private sectors, as was described previously.
- Preparation of a 5-year action program that specifies projects and other actions required to implement the first stage of development (Republic of Ghana/UNDP/WTO, 1996c). The action program indicates the agencies responsible for implementation of each project or action.
- Encouraging official adoption of the plans at the highest levels, which give them a greater legal basis for implementation. It is the intent for the national tourism plan and action program to be adopted by the Cabinet and National Parliament, and the regional plans and programs to be adopted by the regional governments.
- Distribution of the tourism plans and action programs to all the agencies concerned

with aspects of tourism for them to integrate the relevant recommendations into their programs.

- Preparation of a detailed financial plan at the macro-level, based on the overall economic analysis of the tourism sector, and at the project level based on the action program (Republic of Ghana/UNDP/WTO, 1996d). This plan identifies possible sources of project financing.

- Preparation of prefeasibility studies for 10 priority tourism development projects, one in each region, including design concepts, market analysis, and economic/financial analysis (Republic of Ghana/UNDP/WTO, 1996e). All these projects stress involvement of local communities. These studies will provide the basis for final design and development of the projects as models of suitable approaches to tourism development.

- Organization of a donor agency conference, to which international assistance agencies and NGOs were invited, to present the plans and programs and solicit assistance in implementation. The conference was held in Accra in early 1998 and was well attended.

- Formulation of detailed recommendations on attracting private sector investment in tourism. These include improving the institutional framework for investment, simplifying investment procedures, adopting tourism investment incentives that would guide development according to the plan's recommendations on type and location of facility development, establishing a tourism financial credit program, and organizing an international investment forum. Because of limited local financial resources, international investment in tourism must be sought for larger projects but with local and international joint venture investment encouraged. Technical advice and credit facilitation are already available through some local agencies to assist local development of small and medium size enterprises. Several small, medium, and larger hotel projects are underway (in mid-1998) and others have been proposed.

- Establishment of a tourism development fund to be used for tourism project development, training, and marketing. This fund would likely be financed by part of the tourist expenditure tax, which is already in effect.

- Preparation of a marketing strategy and promotion program with cost estimates for the first 5-year period and incorporating this into the action program (Republic of Ghana/UNDP/WTO, 1995a). Prototypical promotional materials were produced by the project as models for good quality promotional material.

- Designation of an implementation unit in the Ministry of Tourism to be responsible for coordination and monitoring of all aspects of implementation.

- Preparation of a tourism awareness program with cost estimates and incorporating this into the tourism action program (Republic of Ghana/UNDP/WTO, 1995c). Some tourism awareness posters have already been produced and distributed. Dialogue has commenced with the Ministry of Education on including the subject of tourism in the school curriculum. A tourist behavior code was also prepared.

- Making land available for tourism through reservation of suitable tourism sites by land use zoning procedures and providing the sites at equitable cost to both the owners and developers. Much land outside urban areas in Ghana is communally owned and controlled by traditional chiefs, and negotiations for land acquisition must take place between the chiefs and tourism developers. In some cases, communal land may be claimed by more than one chief, and arbitration is necessary to decide the rightful ownership before negotiations can take place for sale or lease. A common practice now is to lease land for a long-term period so that the proceeds from development can accrue to the chief and his people over the long term.

- Identification of ways to streamline the tourism project review procedure to make it more effective and expeditious. Also being pursued are drafting and applying historic preservation regulations and slightly modifying existing planning and environmental regulations to be compatible with the plan recommendations.
- Specification of ways to achieve effective human resource development for tourism, especially through development of a new campus for the hotel, catering, and tourism training institute. A suitable site has already been allocated for developing this campus on the outskirts of Accra.
- Identification of specific community-based tourism projects and involving local communities in development of tourist resorts and stopovers in their areas. Utilizing local resources, some craft centers currently are under development (in mid-1998). In 1997, some community-based ecotourism projects were started by a Ghanaian-based non-governmental organization using local resources with some international technical assistance.
- Monitoring the progress of plan implementation and of the economic, environmental, and sociocultural impacts of tourism development, with remedial actions taken for any problems detected. Tourist surveys are a continuing activity.

Management and Follow-Through

The plan stresses the importance of continuous effective management of tourism. The quality of management is dependent in part on having a capable and knowledgeable staff. As referred to previously, the ITDP included an intensive training program for tourism officials of in-country training courses, and out-of-country participation in training courses, study tours, and on-the-job attachments in more developed tourism offices elsewhere in Africa, as well as counterparting with the planning team members. The ITDP also established a tourism information management system in the Ministry of Tourism, which provides a database for tourism analysis and monitoring. The organizational structures of tourism agencies and organization for implementation were examined at both the national and regional levels.

A follow-through project is proposed that will focus on implementation in two areas. One is facilitating development of new, and improvement of existing, tourism enterprises, including organizing an international tourism investment forum, providing higher level training of tourism officials in technical tourism topics, and preparing lesson plans for incorporation of tourism as a subject in the school curriculum. The second area is assisting on development of a network of community-based ecotourism projects throughout the country, which will expand the present ecotourism program.

Conclusions

Several conclusions can be drawn from the experience with the ITDP in Ghana in planning for sustainable tourism while still meeting national objectives for rapid economic development. Many of the approaches used in the Ghana ITDP would seem to be applicable to planning tourism development in other African countries. The terms of reference for the planning project should be carefully prepared before it commences, but there should be administrative and budgetary flexibility to adjust and add to the TOR as the project proceeds. In countries such as Ghana, which look to tourism as a potentially major economic sector, larger as well as smaller scale types of tourism need to be considered. Various types and intensities of tourism development can be developed in different parts of the country based on local tourism resources and capacities to absorb tourism. However, concepts of sustainability can be applied to all locally acceptable types of tourism, with emphasis on conservation of resources, spreading the benefits of tourism geographically, and bringing these benefits to local communities. Developing good quality tourism and maintaining high levels of tourist satisfaction leading to sustaining tourist markets are essential. Plan recommendations should recognize political realities without compromising sustainable development objectives.

Tourism planning must be carried out within the framework of overall national and regional development policy and planning, and tourism must be integrated into overall development planning. If possible, the various levels of tourism planning—national, regional, and community—should be included in one program or in a series of related programs so that they are integrated with one another. Recognizing regional, local, and ethnic identities through tourism development is an important aspect of the tourism planning process.

Technically, the concepts of sustainability must be translated into specific approaches adapted to the local situation. Environmental and social carrying capacity standards should be applied even though based on qualitative evaluation in some areas. Heritage site conservation and interpretation techniques must be specified and community-based tourism and conservation projects identified. Appropriate development standards and design guidelines must be adopted for tourist facilities. Application of the environmental assessment procedure to tourism projects is important.

The planning program must give utmost consideration to means of implementation. All possible techniques of implementation should be considered. Especially important is facilitating financing of public and private tourism projects. Essential to implementation and development of tourism generally is gaining public and political support and commitment, including from religious and traditional leaders. Efforts must be directed to involving all the stakeholders in the planning process and educating them about tourism. In countries where the private sector is still weakly developed and inexperienced, local capital and managerial resources are limited, and there is reluctance to invest in tourism because of the perceived risky nature of this sector, implementation must include mechanisms to encourage and assist local entrepreneurship. Techniques must be specified to encourage community involvement in the tourism development process and generate benefits to local communities.

Because the private tourism sector is often weakly developed and not well coordinated in most African countries, with some facilities and services not meeting good standards or being sustainable, and initiative often not being taken in developing new tourism products and areas, the government must often assume a leading role as a facilitator and coordinator of tourism development. However, the government is often not experienced in tourism or technically prepared to properly handle this management role. The institutional environment must be conducive to developing and managing tourism in a planned and sustainable manner, and improving the institutional factors must be given emphasis in the planning process. Tourism officials may require extensive training in development techniques and exposure to tourism development approaches elsewhere. Organizational structures on tourism may need improvement and greater coordination effected among all the parties involved in tourism. Forging a productive partnership between the public and private sectors is essential. Establishing a sound database on tourism is a prerequisite for achieving successful management. Monitoring the progress of tourism and whether it is achieving its objectives without generating serious environmental or sociocultural problems is an important aspect of tourism management. After the initial planning program has been completed, often there is need for follow-through programs with international assistance to demonstrate how implementation can take place and continue to strengthen the institutional factors.

In this case study of the Ghana tourism planning program, there has not yet been sufficient time to determine how well implementation will proceed. However, some implementation is commencing, the institutional climate is generally favorable, and some financial resources may be available. The private sector is being increasingly responsive to tourism development opportunities but still requires direction. Success in achieving sustainable tourism development in Ghana that also brings substantial socioeconomic benefits to the country and its communities looks promising but is not yet assured.

Author's Note

This chapter is based on the author's experience as Chief Technical Adviser of the Ghana ITDP. The author extends his appreciation to the World Tourism Organization in Madrid, Spain, for permission to use the ITDP documents and draw from his own experience as a WTO consultant in Ghana in writing this chapter, and to the Ministry of Tourism in Ghana for releasing the ITDP documents for public use.

Chapter 7

Planning Tourism in a Reconstructing Economy: The Case of Eritrea

Peter M. Burns

Summary

This chapter critically analyzes conflicting advice on the future development of tourism given to Eritrea, a country at the very start of its planning for tourism. The chapter commences with an examination of national development planning processes. It identifies key issues including sociopolitical structures, participation, and the distribution of economic benefits. For tourism, it is argued that integration of tourism policies into broader national development priorities is essential. The case of Eritrea is an unusual one: a newly independent country with virtually no tourism infrastructure, facilities, or technical knowledge. The main focus of the chapter is on two sets of advice given to Eritrea at its first conference for the development of tourism held in 1993. Neither of these pieces of advice has the capacity to deliver equitable or sustainable development in a way that reflected Eritrea's political ethos of democratic participation in decision-making. The chapter ends with the conclusion that a more effective way of planning must start with convincing tourism planners that there are alternative approaches that can and should integrate processes that such planners would presumably wish for their own countries, namely: participation, democracy, and pluralism.

Key words: Eritrea; Tourism planning; Conflicting advice; Tourism consultants

Introduction

This chapter critically appraises conflicting advice given to the government of Eritrea on the development of its tourism and the role that tourism should play in Eritrea's future. This country makes for a particularly interesting case study because in 1993, when the advice was given, Eritrea was starting its tourism from ground-zero. The chapter commences by asserting that while politics cannot be separated from policies, evidence suggests that at either end of tourism's potential growth spectrum, narrow, self-serving perspectives dominate. The context for tourism development in Eritrea is then detailed along with analysis of the special difficulties in establishing the country's tourism sector. The main part of the chapter deals with two policy advice papers given at Eritrea's first tourism development conference held in 1993. The conclusion poses questions about the appropriateness of advice given in countries like Eritrea, which have been subjected to political, social, and economic devastation of one sort or another.

Planning: A Critical Appraisal

Over the past several decades there is little evidence to suggest that tourism planning in the context of developing countries has adequately dealt with social and political issues (Burns & Holden, 1995; Tosun & Jenkins, 1998). This has not been caused by a knowledge gap where techniques and technologies have had to catch up with tourism development demand, but rather through a lack of willingness to engage with intellectual arguments outside the narrow field of "tourism as industry" (Burns, 1999).

Policies and the planning that arises from them are overt expressions of a particular political position. In the case of lesser developed countries in Africa, development policies are usually stated through a national development plan that covers all sectors and sets targets and goals to be achieved within a set time frame. In the case of Eritrea, no such overall sectoral development plan existed, making it especially difficult to relate tourism to wider social and economic goals.

Externally sourced planning and advice for developing countries (especially aid-assisted master planning) is based on the general idea of using formal plans to stimulate and direct the local economy between the two poles of free market mechanisms on the one hand and a command economy on the other. This balancing approach is one that carries a certain resonance with regard to tourism planning as it is currently practiced. However, what fixes such normative approaches in their cultural and temporal context is not so much the changing global economy where central control is increasingly less likely, but the general lack of reference to people and participation. This top-down approach to tourism planning is about what governments do to their populations, not what populations have their governments do for them. Such approaches have certain characteristics, the main ones of which have been worked into a model for development planning (Figure 7.1).

The model suggests that "guidance" from the World Bank in the form of loans or economic restructuring (i.e., freeing markets, privatization, etc.) is likely to dominate the African development agenda (George, 1989; Harrison, 1993; Waters, 1995). At the next level down in the model, bilateral advice on policy matters is likely to shape economic and social strategies (Hoogvelt, 1982) while aid projects themselves will come into play at the implementation level (i.e., in response to technical assistance requests from governments). It can be seen that an evaluation and feedback loop exists to match outcomes from policies with stated goals, all linked to a central planning office.

Before exploring this aspect of planning further, it is useful to know about the role of the agency that puts such development plans together: the central planning office. Jarman (1980) notes several roles. First, the publication of long-term development plans (the "DPs") sometimes augmented by annual plans. Second, monitoring the accuracy of other ministries' statistical and qualitative research. Third, advising on the integrity of specific projects and seeing how they fit into overall development. Fourth, preparation of feasibility studies, and finally, serving as advisers to elected officials on the coordination of "policy into practice" planning matters.

However, neither Jarman's suggestions concerning the roles of central planning offices nor the model shown as Figure 7.1 illustrate the range of influences on the planning process. Hughes (1980) throws some light on this in a discussion about the deification of economics in general and statistics in particular. In addition to the influences of the prevailing political party or system, and the pervasive influence of elite or "enclave clientele"

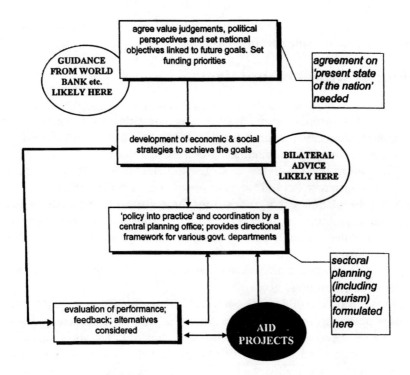

Figure 7.1. Characteristics of contemporary development planning.
Source: from an idea by Todaro (1997, pp. 576–579).

who reflect urban and perhaps colonial attitudes towards rural development, health, and decentralization, Hughes notes four other types of influence (Figure 7.2).

Bubble 1 in Figure 7.2 shows, just as Neuber (1995) suggested some two decades later (Hughes' 1980 paper was first published in 1975), that development plans are "formulated in incremental . . . terms, based on preceding plans" (p. 113). In the case of African nations it may be inferred that the origins of development planning will have been framed by a colonial agenda not unsympathetic to former trading companies and multinational corporations (MNCs). Hughes makes an interesting point about the paucity of regional strategies to deal with MNCs, presently made difficult by national rivalry, and further exacerbated by the failure of regional bodies to adequately deal with this issue. In this interpretation of Hughes' work, his comments concerning presumed attitudes of investors and incentives (bubble 2) and the policies of aid donors (bubble 3) (which, it may be argued, are likely to be aligned with the politico-economic values of the former colonial powers) have been deliberately overlapped.

Finally, the gap between bubble 4 and the interlinked other bubbles symbolically as well as graphically illustrates the disproportionate gap between political responsibility (i.e., policy-making by elected politicians) and what Hughes describes as well-trained and educated civil servants. Hughes cynically and deliberately omits "people" and "community" from his patterns of influences because to do so would encourage what he calls the "grassroots mirage"; the idea wherein "hastily organized tours [of politicians and planners] and committees are set up to gather the views of the people" (Hughes, 1980, p. 20), which, he asserts, can rarely be integrated into the planning process other than at the most superficial level, especially after "the ideas of the people have been assisted in for-

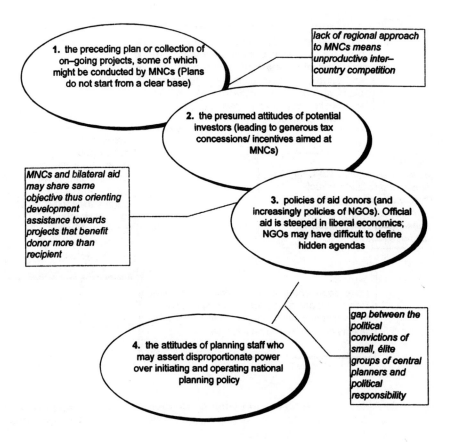

1. the preceding plan or collection of on–going projects, some of which might be conducted by MNCs (Plans do not start from a clear base)

lack of regional approach to MNCs means unproductive inter–country competition

2. the presumed attitudes of potential investors (leading to generous tax concessions/ incentives aimed at MNCs)

MNCs and bilateral aid may share same objective thus orienting development assistance towards projects that benefit donor more than recipient

3. policies of aid donors (and increasingly policies of NGOs). Official aid is steeped in liberal economics; NGOs may have difficult to define hidden agendas

gap between the political convictions of small, élite groups of central planners and political responsibility

4. the attitudes of planning staff who may assert disproportionate power over initiating and operating national planning policy

Figure 7.2. Influences on the development process. Source: from an idea by Hughes (1980, pp. 20–21).

mulation by central politicians and officials and processed by ministries and the planning office" (Hughes, 1980, p. 20).

The results of such planning processes include carrying forward fundamental structural deficiencies such as industrialization versus rural development and the relationship between private and public sector modes of production. These deficiencies exacerbate the dynamics of mal-development within a national system. Neuber (1995) makes a correlation between the rigidity of central planning and deteriorating economic performance, which emphasizes the need to keep planning in perspective, and not ascribe to it the characteristics of a panacea. Too much, as Killick (1995) suggests, depends on the "importance of historical influences on the responsiveness of policy processes" (p. 371) and the legacy of a nation's initial condition. It has been argued that three basic issues arise out of the arguments concerning development and how it is measured. The first relates to the sociopolitical structures under which planning is carried out; the second concerns the extent to which the people are given the opportunity to participate in the formulating of plans; and finally, issues arising out of the distribution and redistribution of the benefits.

Governmental Roles in Tourism Planning and Policy-Making

Formal planning for a sector like tourism represents a type of government intervention. The approach to planning will reflect the role that government assumes with respect to

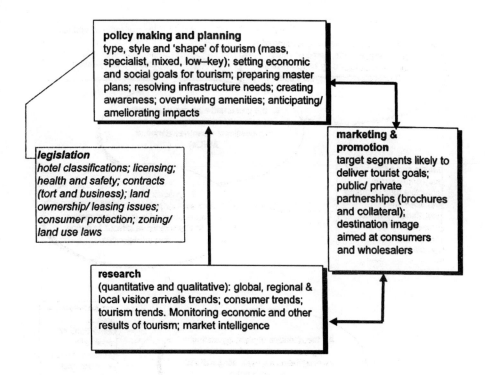

Figure 7.3. Roles of government in planning for tourism. Source: adapted from ideas by Gunn (1998, pp. 21, 141–) and Edgell (1990, pp. 38–30, 104–105).

tourism. Figure 7.3 offers an overview of possible government involvement based on traditional approaches such as those promoted by Gunn (1988) and Edgell (1990). The key feature of this model is the limits it places on participation and interaction: planning being fed by and feeding into marketing; legislation taking account of qualitative and quantitative research while informing the planning process and so forth, but nowhere to be seen are the notions of participation, consultation, or the presence of people at a local level.

In Figure 7.3, legislation is seen as slightly detached from the process, framing rather than informing the policy-making. Edgell (1990, p. 105) suggests a model for the tourism policy development and decision-making processes that integrates three sets of issues for decision-making. First are what Poon (1993) refers to as "frame conditions" (p. 35), second are goals and objectives, and third are resources. Decisions based around the frame conditions will consider social, political, and economic factors. Decisions regarding goals and objectives will contain reference to community benefit, generation of profits and government revenues, and how these should be reached. Finally, resource decisions will include human, financial, and physical factors. Bull (1991, p. 199) attempts to broaden the perspective for policy-making by linking the general tourism policies with general economic policies. However, Bull's model appears to be flawed in that general tourism policies are given the same ranking as national economic policies. According to Bull, the specific economic policies for tourism arise out of the conjunction of these two "equals." This is not, in itself, sufficient. It is fundamental to systematic, integrated national planning that tourism policies should not just be in congruence with national policies, but subservient to them. This point has been made by Getz (1986), who says in relation to goals set for tourism that these should be directly related to the role that tourism is expected to play in overall policies.

Tourism policies should not only be based on market research but framed by *development* needs and contribution to poverty elimination. Policies can then address issues related to legislation, social and economic structures, and physical infrastructures. In general, governments can be seen to have a variety of roles including:

- *entrepreneurial* where domestic investment might be weak or nervous about investing in a sector with no previous significant national track record in owning and operating hotels;
- *stewardship* as an agent for assessing and prioritizing resource allocation;
- *investment* catalyst where the government might both facilitate and stimulate investment through a range of financial and nonfinancial investment incentives.

Given that tourism planning is likely to involve complex education and training rooted in political culture (Burns, 1995), infrastructure and utilities, marketing, public awareness, and impact management, focus at the practical level can lead to loss of sight of the complex interrelationships that exist—both of their interdependence and of the hierarchy of these relationships. Doswell (1978) advocates an overview of the interrelationships of the explicit ("official" politics and policies) and implicit influences (i.e., "hidden" agendas) in the organization and control of national tourism, such as: Who controls membership of the National Tourist Organization? What is the relationship between policy-making and policy implementation (taking into account the national priorities over commercial touristic imperatives)? His model illustrates the consultative and advisory mechanisms, the committees and working parties that operate in some African countries, with functions across most sectoral interests. However, they represent only the means to integration. The initiating role to get them established and operational lies with government or statutory authorities like the National Tourism Organization or economic planning agency. Doswell's conceptual overview model is also flawed in that it infers, rather than directly shows, overlapping responsibilities at the ministerial level. This can cause poor coordination, not to mention compounding the problem of interministerial rivalries. A less hierarchical model with community concerns given representation and commercial sector initiatives recognized and encouraged within a governmental facilitation framework seems more appropriate as we enter the new millennium.

The Case of Eritrea

Short Historical Perspective

Eritrea's 1000-km coastline on the western side of the Red Sea places it in a strategically important position (Figure 7.4). This has drawn expansionist powers over the centuries: the Arabs; the Ottomans; the Egyptians; and, during the European powers' colonialist scramble for Africa, the Italians. Eritrea's existence as a single political entity began in 1889 with the opening of the Suez Canal. This gave Europe easy access through the Red Sea to the rich trade routes of the Indian Ocean. The Italian occupiers changed Eritrea from a subsistence to a market-based economy. During the 50 years of their rule, Eritrea had probably the best communications and transportation facilities in Africa. During the Italian era, a national identity and consciousness was developed. People from diverse economic, ethnic, and religious backgrounds were structurally linked into a national identity within the colonial borders (Government of Eritrea [GoE], 1993).

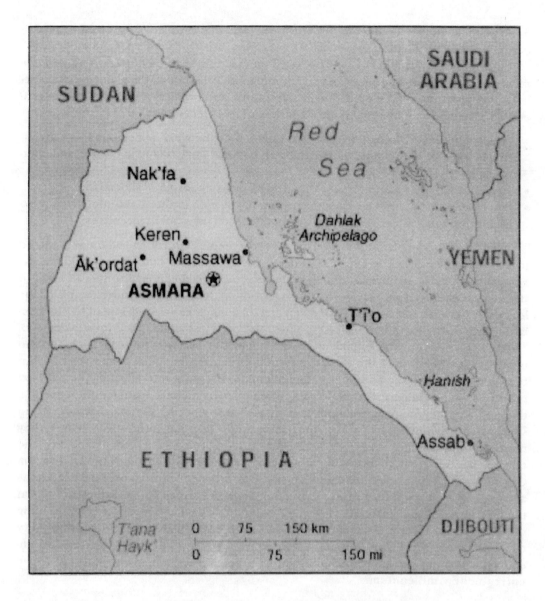

Figure 7.4. Map of Eritrea. Source: www.odci.gov/cia/publications/factbook

Economic, Political, and Administrative Structure

During World War II, most of the infrastructure built under the Italians was destroyed. Following the defeat of the Italians by the Allied forces, there followed a period of neglect under the British Military Administration rule of Eritrea as "occupied enemy territory." This weakness, or seeming lack of commitment on the part of the British, served to heighten neighboring, land-locked Ethiopia's awareness of the country's strategic importance and thus its designs on it.

Against the wishes of the Eritrean people, 75% of whom supported independence (GoE, 1993), and through a blatant piece of horse-trading Ethiopia offered the U.S. full access to the British communications center outside Asmara in return for support in its claim on

Eritrea. At this stage, the United Nations (UN), "under the aegis of the USA government, failed to address the interests and aspirations of the Eritreans. Instead of independence at the end of its mandate UN Resolution 390 (V) [was] adopted . . . by the General Assembly" (Ghebrai, 1993, p. 256). Thus, on December 2, 1950, Eritrea was formally placed in federation with Ethiopia, an event that, according to Ghebrai (1993) "shall be registered in the annals of the UN history as one of the worst political blunders and heinous crime against humanity committed by this world organization" (pp. xvii). The terms of the UN resolution were designed to ensure a good deal of self-determinism for the Eritrean people, and for Eritrea to be "an autonomous unit under the sovereignty of the Ethiopian Crown" (p. 256). However, this did not satisfy Ethiopia's desire for total control. It gradually whittled away the power of the Eritrean administration and violated the people's constitutional rights. In 1962 Eritrea's Assembly was forced at gunpoint to abrogate the Federation and Ethiopia absorbed Eritrea as one of its provinces. Despite being responsible for the legal implementation of the Federation resolution, no UN action followed Ethiopia's annexation of Eritrea ("Eritrea," 1994; GoE, 1993).

Main Development Challenges

Over the next three decades Eritrea, with no international support, waged a struggle against a country of vastly superior military might and financial resources. Ethiopia was supported by the Soviet Union to the tune of $12 billion in military training and equipment. Despite the 1980's cycle of famine in the region, and the loss of more than 5% of its people in the conflict, Eritrea emerged victorious in 1991 and, following a referendum on independence from Ethiopia, became a sovereign state in May 1993.

One of the most remarkable aspects of the protracted war was the close collaboration between the Eritrean Peoples' Liberation Front (EPLF), essentially the army (although EPLF made no distinction between the civilians and "Freedom Fighters"), and the civilian population. The EPLF had a deliberate strategy of involving the ordinary people in consultation and decision-making. They successfully organized literacy programs and education, health and transport systems with minimal resources under constant air attack. They reorganized land ownership on a collective basis and made strides forward in the emancipation of women. The overriding ethos was that of a classless society: this approach did much to consolidate national feeling and create a culture of national solidarity ("Eritrea," 1994).

The qualities that eventually bought victory (determination, discipline, organization, resourcefulness, self-reliance) and the strategic approaches used (consultation at grass-roots level, and the integration of people into the decision-making processes) have great relevance to the planning of Eritrea's reconstruction, with tourism as one of the key components.

The main development challenges, including continued poverty, in common with many other conflict-ridden countries are characterized by the following:

- geographic, linguistic, social, and intellectual isolation;
- limited individual capacity and finance to manage risks such as unexpected drought, pests, illness, unplanned births, and price fluctuations;
- lack of access to resources such as land, credit, technology, useful information;
- demobilization and reintegration of returning Freedom Fighters (those who were at the front during the war);
- disproportionate numbers of widows and other women in female-headed households (FHH);
- the need to find productive employment for the high numbers of amputees and war-wounded;

- the need to motivate (through entrepreneurship and employment) youths to remain in rural areas so as to combat urban drift.

When taken together, it is to Eritrea's credit that the government response to tackling these problems has been, to say the least, robust.

The role of nongovernmental organizations (NGOs) was identified by the government as being essential in their human-centered approach to development. For example, the Eritrean Women's Association and former Women Freedom Fighter's association *Bana* (the exact meaning of this word falls between "shining light" and "dawn") have played a hugely important role in creating microfinance and training opportunities for certain groups.

Current Development Indicators

Determined not to become enslaved to debt repayment, Eritrea has resisted much of the aid assistance offered. The view of the President of the University of Asmara that, "the aid program creates more damage in Africa than the AIDS epidemic," is telling (personal interview, January 1996). To quote Finance Minister Haile Woldense:

> the leadership has been in the countryside, they know the people, they feel their heart beat. We cannot accept that an expert comes here for a few days and dictates terms. We must be the owners of our own programme. ("Survey: Eritrea," 1996, p. 13)

Instead, it is rebuilding roads, including the Massawa–Asmara railway line, which links the main sea port with the capital city, using recycled war materials and the large repository of surplus labor. The Eritrea Community Rehabilitation Fund has acted as the catalyst for communities working together in nation building through projects like the planting of millions of seedlings to replace trees and bush destroyed during the period of war, the integration of the returning Freedom Fighters, and encouraging three quarters of a million or more Eritrean refugees abroad, including the educated diaspora, to return home.

The single-party government, The People's Front for Democracy and Justice, was created by the EPLF in 1994 to transform itself into a mass political party. This is also actively seeking to attract overseas investment, while concentrating on rebuilding the infrastructure that investors require ("Eritrea," 1994). With the 1995 per capita GDP estimated at just US$570, only a handful of government officials and civil servants possessing training or experience for their assigned roles, and skill shortages coexisting with high unemployment, the challenges facing the GoE 5 years after achieving independence remain immense.

The same qualities that gained independence are, however, again to the fore and, until the May 1998 border skirmish with Ethiopia brought unfavorable international media exposure, visitors to Eritrea over the past few years have almost unanimously reported positively on progress ("Survey: Eritrea," 1996).

Tourism Policy and Advice: The 1993 Conference

In October 1993, the Department of Tourism (Ministry of Trade, Industry and Tourism) organized and presented the first conference on the "Consideration of Different Policy Issues for the Development of Tourism in Eritrea." The conference was an early and clear indication that tourism had a distinct role to play in the social and economic development of the newly independent nation. Ten major papers were presented covering a range of topics including social, economic, and environmental issues. Two of these papers are of particular interest because of the completely conflicting messages they carried and will be critically analyzed later in this chapter, forming the thrust of the argument put forward by the present author.

The opening address to the conference stressed that the tourism sector was considered to be a strategic sector by the government and one that would play a critical role in the nation's recovery program (Abraha, 1993). Three broad policy statements were issued. These were concerned with the identification and development of a wide range of tourist sites, the need for a subregional approach (especially with Ethiopia, but also other neighboring countries where possible), and a clear political statement on the role of tourism in developing international and regional relations.

These policies were further elaborated in four detailed paragraphs. First, the call for a detailed assessment of tourism's potential and the identification of factors likely to hold back development. Second, the acknowledgment of Eritrea's cultural diversity and its role in the emerging industry together with the need to develop and restore infrastructure and to ensure that tourism was, from the start, geared towards intersectoral linkages where possible. Third, the need to take a regional and international perspective on the development of tourism, especially through membership of organizations such as the World Tourism Organization. Finally, there was the call for an effective training scheme to balance the need for a professionalized industry against retaining the Eritrean peoples' traditional reputation for hospitality.

These statements, which were general and, in a sense, short term, were then worked into a series of objectives for the Department of Tourism. These included working out a tourism development strategy compatible with Eritrea's national development plan; identifying tourism development areas; providing training in tourism management; encouraging enterprises to expand and develop; creating the necessary conditions to promote internal tourism (thus encouraging Eritreans to develop a positive recreation culture) and facilitating of closer interaction between Eritreans living in different regions of the country to further consolidate their unity; increasing the tourist industry's contribution to national foreign exchange earnings; development of mechanisms to monitor the social impact of tourism; and building up institutional capacity.

With these policy imperatives in mind, the papers by Krippendorf and by Eshel are each discussed in turn.

The Krippendorf Perspective

The first paper under consideration was from Professor Krippendorf, who had made a series of trips to Eritrea, bringing with him a Swiss group who were very positive about Eritrea's future development. He made the point that the success of tourism should be measured by the positive economic and social impacts upon the population weighed against negative social and environmental effects. He suggested that Eritrea should have three objectives for tourism:

- to generate foreign exchange and jobs,
- to promote human development,
- to protect the environment.

In order to promote sustainability, each of these objectives should be treated equally. Krippendorf (1993) further suggested that "tourism development in Eritrea should never be considered as a goal in itself" (p. 73) but that sustainable tourism development should be framed by certain guidelines, which included:

- "small scaled step-by-step tourism development" (Krippendorf, 1993, p. 71) compatible with the nation's stage of development and ability to absorb impacts;

- the formulation of regulations and incentives that encourage development only in allocated sites;
- the targeting of tourists who have moderate physical needs that can be satisfied locally.

By promoting what he has termed "soft tourism" (Krippendorf, 1989, p. 106) he remains focused on the needs of the holidaymaker (to use Krippendorf's own word) and pays only lip service to tourism's capacity to deliver significant amounts of jobs or foreign exchange.

In this sense, Krippendorf fails to address the central paradox of "soft tourism," which is that national development goals concerning the generation of foreign exchange and creation of employment are not easily achieved without tourist arrivals having at least some link to economies of scale. The overriding tone of Krippendorf's approach is patronizing; for example:

> a profound feeling of physical and spiritual well-being and gratitude; combined with many new impressions especially referring to the highly interesting political, social, economical and ecological situation . . . which leads us to some self-critical reflections with respect to our own life and life-style. We feel that other tourists could make similar experiences if they are well informed and guided. That is why we think Eritrea should not try to attract "normal tourists" (who seek nothing more than just to take a break and switch off) but those more rare categories of tourists which are prepared to take their time to experience all this what makes Asmara and Eritrea so unique. (Krippendorf, 1993, p. 80)

This extract raises a number of issues, the first one being the irony whereby visitors from one of the richest countries in the world express what appear to be almost obsequious feelings of "spiritual well-being and gratitude" after exposure to the country and its capital city of one of the world's poorest countries. The second issue arising concerns the activities of Krippendorf's "normal tourist." There is clearly an implied criticism of those "seeking nothing more than a break," a sort of plea to keep Eritrea as it is so that educated and appreciative people can come and gaze upon the curiosities. This "museumization" approach (for, that is, in effect, what it is) echoes Adam's (1990) brief discussion on tourism and indigenous peoples, "it is not the rural poor who will gain most? but the rich consumer in the industrialised North with leisure and wealth to be a tourist" (p. 200); a reflection of First World narcissism: seeking, as Said (1978) would have it "to keep the Oriental-colored to his position of *object studied by the Occidental-white*" (italics in original) (p. 228).

The Eshel Perspective

Eshel, an Israeli tourism expert invited by the Tourism Department to conduct a 10-day study mission in June/July 1993 presented a paper of a very different sort. He started by outlining the general advantages of tourism as an industry; these are worth citing in full:

1. The total capital needs to create one job is lower than industry and agriculture.
2. The capital utilization for each job in tourism is 30 per cent higher than in industry (42 per cent against 33 per cent in Israel) [sic].
3. The quick maturity of the capital investment means almost immediate employment.
4. The indirect ripple effect of two jobs in tourism is an extra job in the general economy.
5. The direct earning of hard currency in tourism turns it into an export oriented cash crop industry.

6. Tourism is one of the few remaining industries in the modern economy with a high manpower demand. (Eshel, 1993, p. 106)

A number of issues arise from this list. Point 1 fails to recognize the capital-intensive nature of tourism, especially the type of mass tourism being proposed by Eshel. Points 2 and 4 may apply to other countries with complex economies (such as Sri Lanka), but Eritrea has an almost unique economy arrived at after a 30-year war of independence during which time the infrastructure and industrial capacity were devastated. Point 3, if the temporary increase in construction and infrastructure support capacity is included, is by no means unique to tourism. Point 5 is weak in that it fails to account for the leakage factor (and dependency) that will occur with the type of tourism he was recommending, which was for winter leisure and vacation tourism on a large scale linked to Israeli and Egyptian tourism developments in the Red Sea Basin.

Eshel goes on to describe, in some detail, Eilat's development profile for the year 2000, which includes (within a 3-km seafront) 10,000 double rooms (in 50 hotels); 1,350,000 arrivals; US$1,350 million foreign exchange and some US$112.5 million of public investment in infrastructure. He then describes Egypt's Red Sea development policy, which is:

> based on the "Eilat Riviera Model" but multiplied 25 times along the 220 kilometre sea front of the Gulf of Aqaba and about 45 times more along the 4000 kilometre of the Western shores along the Red Sea and the Gulf of Suez . . . following public sector investment [of US$5,525 mn.] in the country's infrastructure. (Eshel, 1993, p. 96)

Eshel then uses the following scientific–rational method to arrive at a possibility for Eritrea to develop its own mega-resort on the Red Sea:

> Eritrea's manpower resources from a population of 4–5 million limits its potential for development compared to unlimited manpower resources in Egypt. In a fully developed economy, up to 40% of the entire population could be considered as a national workforce (2,000,000 workers in Eritrea). Suppose the government decides on a maximum 25% of such workforce to be engaged in and around a tourist industry, this gives 500,000 people available. If two thirds of these were to be directed to new Red Sea riviera[s] (330,000 people), then Eritrea could develop 13 riviera [resorts] in a tourism capacity. (Eshel, 1993, p. 97)

Eshel is wrong in his estimates. Eritrea's population is nearer to 3.5 million (World Bank, 1994). Some 85% of Eritrea's population is illiterate, with a labor force of only 732,095, including: 487,212 agro-pastoralists and fishermen; just over 103,000 engaged in nonfarm rural employment; 54,000 registered unemployed; 74,000 civil servants, and 54,000 microentrepreneurs (International Labour Organization, 1994).

Eshel describes the long-term implications of such a development as eventually leading to 130,000 rooms in 650 hotels; 11,700,000 visitors per year generating tourist revenues of up to US$23,400 million (based on a tourist spend of US$2000 per holiday); all of which would be supported by public investment in infrastructure calculated by a rule-of-thumb measurement of total private sector investment, which in this case, using Eshel's calculation of US$100,000 per room, would be in the region of 15% of US$13,000 million. Whether the private sector could be induced to invest before the government built the infrastructure was not discussed. In the short term, Eshel recommends the development of 12,600 new rooms over a 3-year period plus 500 plots for deluxe summer homes. Clearly, this is an example of the capitalization of resources and the setting up of inevitably unequal trade relations.

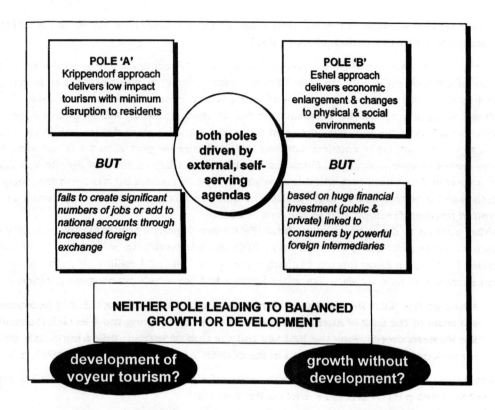

Figure 7.5. Krippendorf–Eshel polarities of tourism policy advice.

Implications for Development

It is clear from the above that policy advice for tourism development has its polarities; in this case Krippendorf at one end and Eshel at the other. The advantages and disadvantages of each are outlined in Figure 7.5.

The polarities outlined in Figure 7.5 demonstrate that a major problem for governments receiving tourism policy or planning advice is that neither extreme will deliver balanced growth; moreover, advice is often driven by the agenda of the advisor. This is why in planning de Kadt's (1992) point about "building the institutions needed for policy implementation" (p. 73) remains so very important. The discussion on the conflicting advice given to Eritrea emphasizes the fact that advice given can range from the development of holiday resorts through to cultural museumization and has very little to do with the central development concerns for most African countries which, as the UNDP states in its revised field manual, must focus on poverty elimination, productive employment, rural development, and the place of women (United Nations Development Program, 1993).

Conclusions

The "solution" (though perhaps not a final one) lies not only in finding a middle way through the two extremes that balances community needs at a local level with the commercial realities of the international tourism system: a kind of tourism advice that empowers local planners through institutional strengthening and embraces local participation.

Such a middle way would not necessarily exclude any particular form of tourism. For example, mass tourism at certain locations might provide part of the solution to development problems (say when the development problem is mass unemployment) just as ecotourism might deliver a solution when the development problem is to do with rural needs. In a way, it is unfortunate that the phrase "alternative tourism" has been subsumed into the ecotourism debate, because clearly "alternative ways" are what is needed if that is taken to mean that the complexities of tourism development in Africa are to be fully acknowledged.

A series of individual studies rather than a large, single "dose" of expertise, such as to be found in the deeply flawed master-planning approach (Burns, 1999), may be more appropriate; using a far broader range of consultants, including those with specific knowledge of the country and its people in tandem with regular tourism experts, may also be valid in places like Eritrea. But whatever the approach, a major challenge remaining for tourism planners is to develop schemes that encourage long-term commitment to the destination on the part of investors based on operating profits, rather than on inflated property prices or land speculation, neither of which brings advantage to the majority of residents. Tourism policies with their associated planning and implementation should be oriented towards anticipating and avoiding (or at least ameliorating) such problems. This approach to tourism planning could act to preserve the long-term viability of tourism and thus the destination, by protecting the components that make up the attraction of a particular area from overuse. However, tourism plans are unlikely to be successful if prepared in isolation; they are most effective when set within the context, and comprising one component, of overall regional or national physical and socioeconomic development plans. By aiming to produce a diverse economy, with tourism as one of a number of prime economic sectors, there is a greater chance of long-term economic (and thus, political) stability. Overreliance on tourism places destinations in a vulnerable position given the fluctuating and often fickle nature of tourist demand.

The foremost concern of contemporary planners is not only the integrative approach (WTO, 1994), but is also to ensure a strategic framework for tourism (Edgell, 1990). Attempts at reaching synthesis between humanistic concerns and "efficient" planning have been made (Murphy, 1985). However, the supply side of tourism requires a complex range of facilities and attractions that are in a fixed location; the "distribution" of a tourism product, as noted above, entails bringing the consumer to the product rather than the product to the consumer. This is a fundamental difference between tourism and almost any other form of economic production–consumption pattern. It is this that makes any "tradeoff" between the human concerns for local populations and economies of scale and other "rational" matters of planning.

Implementing a more effective way must start with educating the donor agencies about tourism and convincing tourism consultant planners that there are alternative approaches that can and should integrate processes that they (presumably) desire for their own countries: participation, democracy, and pluralism. As Davidoff (1965) says in his essay:

> The contemporary thoughts of planners about the nature of man in society are often mundane, unexciting or gimmicky. When asked to point out to students the planners who have a developed sense of history and philosophy concerning man's situation in the urban world one is hard put to come up with a name. . . . We cope with the problems of alienated man with a recommendation for reducing the time of journey to work. (p. 295)

It may be suggested that lecturers in tourism also struggle to come up with names of planners who do more than reiterate old ideas, reify the mundane, or deify the master planning process. To be fair, good planning assumes, a priori, that all is well at the receiving end: that democratic and planning processes within the destination country are effective and functioning. In the case of certain African countries, this is not necessarily so. Minority rights, long-term environmental perspectives, democracy, fundamentalism, continuing food shortages, and tensions between centralizing and decentralizing forces are present in varying forms and will shape the possibilities for more effective planning.

It can be seen from this example from Eritrea, which offers a rare insight into the conflicting advice that may be received by governments, that neither the Krippendorf nor Eshel approaches will help to eliminate poverty or even develop a tourism industry that is sustainable; rather, each has the potential to drive Eritrea into cultural or economic dependency—neither of which has any place in balanced, human-centered growth.

Chapter 8

The Development of Tourism in Namibia

Carson L. Jenkins

Summary

Namibia is a large country geographically (824,000 km²) with a comparatively small population of 1.6 million people, which became independent as a republic in March 1990. Historically, it had been dominated in economic and political terms by its southern neighbor, the Republic of South Africa, to which it is closely associated through currency linkage and a customs union. Namibia, like many other countries in southern Africa, based its development strategy on agricultural and mineral resources. However, as early as 1992 government recognized that tourism could help to diversify the development strategy and consequently designated it a "priority sector." The government sought the help of the European Union to develop tourism. That organization, through its technical assistance programs, has since 1992 supported the tourism sector. This chapter assesses the progress that has been made in this process, examines the nature and impact of the provided technical assistance, and identifies the problems that have inhibited development. These problems are identified further as development issues that may have relevance to other developing countries seeking to define and implement a tourism development strategy.

Key words: Namibia; Tourism; Development; Impact

Introduction

Namibia is an arid country with a considerable geographic variation. It can be categorized into four main regions: the Namib Desert and Coastal Plains along the coast; the eastward sloping Central Plateau; Kalahari sands along the borders with Botswana and South Africa; and the densely wooded bushveldt of Kovango and Caprivi. This geographic variation holds considerable potential for tourism development. The country has 22 national parks with a comprehensive range of wildlife and changing natural environments, including the harsh desert areas and the Skeleton coast.

The economy is dominated by mining, particularly diamonds and uranium, with livestock (cattle and sheep) the next significant sector. Tourism and fisheries are both recognized by the government as having excellent development potential. In an area of 824,290 km² and a population estimated at 1.6 million, Namibia is one of the most sparsely populated countries in the southern African region. However, the agricultural sector already has absorbed its maximum of subsistence-level farming and offers limited potential for further growth. The country is, for historical and commercial reasons, heavily dependent on trade with South Africa. Inward investment is required to help diversify the economy, with tourism having been declared a priority sector by the government.

Namibia became independent on 21 March 1990 and is a democratic republic headed by a president.

Background

After Independence in 1990 the Government of Namibia embarked upon a program of economic development. It was realized that tourism could contribute significantly to the overall development of the country and in 1991 Cabinet declared tourism a priority sector.

In 1992, the European Commission (EC), at the request of the Ministry of Environment and Tourism (MET), allocated funds for technical assistance to Namibia's tourism development. The technical assistance brief was to prepare a comprehensive study on tourism in Namibia, which in early 1993 resulted in the production of a Tourism Development Plan (TDP). This plan provided guidelines, strategies, and targets for implementation of formulated strategies. The TDP was used to form the tourism sectoral content of the government's National Development Plan (NDP1) 1995/96–1999/2000 and further provided the background to the White Paper on Tourism, which was approved by Cabinet in March 1994.

This chapter examines the role and contribution of the tourism sector to the economic development of Namibia. The main features of, and problems in, the sector are analyzed. The technical assistance support for the sector is described, as is tourism's contribution to achieving the national development objectives. The chapter concludes by identifying and discussing the major development issues relevant to the sector and suggests how the Namibian experience can offer valuable inputs to the tourism development process in other developing countries.

Government/Sectoral Policy

The NDP1 contains a 5-year development strategy and is Namibia's first medium-term development program covering the period 1995/96 to 1999/2000. NPD1 was formulated through broad-based participation both inside and outside government. The plan was approved by the National Planning Commission (NPC) and the Cabinet in August 1995 and submitted to Parliament in October 1995. The plan is currently in the process of major revision and update.

Following an analysis of the historical context, government set the following broad national development goals:

- reviving and sustaining economic growth;
- creating employment;
- reducing inequalities in income distribution;
- eradicating poverty.

These broad and ambitious development goals were accompanied by specific performance targets. It was recognized by government that tourism could contribute to the attainment of national development goals and targets particularly in the areas of economic growth, creation of employment and income, and as a means of stimulating regional and, specifically, rural development.

The National Indicative Programme (NIP) for Namibia formulated by the European Union identified two main components in the medium- and long-term strategy:

- poverty alleviation;
- integration into the regional and world economy.

The two objectives support national development policy. It was further agreed that women's role in Namibia's development and environmental issues will be an integrated part of the EC financial program. To support this strategy, the community cooperation policy within the framework of the NIP will be involved in socioeconomic as well as productive sectors and take into consideration some of the sectors that government has designated "priority sectors"; agriculture and rural development, education and training, trade and industry, and services. The NIP is therefore articulated around three focal sectors:

- education and training;
- agriculture and rural development;
- support to productive areas.

Although tourism will contribute indirectly to education and training and rural development objectives, it is specifically mentioned in support to productive areas in the following terms:

> Make the service sector, especially tourism, as a vehicle for economic development with particular importance in areas with limited other economic activities. (European Union, 1996)

This specific objective supports the detailed strategies and policies for the sector set out in the Tourism Development Plan and the White Paper on Tourism. The main constituents of this strategy are given below.

- Support and develop resource management to cope with the increasing pressure on the environment and to secure sustainable and extended tourism development.
- Increase support to research to ensure sustainable development.
- Strengthen conservancy and environmental policy for successful tourism development combined with a strategy to enable communities and commercial farmers to participate more effectively in wildlife and tourism.
- Transfer money and resources from the tourism sector to the protection and enhancement of the environment.
- Properly develop the sector, avoiding the consequences of poor resource utilization.
- Make the 22 government-owned and -operated resorts and camping facilities more commercial and service oriented.
- Improve training.
- Improve management information systems and statistics.
- Promote awareness of the potential for, and the special conditions related to, tourism in Namibia.

These strategic actions will be supported by institution building with the introduction of Namibia Wildlife Resort (NWR), Namibia Tourism Board (NTB), and the strengthening of the Ministry of Environment and Tourism (MET). The NTB will be the means used to more closely involve the private sector in the development effort. MET will concentrate its efforts on the planning of the sector, the coordination of tourism and wildlife policies, and cooperation with other ministries.

General Context

There is a coherence between the stated macrodevelopment objectives in the NDP1 and the objectives established for the tourism sector. What has not received sufficient emphasis is the comparative advantage that tourism often enjoys in areas where activities such as small-scale manufacturing and agriculture are difficult to develop. In an arid country like Namibia with vast distances and a small population base, small-scale manufacturing and agriculture are likely to have limited development potential. As the Director of the Namibian Economic Research Unit stated:

> the marginal nature of farming does not provide a substantial livelihood for farmers and was not a full-time occupation for most people. ("Development Issues in Namibia," 1997)

With the same source estimating the combined rate of unemployment and underemployment could be as high as 60% of the adult population, the need for job creation is obvious. Much of the mineral extraction activity is highly localized and capital intensive; therefore, it is not able to contribute in any substantial way to either job creation or rural development.

Tourism can utilize the natural endowments of the country, its scenic attractions, and, by tourists traveling to attractions, create economic impact in situ. As most Namibian tourist assets are based on wildlife and environmental attractions—essentially in rural locations—this permits tourism to directly inject economic benefits through employment and income into these communities. The location of these assets therefore directly supports national development objectives and macroeconomic policy. A further consideration is that much of the tourism activities take place within the national parks, thereby creating an important revenue source for government.

The government's stated policy—as set out in the White Paper—is to make more efficient uses of these resources by transferring the lodges and camps to the proposed NWR. This is part of a strategy to commercialize the management and operation of these resorts to control costs, generate higher revenues, and generally to make better and more efficient use of prime tourism assets. The commercialization process is a foundation stage that can eventually facilitate the privatization of these assets. There is not yet any government commitment, either to the eventual privatization of these assets or to what pattern of privatization might be chosen. Although government is encouraging private sector investment and involvement in tourism, at present it is reserving development within national parks for the proposed NWR. The new management, when eventually appointed, will have a major task in converting what is generally regarded as a loss-making operation into a profitable company capable of being sold in part or in whole to private sector investors or through joint ventures.

Features of the Sector

Having been politically independent for just 8 years, Namibia's tourism industry is very much conditioned by its historic links with the Republic of South Africa (RSA). It remains an industry dominated in terms of investment, ownership, and management by the white minority. It has a very small domestic market and it is heavily reliant on South Africa and European source markets to generate visitors. Although international visitors expect international standards, they are not always available in Namibia. There is a widespread need to provide training in the tourism sector, often at a very basic level, and to upgrade these skills. Training for middle and upper management is a secondary priority.

Institution building for the tourism sector is needed to support development and to facilitate the government's commercialization policy. This institutional support will also facilitate the implementation of the strategies and actions set out in the Tourism Development Plan and the Tourism White Paper. In turn, these strategies need to be supported by the introduction of a reliable and user-friendly system of statistics.

Future tourism development is expected to be closely managed with priority and continuing emphasis given to high-quality tourism based on the important concept of localized carrying capacity. Resource utilization will be monitored and a high priority afforded to the involvement of local individuals and communities in the tourism development process and in benefits sharing. The major potential for tourism development is related to the country's environment, wildlife, landscapes, and cultural heritage.

Namibia's existing tourism product has been developed for the local and regional market (i.e., intra-southern Africa) (e.g., self-catering facilities for local and regional customers). The main requirement in the future, however, is to clearly identify and market new facilities for overseas customers, to improve existing facilities, and to separate the two major market segments and products. The TDP identified that Namibia has the potential to develop an international tourism product of high standard but that major product and human resource development is required. The TDP suggested that Namibia could increase the number of international tourist arrivals from 280,000 in 1992 to 400,000 in 1997. Target earnings from tourism were forecast to increase fourfold from 1992 to 2002 in real terms to make tourism the second or third most important economic sector in Namibia (Government of Namibia, 1993a).

Although these forecasts have to be interpreted cautiously due to the unreliable statistical data, if the basic sectoral weaknesses can be overcome, there is considerable opportunity for tourism to contribute to both national and sectoral objectives.

Development Problems

Problems to be Addressed

It is recognized by government and the international travel trade that Namibia has the potential to become one of southern Africa's outstanding ecotourism destinations. At present, due to inconsistent marketing, indifferent product standards, and previous ad hoc development decisions, the tourism sector is not attaining its potential. The potential benefits to be derived from a successful tourism sector have to be seen in the context of regional competitors, with, arguably, the Republic of South Africa, Botswana, and Zimbabwe already established destinations. To meet this regional challenge and contribute to national development objectives there are a number of constraints and problems to be addressed. Some of these constraints are discussed below.

Institutional Framework

The present institutional framework for the tourism sector is in a transitional stage. As an output of the TDP and the White Paper on Tourism, the parastatal NWR and the NTB will be incorporated. Until this legislation is approved by Parliament, the lack of these organizations will continue to frustrate the restructuring of the tourism sector and some of the activities of the Foundation Phase program. A substantial amount of preparatory work has already been done to support these proposed organizations, and it is anticipated that the legislation will be submitted to Parliament in 1998.

Without the NWR the intended commercialization of the government's resorts cannot proceed nor can the tackling of the many problems associated with that operation. The NTB is likewise needed to properly market the Namibian tourism product. The NTDP Phase II program has identified technical assistance needs to support both organizations.

Human Resource Development

To develop a quality tourist product—an objective laid down in the NTDP and the White Paper on Tourism—Namibia has to address its human resources problem. There are plenty of people able and willing to work in the tourism sector but there is a severe shortage of trained and skilled workers, which consequently affects the level of service offered. Reports compiled as part of the preparation phase of the NTDP and subsequent surveys carried out confirm the existence and continuation of some fundamental problems.

Although these problems are too numerous to detail here, among the most significant are the following. First, at the government resorts virtually no staff training had taken place before the current ongoing program, with a consequent lack of skills, motivation, and the creation of attitudinal problems. Second, staff have only recently, as part of the Foundation Phase Stage II, been introduced to motivational training and customer care skills, both of which are major deficiencies in the general industry. Third, the absence of a basic workforce with skills and training makes it difficult to select and train people for supervisory and middle-management positions. Fourth, most in-industry training has been carried out by the large hotels to meet their own needs; few programs have yet been developed to train workers in situ (i.e., in the rural areas, camps, and communities where the Namibian tourism product is found).

There is no doubt that human resource development in tourism is a priority issue. Without substantial and widespread improvements in training, attitudes, and delivery of high standards, Namibia will not be able to achieve a high-quality tourism product with a commensurate high price. Current activities in the Foundation Phase Stage II program are beginning to address these issues through institution building of the Hospitality Training Centre (HTC) and the Namibian Academy of Tourism and Hospitality (NATH). The mobile unit now available to the HTC will facilitate training programs to the regions and communities.

Finance

With the exception of some of the large hotel companies, which have their own financial sources, finance is a difficult area for the tourism sector. Interest rates are high, much higher than international rates. The cost of business borrowing is further exacerbated by the decline and fluctuations of the rand, to which the Namibian dollar is tied.

A further problem is the lack of finance for small business development. Without experience and a proven track record in business, it is very difficult for local entrepreneurs to source capital at an affordable rate. This is a particular problem that will have implications for the development of community-related tourism businesses where problems are compounded by the difficulty in the communal areas of establishing formal ownership of sites, necessary to provide collateral for commercial credit.

Lack of Local Participation

One of Namibia's development objectives in tourism is to widen the participation base to include those living in rural communities and women, and to encourage more entrepreneurial activity. This is a laudable but difficult objective to achieve. It will require strong positive actions in the areas of human resource development, access to finance, management skills training, and, above all, an understanding of how tourism can contribute to rural incomes and development. This will be a long-term objective, and although the Foundation Phase Stage II addresses some of these issues, more needs to be done to develop models to encourage and secure wider participation in the tourism sector.

Lack of Planning and Development Information

The NTDP indicated an approach to regional development planning for the tourism sector. As yet little follow-up has been done to develop this base information. A recent study in the Caprivi area has been suggested as a model for tourism planning. Until more widespread planning exercises can be achieved there is a continuing vacuum in this important aspect of development. Planning should be based on prioritized locations as identified in the NTDP and supported by necessary institutional and infrastructure developments. It is further essential to balance the demands of tourism development against the need to respect sociocultural and environmental concerns in the selected areas.

The limited availability and, often, unavailability of tourism data and statistics continues to frustrate planning of the sector. These problems are addressed in the Foundation Phase Stage II program, which should provide at least a recommended system to facilitate data collection in the future together with statistics on visitor arrivals and some economic impact data. Coverage of accommodation statistics is good, with comprehensive data available on a regular basis.

Product Development

The aforementioned problems all, in various ways, act as constraints on the present utilization and future development of the tourism product. The need is for concentrated actions to alleviate or remove them. Without a comprehensive approach it will be difficult to develop a high-quality product, regionally competitive and able to fetch a high price in the international market. As the Namibian product is based on wildlife and the natural environment, particular care is required to balance tourism with conservation; and land utilization, with its conflicting claims, is a major problem. In many areas, tourism is likely to generate more value added than agriculture. More has to be done in rural areas to spread an understanding of tourism's potential to increase incomes. This has been recognized by some commercial farmers who operate game ranches, which demonstrates the symbioses between environmental quality, wildlife, and tourism.

Development Assistance

As a Foundation Phase, the Work Programs sought to establish a sound basis for the development of tourism in Namibia. The four main components of the Work Program were: Training and Manpower Development; Regional Planning and Development; Statistics and Research; and Institution Building. These components are regarded as essential inputs to achieve future sustainability in the tourism sector. It was recognized by government that tourism could contribute to the achievement of national development goals, which are to revive and sustain economic growth, create employment, reduce inequalities in income distribution, and eradicate poverty. The success of the tourism development effort would depend on widening participation in the tourism sector. A particular concern was to involve communities in tourism businesses to directly generate benefits to improve rural living standards.

The four main component activities sought to redress the main problems in the tourism sector, which included institutional deficiencies, a widespread need for human resource development, development of a comprehensive and reliable system for compiling and disseminating tourism statistics, and inadequate product development. These issues were addressed through a combination of technical assistance and project activities.

The action program recommended in the TDP formed the basis of a Namibia Tourism Development Program (NTDP) further funded by the European Union. The NTDP comprised two phases: a Foundation Phase (Phase I) with a Work Program due for completion in September 1997, and an anticipated Development Phase (Phase II) to be implemented with the financial support of the European Union.

The NTDP Foundation Phase was divided into two stages. The first stage, covering the 6-month period November 1995 to April 1996, concentrated on institution building of NWR and NTB, and training and accounting support for the proposed institutions. The work program for Stage 1 consisted of 19 activities divided into the following components:

- provision of a business operation base for NWR;
- transfer of government resorts to NWR;
- creation of the NTB;
- human resource development and training for NWR and NTB staff;
- legal assistance to the establishment of NWR and NTB;
- assistance to the Policy, Planning Management Information Unit (PPMIU) located within the MET.

The second stage, covering a 14-month period, commenced in mid-July 1996. The four main components for Stage 2 of the Project comprised the following activities:

1. Training and Manpower Development
   - basic education skills;
   - hotel and catering in-service training;
   - assistance to the Hospitality Training Centre and tour operation and guiding.
2. Planning and Development
   - regional planning;
   - product development and economic linkage development;
   - assistance to investors;
   - community participation.
2. Statistics and Research
   - visitor arrival statistics;
   - visitor surveys;
   - accommodation and employment statistics;
   - economic impact study.
4. Institution Building
   - establishment of a planning and statistics section in the MET;
   - support to the NTB;
   - support to NWR.

As a Foundation Phase Project, the Stage 1 and 2 Work Programs have sought to establish a sound basis for the future development of the tourism sector. By utilizing the research and work accomplished under the preparation of the TDP, the four broad components noted above have been prioritized. Institution building will provide the necessary administrative and legal framework to permit the transfer of wildlife and resort assets to the proposed NWR. This is a key institutional development as it is the means chosen to commercialize government's tourism activities. The proposed NTB will work jointly with MET, NWR, and the private sector to provide a sharper and more competitive focus to the promotion of the Namibian tourism product.

The Work Program on Statistics and Research has two broad objectives: first, to implement a system able to provide on a regular basis necessary statistical data to inform tourism decision-making, and second, through an economic impact and visitor survey study, give an indication of the current impact of tourism on the economy of Namibia. The provision of a comprehensive and reliable data source would be a major input to the effective functioning of the proposed NWR and NTB. Both these organizations will be required to upgrade staff skills, and this activity is included in the Foundation Phase Project.

The main focus of the Training and Manpower Development activities is to create, through the HTC, a sustainable vehicle for future training provision in the tourism sector. Close cooperation with the private sector is an integral part of this activity and is a key element in future sustainability. The ability of the HTC to operate a mobile training unit is equally a key measure in taking training to the rural communities to facilitate human resource development, which is a stated objective of the NDP1.

The Regional Planning and Development component builds on the information and recommendations set out in the NTDP and the guidelines established in the White Paper on Tourism. The main focus is to facilitate regional tourism development that meets the objectives of involving rural communities in the development process, creating employment and entrepreneurial opportunities for rural residents, and to do so with due regard to the social and environmental parameters necessary for sustainable tourism. In particular, this will require the expected economic benefits accruing from tourism to be balanced against the need to maintain ecological diversity and respect the ethic of nature conservancy.

As tourism is a multisectoral activity, its development inevitably impinges on the responsibilities of ministries other than the MET, and it will require for its sustainability inputs from, and coordination with, the private sector and nongovernmental organizations (NGOs). Effective interministry cooperation, and coordination between the MET and the proposed NWR and the NTB, will be important elements in furthering the development of the tourism sector.

Contribution to Development

The product in tourism is a composite one to which the concept of a value chain applies. It consists of many diverse services, such as those generated in transport, accommodation, restaurants, travel trade, attractions, entertainment, and ancillary services. The diversity of component services is the main reason why measurement of total tourism activity and its economic impact has proved to be so illusive, and its results often controversial. This situation is noted in the following comment:

> The growth of the tourism industry is reflected in the high annual growth rate of hotels and restaurants. However, this is only part of tourism, which also contributes to, inter alia, financial services and transport. Thus far, it has not been possible to determine to what extent other activities are influenced by tourism; thus, the exact contribution and growth of the total tourism industry remains unknown. (Government of Namibia, 1995a, p. 9)

The paucity of both tourism and general statistical data required the initial consultants (NTDP) to undertake survey work to establish at least some basic parameters of tourism activity in the country. The estimate was that 280,000 visitors arrived in 1992. The consultants noted that the Republic of South Africa (63%) and Germany (14%) generated almost 80% of arrivals between them. There was an expectation that the European market led by Germany would increase its share in the future.

Some estimates have been made for 1996 of tourism's economic impact on the economy of Namibia. Data are based on the various surveys undertaken as part of the NTDP (Foundation Phase) including a Visitor Survey, an Employment and Tourism Business Survey, and a sample analysis of the 1996 visitor arrivals data collected by the Ministry of Home Affairs.

It is usual to segment the economic impact of tourism into four main components; impact relating to the earnings of foreign exchange; contribution of tourism to national income; creation of employment; and contribution to government revenues. Tourism will have direct, indirect, and induced effects on the economy, creating a "multiplier" impact; that is, the additional incremental expenditure by tourists will circulate through various sectors in the economy, creating a total impact greater than the initial incremental expenditures. Multiplier analysis is much used in tourism but the quality of its outputs (i.e., the final estimates) are always qualified by the availability and quality of the data used in the process. Where available, this output can be compared with the results of input–output analysis. In Namibia at present, there are no input–output tables available and the data for multiplier analysis are variable in both quality and coverage. The following information, therefore, should be interpreted cautiously.

Earnings of Foreign Exchange

In most developing countries the limited availability of foreign exchange is recognized as being one of the major barriers to development. Both government and the private sector need foreign exchange to purchase imports of goods and services to initiate and sustain the development process. In most developing countries the export economy is narrowly based, often dependent on primary agriculture and minerals. In the last decade the terms of trade have progressively moved against the developing countries' creating a situation where greater volumes of exports have had to be exported to sustain a level of foreign exchange earnings. As most exports are constrained by quotas and duties imposed by the importing countries, it has been very difficult for developing countries to increase both their levels of exports and earnings of foreign exchange.

This worldwide situation has persuaded many governments to support and invest in tourism. Tourism, as a trade in international services, does not face either quota or tariff restrictions on international travel; with few exceptions, tourists are free to travel where they want to go, as often as they want to do so, and to spend whatever amount of money they wish. As most international tourists live in developed countries they usually travel with the "hard" currencies characteristic of these countries (e.g., the Deutch mark, United States dollar, pound sterling, etc.). For many developing countries, including Namibia, receipts from international tourism constitute an important source of foreign exchange earnings.

In 1996 it is estimated that 420,000 visitors arrived in Namibia staying an average 12.3 nights and generating N$801 million in gross receipts. From this gross receipt figure should be deducted a percentage to represent "leakage" (i.e., the amount spent on importing goods and services to meet the needs of international tourists). There is no reliable estimate of what this leakage factor may be. The TDP (1993) used a leakage factor of 20%. If this is applied to the 1996 figure (N$801 million – 20%) the estimated net receipts would be N$640 million.

In 1996, therefore, the gross estimated receipts from international tourist arrivals constituted the third largest export sector after mineral products (N$3,357 million) and food and live animals (N$2,096 million). The level of official reserves was N$906 million in the same year. The receipts from tourism also made a substantial contribution to the Balance of Payments. The Bank of Namibia provided the estimate shown in Table 8.1.

It should be noted that the estimate of receipts *excludes* international fare payments, which are recorded in the Transportation Account. One of the enduring difficulties in

Table 8.1. Contribution of Tourism to the Balance of Payments

	N$ Millions
Net	574
Credit	894.5
Debit	321.0

Source: Bank of Namibia (1996).

estimating tourism's economic contribution to an economy is not only its multisectoral nature, but also the absence of a Tourism Account in the National Accounts framework as formulated by the United Nations Statistical Commission.

The earning of foreign exchange from tourism is influenced by three variables: the number of visitor arrivals, length of stay, and per diem expenditure. Multiplying the three variables provides gross expenditure. These expenditures should be modified to reflect the leakages from the economy. All three variables are important to marketing strategies and to economic impact analysis, and are described below.

Number of Visitor Arrivals

The visitor arrivals figure is that used to measure the "growth" of international tourism and the success (or otherwise) of promotional strategy. In some countries with extensive resources, a high volume of tourist arrivals is a desired outcome from a promotional campaign (e.g., South Africa). The question of market targeting is not primarily an economic consideration, although the actual volume of visitor arrivals provides the basic financial injection into the economy, which will trigger the multiplier effect.

Visitor arrival figures for Namibia include three market segments: business travelers, visiting friends and relations (VFR), and leisure travelers. The figures exclude the cross-border travelers on foot from Angola, Botswana, and Zambia who cross the border but do not fit into any of the three categories. From the perspective of economic impact, each category of traveler will have different expenditure characteristics, which have important policy implications. The business traveler is likely to have a relatively short length of stay in a country but with a higher per diem (and sometimes a higher per visit spend) than the other two categories of travelers. These business travelers may potentially become "leisure travelers" by adding some nonbusiness days to their stay. This is a possibility particularly when the business traveler is on a long-haul journey (e.g., Europe to southern Africa).

The VFR traveler is usually given a low priority when economic impact measures and policies are being considered. This low priority arises from the fact that, by definition, this category of traveler does not buy accommodation (which averages between 30% and 40% of holiday expenditure). However, it may be that this group will use its nonaccommodation expenditure for other purposes (e.g., shopping, excursions) and may therefore have a per visit spending that is not far from the average for all visitors.

The third category—the leisure traveler—is the genuine holiday-maker and the traveler most susceptible to motivational manipulation. It is this traveler whom the industry most seeks to influence. However, as this brief introduction to market categorization suggests, simply increasing the number of tourist arrivals may not be a viable option without careful analysis of the arrivals data to include country of origin, expenditure profiles, and the impact of rising visitor arrivals on capacity. In Namibia, the White Paper on Tourism (Government of Namibia, 1994) strongly recommends that "low volume high per capita spend" tourists are the preferred market target. Volume considerations have to be tempered by length-of-stay and expenditure profiles.

Length of Stay

The length-of-stay statistic is one of the most important analytical factors in formulating policies for tourism development. The simple proposition is that the longer the length of stay the greater the per visit expenditure is likely to be. In the context of Namibia, which is both a single and multidestination country, efforts have to be made to increase the length of stay, which, on average is 12.3 nights. Multidestination visitors will obviously have a shorter length of stay and, if they are package tourists, it will be impossible to change itineraries to increase length of stay. Substitution of one destination for another can only be done through the tour operator. Independent travelers have the freedom and flexibility to change their personal itineraries. By whatever means, any increase in the average length of stay of visitors is likely to increase per visit expenditure and it can increase economic impact without necessarily increasing visitor numbers.

Per Diem Expenditure

Per diem expenditures are influenced by many factors (e.g., costs of accommodation, discretionary spending opportunities, local transport, etc.). Namibia is sometimes described as an expensive destination with tourist services provided at a high price. Whether the country is or is not an expensive destination will depend very much on the tourist's comparative evaluation of Namibia's product vis-à-vis that of perceived competitors. What is important is to provide a "value for money" service that includes opportunities for tourist-related expenditure (e.g., shopping, car hire, gifts and souvenirs). Again, the three identified categories of visitors will each have different expenditure profiles. Economic impact from tourists' expenditures will depend ultimately not only on the number of visitors arriving and their length of stay, but also on their income levels and propensity to spend.

From the survey data Table 8.2 shows, for 1996, tourist arrivals and tourist receipts by country of residence.

Despite the growth of tourist arrivals and receipts during the period 1992–96 there remain opportunities to improve on this base. One opportunity is to reduce the import of goods and services to the tourism sector. Namibia is very dependent on South Africa for supplies of goods. If these imports could be identified through refinement of the statistical data relating particularly to hotel operations, then opportunities to create intersectoral linkages might occur. This is always a problematic area as intersectoral linkages should be viewed in relation to the stage of development of a country. However, little is known about this matter and it should receive future attention.

In Namibia, and particularly outside the capital Windhoek, tourism is mainly an activity dominated by small-scale businesses. It is these types of businesses, which are family owned and managed, that are most likely to use local inputs to provide the goods and services required by tourists. It is one of the government's national development objectives to improve incomes and standards of living in rural areas. Community-based businesses can create not only jobs but also stakeholding in tourism through entrepreneurial opportunities, albeit on micro-scales. In cooperation with private sector tourism operators and assisted by NGOs like the Namibia Community-Based Community Association, some tourism projects have begun to operate.

Table 8.2. Tourist Arrivals and Tourist Receipts by Country of Residence

	Southern Africa	Germany	Other Europe	Other	Total
Foreign tourist arrivals	396,205	69,719	68,573	25,705	419,502
Percent by region	61%	17%	16%	6%	100%
Average length of stay (nights)	11	13.5	13.1	14.8	12.3
Total receipts, excluding international airfares (N$)	339.9M	231.5M	162.1M	67.5M	801.0M
Percent by region	42%	29%	20%	8%	100%
Receipt per tourist (N$)	1,330	3,320	2,363	2,625	1,909

Source: Project survey data (Government of Namibia, 1997).

Contribution to National Income

The incremental expenditure injected into the economy by tourists will trigger a multiplier effect that will have impacts on personal and company incomes, government revenues, and employment. To calculate a multiplier requires the input of quite comprehensive data, which at present are not available in Namibia. The limitations on the extent and quality of the existing data make any estimation of tourism's contribution to government revenues very hazardous. Background papers for the TDP of 1993 used a multiplier coefficient of 0.7. If this figure is applied to the gross tourism receipts of N$801 million it would have the effect of "multiplying" tourism's contribution to national income to $1,362 million. However it is emphasized that this figure is an estimate and can only be verified once a rigorous multiplier analysis has been carried out.

The Bank of Namibia estimates that tourism contributes 6.4% gross and 4.1% net to gross domestic product. Results from the Visitor Survey indicate that the contributions are 6.8% gross and 5.5% net.

Employment

As a service-intensive activity tourism is regarded as an effective option to create jobs. In most developing countries with relatively high rates of increase in population, absorption of young workers into the labor force is a major problem. In Namibia, with a small population base, a marginal agricultural sector, and limited opportunities for development of small-scale manufacturing industry, tourism has a comparative advantage to create jobs particularly in the rural areas where most tourism activity takes place.

An Employment Survey completed in July 1997 indicated a growth in employment in the accommodation and tourism operations sector of 10.6% since 1992. If this estimate is applied to the 1992 data, which calculated that there were 10,000 direct jobs in the tourism sector, the estimate of direct jobs in 1996 would be 11,052 employees. As there is no evidence available to contradict the 1992 contention that the ratio between direct and indirect jobs is 1:1, then total employment in the tourism sector in 1996 is estimated at 22,100. The figures derived from the Employment Survey are quite robust and suggest that the estimate for 1996 is sound.

Contribution to Government's Revenues

Tourism's direct contribution to government revenues is estimated at N$63.965 million. This figure is derived as shown in Table 8.3.

This contribution is likely to be an understatement for a number of reasons. It does not include a proportion of government revenues from company and personal taxation generated by activities related to and employment in tourism. It also does not include an estimate for revenue generation accruing from tourism-related activities in transport and retailing, for example. The estimate of tourism's contribution to GST was an "informed guess" provided by the Ministry of Finance.

These estimates provide some indication of tourism's contribution to the Namibian economy in 1996. Although they have to be interpreted with caution, they provide a base for future research and updating.

Development Issues

Arising from the tourism development experience of Namibia over the last 8 years are a number of issues that may have relevance to other countries in the initial stages of devel-

Table 8.3. Contribution to Government Revenues: 1996

	N$ Millions
Acutal revenues: MET	23.500
Annual levy on gambling income	.737
Liqour licensing	.308
Hunting and fishing licenses	.176
Gambling licenses	2.357
Tourism concessions	.155
Airport departure taxes[a]	6.022
Contribution to general sales tax[b]	30.710
Estimated total	63.965

[a]International departures from Windhoek International Airport (172,858), Eros (6,292), and Walvis Bay (21,582) = 200,734 × N$30 (combined departure and security tax added to ticket price).
[b]Estimate of 5% of GST for 1996.
Source: Government of Namibia (1996).

oping their tourism sectors. Although identified within the particular circumstances of Namibia, these issues are perhaps not uncommon in other developing countries.

Macro Planning

At the initial stages of developing the tourism sector it is usual to prepare a tourism development plan that provides a prioritized and coherent framework to guide investment and development generally. Many developing countries have plans that are inevitably macro in focus. Such plans take a medium- to long-term view and are mostly concerned with strategies to achieve these objectives in the future. This type of plan does not provide any immediate return to the ultimate beneficiaries of the endeavor, which in this case are the people of Namibia. In the future, plans should incorporate some microprojects that can be implemented to demonstrate the benefits that tourism is said to bring—employment, income, and rural diversification in this case. After almost 8 years of sound development planning in Namibia no direct benefits to target communities have arisen through the creation of tourism businesses in the community. This situation tends to generate what might be called "promise fatigue." In Namibia some prime tourism development land near the Caprivi strip was appropriated by the Prisons Department to extend an existing prison farm while debate about its potential tourism use continued!

Human Resource Development

As tourism in Namibia is essentially a rural activity based on wildlife and the environment, training needs to be given to local people who are capable of taking advantage of business opportunities. Of necessity, much of the training that was done under the Foundation Phase of the TDP concentrated on institution building, particularly of the Namibia Hospitality Training Centre. This centre now has the capability to take to the rural areas a wide range of training courses especially adapted for local conditions. The Namibia Community-Based Tourism Association supported by technical assistance funds has also been able to provide training and technical assistance to community-based business development initiatives. The combination of a government-sponsored institution and a NGO is a good example of cooperation aiming to utilize all available resources. Both organizations also have the sociocultural knowledge within which training has to be given. Much remains to be done, but a start has been made on taking training to the local communities, where it is most required. It is envisaged that this training will be supported by a series of "community awareness" programs to inform people of the nature and impact of tourism development.

Employment and Entrepreneurial Opportunities

Tourism, as a generally recognized labor-intensive activity, has particular advantages in many developing countries including Namibia. The marginal nature of the agriculture sector in Namibia makes it difficult to absorb more workers onto the land. Tourism has been recognized as being one means to help diversify the rural economy. In some areas this process has already begun with local people supporting tourism with supplies of foodstuffs, laundry services, accommodation supply, and handicrafts. These in situ developments are essentially microprojects that, although sometimes appearing insignificant, do provide local people with entrepreneurial opportunities, which are the first rung on the development ladder. This creates some sense of ownership within the local community, which is one way of helping to support tourism as a sustainable activity.

Tourism and the Environment

There is a close relationship between tourism and the environment within which it takes place. In Namibia, where many of the prime areas for tourism are ecologically and sometimes socially fragile, care has to be taken in selecting the appropriate scale and type of development. There is perhaps an inevitable tension between environmentalists and tourism developers. There are many examples worldwide of tourism projects that have been inappropriate and insensitive to various locations. However, with sound planning and cooperation between the various government ministries and local communities, these difficulties can be mitigated. However, environmentalists must realize that in Namibia tourism will inevitably be based on wildlife and other natural attractions. A dominant conservation ethic that is not tempered with commercial reality will create only an "ecolaboratory" and have limited or no developmental impact for people. The proposed Namibia Wildlife Resorts will take over from government the operation and development of tourism in the park areas. One of its main tasks will be to seek a balance between tourism development and conservation needs to ensure that the national objectives of economic progress with sustainability are met.

Sustainable Development

Perhaps too often in the tourism literature the concept of sustainability has been too closely identified with environmental protection and the use of present resources with a view to ensuring their availability for future generations. Any development will use present resources but hopefully in a sensible way. In Namibia there is a policy on environmental protection that has been given prominence by government. But sustainability also has to embrace the requirements of the present generation. Without the present generation being able to derive benefits from development, it will not be sustainable. Sustainability must incorporate both economic enhancement and financial betterment for individuals and communities. Examples such as the Campfire scheme in Zimbabwe illustrate how village communities can become involved in environmental protection and antipoaching measures when it is demonstrated that the measures will benefit them from their support.

In Namibia sustainability of the tourism sector depends not only on government policies but also on the support of the private sector and communities. The proposed Namibia

Tourism Board will be the means to more closely involve the private sector in both tourism policy-making and in the critical area of marketing. In the changing social and political environment the private sector is not expecting government to dictate the private sector's role; it is expecting to be involved in the determination of that role.

The experience of Namibia is that institutions take time to develop. At the end of the Foundation Stage project the two key organizations—Namibia Wildlife Resorts and the Namibia Tourism Board—had still not been enacted with a consequent knock-on effect for the project. For this reason, any examination of institutional arrangements in the tourism sector should be at the first stage of the project, to ensure that any changes necessary to the existing structure could be debated and made in a timely fashion. Such an analysis would also examine interministry links where lack of cooperation is so often the source of frustration and project delay.

External Assistance

Much has been written about the dependency of the tourism sector on external assistance, be it in the form of financial aid and/or technical assistance. For a country like Namibia, in the initial stage of the development of its tourism sector, such assistance is crucial. Without the assistance of the European Union, development planning for tourism would have been beyond the resources and capacity of Namibia. The assistance given has been closely related to national development objectives and, hopefully, further assistance will be forthcoming to implement the strategies already proposed.

Conclusions

An analysis of the tourism sector in Namibia has shown that many of the development problems it faces are typical of the developing world. What is perhaps unusual is the acknowledged lack of capacity in the agricultural sector to absorb more workers without adding to the problems of underemployment. Tourism does offer a means of diversifying the general economy and improving the standards of living of rural people, who are usually the poorest in the country. To sustain this development will require a tripartite contribution of effort and resources by government, the private sector, and participation from local communities. As part of the sustainability effort, the required institutions need to be put in place and supported by trained staff. Namibia has much of the required planning infrastructure and institutional support in place and now faces the challenge of implementation.

Chapter 9

Tourism Development in Kenya

Isaac Sindiga

Summary

Tourism is the second highest foreign exchange earner and the sector contributes about 11% of Kenya's gross domestic product (GDP) according to the latest statistics. This chapter discusses the origins and development of both wildlife and beach tourism in Kenya, analyzes the role of tourism in the economy, and outlines the challenges of the country's tourism industry at the end of the 20th century and the prospects in the new millennium. The findings show that tourist numbers increased rapidly in the postindependence period as did investments in the industry. However, per capita real earnings in tourism have been declining over time. Further, contrary to popular belief, tourism generates little employment and on average pays wages below the modern sector economy as a whole. Yet tourism is essential to raising the levels of income and developing certain remote areas of the country. Government commitment to addressing the problems of the industry through repairing the damaged road infrastructure, ensuring peace and security, allocating more resources to security services, providing stable funding for the Kenya Tourist Board (KTB), encouraging locally financed tourist hotel development through tax incentives, and comprehensive tourism planning could change the image of tourism and secure the place of Kenya as a competitive African destination.

Key words: Beach tourism; Development; Economy; Kenya; Tourism; Wildlife

Introduction

Kenya is one of the most developed tourism destinations in sub-Saharan Africa.[1] Although the country's tourism product began to decline from 1990 because of a deteriorating infrastructure, an uncertain political future caused by political pluralism, and poor security, the tourism sector still retains second position as the highest foreign exchange earner after agriculture (Republic of Kenya, 1998a, p. 174). The tourism sector contributed 11.2% of the GDP and 18% of the country's foreign exchange earnings in 1996 (Republic of Kenya, 1998b). In 1997, Kenya attracted about 3% of the 23 million tourist arrivals to Africa (World Tourism Organization [WTO], personal communication, June 1, 1998). In terms of international tourism receipts (excluding international transport), Kenya was second to Mauritius in sub-Saharan Africa outside South Africa. Kenya is thus an important African tourist destination.

This chapter provides a case study of tourism evolution in Kenya by analyzing the current tourism situation, its historical development, and future prospects. Tourism's contribution to the Kenyan economy is also discussed. Tourism in Kenya is considered within the regional context of East Africa and the contribution of British colonialism to contemporary tourism in the region. The chapter then analyzes the challenges facing Kenya's tourism at the onset of the third millennium. The future prospects of the tourism industry in Kenya are also considered.

Location

Kenya, with a territorial area of 582,646 km² in eastern Africa, is about 2.4 times the size of Great Britain. Some 11,000 km² (or 2%) of Kenya is covered by the water of the Indian Ocean, Lake Victoria, and several inland lakes, especially in the Rift Valley. The country lies across the equator between 4°21′ north and 4°28′ south latitudes and 34° and 42° east longitudes. Kenya is bordered by Somalia and the Indian Ocean to the east, Uganda to the west, Ethiopia and Sudan to the north and northwest, and Tanzania to the south.

Government and History

Kenya is divided into eight administrative provinces, each of which is further divided into districts. Each district in turn has divisions, locations, and sublocations. Superimposed on this central government structure are local government authorities. In practice, each district is also a county council. Urban areas are run either as urban council, town council, municipal council, or city council in order of size, population, significance, or political expediency. Nairobi is the only urban area with city status.

In the colonial period, provincial and district boundaries were drawn along ethnic lines. A single ethnic group was usually bound in an administrative area. Although some provinces and districts were cosmopolitan, the official divide and rule policy tended to emphasize ethnic exclusiveness and this carried forth to independent Kenya with the potential to threaten the unity of the new nation-state.

Kenya was a British protectorate between 1895 and 1920, when it was declared as a colony. During the first half of the 20th century, the Kenya colony was dominated by a small group of European settlers who came primarily from Britain and South Africa, with small groups arriving from Australia, New Zealand and Canada (Ogot, 1974). These settler farmers were quite wealthy and controlled the colonial government. Below this group in the socioeconomic hierarchy were Indians, who worked as shopkeepers and traders. Some Africans, initially the Washwahili, Somalis, and the Sudanese, served as policemen, porters, and soldiers. At the bottom of the wrung were the majority of the Africans) This group suffered the brunt of British colonialism; it lost fertile land in the highlands, which was expropriated to give way for European settlement, and paid taxes to the government.

The colonial arrangement in Kenya provided a socioeconomic class of people with the resources for starting domestic tourism in the country. As will be shown below, this wealthy class of European farmers could afford the time and resources to create the demand for and undertake internal tourism activities.[2] Settler colonialism pushed for the creation of national parks and reserves after an initial period of carefree hunting. The purpose of protecting wildlife was to regulate sport hunting and the collection of trophies. In time, accommodation facilities, camping grounds, and basic tourism infrastructure were created and these would become the basis of a thriving tourism industry in independent Kenya.

Kenya regained its independence in 1963 and became a republic in 1964 under an executive president. Since independence, Kenya has had elected governments after every 5 years. Except for a brief period between 1966 and 1969, Kenya developed as a de facto one-party state, a status that was legalized in June 1982 with the Kenya African National Union (KANU) monopolizing political power. This was maintained until 1992 when a multiparty parliamentary system was established.

Under one-party rule, certain basic freedoms such as speech and public assembly were circumscribed. Matters came to ahead in 1982 when Kenya was declared a single-party state by law. To many people, the legalization of the one-party state meant the criminalization of free speech, association, and political dissent. The ensuing political tension led to a coup attempt against the government organized by junior officers of the Kenya Air Force on 1 August 1982, almost 2 months after the country became a *de jure* one-party state. Although the coup attempt failed, the government clamped down on all dissent, leading to the intensification of political suspicions in the country.

Despite the country's political problems in the period up to 1990, Kenya's economy remained reasonably sound. There was also a perception of political stability, at least in comparison to many countries in the sub-Saharan Africa region. Also, in the era of the Cold War, Kenya always was a supporter of the West in a continent characterized by socialist and Marxist expansion. This background made Kenya a favorite of Western governments. This Western support and the country's relatively well-developed tourism infrastructure led many international visitors to the country. An observer of the African scene notes a number of reasons for Kenya's economic success, especially during the first two decades of independence. Among these is the fact that at independence the country retained white settlers who, arguably, had technical and management skills, thereby maintaining production and capital formation; consequently, "Kenya operates far more efficiently than most African countries, and foreign investment and tourists from the West have poured into the country, providing great economic stimulus" (Lamb, 1982, p. 64). Further, Kenya gave top priority to the agricultural sector, developed the social infrastructure (especially health care and education), kept defense spending low, and maintained a capitalist model of development with a monetary reward system for initiative (Lamb, 1982).

Kenya's relative economic and political stability assisted the tourism industry until 1990, when the tourism numbers began to decline. One estimate put the decline of the country's tourism industry at 40% in 1992 alone, partly because of political violence and insecurity associated with the democratization of the country's political space (National Election Monitoring Unit, 1993, p. 3). As happens in similar situations, where the security and personal safety of tourists cannot be guaranteed, international tour operators swiftly blacklisted Kenya as a politically unstable destination.

Kenya's transformation from a single-party to a multiparty parliamentary system did not come with peace and tranquility. The democratization process brought into the open traditional ethnic rivalries and competition over resources, notably land. As a result, opposing political forces formed along ethnic lines, leading to violent conflict with each other. These ethnic clashes started towards the end of 1991 and continued sporadically ever since. By 1997, ethnic violence engulfed Kenya's coast, the most popular international tourism destination. And in 1998, fresh ethnic clashes erupted in Laikipia, Nakuru, Trans Nzoia, West Pokot, and Marakwet districts in the Rift Valley province. This context of Kenya's government and history is important in comprehending the later discussion of the contemporary challenges of the country's tourism industry.

Geography of Tourism

There are no accurate statistics on various tourism indicators in Kenya. Government publications tend to carry different figures for a given indicator for a given year. Sometimes provisional results are used, which may be significantly different from final tallies for the year. The statistics used in this chapter may not be accurate in an absolute sense; nevertheless, they are useful in clarifying the extent and magnitude of tourism.

Kenya's tourism arrivals rose from 65,000 in 1964 to 444,000 in 1972, 512,000 in 1984, and 814,000 in 1990. The arrivals declined to 699,000 in 1992 and thereafter increased marginally. The numbers dropped to 691,000 in 1995 and rose again slightly to 717,000 in 1996 and 700,000 in 1997 (WTO, personal communication, June 1, 1998). These statistics show an unstable picture of the arrival of international visitors to the country and attest to the difficulties facing Kenya's tourism in the 1990s.

It is fortuitous that Kenya has rich wildlife resources that attract visitors to the national parks and reserves.[3] Another major attraction is the beaches of the Indian Ocean coastline. Both wildlife and beach tourism are complemented with museums and historical sites, urban tours, particularly in Nairobi and Mombasa, and conference tourism in these cities.

In terms of regional concentration, the largest share of tourism bed-nights is at the coastal region followed by Nairobi (Table 9.1). Nairobi is a principal business center and the air transportation hub in eastern Africa and has been able to attract some conference tourism. In addition, visitors to Nairobi can view wildlife within a short distance of the

Table 9.1. Hotel Bed-Nights Occupied by Country of Residence: 1997

Country of Residence	Nairobi (000s)	Coast (000s)	Lodges (000s)	Others (000s)	Total (000s)
Permanent occupants[a]	14.6	11.2	1.3	1.2	28.3
Germany	46.1	1,036.7	43.5	8.8	1,135.1
Switzerland	12.3	244.2	13.6	2.5	272.6
United Kingdom	148.6	714.2	64.4	28.8	956.0
Italy	22.4	214.0	10.9	2.0	249.3
France	37.3	184.1	38.7	7.5	267.6
Scandinavia	34.2	98.1	15.5	4.3	152.1
Other Europe	77.0	209.2	26.4	9.3	321.9
Kenya	262.3	291.8	29.8	192.9	776.8
Uganda	22.3	9.9	0.3	4.1	36.6
Tanzania	24.3	11.7	1.1	3.5	40.6
East and Central Africa	41.1	7.6	0.2	1.3	50.2
West Africa	18.6	2.1	0.7	0.3	21.7
North Africa	12.4	1.6	0.4	0.6	15.0
South Africa	29.2	13.1	0.8	0.5	43.6
Other Africa	45.5	16.7	0.7	1.5	64.4
United States	118.8	26.8	66.2	13.9	225.7
Canada	18.1	6.3	3.9	1.6	29.9
Other America	11.4	4.6	4.3	2.9	23.2
Japan	29.8	4.9	10.7	4.2	49.6
India	18.4	8.0	3.3	1.4	31.1
Middle East	23.0	3.9	5.3	2.4	34.6
Other Asia	13.8	8.0	2.8	1.6	26.2
Australia and New Zealand	19.5	2.9	5.7	2.1	30.2
All other countries	12.1	14.5	0.7	0.7	28.0
Total	1,113.1	3,146.1	351.2	299.9	4,910.3

[a]Persons staying 1 month or more in one hotel; includes block bookings for aircrew.
Source: Republic of Kenya (1998a, p. 181).

city center at the Nairobi National Park, and go to the Kenya National Museum, including the Snake Park and the Karen Blixen Museum.

Lodges are dispersed around the country within or adjacent to wildlife protected areas. However, only about seven parks receive the preponderant number of visitors to Kenya. The following receive over 100,000 visitors each per year: Nairobi, Amboseli, Tsavo West, Tsavo East, and Lake Nakuru national parks; Maasai Mara national reserve, and the Nairobi Animal Orphanage (Table 9.2).

The data on bed-nights occupied by country of residence of the visitors and the Kenya tourism region visited show differences in tastes and preferences of the visitors (Table 9.1). Visitors from continental Europe appear to prefer a beach holiday whereas those from other countries go to the Nairobi area and the national parks.

In general, Europe dominates all other regions of the world as a source of tourists to Kenya (Republic of Kenya, 1998a). In 1994, for example, Europeans spent 2,220.7 thousand bed-nights in the country (Republic of Kenya, 1995, p. 165). Of the 5 million hotel bed-nights occupied by country of residence in 1995, 24% came from Germany, 19% from the UK, 6% each from France, Italy, and Switzerland, and 5% from the U.S. (Kenya, 1996a, p. 178). Beginning in 1983, Germans were the leading single group visiting Kenya, as shown by the number of bed-nights. Since 1983 they have occupied over 1 million bed-nights each year. This peaked at 1.8 million bed-nights in 1991, although there was a downturn in

Table 9.2. Number of Visitors to Parks and Game Reserves: 1993–1997

	1993 (000s)	1994 (000s)	1995 (000s)	1996 (000s)	1997 (000s)
Nairobi	164.6	163.2	113.5	158.3	149.6
Animal Orphanage	155.3	182.0	212.1	210.6	193.7
Amboseli	121.1	159.5	114.8	109.1	117.2
Tsavo (West)	102.9	105.4	93.1	93.6	88.6
Tsavo (East)	135.8	132.4	228.8	137.5	123.2
Aberdare	60.8	60.2	70.1	60.2	59.0
Buffalo Springs	—	—	—	—	—
Lake Nakuru	178.6	164.3	166.8	156.9	132.1
Maasai Maru	133.1	138.2	133.2	130.3	118.3
Bamburi Nature Park	93.2	98.9	109.2	107.0	86.8
Malindi Marine	41.1	39.4	38.8	38.3	27.0
Lake Borgoria	37.2	43.2	14.2	14.2	24.5
Meru	7.4	7.9	7.3	7.8	4.1
Shimba Hills	24.8	31.6	20.0	23.4	22.5
Mount Kenya	18.0	17.2	17.2	17.1	14.8
Samburu	21.5	9.2	9.1	9.1	8.3
Kisite/Mpunguti	27.5	34.8	32.4	39.9	35.1
Mombasa Marine	43.3	48.0	23.9	21.7	15.2
Watamu Marine	31.7	32.1	16.1	20.2	19.4
Hell's Gate	47.4	44.9	50.1	52.1	47.2
Impla Sanctuary (Kisumu)	59.1	5.5	3.5	65.6	62.4
Other[a]	16.6	9.6	18.9	14.8	15.5
Total	1,521.0	1,527.5	1,493.1	1,488.7	1,364.5

[a]Other includes Mount Elgon, Ol Donyo Sabuk, Marsabit, Saiwa Seamp, Sibiloi, Ruma National Park, Mwea National Reserve, Central Island National Park, Nasolot National Reserve, and Kakamega National Reserve.
Source: Republic of Kenys (1998a, p. 182).

Table 9.3. Kenya National and Marine Parks and Reserves

	Area (km²)	Year Established	District
National Parks			
1. Sibiloi	1,570	1973	Marsabit
2. Central Island	5	1983	Turkana/Marsabit
3. South Island	39	1983	Marsabit
4. Malka Mari	876	1989	Mandera
5. Marsabit	360	—	Marsabit
6. Mount Elgon	169	1968	Trans Nzoia
7. Saiwa Swamp	2	1974	Trans Nzoia
8. Meru	870	1966	Meru
9. Kora	1,787	1989	Tana River
10. Mount Kenya	715	1989	Nyeri/Meru
11. Ndere Island	4	1986	Kisumu
12. Mau[a]	—	—	—
13. Lake Nakuru	188	1967	Nakuru
14. Aberdares	715	1950	Nyeri
15. Ruma	120	1983	Homa Bay
16. Hell's Gate	68	1984	Nakuru
17. Longonot	52	1983	Nakuru
18. Fourteen Falls[a]	—	—	Thika
19. Ol Donyo Sabuk	18	1967	Machakos
20. Nairobi	117	1946	Nairobi
21. Amboseli	392	1974	Kajiado
22. Tsavo West	9,056	1948	Taita Taveta
23. Tsavo East	11,747	1948	Taita Taveta/Kitui
24. Arabuko Sokoke	6	1991	Kilifi
25. Chyulu	471	1983	Machakos
Marine Parks			
26. Malindi	6	1968	Kilifi
27. Watamu	10	1968	Kilifi
28. Mombasa	10	1968	Mombasa
29. Kisite	28	1978	Kwale

Continued on next page

subsequent years (Republic of Kenya, 1995). Residents of the U.K. have been second ranking to the Germans since 1986. This is probably because of Kenya's history as a British
colony, which makes the country well known in the U.K. Also there are significant British
investments in the country. Kenya needs to market its tourism in other parts of the world
to improve the geographical coverage as insurance against the risks associated with a
narrow market.

Although many visitors from the U.K. go to the coast as well, a significant number still
opt to stay in Nairobi. Most visitors from North America and Asia choose Nairobi and the
game lodges. This European domination appears to be related to foreign capital and expertise in the country's tourism industry (Dieke, 1991). Most tourism enterprises in Kenya,
especially in the accommodation and tour operation sectors, are foreign owned, with European companies having substantial shares. Among African countries, most tourists come
from Tanzania followed by Uganda (Table 9.1). As discussed below, there is a basis for
regional tourism development within East Africa. Besides, this can also encourage visitors
from outside the region to make an East African rather than a single country tour.

Table 9.3. Continued

	Area (km²)	Year Established	District
National Reserves			
30. Marsabit	1,198	1962	Marsabit
31. Nasolot	92	1979	West Pokot
32. South Turkana	1,091	1979	Turkana
33. Losai	1,806	1976	Marsabit
34. Kerio Valley[a]	—	—	Baringo
35. Kamnarok	88	1983	Baringo
36. Kakamega	4	1985	Kakamega
37. Lake Borgoria	107	1970	Baringo
38 Samburu	168	1963	Samburu
39. Shaba	239	1974	Isiolo
40. Buffalo Springs	131	1963	Isiolo
41. Bisanadi	606	1978	Isiolo
42. Rahole	1,270	1976	Garissa
43. North Kitui	745	1979	Kitui
44. Mwea	68	1976	Embu
45. Maasai Mara	1,510	1974	Narok
46. South Kitui	1,833	1979	Kitui
47. Arawale	533	1974	Garissa
48. Boni	1,339	1976	Lamu
49. Dodori	877	1976	Lamu
50. Tana River primate	169	1976	Tana River
51. Shimba Hills	192	1968	Kwale
Marine Reserves			
52. Kiunga	250	1979	Lamu
53. Malindi	213	1968	Kilifi
54. Mombasa	200	1986	Mombasa
55. Watamu	32	1968	Kilifi
56. Mpunguti	11	1968	Kwale
National Sanctuary			
57. Maralal	6	1968	Samburu

[a]In the process of being established.
Source: Sindiga (1995, pp. 46–47).

Development of Tourism

Colonial Roots of Kenya's Tourism

As noted above, Kenya's European settler community played an important role in spurring tourism-led conservation. The country's rich wildlife resources provided the base on which the country's tourism was founded. Since 1946, when Nairobi National Park was established, followed by Tsavo in 1948, the Aberdares in 1950, Meru in 1966, and Lake Nakuru National Park in 1967, the government has adopted a policy of game protection and opening up these areas for tourism (Table 9.3). The national park concept goes back to the 19th century with the creation of Yellowstone National Park in the U.S. In Kenya it became necessary to establish parks for the preservation of wildlife, which had suffered destruction from hunting, especially with the use of firearms following the establishment of British rule (International Bank for Reconstruction and Development [IBRD], 1963, p.

173; Ouma, 1970). Initially, a number of ordinances were established to restrict killing game, but these did not always stop the poachers (Ouma, 1970, p. 50). These ordinances included the game ordinance of 1903, the East African wild bird protection ordinance in 1903, the game ordinance of 1909, which created the southern reserve (Maasailand) and the northern reserve; others were the game ordinance of 1921 and the Kenya colony and protectorate ordinances and regulations of 1937 (Ouma, 1970, pp. 41-42). Before 1930, most of the overseas visitors to Kenya were wealthy Europeans and Americans who could afford the time and resources to undertake the long sea voyage.

In subsequent decades Kenya established additional protected areas to enhance wildlife conservation. A recent count reveals 25 terrestrial national parks, 4 marine parks, 22 national reserves, 5 marine reserves, 1 animal orphanage, and 1 national sanctuary (Table 9.3). These parks cover about 8% of Kenya's land area and host a wide variety of wildlife, including the rare roan antelope, the Hirola antelope, and bongo, the forest antelope.

Classification of Wildlife Conservation Areas

The categorization of protected areas in Kenya requires some clarification. The classification of wildlife conservation areas as national/marine parks, national/marine reserves, and game reserves implies a concept of the ownership and management of wildlife conservation areas that is important for the relationship of local people and protected areas and the benefits accruing therefrom (Sindiga, 1995).

National parks are state lands that are managed exclusively for the conservation of fauna and flora (Republic of Kenya, 1975, 1985a, 1989). Government policy explicitly states that parks are to be used for many purposes including educational, recreational, and tourism (Republic of Kenya, 1975). As such, activities such as cultivation, livestock herding, timber harvesting, and consumptive wildlife utilization (e.g., sport hunting, live animal capture, cropping for meat and trophies, and game ranching) are excluded from parks. Kenya banned sport hunting in 1977, followed by an embargo on the sale of curio and animal parts in 1978. Several attempts to revive limited hunting since then have not been successful. In contrast, national reserves are declared by the government with the consent of a local authority on any type of land. The difference between reserves and parks is that certain land uses, such as herding and wood fuel collection, may be allowed in reserves. However, the entire wildlife management in Kenya is vested in the Kenya Wildlife Service (KWS) (Kenya, 1985b), which also collects licensing fees for tourism facilities located in protected areas.

Marine parks are similar to national parks in administration and management. Kenya established its first marine parks in 1968, the first country in the world to do so following an International Union for the Conservation of Nature (IUCN) resolution in 1962 (Jackson, 1973). This was done to conserve fragile marine ecosystems, a recognition of the degradation of coral gardens in the reef by tourists collecting corals and shells and other ornamental marine life (Musyoki, 1992). Marine parks are of varied size and start at the highest spring watermark and extend some distance. The marine reserves extend beyond the parks. Both marine parks and reserves are managed by the KWS. Certain types of fishing by local people are allowed in the marine reserves.

Finally, wildlife is also conserved in forest reserves owned by the state or individuals, trustlands or land held in trust for local people usually by a local authority such as a county council, and in private farms and group and private ranches. Wildlife has protection under the laws of Kenya and may not be killed even when present on private land. So far, forest tourism remains underdeveloped (Kenya Wildlife Service [KWS], 1990; Republic of Kenya, 1994c). This is partly because wildlife and forest management are housed in different government ministries and their aims and objectives are not always shared. The forest department concedes that deforestation, including the indigenous species, is a continuing problem (Republic of Kenya, 1994c, p. 14). Yet the value of forests for biological diversity and nature tourism cannot be overemphasized (KWS, 1990, p. 45).

Although initial wildlife conservation was to be closely intertwined with the development of Kenya's tourism, the goals of conservation have always been much broader. The 1945 Kenya national parks ordinance, for example, outlined the goals of the parks to be "the preservation of wild animal life, wild vegetation and objects of aesthetic, geological, prehistoric, archaeological, historical, or other scientific interest therein, and for incidental matters relating thereto" (quoted in Ouma, 1970, p. 40). Unlike the Wildlife Act of independent Kenya noted above, tourism activity was not purposely included; it can be inferred, however, that tourism was one of the incidental aspects of wildlife conservation. As such, the intensive tourist visitation that occurred in the parks in later decades had not been planned for. Lack of roads, airstrips, and lodging facilities presented the greatest difficulty for national parks as tourist destinations (Ouma, 1970, p. 50). Later, on tourist demand, when such facilities were established, they were superimposed on an existing park without prior planning. This had potential for problems.

The first visitors to the parks in the 1950s and 1960s were interested in sport hunting, sport fishing, collection of trophies, and generally experiencing the wild. The activities included slaughtering game for food, skins, and ivory; capturing live animals for sale abroad; and photography. Kenya became world famous for sport hunting and tourism in general following the visit of American President Theodore Roosevelt earlier in the century and of Queen Elizabeth II of the U.K. As noted above, the creation of national parks was a step in biodiversity conservation. It was not intended expressly to serve the needs of the incipient wildlife-based tourism. In the initial period of tourism development, the government role was somewhat limited. This might explain the later ambivalent attitude towards tourism planning.

Before 1940 Kenya had no tourism policy and there was no organization dealing with tourism. The East African Publicity Association (EAPA) was formed in 1938 to coordinate tourism activities not only in Kenya but in East Africa as a whole. The outbreak of World War II did not allow the body to function. EAPA was succeeded by the East African Tourist Travel Association (EATTA) in 1948 to coordinate tourism business (Ouma, 1970). Over the next one and a half decades, EATTA was involved mainly in matters of tourism promotion and transport. There was relatively little done to plan and develop tourism as part of the colony's sectoral planning. This was the state of Kenya tourism at independence. The major preoccupation appeared to be opening up access roads in the parks to allow tourists to visit in both the wet and dry seasons (Popovic, 1972). One thing is clear, however. Virtually all tourism income to the country was associated with wildlife (IBRD, 1963, p. 173). The money was drawn from transport, tour guides, professional hunters, and equipment and materials for hunting and photography procured from Kenyan firms. Income was also obtained from the sale of safari clothes, shoes, and arts and crafts.

Origins of Beach Tourism

Parallel to the development of wildlife tourism was beach tourism at the Indian Ocean coast. Although it expanded to become a crucial part of the country's tourist industry, beach tourism also started without much planning (Popovic, 1972, p. 99). This raises interesting questions about its origins and how it could expand quickly to claim more than 60% of all bed-nights occupied in Kenya in the 1990s.

The Kenya coast has been in contact with other parts of the world for more than 2000 years. Sailors came in from the Middle East, the Orient, and from southern Europe in dhows (i.e., Arab coastal vehicles with triangular sails), which were driven by the Monsoon winds. These people mixed with the local Bantu groups and founded trading settlements dotted along the coast. These contacts led to the growth and development of the Swahili civilization. The Swahili participated in the mercantile trade on the Indian Ocean and founded an urban, literate, Islamic culture (Middleton, 1992). Such towns as Lamu, Malindi, Gedi, Mnara, Pate, and Mombasa were founded by the Swahili and prospered in the 14th and 15th centuries. Between the 16th and 18th centuries the Swahili coast was conquered by the Portuguese followed by Omani Arabs (Salim, 1992). These contacts with the outside world abated some form of early tourism. Except for, perhaps Mombasa, the fortunes of the coast declined greatly by the end of the 19th century. The British colonized the coast but then ignored it (Memon & Martin, 1976). In subsequent years, coast development tended to lag behind the interior, especially in areas of European settlement. It was during the 20th century when tourism began to develop at the coast. Interest in the coast started following Mombasa's development as a deep-harbor port serving East Africa. This role was enhanced by the construction of the Kenya–Uganda railway, which began at Mombasa in 1896. In time, Mombasa grew into a big town.

A few decades after the beginning of the British period, the coast began to attract resident Europeans from the interior as an ideal place for holiday-making. Lacking other alternatives, these people were attracted by the sandy beaches and the warm climate. But, rather than end their trips in Mombasa, these domestic tourists ventured to the north coast and went to Malindi, which provided a beautiful seaside, sandy beaches, and opportunities for deep-sea fishing (E. B. Martin, 1973, p. 103). This early beach tourism was spontaneous. There were not even hotels until well into the 1930s when Brady's Palm Beach and Lawford's hotels were put up as family ventures in response to a perceived need (E. B. Martin, 1973). The early tourists to Malindi pitched tents on the beach.

In subsequent decades, Mombasa and Malindi also attracted a resident European population of retirees. This was especially so after the World War II. According to E. B. Martin (1973), Malindi became the choice retirement place because it was cooler, and housing and labor were relatively inexpensive. This trend continued in the 1950s and by the early 1960s many European farmers were moving to settle at the coast permanently on retirement. Others would go there on vacation during Easter and Christmas holidays. As Kenya became independent, coast tourism could be summarized as a place for resident Europeans to spend their holidays.

Postindependence Developments

Foreign visitors started coming to the coast on the first all-inclusive package holidays after 1962 (Jackson, 1973). These tourists, mainly Germans and Italians, took advantage of the relatively cheap charter flights to Mombasa. This marked the beginning of mass tourism in Kenya. The numbers of the visitors increased tremendously after 1965.

As this influx of visitors had not been planned for, private investors made ad hoc responses to meet the demand. For example, up to 1970, most of the bed space expansion took the form of alterations and extensions to existing hotels (Republic of Kenya, 1971a). Coast tourism at this stage attracted little new investment because of the relatively underdeveloped physical infrastructure. Water supply was inadequate, the access roads were poor, and communication facilities meager. Mombasa airport had poor facilities for handling aircraft. Further, there were delays and uncertainties in ferry operations, especially across the Likoni channel connecting Mombasa Island to the south coast and across the Kilifi creek connecting Mombasa and Malindi. The government moved in, for the first time, to attempt to salvage the situation with some kind of planning for existing tourism and for future development (Republic of Kenya, 1971a). A plan for 3100 new beds at the coast by 1974 was inaugurated (Republic of Kenya, 1970). In addition, an interministerial working party was established to map out strategies for future development of coast tourism (Republic of Kenya, 1971a). Consequently, the physical infrastructure, such as roads, electricity, and water, was expanded in the 1970s. Also, the government encouraged private developers and investors to participate in coast tourism. The Kenya Tourist Development Corporation (KTDC), which was established in 1965, provided the required investment finance. In the meantime, private investors moved in and constructed hotels along the beaches wherever they could obtain land. There was neither government control nor regulation. The result was a ribbon-type spatial structure of hotels along the coastline. The government merely responded by providing infrastructure after investment decisions and actions had been made without prior planning.

For Kenya as a whole, tourism grew rapidly in the immediate postindependence period. The number of visitors increased by 24% in 1965 over the previous year. This was the highest rate of increase achieved over a period of 10 years (Republic of Kenya, 1966b, p. 51). The number of visitors multiplied many times in the next few years, rising from 80,000 in 1965 to 339,000 in 1970 (Republic of Kenya, 1966b, p. 51, 1971b, p. 123). This phenomenal increase in tourist numbers was regarded favorably by the government because it was associated with employment opportunities. Tourism led to 20,000 additional jobs in direct employment between 1968 and 1974 and a further 7000 in agriculture and distribution (International Labor Office [ILO], 1972, p. 211). In addition, tourism induced a demand for other services in accommodation, entertainment, and distribution.

Before discussing the role of tourism in the Kenyan economy, it is instructive to further discuss Kenya's tourism in its East African regional context. Below is sketched the evolution of tourism in East Africa since the colonial period in order to expose the potentials and limitations of regional tourism development for Kenya.

Development of Kenya Tourism in the East African Context

Kenya's tourism in the colonial and the immediate postindependence period did not develop in isolation. It was closely linked with tourism development in East Africa as a whole. The countries of East Africa, namely, Kenya, Uganda, and Tanzania, were under British colonial rule. This common colonial history assisted in developing a regional tourism package by which tourists could move freely within the region. A formal regional cooperation structure, which was established in 1948 as the East African High Commission (EAHC), assisted in the effort. The EAHC was transformed into East African Common Services Organization (EACSO) in 1961. It became the East African Community (EAC) after the East African countries attained their political independence in the early 1960s.

The EAC became the most promising economic community in sub-Saharan Africa and boasted a common currency, a regionally coordinated infrastructure, harmonized economic policies, a system of common institutions, and labor mobility within the region (World Bank, 1989). Among the very successful ventures were the railway system and the common airline, East African Airways, both of which assisted in intraregional trade flows and movement of tourist traffic. The airline, in particular, had become a smooth-running, profit-making venture, capable of competing with world-class airlines (Tibazarwa, 1988).

As noted above, tourism emerged as an important industry in East Africa just before World War II. However, the war period slowed down tourism until it was taken up again by the East African Governors conference in 1947. The Conference formed a representative committee of the EAHC to oversee the matter and set up an interim office of EATTA. The latter was incorporated in 1948 as a semiofficial organization with a central role of developing and promoting tourism in East Africa. EATTA prepared a document on tourist attractions in East Africa and the road travel conditions. This was the first document of its kind in the world and was published both in English and French in 1951 (Ouma, 1970, p. 10). The association then opened tourist offices in Nairobi, Kampala, Dar es Salaam and Mombasa. In subsequent years, EATTA launched a carefully prepared publicity campaign for East African tourism at home, in the rest of Africa, and in the world by the use of published material, mass media, and through conferences and representations (Ouma, 1970).

On the operational side, tour operators based in one country could take tourists to any of the other countries. Apart from EATTA, which handled all the promotional matters, trade associations, including hotelkeepers, tour operators, travel agents, and professional hunters, also worked jointly on a regional basis. This was possible because the EACSO had removed all administrative obstacles that could make such cooperation difficult.

It did not take a long time after the independence of the East African states before cracks began to appear on regional cooperation in tourism. Uganda and Tanzania felt that the cooperation was benefiting Kenya at their expense. Mitchell (1970, p. 4) estimated that of all the tourism receipts in East Africa in 1967, about 59–64% went to Kenya, 22–33% to Tanzania, and 13–19% to Uganda. This distribution of benefits appears to have been the underlying element in the complaints lodged by Uganda and Tanzania.

Uganda abandoned EATTA in 1963, arguing that the benefits it derived from regional tourism cooperation relative to its subscription was less than the same ratio for the other members (Mitchell, 1970). The country saw itself in a disadvantageous position and had always tended to remain at the backwaters of East African tourism activity. Most tourists started their journeys in Nairobi and then moved to Tanzania and later to Uganda, if at all. Lacking in firm support from the member states, EATTA collapsed in 1965.

As a result, individual countries imposed administrative barriers, which made the free flow of people impossible. Immigration controls were set up at the borders of each country in 1966 and 1967. This made tourism movement from one country to another somewhat cumbersome and impeded tourist flow. Uganda then imposed sales tax and a requirement for local registration of vehicles in that country if there was more than one visit in a year. The immediate impact of this was the raising of the cost of conducting tour operations business. Also, Tanzania required tour firms taking tourists to that country to be registered there and imposed stiff penalties for those that did not meet the conditions. Most tourists from Kenya flew into Tanzania on chartered aircraft for 1 or 2 days and then returned to Nairobi. The new requirement was clearly intended to undermine Kenya's leading position in the tourism business in the region. It was a matter of time before regional tourism in East Africa collapsed. This came in 1977 when Tanzanian president Julius Nyerere sealed the Kenya–Tanzania border. The EAC broke up and with it most of its structures, including the subcommittee on tourism.

Since the 1970s there has been little regional cooperation in tourism in East Africa. Of the three countries, only Kenya has cooperation packages involving tourism marketing and promotion with the Indian Ocean islands of the Seychelles and Mauritius. Comprehensive regional tourism packages among the three East African countries are hampered by immigration and customs regulations, which make it difficult to move people and vehicles between countries. Clearance procedures are long, tedious, and cumbersome. It is especially difficult to move automobiles from one country to another. Further, tour operators cannot remit their money from one country to another.

Yet, there is great demand for multidestination tourism within East Africa (Republic of Kenya, 1994b). And there are healthy signals for the growth of tourism in each of the three

East African countries. In 1993, tourism contributed 6.1% to the GNP in Kenya, 5.3% in Tanzania, and 1.4% in Uganda (Fair, 1996, p. 156). As Kenya's tourism underwent relative decline in the 1990s, tourism in Uganda and Tanzania began to recover. In Tanzania, World Bank assistance is being used to upgrade the tourism infrastructure, including accommodation in the protected areas, access roads, and passenger facilities at harbors and airports. Similarly, the rehabilitation of the tourism infrastructure in Uganda has provided the impetus for a revitalized tourism sector. In its effort to encourage tourism, Uganda has abolished visa requirements for citizens of 33 countries and is encouraging direct air links to the country (Fair, 1996).

The revitalization of the tourism industry is an excellent sign for the region and offers a basis for regional cooperation in the sector. While an impression might be created that the East African neighbors are benefiting from Kenya's tourism decline in the 1990s, "Experience has shown that well established tourist countries have nothing to fear from development of tourism in neighbouring countries" (Popovic, 1972, p. 55). Only vibrant and competitive tourism sectors in the East African countries could become a basis for future cooperation. A positive image of the region can attract greater numbers of tourists who will have greater flexibility on the places and countries to visit. Ultimately, this should remove the fear that one country will take a larger portion of the tourism proceeds and should encourage cooperation.

Some work towards the goal of regional cooperation has been done within the framework of the new East African Cooperation Agreement, which was signed by the three heads of state on November 30, 1993. A draft treaty on East African Cooperation was published in 1998 with the aim of gradual integration through the creation of a common market, monetary union, and ultimately political federation. The draft treaty provides for a coordinated approach to the promotion of quality tourism and wildlife management. This will allow for a framework of cooperation in tourism by ensuring that the benefits from the industry are equitably distributed. Once the East African Cooperation Agreement becomes operational, the administrative barriers to cross-border tourism activities are expected to be eliminated, thereby enhancing regional tourism activity.

It has been suggested elsewhere that for such regional cooperation to succeed, it is important that the lessons of the collapse of the previous EAC should be learned: "the need for sovereign states in Africa to make political concessions; to show great statesmanship; and to set aside national interests in order to serve continent- and sub-national-wide development goals" (Dieke, 1998, p. 43).

In the preceding sections, this chapter has discussed the development of tourism in Kenya with special reference to its colonial foundations and regional context within East Africa. This is the basis for the analysis that follows on the contribution of tourism in the Kenyan economy. Ultimately, the chapter discusses the problems of Kenya's tourism at the dawn of the 21st century.

Tourism and the Kenyan Economy

On independence in 1963, Kenya had a growing tourism sector. Recognition of the economic benefits of tourism led the newly independent government to create a Ministry of Tourism, Forests and Wildlife. This emphasized the environmental and especially the wildlife basis of the country's tourism industry. A World Bank economic development mission at the dawn of independence in 1962 set the tone of Kenya's future tourism policy. Tourism would be nurtured because it was an important foreign exchange earner, would stimulate domestic income, and generate employment in other areas related to tourism (IBRD, 1963, p. 170). These objectives, which were further elaborated and articulated by the subsequent national development plans (Republic of Kenya, 1966a, 1970, 1974, 1979, 1984, 1989, 1994a, 1997), can be summarized as follows:

- to increase the contribution of tourism to the growth of the country's gross domestic product (GDP);
- to increase foreign exchange earnings from the sector and maximize the retention of foreign exchange in the country;
- to create and expand employment opportunities;
- to improve the quality of service offered by tourism enterprises;
- to conserve wildlife and protect the environment.

These objectives show the Kenya government's continued enthusiasm in tapping tourism's economic outcomes and preserving biodiversity. However, these objectives ignore the role of local people and communities in tourism development. Biodiversity preservation cannot be sustained if the participation of local communities is ignored.As Murphy (1985) notes, "where development and planning does not fit in with local aspirations and capacities, resistance and hostility can raise the cost of business or destroy the industry's potential altogether" (p. 153).

The Kenya national economic statistics published in various government policy documents do not show tourism as a separate category in the national accounts (e.g., Republic of Kenya, 1994d, 1997). Tourism statistics tend to be subsumed under services. Over the period 1982 to 1993, the absolute size of the tourism sector using 1982 constant prices grew from K£306.7 million to K£479.6 million, representing an annual growth rate of 4.18% (Japanese International Cooperation Agency [JICA] & Republic of Kenya, 1995b).[4] The share of tourism in the GDP increased from 9.97% to 11.06% or an average of 10.9%, over the same period. In relative terms, the share of the tourism sector in real GDP was ranked fourth after agriculture (28.5%), government services (15.3%), and manufacturing (13.1%) (JICA & Republic of Kenya, 1995b). As noted above, the tourism sector contributed about 11.2% of the GDP in 1996. This shows the important contribution that tourism makes to the Kenyan economy. Below, this contribution is examined more closely by focusing on tourism's foreign exchange earnings, employment generation, and its share in government revenues.

Foreign Exchange Earnings

Since independence, tourism has played a leading role in the country's foreign exchange income. It has maintained its position among the three leading export earners; the others are coffee and tea.As such tourism is an important contributor to the GDP and the foreign exchange reserves necessary to allow the importation of capital goods required for development and to service foreign debts.

Over the years, however, real dollar tourism earnings have been declining, essentially because of the depreciation of the Kenya shilling (Sinclair, 1990). Also, per capita real earnings in tourism have been declining (JICA & Republic of Kenya, 1995b; Sinclair, 1990). The foreign exchange earnings per foreign tourist per day in 1993 was Kshs.500 calculated on the basis of constant prices for 1982 (JICA & Republic of Kenya, 1995a). This figure, which has been stable over the years, represents US$8 at 1998 foreign exchange rate and demonstrates the low earnings per tourist for Kenya from international tourism. Also, although the absolute size of foreign exchange receipts from tourism grew by a compound annual growth rate of 3.97% between 1982 and 1993, average per capita tourist receipts declined by an annual compound growth rate of -2.09% (JICA & Republic of Kenya, 1995b).

Table 9.4 shows the gross tourist per capita expenditure per day over a period of some years. Although these are crude figures, they do, however, emphasize the fact that the phenomenal increase in the numbers of tourists over the past three decades has not translated into high foreign exchange earnings for the country. This is related to the dominance of all-inclusive package tourists. For example, although tourist expenditure rose from K£16.7 million to K£18.5 million between 1969 and 1970, the average expenditure per visitor day declined from Kshs.135 in 1969 to Kshs.120 in 1970 (Republic of Kenya, 1971b, p. 123). Ten years later, the problem of lack of real growth in receipts persisted. This was attributed to many tourists resorting to package and charter arrangements. In 1979, the ratio of private to package tours was 5:3; about 40% of the tourists came on package arrangements (Republic of Kenya, 1980, p. 160). The recognition of the problem did not lead the government to reverse mass tourism. Instead, it opted for lower spending package tourists in earnest. The government proceeded as follows:

> In order to maintain growth in tourist earnings and achieve the Development Plan targets, it will be necessary to attract such tourists in larger numbers in the face of powerful competition from other tourist areas in the world, and it will be increasingly important to offer them good value for money on their visits here. This means that publicity overseas will have to be stepped up, more tourist attractions developed, greater attention paid to ensuring that all tourists feel they are welcome as visitors in Kenya, and prices kept as low as possible, consistent with providing the facilities tourists expect, and the returns to investment which the economy needs. (Republic of Kenya, 1971b, p. 123)

The government challenge to allow more tourists may be understood from the perspective of increasing economic benefits from tourism. However, those benefits were not commensurate with the price that the country was paying to sustain mass tourism in terms of

Table 9.4. Average Expenditure of International Tourists to Kenya (Excluding International Travel)

Year	Average Length of Stay (Days)	Total Expenditure per Person (US$)	Expenditure per Person per Day (US$)
1982	16.2	—	—
1983	15.9	—	—
1984	15.9	—	—
1985	15.9	—	—
1986	15.9	—	—
1987	16.0	536	33.5
1988	16.0	567	35.4
1989	14.4	571	39.6
1990	14.4	572	39.8
1991	13.7	537	39.0
1992	13.4	565	42.2
1993	13.9	500	36.0
1994	13.6	488	35.9
1995	12.2	657	—
1996	13.3	554	—
1997	11.8	—	—

Sources: WTO (personal communication, 2 April 1997); various issues of the *Economic Survey* issued annually by the Kenya government.

infrastructure development and maintenance (roads, airports, public utilities, national park development, hotels, air travel, tour operations, and personnel training) and the serious social and environmental impacts created (Hazlewood, 1979; Mitchell, 1970; Sindiga & Kanunah, 1998). Indeed, during the 1970s, the Kenya government made very large investments in airports. This included reconstructing Mombasa airport between 1976 and 1978 at a cost of K£11 million so that it could handle direct flights from Europe; and building a new terminal at the Nairobi airport at a cost of K£28 million in order to deal with large tourist flows (Hazlewood, 1979, p. 105). Also, Kenya has tended to emphasize large hotel structures, which require imported materials and drain on foreign exchange reserves (Elkan, 1975).

Nonetheless, the government appears to have fully come to terms with the problem when it complained that

> The fees and taxes levied on foreign tourists are heavily subsidised and do not reflect the true cost to the Kenyan tax payer of developing and preserving tourist attractions. (Republic of Kenya, 1989, p. 187).

In addition, it appears that the average spending per tourist day of Kshs.630 recorded in 1987 was not sufficient to pay for even a domestic tourist (Republic of Kenya, 1989). This problem of "package" tourism in Kenya is discussed further in the next section.

Kenya is, however, fortunate in the sense that its economy is reasonably large and can save some foreign exchange earnings by reducing imports for the tourist industry. Unlike many of its neighbors, most of the food and beer used in tourism enterprises are produced in the country. Summary (1987) found high backward linkages in food manufactures, baking, hotels, and restaurants, and high forward linkages in agriculture, paper products, metal products, petroleum, trade, transportation, and other miscellaneous services. While noting that petroleum is imported and the country spends a large amount of foreign exchange to do so, she was able to conclude that the "tourist industry has increased its linkages with other important sectors of the Kenyan economy since 1968. Imports of intermediate goods by the tourist industry are not excessive, at least when compared to the economy as a whole" (Summary, 1987, pp. 538–539).

Although tourism's backward linkages with agriculture are strong, it appears that these links are forged between large hotels and large agricultural producers, thereby excluding small-scale farmers (Rajotte, 1983). This may minimize tourism's trickle-down effect to the many peasant producers in the country. In this sense, the economic impact of tourism may not be directly felt by the majority of the Kenyan agricultural population.

Employment

Knowledge of the employment record of a sector of the economy is important for socio-economic development and the well-being of the people. The more the jobs created, the greater the multiplier effects of the sector to the rest of the economy. Employment allows people to participate in ordered economic activity with dignity and in a productive way. For tourism, it is necessary to know its capacity for employment generation because of the immense investments in infrastructure and the opportunity cost that local people forego for tourism-related conservation and for hosting tourists. Such resources could be invested in alternative sectors that promise higher returns. Finally, it is relevant to inquire into tourism's employment record because of the relatively high unemployment level in Kenya. In 1996, it was estimated that 2 million people were unemployed; however, the unemployment level in the urban areas was about 25% (Republic of Kenya, 1996b, pp. 5–6). Kenya must create half a million jobs every year to the year 2010 if it is to keep up with the population growth (Republic of Kenya, 1994b, p. 42). Such unemployment and under-employment could stifle economic development because of high dependency on a relatively small productive sector.

Table 9.5 shows employment figures in tourism in Kenya for a number of years. Direct employment in tourism appears to have increased from 20,000 in 1970 to 170,000 in 1994. Tourism employment formed about 7.6% of the modern sector wage employment in the country in 1988. This figure shows a slight improvement of 9.1% in 1996. This is because the growth in the tourism sector has declined since 1990. In general, 93% of the employment generated in tourism is in the private sector, with a small proportion in the public sector.

Employment figures in tourism are not disaggregated in any sense. This makes it difficult to obtain a detailed picture of the industry. For example, hotel and restaurant figures are usually lumped together and so are laundry and housekeeping. However, the accommodation subsector tends to generate the most employment. Of the 170,000 workers in tourism in 1994, 61% were in accommodation establishments, 16% in tour operations, 6% in travel agencies, 11% in curio shops and entertainment, and 6% in the central government (Sindiga, 1996a, p. 19). In addition, there is little information on nationals and expatriates, and supervisory management ranks and those in subordinate positions. If such data were available, they would provide invaluable insights into the employment structure of the tourism industry. The aggregated data at hand are nevertheless useful for indicating the general magnitude of employment in tourism.

Tourism is thought to create employment in other sectors of the economy; however, there are no precise figures to show the extent and magnitude of such job creation (Sindiga, 1994). Usually, direct employment in tourism is highly variable with one hotel bed estimated to create from 0.80 to 3 jobs. Elkan (1975) estimated one hotel bed for 0.84 jobs for Kenya, whereas another estimate gives 1.4 employees per bed (Economic Intelligence Unit [EIU], 1991). In his study of Malindi at the Kenya coast, Bachmann (1988a) estimated 0.6 additional jobs in the tourism sector for each hotel bed. His estimate includes informal types of work such as tour guiding, especially along the beach, professional friendships and following tourists, and prostitution. In addition, one job was indirectly created in agriculture, trade, and handicrafts. Bachmann concluded that 20–25% of the Malindi population derived a livelihood from tourism. However, the figure went down to 9–10% for Malindi division as a whole and merely 5% of the population in Kilifi district (Bachmann, 1988a, p. 281). The employment contribution of tourism is not very high. In fact, Summary (1987) also found that the wages paid by Kenya's tourism industry are rather low. She argues that:

> Employment generated by tourist expenditures is below what would be predicted by tourism's share of Gross Domestic Product (GDP). Wages and salaries paid directly and indirectly are slightly below what would be predicted by tourism's share of total employment. (Summary, 1987, p. 538)

She concludes that the "tourist industry is less labor absorbing than the overall economy, and that wages paid in the tourist industry are below the average for the modern economy as a whole" (p. 538).

Kenya's tourism industry is unable to generate many jobs partly because of the structure of the industry, which allows some of the employment to be generated abroad. Tour operators located in developed countries usually supply inclusive holiday packages to travel agents also located there. They obtain block airline seats on scheduled flights or charter aircraft. Travel agents in turn retail the tour packages to individual holiday-makers at a commission—usually 9% for the economy class and 24% for a first-class ticket in a nonpackage trip (Sinclair, Alizadeh, & Onunga, 1992). These negotiations and transactions

Table 9.5. Direct Employment in Tourism in Kenya

	1984	1985	1986	1987	1988	1989	1990	1991	1992	1993	1994
Modern sector employment (100s)	1,119	1,174	1,277	1,274	1,345	1,388	1,409	1,442	1,463	1,475	—
Tourism public sector	5,600	5,900	5,300	8,200	8,400	8,900	9,300	7,900	7,800	7,000	—
Tourism private sector	79,200	83,800	88,100	92,700	98,000	101,400	104,600	108,800	110,900	114,100	—
Total	84,800	89,700	94,400	100,900	106,400	110,300	113,900	116,700	118,400	121,000	170,000
Average tourism sector employment (%)	7.6	7.6	7.7	7.9	7.9	8.1	8.1	8.1	8.1	8.2	—
Public sector share (%)	6.6	6.6	6.7	6.1	7.9	9.1	9.2	6.8	6.3	5.8	—
Private sector share (%)	93.4	93.4	93.3	91.9	92.1	91.9	91.8	93.2	93.7	94.2	—
Growth in tourism sector employment (%)		5.78	5.24	8.89	5.45	3.67	3.26	2.46	1.46	2.28	—

Source: JICA & Republic of Kenya (1995b, Annex 4–81); Republic of Kenya (1994b, p. 73).

are done abroad without reference to local tour operators in Kenya. The international tour operators then make block bookings of hotel rooms in advance and obtain large discounts due to their bargaining power and ability to source the tourists (Sinclair, 1990). The accommodation prices are usually negotiated in Kenya shillings, thereby allowing the overseas operator to pay less because of frequent currency depreciation. Typically discounts of up to 30% less the price in Kenya shillings are obtained in midseason and up to 50% during the low season (Sinclair et al., 1992, p. 58).

Kenya's tourism industry loses much revenue through prepaid all-inclusive tours arranged overseas. Although contractual relations allow the overseas tour operators to pay more than 1 month after the tourists have left Kenya (Sinclair, et al., 1992, p. 58), a large proportion of the money paid abroad never reaches the country (Republic of Kenya, 1991; Sinclair, 1992, p. 557). This means that many local tour operators merely act as agents to the overseas tour operators. Their role is relegated to meeting and transporting tourists from the airport to hotels and sometimes acting as tour guides (Sinclair et al., 1992). Also many of the Western tour firms have their own locally registered tour companies that take care of the ground logistics of the tourists while in Kenya. Such include Jetset, Universal Safari Tours, Franco Rosso, Kuoni. I Grandi Viaggi, Touristic Union International (TUI) of Germany, Pollman's (owned by TUI), Hayes and Jarvis, United Touring Company, British Airways Speedbird, and so on (Jommo, 1987; Sinclair, 1990; Sinclair et al., 1992). There are other instances in which Western tour firms or airlines also own accommodation facilities in Kenya. It should suffice to say that the transnational nature of the tour operations business heavily reduces foreign exchange retention within Kenya and this makes it difficult to generate much local employment.

In terms of quality of employment in tourism, it has been noted that supervisory and management positions both in accommodation facilities and tour operations are held by expatriates. Like in other African countries, this leaves subordinate roles as drivers, porters, waiters, laborers, and housekeepers for local people. These low-level jobs are very poorly remunerated and produce limited multiplier effects (P. K. Ankomah, 1991; Farver, 1984). Farver argues that subordinate tourism jobs are not productive and make little contribution to the economy.

One of the reasons that is frequently advanced to explain expatriate domination in the managerial and supervisory positions is that there are no local skills (P. K. Ankomah, 1991). Although this might be true for sub-Saharan Africa in general, it is not so for Kenya where tourism education at the certificate, diploma, and degree levels is well established (Sindiga, 1996b). Despite the government's stated policy of Kenyanization, expatriate personnel come with the substantial foreign investment in tourism in the country. Most of the large tourism enterprises are joint ventures with local capital and are managed through management contracts that cover "financial arrangements, government concessions, level of protection and fees to be paid to the parent company for technical and management services. It is obvious that foreign firms will push for the highest fees possible and for quite a high level of management control (particularly at senior levels)" (Swainson, 1980, pp. 230–231). The management contract will therefore specify the number of expatriate technical and managerial staff for a given venture and this tends to perpetuate expatriate presence even in the face of a supply of local skilled personnel. The solution to the problem therefore lies in the progressive indigenization of the ownership of tourism enterprise.

Also, tourism employment in Kenya tends to be seasonal, reflecting the annual pattern of tourist visits. The peak tourism season is September to March. The volume of traffic flow is very small between April and July. This affects tourism enterprises, especially accommodation facilities, because very few beds are occupied. This leads to many employees being declared redundant. Such workers in casual employment are not well paid and their termination seriously affects their family welfare.

Government Revenue

Apart from injecting foreign exchange earnings into the economy, tourism generates government revenues through various taxes. Such include customs and excise duties for imports; sales tax and value-added tax for goods bought in the local market; accommodation tax and training levy on hotel guests; concessional or rental fees paid by game lodges and camp sites; and trade licenses and company taxes paid by various tourism enterprises. The government also charges income tax on the personal emolument of the employees in the tourism sector. However, government tourism revenue is much smaller. Most of the earnings accrue to the private sector, which controls the industry.

Challenges of Kenya Tourism

The discussion in the preceding section shows that Kenya has not done profitable business in tourism. This is partly because the country did not conduct comprehensive tourism planning. The country simply reacted to the influx of mass tourists. Unable to control it, Kenya decided to expand that market segment in the belief that foreign exchange earnings would grow with the numbers. As a result, the country's tourism resources were stretched to the limit and the quality of the tourism product began to decline. In addition to the economic difficulties illuminated above, Kenya's tourism faces a number of major challenges—which must be addressed if it is to remain a major export sector for the country in the new millennium. The crisis facing Kenya's tourism is a result of the breakdown of the physical infrastructure, biodiversity degradation, especially in protected areas, political violence, uneven distribution of benefits especially to local communities, foreign ownership and management of tourism enterprises, and a small domestic and regional tourism base. A brief analysis of each is given.

Breakdown of the Infrastructure

Kenya's road network has virtually collapsed after years of neglect. The maintenance standard is very low. The situation was worsened when the El Nino rains of 1997 floodwater washed away bridges and sections of the roads. This leads to very high transportation costs. Also, traveling becomes unpleasant because of personal discomfort, the high probability of road accidents, and the enormous amount of time consumed in traveling.

The government will need to pay greater attention to the maintenance and rehabilitation of the existing road network and to open up new roads in order to improve the efficiency of the country's productive capacity and to enhance the movement of tourists. This applies both to the roads connecting Kenya's network of protected areas and within them. Kenya's railway system, which was planned for different purposes, is unsuited and too slow for tourism. Also, most long-distance trains currently travel at night, thereby making it difficult for tourists to enjoy the country's varied physical geography.

Also, water and electricity are a persistent problem because of insufficient and irregular supply throughout the country. Further, telecommunication services lag behind in this era of electronic mail systems, facsimile technology, and telex. These services require adequate telecommunication lines, which are lacking.

Biodiversity Degradation

Large tourist numbers have exerted enormous pressure on the environment, especially in the conservation areas. Overexploitation of park resources has been observed in Nairobi,

Amboseli and Lake Nakuru national parks, and Samburu and Maasai Mara national reserves (Muthee, 1992). This is because the tourist population is concentrated in a few places at the coast and in selected parks. In fact, 98% of the wildlife safari visitors go to only seven: Nairobi, Amboseli, Tsavo East, Tsavo West, and Lake Nakuru national parks; Maasai Mara national reserve; and the Nairobi animal orphanage (Table 9.2). The popularity of these parks has attracted the concentration of lodges and tented camps in a number of them, especially Amboseli and Maasai Mara. This has led to the deterioration of environmental quality. Other problems include overcrowding of minibuses, poor waste disposal, water pollution, soil erosion, and trampling—all leading to the loss of biodiversity and aesthetic quality.

Political Violence

Perhaps the most important factor explaining the decline of Kenya's tourism in the post-1990 period is local insecurity associated with political violence. As noted above, ethnic clashes broke out in the country at the end of 1991 in the former white highlands where many ethnic communities had been resettled after independence. In subsequent years, ethnic violence flared up sporadically in one part or another of the country, thereby seriously affecting tourism activities. Although the causes of the clashes are multidimensional and complex (Republic of Kenya, 1992), the main causes are related to the democratization process in the country. Traditional ethnic rivalries and competition over resources that had been suppressed in the postindependence period were activated by opposing political forces at the onset of multiparty politics.

Although tourists or tourist establishments have so far not been targeted by the raiders, there was a drastic fall in tourist numbers. As happens in similar situations, international tour operators and travel agents swiftly blacklisted Kenya as a politically unstable destination. With the decline in tourist arrivals was a decline of tourist income. The Kenya Tourism Board (KTB) estimated a loss of about US$280 million in tourist earnings between mid-1997 and mid-1998 because of the violence at the coast and the insecurity associated with the 1997 general elections ("The Tourism Industry on the Mend," 1998). Bed occupancy at the coast fell to as low as 24% in April 1998 compared to 52% in the previous year ("Bed Occupancy Falls," 1998). Many tourist hotels drastically reduced their tariff whereas others closed down for renovation. In the process, many tourism workers lost their employment. The efforts of individual tourism establishments will, however, not bear fruit until political violence, ethnic tensions, and general insecurity have been addressed satisfactorily by the political establishment.

As part of the Kenya government solution to political violence, it established a judicial commission of inquiry into tribal clashes in the country on July 1, 1998 (Republic of Kenya, 1998c). The commission was created to investigate the ethnic clashes from 1991 to 1998. Specifically, the commission will establish the origins, causes, and handling of the clashes by the law enforcement agencies. Although its establishment was somewhat belated, the commission's report may recommend prosecution or further criminal investigations of the perpetrators and ways, means, and actions to be taken to prevent such happenings in the future (Republic of Kenya, 1998c). The mere fact that this commission was created shows government determination to deal with the matter of political violence, which has had serious consequences to the country's tourism industry.

Uneven Distribution of Benefits

As noted above, most of the proceeds from Kenya's tourism go to multinational corporations rather than to the country. Sometimes the leakage of total tourism revenues is as high as 70% for beach-only tourism; however, the leakage falls substantially for safari visitors because of the element of local travel (Republic of Kenya, 1991). As already noted, the problem of leakage is exacerbated by the foreign ownership and management of most of Kenya's tourism enterprises.

It has been suggested that small African economies can mitigate against the inequitable division of benefits from tourism through negotiated agreements (Green, 1979). Such negotiations must be done by highly skilled people. This will stop the tendency in Africa of signing agreements that are written in general terms and later provide multinational corporations with the opportunity to work in their own interest with negligible benefit to the host country. In Kenya graduates trained in tourism are expected to replace expatriate personnel and to start indigenously owned tourism enterprises. Ultimately, controlling the ownership of major subsectors of tourism will lead to more equitable distribution of benefits (Lea, 1993). But without policy resolution, this would be difficult to achieve in the short term because it involves competition with multinational companies, which are better endowed with development resources.

Domestic Tourism

Kenya's international tourism is highly seasonal. The so-called high season for arrivals starts in September and lasts until March. This flow of tourists dries up during the period April to August. This seasonality is reflected in employment because workers must be laid off in the low season. As a result of this pattern, the country established a domestic tourism policy in 1984 to encourage residents to travel locally, especially during the period April to August.

Although domestic tourism is supported for a variety of reasons, the central objective is to even out the seasonality pattern, thereby preserving jobs year round. Another reason is that domestic tourism can maintain the continuity of the sector whenever international tourism slumps, as happened in Kenya in the 1990s. Also, it has been argued that a country must have a culture of domestic tourism as a basis for international tourism. Indeed, beach tourism in Kenya developed from a vibrant domestic tourism sector. This led to the creation of a basic infrastructure using local resources and personnel upon which international tourism was established.

Domestic tourism can also be supported on the basis of the model of social tourism that evolved initially in Europe and later in the United States, which stimulated travel by low-income people. This is done by organizing children's camps, low-cost accommodation in colleges and universities, especially during vacations, and through the creation of employee travel associations (Gunn, 1988).

Despite government policy on promoting domestic tourism, the mechanisms to do so are not in place. So far, the strategy has been for tourism accommodation facilities to reduce their tariff during the low season of international tourism. Domestic tourism has some impediments. There are no tourism offices in the country except perhaps for Mombasa and Malindi. In addition, almost all tour operators and travel agents serve the needs of international visitors. It is therefore not surprising domestic tourism in Kenya is rather weak.

Future Prospects of Kenya Tourism

Kenya's emphasis on numbers of tourists rather than per capita foreign exchange earnings in the period between independence and 1990 partly led to the overexploitation of the tourism resources in some parks and at the coast. As a result, a number of challenges stand in the way of Kenya's tourism in the 1990s, leading to the deterioration of the tourism product. Although government explanation for the decline of the tourism industry tends to emphasize external factors, such as competition with other countries like South Africa and Zimbabwe and adverse publicity abroad on the security situation (Republic of Kenya, 1994e), it is recognized that the problem is largely internal. The internal factors are the breakdown of the infrastructure (especially roads), biodiversity deterioration, and the degradation of attractions including beaches because of overcrowding, and fears about personal security.

Despite the problems faced by Kenya's tourism, it is likely to develop further in the future with the upgrading of the quality of the tourism product and more aggressive promotion and marketing overseas. So far, such promotion and marketing has been weak because of budget constraints for the government department of tourism. In 1996, however, the government established the KTB with the responsibility of coordinating tourism promotion (Republic of Kenya, 1998a, p. 184). The KTB is expected to take over the responsibility of packaging and marketing Kenya's tourism product from the Ministry of Tourism and Wildlife. KTB is a quasi-government body with a number of other responsibilities, among which are: to establish public relations services to address issues raised by visitors and to facilitate conflict resolution among the stakeholders in the tourism industry; to monitor the quality and standards of facilities available to tourists and advise both the private sector participants and relevant government agencies; to work in partnership with national, regional, and international organizations and local authorities to improve the tourism business environment; and to initiate education and awareness programs locally and abroad, to develop and maintain the capacity for quick, professional, and effective responses to issues that adversely affect Kenya's tourism. To discharge these heavy responsibilities, KTB will be funded from the catering training and tourism development levy on accommodation and tourist establishments, and an endowment fund provided by the European Union (Republic of Kenya, 1998b; "The Tourism Industry on the Mend," 1998). Should the KTB succeed in its mandate, Kenya's tourism will be better marketed abroad and this may assure sustained tourist flows into the country.

Also, the government has established a tourist police unit to attend to the special security and other needs of tourists. Initially, personnel from this unit were deployed along the beaches where the so-called beach boys harass tourists. Beach boys are informal hawkers of merchandise at the Indian Ocean coast beaches and provide a range of other services, including drugs and prostitutes. They are known to pester tourists to purchase their curios. In time, the tourist police unit will be expanded to cover all the major concentrations of tourist activity in the country. As the unit works specifically on tourist matters, it is expected that personal safety and security will be assured and the country's image will improve. Yet, a better assurance of security for tourists requires that the environment in which all Kenyans live is peaceful and stable. As indicated in this chapter, the political instability, ethnic divisions and violence, and political power rivalries associated with the country's democratization process must be addressed satisfactorily in order to restore a stable political and economic environment.

One of the issues that must be addressed in order to secure Kenya's future tourism is to diversify the sources of tourists. As noted elsewhere in this chapter, Kenya's international tourists come from a very narrow market in Western Europe and North America. This market must be diversified to ensure stability of tourist flows. The Far Eastern market (Japan, Korea, Australia, New Zealand) and the Middle East, for example, have not yet been systematically exploited. Other potential markets are Canada, Southern and Eastern Europe, and South Africa.

Similarly, Kenya's tourism product is rather narrow and emphasizes coastal beaches, wildlife safari, and urban tours in the primary towns. Yet there is potential for diversifying the attractions to include horse riding, camel safaris, polo hunting, fishing, mountain climbing, cruise ship, sporting, and conference tourism (Sindiga, 1996a). These could be developed to provide a large diversity of products in different geographical areas of the country for different market tastes and economic classes.

In an effort to further develop Kenya's tourism the country must prepare a tourism master plan to guide proposed actions. Kenya's lack of a tourism plan suggests that the challenges the tourism industry has been undergoing were not anticipated.

Finally, the Kenya government is committed to further development of the tourism industry by facilitating investment in the sector. With this regard, the government has identified KTDC as a strategic quasi-government institution (Republic of Kenya 1998a, p. 184). Its functions will include investment in the tourism industry, provision of information to domestic and foreign investors, and acting as a confidence builder attracting both local and foreign private investment in the industry (Republic of Kenya, 1998a). Should government plans to transform the KTDC into a tourism development bank (Republic of Kenya, 1994a, p. 196) succeed, the tourism industry will be assured of development finance. The future growth of tourism will thereby be secured.

Conclusion

This chapter has discussed the development of Kenya's tourism since the colonial period. Both beach- and wildlife-based tourism were started from a demand from the European settler population. This was assisted a great deal by the regional cooperation among the three British colonies of Kenya and Uganda and the Tanganyika protectorate. Although this East African cooperation continued for a few years in the postcolonial period, it finally collapsed in the mid-1970s.

Kenya's postindependence tourism history shows a great increase in the numbers of tourists. However, per capita real earnings in tourism have been declining over time. This suggests that the Kenyan taxpayers who have put up expensive infrastructure such as airports, large hotels, national parks and reserves, and roads for the tourism industry actually subsidize the all-inclusive package tourists. This matter would need to be addressed together with the foreign domination of the industry. The structure of Kenya's tourism industry, which provides room for heavy financial leakages in favor of the international tour operators and to the disadvantage of the country, must be changed to redress the imbalance, thereby assuring local support for tourism. Tourism generates little employment and on average pays wages below the modern sector economy as a whole. Also, management-level positions tend to be occupied by expatriates, leaving menial support jobs to the local people.

A number of challenges in the 1990s threw Kenya's tourism into a crisis. Yet tourism is recognized as essential to raising the levels of income and developing certain remote areas of the country (Republic of Kenya, 1998b). Government commitment to addressing the problems of the industry through repairing the damaged road infrastructure, assisting the KTB in marketing and promoting tourism, ensuring peace and harmony, and certain tourism-specific measures (Republic of Kenya, 1998b) could secure the future of the tourism industry. The country's well-developed tourism infrastructure will be a boon to further development.

Notes

[1] This chapter is drawn from my manuscript entitled "Tourism and African Development" (Leiden, African Studies Centre, forthcoming), which was prepared when I was in resi-

dence as a visiting research fellow at the African Studies Centre at Leiden, The Netherlands, in 1997. I am grateful to the African Studies Centre for facilitating the research.

[2]The term European as used in Kenya means any white person, notwithstanding the country of origin. In the usage here, it includes Australians, Canadians, South Africans, Americans, etc.

[3]Throughout this chapter, wildlife is used to mean wild animals. In some instances, as the context allows, the term refers to both plants and animals.

[4]Kenya currency is denominated in shillings. Twenty shillings make one Kenya pound. In 1998 the exchange rate was Kshs.60 to US$1.

Chapter 10

Tourism Development in Botswana: Problems and Potential

Adams Dambe Chilisa

Summary

This chapter catalogues and assesses the effect of tourism development policies and programs in Botswana. It highlights the inherent problems associated with tourism in this country and their probable causes against the backdrop of a desired sustainable tourism development. In the context of Botswana's tourism development policy objectives, the chapter discusses the potential of tourism and also analyzes government policies and institutional inputs and initiatives that support tourism development. It argues that tourism development policies should be complementary and advocacy in nature, reinforcing the national development objectives. This approach would be embraced in the tourism master development plan that seeks to address those issues within the context of both the internal and external environment and national economic goals.

Key words: Botswana; Tourism development; Tourism potential; Tourism policy

Introduction

In the context of this chapter, the focus is to provide some perspectives on the development of tourism in Botswana: what the main problems are; and what the future direction of the tourism sector might be, particularly relating to cooperation between the public and private sectors. As a starter, perhaps a brief background to this country seems necessary.

Botswana is a landlocked African country, bounded by Namibia in the west, Zambia in the north, Zimbabwe in the northeast, and South Africa in the east and south. Its physical features are its large size, with total surface land area of 582,000 km², its aridity, and, by any comparative standard, a low population density, as its population is approximately 1.5 million people. A former British protectorate, Botswana gained political independence and, subsequently, on September 30, 1966 became a republic with an executive president. The country has an independent judiciary and a legislature modeled after the British Westminster type political and judiciary systems (Government of Botswana, 1965).

Like other African countries, this country's economy is undiversified, with mineral (essentially diamonds) and, to some extent, the motor industry the dominant export sectors

(Government of Botswana, 1999). With up to 25% of the labor force being unemployed and, considering the fact that the agricultural sector offers formal employment to less than 15% of the total labor force in this country, a potential export sector was to encourage tourism. Therefore, to broaden the economic base of the country and thus enhance employment opportunities, the government has recently more concertedly supported the development of tourism as is reflected in the sector's inclusion in the country's 5-year development plan (Government of Botswana, 1997).

The government has sought to boost investor confidence through a series of incentive schemes that, although limited in variety and scope, have been successful in demonstrating government commitment to tourism. The removal all forms of foreign exchange control measures has somewhat become an indication of Botswana government's move towards complete liberalization of its foreign exchange and economy. In one sense it can be argued that the efforts to promote tourism in the country have been successful; there is evidence, however, suggesting that the future success or even sustainability of the tourism industry requires a more creative approach (Chilisa, 1996a). As a member of the Southern African Development Community (SADC), Botswana will play a useful role in strengthening this particular development initiative and impetus. This chapter discusses these issues within the context of cooperation between the public and private sectors.

Developing Tourism in Botswana

Many African countries, including Botswana, welcome the development of tourism because of the positive contributions the sector can make to their development efforts. Such contributions are well known and do not need repeating (see C. L. Jenkins, 1991; McIntosh, 1990). However, it should be stated that whatever the potential benefits arising from tourism, it should be emphasized that ultimately the real benefits of tourism should be on the improvement of living standards for most people in Botswana, if not all Batswana. This could be through subsectoral expansive linkage possibilities. Tourism is also nonconsumptive in nature generally and, in certain cases, it is indeed a renewable resource that has the capacity to grow. It has a feature of low marginal cost relative to investment in other sectors (Hermans & Stone, 1990), and this offers competitive advantage over other service sectors. However, it is not a sector without its peculiar problems. For example, it is restrained by its large capacity for leakages, inflationary tendencies, structural imbalance, low linkages, high training costs, customer moods swings, etc.

Despite these difficulties, tourism as a development strategy has positive input to a country's overall economic goals. It has been known to add value to a well-run economy, industrial harmony, excellent relations, leading to a good trading with lending partners, to skilled manpower, and political and social stability. It has made the political leaders understand and accept the desire for sound macroeconomics management. Botswana has, as it were, strived to strike a balance between transformation and industrial and political conflicts, on similar lines that highlight the distinction between the issues commonly referred to by students of social sciences as "macropolitics" and "micropolitics." The development and implementation of rules for resource allocation through a process of interaction with various societal groups (Baranizini, 1991) has been a common feature of tourism development.

Characteristics of Botswana's Tourism

Botswana's tourism private sector has argued that the country's tourism product, although somewhat unique and well sought after by its niche market, it did not meet the cost criteria for promoting Botswana as an independent tourist destination, particularly in the short term. The situation was also exacerbated by the marketing of the tourism product, as a "high-cost" and "low-volume" product. This means Botswana is, effectively, an expensive destination. In fact, none of the SADC region countries can be marketed successfully as single destinations, as the tourist product is not complete without its regional generic permutation. It is against this backdrop that the region's product marketing and promotion has been done collectively, and its development should experience combined regional effort and resource allocation and utilization.

Government Policies on Tourism

Public policies do impact, one way or the other, on tourism. One such policy that impacts on tourism is land policy: it determines and spells out its enabling character on the present and future of tourism. The land earmarked for tourism development has been the subject of discussions at workshops, particularly the issues of its management plans and environmental assessment investigations (EAI), which cover:

- land utilization specifics, tenancy, guarantees, including assessment for suitability, compliance with existing guidelines, and/or regulations;
- conservation, pollution, preservation;
- equitable distribution methods—revenue, rental, royalties, license fees;
- employment creation, training programs' existence, and citizen empowerment;
- definition of relations between landlord (community ownership);
- future development, lease periods, development covenants, etc.;
- member and size of tourist establishments per a concessionary area, etc.

The main reason for this policy approach, it would appear, has to do with the need for orderly tourism development—a balance between competing needs, for example, the cattle industry and tourism, and/or other traditional uses of land.

The main reason for the government tourism development policy is to ensure that economic activities complement the main economic mainstream policy objectives. This would lead to the proper tourism development and management of natural resources (disease control, culling, overstocking controls), conservation, tenders for concession areas and administrative procedures such as licensing, and detailed criteria for awarding the photographic and hunting concessionary areas.

As a result of the public and private sectors' consultations, tourism development needs prompted the parties to agree to deal with specific and major issues of concern to the private sector, such as provision of infrastructure:

- **soft infrastructure**: enhancement of opportunities for consultations and interactive dialogue process, including joint consultative works committees, between public and private sectors and/or labor to create the enabling environment.
- **hard infrastructure**: advocated for the promotion of coordinated regional communications link, with bias towards satisfying the traditional tourism supply equation (McIntosh, 1990) (e.g., telecommunications network, roads to the tourist areas, etc.).

This approach gave birth to common areas of interest between the public and private sectors and labor, which can be summed up as promoting the maintenance of economic stability, creation of employment, and maintenance of industrial peace, with the goal of profit optimization and effective management of operational costs (where appropriate).

This paradigmatic shift heralded an important stage in the tourism development process, as the parties in Botswana realized the need to do something to manage the current hindrances to the development of tourism, and this included:

- lack of access to capital, particularly venture capital;
- lack of collateral for bank loans by citizens;
- distribution of businesses and entrepreneurial management skills (there are instances where the number of businesses are skewed in favor of first world nationalities, operating in the SADC countries).

It is necessary to understand what has been the actual tourism development policy in the 30 years of Botswana independence. In the National Development Plan 8 (Government of Botswana, 1997) the tourism policy objectives are:

- the creation of economic opportunities, jobs, and income for the rural population in particular, and the national economy in general, this contributing positively to the long-term diversification of the country's economic base;
- the enhancement of environmental stability and quality;
- the conservation of the reservoir of generic resources and essential life support systems;
- potential sustainability in the development of the tourism industry, a potential engine of growth;
- the protection of aesthetic, scientific, cultural, national, and educational values.

Effectively, the policy objectives of tourism development over the years have grown from what they were at the time of independence. Then there was a mere statement that wildlife would contribute to tourism through the "attraction of tourists," and now there are very concrete statements of intent (e.g., "Tourism is all our business" and its benefits should accrue "to all of us") and therefore the national plans should spell out specific actions that have to be embarked upon in order to achieve the tourism development goal.

Admittedly, the Tourism Department budget has been fairly small, and did not enable the department managers to make creative decisions. It was only upgraded to a full-fledged departmental status in 1994–95. Creative decisions in the development of tourism are necessary. In fact, the tourism marketing and investment promotion budget was so small that the private sector had to ask government to increase it. The process has since continued.

Development of Tourism Facilities

Botswana's existing tourism product has been developed mainly for local/and regional business transient market segments. The major need in the future is to develop other facilities for leisure visitors (tourists) and to separate the two market segments in our sales and marketing efforts, as their needs and market orientation are different. Botswana needs quality in low-, medium-, and high-cost accommodation facilities. The citizens of the country are increasingly becoming entrepreneurs and most of them fall under the small to medium entrepreneurs category, and they are interested from an affordability perspective in the small to medium hotel/lodges/motels type of accommodation facilities.

Tourists patronize small, medium, and large up-market accommodation facilities (hotels, lodges, camps, camp sites, etc.) as long as they provide personalized services at the right prices, with appropriate privacy and comparable standards. There is evidence that Botswana is also visited by an international niche market, which has the propensity to spend on high-cost tourist products, including the high-cost lodges, camp accommodations, transport costs, etc.

Botswana's Type of Tourism

The permutation of the hotel and tourism association of Botswana (HATAB) members and their product is very diverse. It is that diversity that explains the impact of tourism on other subsectors, and also explains the uniqueness of the sector to most developed and developing countries. The membership of HATAB is drawn from nine sectors of the tourism industry, which are: hotels, lodges, camps, airlines, tour operators, services, hunting, mobile safaris, air charter, and restaurants.

Botswana tourism product is wildlife based; however, the country's wilderness and historical sites and monuments are important and complement each other in the provision of tourist attractions. They add value to the tourist product of the country. What needs to be added to this tourist product is quality service that is oriented directly to the tourist needs, such as conference venue, culture center, food, transport and communication links, entertainment, generic hospitality facilities, etc. In addition, at the secondary level services need to increase to tourist service providers, such as hotels, tour operator, etc. At the third level, entrepreneurs can provide raw materials that are part of the manufacturing process. Botswana has very popular stone carvings, handicrafts and baskets weaved in most parts of the country. These form the products of traditional village market produce to tourists from the rural areas. Traditional folklore is very rich and widely accepted by tourists to Botswana.

Statistics of Tourism Development

Tourism statistics in Botswana are generally not available, and to find reliable tourist statistics is even more difficult (Hermans & Stone, 1990). However, international tourist arrivals for 1994–1997 (Table 10.1) give some indication of past growth, and the projection of international tourist arrivals (Table 10.2) predicts continued growth. The future of the southern Africa tourism sector thus shows potential for growth. It has the capacity to grow in terms of both product variety and distribution (i.e., accessibility to the existing and new locations of the diversified tourism products). When these are converted into monetary terms, tourism is a significant contribution to the economy in both economic and social terms. It is this potential that has to be communicated to Botswana, in the tourist regions of the country, in order to inculcate a receptive attitude towards tourism and tourists.

Batswana are increasingly realizing the value of conservation and preservation programs as part of national tourist assets, particularly wildlife and land, historical sites, etc. The transposition of the estimates of tourism growth in southern Africa to Botswana suggests that the country is likely to see an increase in tourists and, therefore, tourist facilities might have to be increased. These projections are a strong indication that Botswana's tourism has a future and as such Botswana need to prepare for it, as was the case in Kenya, Zimbabwe, Mauritius, etc., through the camp fire communication strategy (see Chapters 5, 12, 19, and 21).

Table 10.1. Botswana International Tourist Arrivals

Year	Numbers	Growth Rate
1994	625,000	
1995	644,000	3.0%
1996	707.000	9.8%
1997	728,000	3.0%

Performance before southern Africa became a popular destination.

Administrative Structure for Tourism

The most active and organized private sector structures, working at promoting tourism development, the selling and marketing of the country's tourist product, individually and collectively, are HATAB members. This is not to suggest that there are no other individual tourist enterprises engaged in similar roles. The Ministry of Commerce & Industry, through its Wildlife and Tourism departments, implements government policies that relate to the past, present, and future of tourism, including the development of infrastructure. Various initiatives have been taken by these departments; of significance have been the "Tourism Symposium" of 1990 and the workshop on "Strategies for Wildlife Utilization in the New Millenium."

The Tourism Symposium gave birth to some main policy documents (other policy documents are in the making):

- National Conservation Strategy
- Tourism policy 1992
- Tourism Act 1994
- Wildlife, National Parks and Management plans

These documents have been pivotal in providing the much needed cohesion, direction, and short-term initiatives towards making the industry an asset to the economy. The future of the industry has been somewhat defined, and the guidelines regulating the industry have been provided. The workshop on the strategies for wildlife utilization provided stakeholders with the opportunity to review past experience and to define and devise the path for future tourism development.

The EU-funded project, called the Botswana Tourism Development Programme, was initiated by government and has four components that in essence will undoubtedly help the country overcome current major constraints and lack of tangible economic and financial benefits from tourism. The program also should create within the public and private sectors efficiency and effectiveness in the organization and management of tourism promotion, communication, and feedback processes; should help to establish reliable tourist data on arrivals, receipts, linkages, leakages; and should help to develop the tourism product on the basis of opportunities for participation by citizens, etc. The program essentially lays the foundation for the future tourism development path.

These parameters highlight the importance of tourism to government and its possible positive impact on the people, and defines support to national economic growth objec-

Table 10.2. Botswana International Tourist Arrivals: Projections

Year	Projected Growth	Projected Growth %
1997–1998	750,000	4.8%
1998–1999	850,000	5.5%
1999–2000	950,000	6.5%
2000–2001	1,050,000	6.5%
2001–2002	1,118,250	6.5%
2002–2003	1,190,940	6.5%

Based on WTD 1994 Africa Focus discussions on ITB Berlin, Germany.

tives. The creation of employment, particularly for rural people, through income generation for rural dwellers is viewed as a priority by the government.

There are also specific public and private sector bodies that contribute to the policy implementation, such as the Tourism Advisory Board, the Tourism Licensing Board, and the ministerial and high-level consultative fora. While presently there is no tourism board/authority, the private sector is on record as having called for the establishment of such an autonomous body (Chilisa, 1996c).

Botswana's tourism is not working as it should, and the biggest hurdle to progress is the apparent lack of coordination and harmonization of different polices that impact on tourism. The private sector has attributed this failure to the lack of an enforcing body (structure) that is credible in the eyes of both the public and private sectors. A Tourism Board/Authority, which would be autonomous and have representation of respected individuals and appropriate expertise, is overdue in Botswana. The body would devise and implement strategies that define the overall tourism policy in the short, medium, and long term. There have been delays in the implementation of the recommendations for a Tourism Board/Authority, probably mainly because of a lack of skilled manpower and/or budgetary constraints, and/or readiness to enter the highly competitive market of international tourism, which has its own set of challenges.

The Challenges and Problems of Tourism Development

Botswana, like most SADC, has problems of its own making, with other problems being of an external influence. These challenges are typical to a tourism industry that has full potential. These challenges are diverse and cannot be classified into a single generic grouping. The tourism private sector, particularly HATAB, has been in the forefront in tackling the problems and engaging government in discussions to jointly solve the tourism problems. The following were the direct result of their tourism initiatives:

- Government tourism support programs—scarcity of development resources such as investment capital, investment incentives schemes (fiscal exemption and tax relief or financial nature).
- Specific tourism manpower policy—involving the rationalization of work and residence permits for investment; the manpower planning centers to directly supply skilled citizen manpower; training for local-level labor for supervisory and management positions; and planned manpower forecasts for future growth of the industry and the associated manpower training and development programs.
- International character of tourism—the economic and social forces in the main tourist-generating countries, including the determining of the standards.
- Competitive nature of tourism market—no single country within the SADC countries offers the optimal mix of product transactions and price; hence, the need to market the SADC region as a single destination, "to avoid the real challenge of destination substitute" (Dieke, 1993b). This is a reality in SADC, as most countries of the region offer a single product, mainly wildlife. Hence, marketing efforts and cooperation to achieve a large share of Africa's tourist market is certainly a priority for the SADC region.

At the micro-level (as it were) the problems of tourism development in Botswana are similar to those in most SADC countries and to some extent the developing countries. The only difference is that wildlife-based tourism has its own type of problems, which are dissimilar to, say, beach tourism. These problems are similar to those of Kenya's, namely: rapid growth and uncontrolled development (Richards, 1980), impact of recession (Godfrey, 1986), and land use patterns (Ambrose, 1980).

In Botswana at independence tourism was regard a white man's business but was relatively small in size and in the number of tourist enterprises available to service the sector. The situation changed when government provided costly but improved infrastructure for the industry. The industry made increased demands on government for a favorable environment in which to do business.

In contrast to Kenya, there was always a realization that tourism enterprises had problems relating to equity (President Masire, opening of Maun International Airport). Nonetheless, the industry grew, but its format was mainly the small lodges and camps.

The emergence of both regional self-drive tourists from the Republic of South Africa and international inclusive tours resulted in the noticeable increase in tourist numbers and associated revenues. There was increased need for tourist facilities in parks, and this resulted in unplanned but considerable investment in infrastructure, hotel and lodges/camps, game parks and reserves, and the supporting services, such as petrol stations, handicrafts/curio shops, roads, etc. The main growth tourist areas have been the Delta and the Chobe National Park and its vicinity (Savuti), and the hotels along the railway line in the eastern part of the country.

The hotel and tourism association of Botswana and government were both concerned about the lack of tourism content and/or the somewhat unplanned development, particularly in the national parks. In the late 1980s the industry called for the embargo on new tourist enterprises and a ban on safari hunting. This was in response to the outcome of unplanned tourism expansion. Although the scale of tourism activities and development was small, it nevertheless represented growth of a scale that had not been planned.

The impact of the world economic recession in 1972–76 and 1980–84 affected the growth rate (inflow) of international holiday-makers, particularly most long-haul holiday markets (Godfrey, 1986), really recovered only after the stagnation in real incomes and high unemployment overseas, particularly in the U.K. between 1978 and 1983. During these times the industry relied mostly on regional tourists. The international tourists inflow in the region was also somewhat affected by the bush wars in Rhodesia (Zimbabwe), South West Africa (Namibia), and South Africa.

The policies of destabilization of the black independent states by South Africa in the 1980s also contributed to the reduction of international tourism to the region. The problems of Botswana tourism varied as a function of time, with some problems related to lack of appropriate enabling macroeconomic environment, while other problems were of an external nature:

- inconsistency of land utilization master plan—the industry has problems with the land utilization plans, particularly with size of tourist establishments, tenure, royalties, and fees, etc.;
- lack of realization and/or appreciation by some Botswana structures of the contribution/value of maintenance of economic stability, employment, and industrial peace;
- tourism contribution to the creation of wealth;
- access to capital, particularly venture capital;
- lack of skilled manpower relevant to maintenance of standards in tourism enterprises;
- lack of SADC funding for the Regional Tourism Organisation of Southern Africa (RETOSA) in order to effectively promote southern Africa as a single destination;
- funds for provision of and/or upgrading of tourist infrastructure and diversification of tourist product programs, through commercial banks;
- perceived restrictive policies and decisions regarding permission for new tourist establishments, particularly in parks;

- tax subsidies or credits for the marketing of the country as a tourist-receiving destination;
- unfavorable attitudes and perceptions towards tourism;
- inadequate consultative forums, local authorities (regional and governmental), and establishment of tourist offices and authorities (local, regional, and central governments); more consultative structures are needed at the bottom than at the top (the high-level consultative structure works fine);
- efficiency in some local, regional, and central government offices;
- inequitable air transport and aviation regulations;
- tax imposition on tourism products vs. competitiveness of the region;
- national master tourism plan, tourism authority/board (credible structures to drive tourism development);
- implementation capacity;
- harmonization of government role towards tourism and policies;
- master tourism planning and development, tourism sales, marketing and promotion, tourism information (statistics), and human resource development;
- lack of government subsidies, credits, soft loans, interest rebates, etc.

Botswana Tourism Potential

Given the deficiencies and constraints of its tourism sector, Botswana has actively sought to expand tourism and reach international tourism management standards. These standards are, of course, dictated by the tourist-generating countries. The international tourist market is very susceptible to customer satisfaction needs, particularly price and variety. This implies that if tourist needs are not met in Botswana (or the region for that matter) then tourists will switch to other similar destinations from price and product perspectives.

It therefore follows that the "value for money" criterion is very important, and that it promotes the tourist-receiving country's image of a popular and "value for money" destination. Botswana's tourist attractions are varied and plentiful. They are perceived by the tourist wholesalers as a unique product, which should be marketed and supported by the creation of enabling and facilitative infrastructures, such as economic and political stability.

The country's level of infrastructure development affects tourist demand for a location (Dieke, 1991), and as Botswana has a highly developed infrastructure, this influences the country's tourist inflow and in a way defines the tourism potential of the country. The industry has continuously advocated for the easing of constraints to tourism development, through functional, coordinated plans, high operational standards, and implementation of favorable legislation and provisions of skilled manpower, to manage self-sustaining tourist enterprises.

Ideally, Botswana tourism should have the potential to contribute to the economic benefits that produce high GNP per capita and that facilitate the positive human development index. These are some of the parameters that are fundamental in contributing to the desired future potential of tourism, as they are a function of good management practices of foreign exchange and/or foreign reserves accruing from the tourism industry, in cases where there is a surplus between export earnings and import deficits. This has led to the establishment of investment policies that seek to: "Stimulate investment in the tourism sector, and ensure a sustained tourism development increase efficiency and effectiveness regulations" (Dieke, 1993, p. 445).

HATAB has called for sound incentive programs to lure potential investors with their foreign capital and expertise. They have also appealed for a better monitoring mechanism of the financial assistance program that has been extended to the tourism industry, including improvement of measures intended to support the effective management of the tourism program (Dieke, 1993, p. 445). The call for transparent, direct or indirect participation in the ownership and management of the industry by the citizens of Botswana is vital, and should encompass:

- special concessions for tourism land purchase;
- fiscal aid;
- relief for operating costs;
- training and development of tourism services staff;
- employment—contribution by tourism at the macro-level;
- joint marketing efforts (collective and regional promotion);
- cooperation in the design of product and services according to tourists' demand;
- joint problem solving;
- bilateral and multilateral agreements with industrialized countries;
- promotion of cohesive regional tourism promotion policy.

It is probably on the basis of the above approach to tourism management that the national economic objectives (guidelines) of tourism are formulated, and the Botswana National Development Plan chapter on Tourism, in the 1970s, had the following objectives:

- the provision of a framework for raising the living standard of the people through the economic benefits of tourism;
- development of an infrastructure and provision of recreation facilities for visitors and residents (tourists);
- ensuring that types of development to tourist-receiving countries are appropriate to the purposes of those areas (relevance of tourism projects);
- establishing a development program consistent with the cultural, social, and economic philosophy of the government and people of the host country or area.

An evaluation of these objectives clearly points out the consistency of the Botswana official document, to the guidelines offered by McIntosh (1990), on the ideal economic objectives of any tourism development, as a strategy for economic development, namely:

- improvement of quality of life of the tourist-receiving countries and people;
- infrastructure development, conservation of environment, and preservation of culture;
- the tourism industry as an economic activity that has *potential* for growth, expansion, and self-sustainability.

The creation of a tourism authority body, with responsibility to implement the tourism policy of the country and that has specific responsibility for marketing to specific target niche markets and selected secondary markets, must be given consideration. It is this author's view that the Switzerland Tourism Authority model should be considered in the establishment and/or revitalization program of Botswana's body dealing with the wider spectrum of tourism status and its future.

The objectives of such a tourism body could broadly be inclusive of some of, or all, the objectives found in the National Development Plan Seven of Botswana, here restated for comparison:

> make tourism, self-sustainable and a significant contributor to the economy, including the upliftment of the quality of life of indigenous people; develop and diversify the tourist product range, and to sell, market and promote the product to both the domestic region and outside world, and to project a favourable image of the country; improve the quality of the tourism products, and make the product competitive, in terms of quality, accessibility, price, opportunities; achieve sustainable growth of the

tourism sector in terms of visitor numbers, duration, multiplier effect; benefit the indigenous people where tourists activities take place including their direct participation as employees and stakeholders; sustain projected tourism planning, and utilisation levels and conservation of tourism resources.

The specifics of the EU-funded Botswana Tourism Development Programme appear to have been of a problem-solving approach, and are restated for comparison: "Tourism planning and development; Tourism sales, marketing and promotion; Tourism Information (Statistics); and Human Resources Development."

These components of the master tourism plan appear geared towards redressing deficiencies and/or inadequacies in the current tourism development plan. The lack of reliable touristic data is a major constraint that is hindering effective planning. Every SADC country has its own tourism project(s) that contribute to the regional tourism development objectives. The trans-frontier ecotourism projects, like the Spatial Development Initiatives (SDIs), including the SADC regional wildlife management approaches to some of SADC countries, have important significance to the region. SADC governments have sound working relations with their private sectors, as evidenced by the success of the Smart partnership dialogue outcomes. The region is aiming at tackling touristic projects in which they have competitive advantage and opportunity to succeed. Such coordination has led to self-policing by the industry against poaching, overselling of prime tourist areas, and avoiding running down the tourist product. The industry has in two instances successfully lobbied government for the banning of hunting. The joint management consultative forums for the joint projects in Botswana's case are mechanisms for planning and control:

- product price management;
- identification of product expansion options;
- reasonable land prices;
- inventory of potential national and regional tourist resources;
- tourist trade fluctuations—quality and quantity;
- standardization of tax, structures (safaris rental, royalties, management fees), and double taxing;
- fiscal policies;
- export value of tourism;
- constructive publicity campaigns—backup financial resources;
- socioeconomic development;
- Customs & Immigration and police liaison;
- seasonality of product and its impact on employment standard practices;
- transportation issues (whole spectrum);
- tourism master plan—with transport issues such as master physical infrastructure;
- travel-associated properties, including others;
- communication-related facilities.

Usually, the scope of the development work for a tourism project is preceded by feasibility studies and a comparison of determined characteristics, indicating order of magnitude, technical, economic, and financial impacts. The Botswana trans-frontier ecotourism project either in Gemsbok or Tuli block should be subjected to these techniques to ensure its relevance, maximization of opportunities, and potentials, on both the economic and social scale.

It should be pointed out that the tourism project evaluation system within the SADC countries may or may not take the form of specific assessment dimensions, such as the known standard ones above, but the evaluation has placed emphasis on the management of the project and an equal emphasis on the sensitivity to both political and economic issues involved in the project, such as:

- choice of preference—development of export-oriented tourist attractions versus domestic-oriented tourist attractions;
- general public funding of projects policy versus private sector investment and provision of *credits*, including public service debt (psd) funds, institutional funding, and/or tax credits and incentive plans, such as financial assistance programs, to engage private investment;
- private sector versus public sector potential to fund projects (private sector capital investment—introduction of tourist preferential area with special development funding, free trading zones with special infrastructure roads/airports linking with more established ones, tourist micro urbanization);
- data on features such as cost–benefit analysis, incentive schemes, venture capital availability.

Role of Government in the Tripartite Relationship: Policies, Regulations, and Laws

The Botswana government has a major role in the development of tourism, and as already broadly described, in the soft and hard infrastructure approach. The detailed role of government in an "enabling environment" of tourism development has been identified by McIntosh (1990) as having to do with all or some of the following:

- creation of the enabling business environment and positive investment climate;
- existence of judicious system of regulations and laws;
- harmonization of policies and roles played by different ministries and departments that impact directly on the delivery of tourism and services as an economic sector in a diversified economy;
- creation of credible consultative structures between public and private sectors;
- creation of responsive attitude by the public and private sectors on tourism industry-sponsored issues;
- established government policies and regulations that are investor-friendly and deliberately made to attract and retain investors and instill confidence in the present, and future of government, in the country/region and the economy;
- participation in the creation of national and regional tourist bodies and the workings of such bodies and where possible involvement of private sector in the driving seat of the quasiboard once established, particularly the funding and legal infrastructure;
- existence of preferential financial regulations and institutions that fund tourism development projects and related infrastructure development and provision;
- specific incentives to the private investment in tourism;
- concessionary arrangements to mobilize capital investment into the tourism sector, as identified in the national tourism plan;
- reduced/relaxed (enabling) foreign exchange regulations to allow greater rate of capital formation and high rate of return such as necessitated by the devalued local currency against the currencies of the countries of potential sources of investment (investors) and tourist-generating countries;
- bilateral agreements that promote the development and promotion of tourism, its potential, and management of its hindrances (problems), etc.

In this volume, as elsewhere, C. L. Jenkins (1994) has also highlighted such issues.

Conclusions

The Botswana government has in its various roles indeed facilitated and strengthened tourism development. However, it remains to be established whether the sector has contributed to the rural development and wealth creation objectives of government. We still need to measure the real effects of the "multiplier effect" in terms of contributions to economic output and national income, or employment creation and value added to quality of life of citizens, particularly in the outlying rural communities that have "forgone" land to tourism development that would have been used for other development needs.

There is evidence that provision of tourist accommodation facilities and the supporting services is on the increase and will no doubt popularize our tourist destinations, and this must be matched appropriately by an increase in the number of tourist attraction facilities. In addition to the diversification of the economy into tourism, there is a need to diversify the tourist product, individually and collectively in the parks, at hotels, game lodges, guesthouses, safari camps, gambling houses, etc. The contribution of tourism to the size of the economic growth is associated with an approach that seeks to expand and maximize tourist arrivals and/or arrival points. However, it must be noted that the "scale of tourism development" (Dieke, 1989, p. 286; C. L. Jenkins, 1982) is influenced by factors mostly determined by the tourist-generating countries. The participation level of citizen enterprises in the tourism industry continues to increase, even if it is small, relative to the quantum of foreign ownership and investment in the sector. The majority of citizens, however, occupy "most jobs/employment" in the tourism industry. On the whole one can safely conclude that the level of Botswana tourism development has brought balanced economic gains against its costs, and large-scale tourism development might bring with it efficient and cost-effective use of resources through economies of large-scale production. What remains, therefore, is to determine the time lag appropriate for bringing new tourist units.

Second, the need for Botswana to expand its conference and exhibitions trade rapidly cannot be over emphasized. The rate of the planned tourism growth will be achieved by a diversification approach that seeks a bipronged approach to achieve a growth rate that is linked to the expansion of international tourists looking for attractions in southern Africa, including international tourists looking for an appropriate venue for international conferences.

The development of the tourism sector is not without its problem, some of which are imported and others that are of a local nature, particularly its price sensitivity and standards determination. Internal constraints include lack of skilled manpower, restrictive policies, and lack of harmonization of policies and legislation that impact on the operations of an efficient tourism sector. An enabling land use policy that is rational and promotes priority of decision-making in favor of tourism development when there are competing needs for land use has been determined as characterizing the new role of Botswana government on matters of tourism development.

Tourism planners in Botswana's public and private sectors have to respond and adapt to changing market conditions. They not only have to carefully monitor and evaluate tourism programs, but they have to be flexible in their decision-making process and match development priorities with available resources in a realistic planning framework of the tourism investment and development plans and objectives.

The enabling and facilitative environment is definitely on the increase, with both private and public sectors being keen to have creative drivers and catalyzers who proactively steer the engine of economic growth, in a development-oriented path, and adding value to the planned economic growth and development objectives.

Chapter 11

Ecotourism in Zanzibar, Tanzania

Ahmada H. Khatib

Summary

Zanzibar island of Tanzania has recently embarked on tourism as a means to diversify the island's monocrop economy, mainly related to agriculture, which has suffered from the world economic recession. Given the island's fragile ecosystem, its small size, and the need for conservation of its cultural heritage, the island city-state is in the process of searching for an appropriate type of tourism. Ecotourism has been seen as one of the best options, which could at least minimize problems associated with other types of tourism. In consequence, ecotourism has been adopted as a national strategy. This chapter explores the Zanzibar experience of ecotourism by analyzing some policy issues arising from its development and assesses both the existing and future potential for the development. The argument is that there is good potential in terms of attractions, both terrestrial and marine, but there has always been difficulty in balancing the conservation needs and promoting tourism as a business. A suggestion to enable this balance to be struck is made, especially in making the project self-sustaining, involving the local community of the surrounding area, and making tourism directly contribute to the conservation and livelihood of the community.

Key words: Ecotourism; Community participation; Conservation; Island; Ecosystem; Management

Introduction

Early travel began when mankind went in search of commerce and trade. This was the time when long caravans went across Asia, North Africa, and other parts of the world. The World Tourism Organization has conducted two projects tracing the slave and silk routes of that time (WTO, 1997d, p. 12). Exploration by early travelers mainly came as a quest to increase trade and commerce, and then later for religious and political reasons, but had little economic impact. After industrialization, due to improvements in communication and transport facilities, people from European countries began traveling for leisure purposes. Thus began the age of mass or conventional tourism. This modern form of tourism is alleged to be a source of prejudice, degradation of environment, and acculturation of some destinations in developing nations. For example, the Diani area on the Kenya coast is dedicated to tourism but its residents are still poor and economically backward, implying that tourism has done little to benefit the local community. Such tourism is also Eurocentric, and is controlled by a limited number of companies.

In the early 1990s people started to become more aware of the problems faced by many areas of the world. The Rio de Janeiro Earth Summit was convened in 1992 to address the problems of poverty, degradation of environment, misuse of natural resources, overcrowding, and pollution. Agenda 21 of the Earth Summit, which was unanimously adopted by 182 nations, calls for action plans toward a better and healthier world in the next century. Tourism is one of the industries that was identified as having potential to provide the means to conserve the environment, natural resources, and traditional way of life. As a result of the Summit, the tourism industry has adopted a program to encourage sustainable development through international organizations and governments formulating regulatory measures, guidelines, and more sound environmental projects in nature-based destinations.

Against this background, ecotourism is seen as a panacea of most problems caused by mass tourism, particularly with its principles of putting more emphasis on the improvement of livelihood, involvement of community, conservation, and better use of land and other resources. This chapter therefore explores the applicability of ecotourism in a small island environment that views tourism as a source of earning, environment conservation, and community involvement. The sustainability of ecotourism is also assessed. Zanzibar, a small island in the Indian Ocean rim, identified tourism as a possible way to develop economic diversity and is now investigating an appropriate form of tourism for the island.

This chapter first attempts to define ecotourism itself, within the context of tourism in general. Some perspectives on ecotourism experiences worldwide are given. The chapter then identifies government policies, objectives, and potential problems in relation to developing ecotourism in Zanzibar. A case study of the Jozani Forest Reserve is highlighted. The chapter concludes with future prospects and recommendations.

The Search for a Definition

The American Society of Ecotourism defines ecotourism as responsible travel to nature areas that conserves the environment and improves the welfare of the local people. The WTO (1993) defines ecotourism as traveling to nature-based areas to study, admire, and enjoy nature. Both definitions recognize ecotourism as a movement of people to nature-based attractions; the latter emphasizes its impact on the destination and the former emphasizes tourists. These definitions answer the questions of why people travel, where they travel, and what is the impact of their travel.

Weaver (1998b) defines ecotourism as any form of development that incorporates the entire spectrum of activity, from passive to active, with the proviso that host communities be included along with natural environments as aspects of the destination that are not negatively affected. This definition tends to be more inclusive by making the passive and active tourist responsible, but it also recognizes the importance of conservation of the environment and the local participation.

The problem of defining ecotourism is that the boundary line between ecotourism and other forms of tourism is not clear. It becomes more complicated by the fact that even the tourists themselves have more than one goal at a destination. For example, a tourist may visit a protected area, a historic city, and then relax at a beach.

In this chapter ecotourism is defined as a form of tourism involving travel to nature and cultural areas, focusing benefits on the resident's livelihood, nature conservation, and enhancement of the visitor experience. The causal relationship of the three components—tourist, resident, and nature—is mutual in character, as seen in Figure 11.1.

Ecotourism is a set of principles that calls for friendliness to the environment, economic viability, sociocultural compatibility, and community involvement. These principles

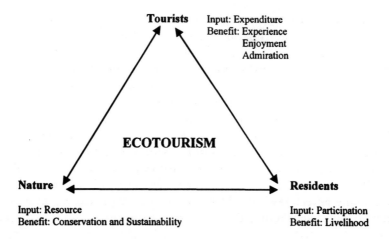

Figure 11.1. Ecotourism model.

relate to sustainable development, and therefore ecotourism is not restricted to nature areas but is extended to cultural areas, where the community becomes the main actor and benefit sharer.

Ecotourism Perspectives

The benefits of general tourism are also applicable to ecotourism: creation of employment, generation of income, foreign exchange earnings, stimulation of local economy, conservation of culture and environment, provision of infrastructure and amenities, better use of resources, etc. Ecotourism is particularly important for its emphasis on the shared benefit and mutual responsibility between the local community, environment, and the tourists themselves.

As a business, ecotourism creates profit, some of which is spent to sustain development, conserve the environment, and fund community development projects in surrounding areas. The Rio de Janeiro Earth Summit gave new impetus to ecotourism worldwide. Since the Summit different actors have responded differently but positively.

In 1997 about 20% of 620 million international travelers spent their holidays on ecotourism and other nature-related forms of vacation (WTO, 1998d). Brazil spent US$200 million in launching a program on ecotourism in the Amazon. Bwindi and Mgahing National Parks in Uganda, famous for mountain gorilla, are open to tourists for only 1 hour a day, allowing not more than 12 tourists at a time (WTO, 1993). The income obtained from visitation is spent on upkeep and managing the park, and 12% of the gross income goes directly to projects for the local residents near the park. The residents in return are obliged to control poaching, encroachment, and timber exploitation in the area.

An ecotourism resort, the Maho Bay in St. John Virgin Island, has over 113 tents within a National Reserve and is visited by more than 1 million nature tourists each year (Maho Bay Brochure). A private-owned resort, tents are made of simple and environmentally friendly materials with design and architecture fitting well into the environment, with minimum disturbance to the ecosystem. To conform to the principles of sustainable development, Maho Bay minimizes impact on the environment, encourages conservation of natural resources, conducts education programs, and in a number of ways contributes to the local community. Garbage waste is recycled, used papers are turned into scratch pads, food remains are converted into compost, glass materials are used to make cement, sewage water is used for irrigation, and solar power is used for most of the work. Biocompatible materials are encouraged, elevated walkways help preserve the ground cover and prevent soil erosion, and there is biological control of the insect population.

At Maho Bay there are regular evening programs using slides and overhead projectors to educate guests on various environmental issues. Guests are encouraged to become part of the delicate ecology and to observe the right of mutual survival. Maho Bay uses local suppliers, distributors, and other service providers. A percentage of the profits is directly donated to funding scholarships to the Virgin Island University and to funding of victim advocacy, among others. Guests are also requested to make a voluntary donation of US$0.30 to the Friends of the National Park Programme. Local musical groups perform for evening entertainment. Diverse activities are provided at the camps, including scuba diving, night snorkeling, sport fishing, rafting adventures, historical and site-seeing tours, kayaking, etc.

The South Luangwa National Park of Zambia allocates 35% of its revenue to the local village community. In Kichwa Tembo and Siana Spring, both in Masai Mara, Kenya, and Grumet River Camps and Ngorongoro Crater Lodge, all under the Conservation Corporation Africa, a company based in South Africa, the land title deed agreements are between the Masai communities of the areas. Money goes directly to community projects, such as improving roads and schools or assisting women's groups. In these different examples, community involvement in decision-making, implementation, and benefit sharing increases the possibility of sustaining development.

There are also cases where the local community makes its own decision on the type of project suitable for the area. In Auyuitting in Canada (WTO, 1993), the local Inuit residents limit tourists to small groups of 10–15 people a day. Through their involvement, the Inuit people set aims and objectives for tourism that include:

- Promoting development that is compatible with subsistence and hunting activities and that respects traditional Inuit lifestyles.
- Promoting development that provides jobs and reduces dependency on social assistance.
- Promoting cultural programs and facilities that benefit both tourism and local development.
- Encouraging local ownership, decision-making, and skill development in managing tourism business.
- Encouraging long-term self-sufficiency for the community.
- Facilitating cross-culture learning and providing opportunities where Inuit can get to know each other, so local people can develop skills in dealing with non-Inuit people.
- Developing awareness so that residents can make informed decisions regarding tourism development. (WTO, 1993, pp. 114–115)

As with many other new concepts, ecotourism has some limitations that may hinder implementation. Ecotourism lacks the comparatively long accumulative experience enjoyed by other types of tourism (e.g., convention tourism, which has been conducted for quite a long period and has gained considerable experience with time). Because of the short ecotourism life span, applicability to different environments is untested. Ecotourism uses scarce, sensitive, and fragile resources, such as natural environments, protected areas, marine habitats, cultural sites, and endemic species of fauna and flora. These fragile resources are limited in number and, if damaged, recovery could take a lifetime. For example, The National Maho Bay Forest Reserve is the only one of its kind on the island.

Since the Rio de Janeiro Summit, tourists have become more environmentally conscious. But there is also the danger that the ecotourism concept could be abused by international tour operators who might use it as a marketing tool rather than observing the principles upon which it functions.

Tourism in Zanzibar

Zanzibar, consisting of two sister islands, Unguja and Pemba, is part of the United Republic of Tanzania, which was established in 1964 when the former Tanganyika and Zanzibar merged. Under the Union constitution Zanzibar has its own House of Representatives whose members are popularly elected. It also has its own government with a democratically elected President. The government of Zanzibar has jurisdiction for all matters that are not Union affairs, such as trade, commerce, social welfare, etc.

The island is located at 39° east of Prime Meridian and 6° south of the Equator (Figure 11.2). With its location along the Equator, the climate is mostly affected by the southeast, and northeast monsoons, with very heavy rains during March through May and less rain in October through December. The highest temperature is experienced in February and the lowest in August. Humidity is high throughout the year.

According to the 1988 census, Zanzibar had a population of 640,578, increasing at 3% per year, and by the year 2000 it is estimated to reach over 1 million.

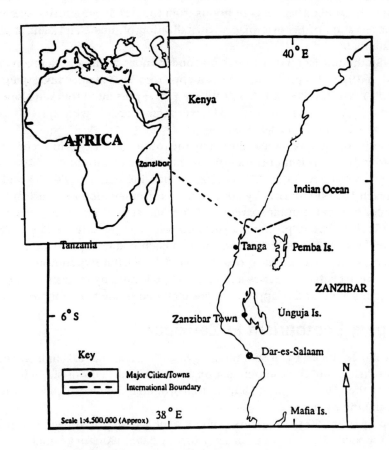

Figure 11.2. Location of Zanzibar.

The economy of Zanzibar is typical of a small island that has depended on a monocrop (i.e., cloves) for many decades. In the 1980s the world economic recession had a profound impact on Zanzibar as prices in the world market declined, seriously affecting the economy. During these traumatic years productivity fell, resulting in poor performance.

The Economic Structural Programme recommended a move towards a free market economy, which led to a Trade Liberalization Policy in 1985, encouraging private initiatives. The government gave up areas of the economy in which the private sector could perform more efficiently and profitably. The Investment Act was approved in 1986, which provides incentives, procedures, and formalities and facilitates investment in the designated sectors. In the same year, the Zanzibar Free Economic Zone Policy was conceived and its Authority formed in 1992 (Zanzibar Free Economic Zone Authority, 1997).

The Economic Processing Zone (EPZ) operates Amaan Industrial Park and Fumba and Micheweni zones. Both the Investment Act and the EPZ are part of the economic diversification program. In the process of diversification and in realizing tourist potential, Zanzibar envisaged tourism as a panacea for the crippled economy.

With help from United Nations Development Program (UNDP), Zanzibar established a Tourism Master Plan in 1983 (WTO, 1993). The plan was not fully implemented under the centralized state economy in which the public owned, managed, and ran all major economic activities. However, the plan has many elements and recommendations that are still valid and appropriate to Zanzibar. For example, the use of local architectural designs and styles in hotels and tourist facilities makes them fit into the local environment and helps the preservation of the traditional heritage. Other examples are proper solid waste disposal, limit of height and setbacks of hotels from the beach, monitoring of environmental impact, conservation of historic places, revitalization of music and dances, and improvement of handicrafts.

Since 1986 the tourism industry has responded more positively than any other sector. By the end of 1996, 208 projects had been approved by Zanzibar Investment Promotion Agency (ZIPA), worth US$349,476,419, where 50% represented tourism alone (hotels and tour operations), 14% were industries, 31% were transport, 4% were agriculture and fisheries, and 1% was business and services.

The better investment response shown by the tourist industry is in accordance with the very fast growth of tourism currently being experienced. Although in 1987 only 20,011 tourists were registered, in 1997 this number had increased to 86,495 and this is estimated to reach 100,000 tourists by 2000 (Zanzibar Commission for Tourism [ZCT], 1998).

Lack of control and nontransparency of the Ministry of Finance and Revenue Board make it difficult to obtain proper statistics on tourist expenditures. The 1998–99 figures for the hotel levy (which is 15% of the value of each bed occupied) alone was estimated by the Commission for Tourism to reach US$4,271,000. But expenditure on accommodation is just one aspect; other taxes and direct expenditure by tourists on meals, domestic transport, sightseeing, and shopping are not included in the above figure (Table 11.1).

Developing Ecotourism in Zanzibar

After the Rio de Janeiro Earth Summit in 1992, in Zanzibar the real landmark in ecotourism was the workshop on Environmental Conservation and Ecotourism, which was jointly organized by the Commission of Land and Environment and the Commission for Tourism in 1994 at the Inn by the Sea.

Attended by over 150 participants from all over the world, the workshop adopted the President's speech (The President of Zanzibar, Dr. Salmin Amour), which emphasized the government's intention to develop high-class environmentally sensitive tourism that ben-

Table 11.1. International Tourist Arrivals by Nationality: 1988–97

Year	Scand.	Germany	U.K.	Italy	France	Other Europe	U.S. & Canada	Other Amer.	Kenya	Other Africa	Japan	South Africa	Other Asia	Australia & New Zealand	Total
1988	2,655	2,448	3,278	3,778	755	7,054	3,222	838	815	2,189	813	—	4,274	—	32,119
1989	3,908	4,370	4,560	3,144	1,498	6,563	4,286	378	903	3,089	982	—	1,833	2,336	37,850
1990	4,238	4,148	5,584	4,345	2,174	6,838	4,677	496	1,228	1,608	1,088	—	2,165	3,552	42,141
1991	4,669	5,331	7,790	5,174	2,529	8,400	4,998	—	1,920	1,877	1,048	—	2,524	4,567	50,827
1992	5,991	7,223	9,139	6,625	2,928	8,519	5,664	—	1,552	2,606	2,441	—	3,031	4,028	59,747
1993	5,354	7,192	6,272	13,920	4,348	7,925	5,067	1,728	2,890	3,916	2,543	—	3,773	3,669	68,597
1994	3,684	5,737	6,377	3,004	2,600	6,893	4,002	—	1,075	2,547	1,102	—	2,047	2,365	41,433
1995	4,362	4,942	10,391	8,922	2,996	6,582	4,804	369	2,727	1,863	876	2,090	1,998	3,493	56,415
1996	6,873	5,414	11,909	13,502	4,121	7,261	5,682	253	2,034	1,996	917	2,358	2,349	4,490	69,159
1997	7,767	5,531	14,884	19,583	4,876	8,297	7,603	341	2,890	2,161	1,016	2,971	2,652	5,923	86,495
Total	49,501	52,336	80,184	81,997	28,825	74,332	50,005	4,403	18,034	23,852	12,826	7,419	26,646	34,423	544,783

Note that an abrupt change in 1993 to 1994 is due to the adjustment of recording. Source: Zanzibar Commission for Tourism (1998).

efits both the nation and the local community as the basis for tourism in Zanzibar. The workshop also adopted "ecotourism as responsible travel to natural areas which conserves the environment and improves the welfare of local people" as a working definition of ecotourism in Zanzibar. The workshop recommended:

- The growth of tourism development in Zanzibar has to be controlled. Target for the years 2000 and 2015 of 6,000 and 15,000 beds, respectively, were considered adequate for Zanzibar.
- Instead of marketing Zanzibar as an ecotourism destination, emphasis is on the principles of ecotourism and sustainable development.
- All projects should involve community, from decision-making to implementation to benefit sharing, and residents are the center of the development.
- The establishment of the Nature Conservation Areas (NCAs), which would act as the basis for resource utilization and conservation and at the same time act as demonstration or pilot projects.

The workshop had a big impact on influencing policies and programs and, as a result, environmental issues were considered. The Environment Policy, The Forestry Policy, Integrated Coastal Management, and Biodiversity Programs, which were either formulated concurrently or later, recognize ecotourism as an appropriate form of development for this destination. The Zanzibar Ecotourism Association (ZEA), for which the idea originated from the workshop, was registered in 1996 as a response by the private sector. The major aim of ZEA is to support government efforts in promoting a responsible tourism that considers its fragile ecosystem, cultural mix, and the need to conserve them for posterity.

But how is this form of tourism appropriate to Zanzibar? The island ecosystems took millions of years to develop. To damage or destroy an ecosystem would take a fraction of that time. Coral reefs, for example, are created by tiny creatures over long periods, and they make diving and other sea sports enjoyable. Coral reefs also help create and protect sandy beaches, which are another tourist attraction. Yet coral reefs worldwide are in danger.

There are some primary attractions in Zanzibar that are also fragile and need to be protected, such as the red colobus monkeys and flying fox. Also small islets are fragile and abuse could seriously affect them.

Zanzibar has the highest population density in East Africa of 900 residents per square mile, increasing at 3% per year. Unless proper land use management programs are put in place, land scarcity is eminent. Ecotourism is seen as a possible solution.

The age of purely leisure tourism is ending and the motivations of international tourists are changing. Tourists now travel to enrich themselves with knowledge of the environment, to admire and appreciate nature, to learn about other people's way of life, and to share their feelings with others.

Ecotourism Potential

Zanzibar has much to offer ecotourists, not just history and culture, but also opulent spices, fruits, flowers, medicinal and cosmetic plants, herbs, and small islets. Also important are its marine parks and unpolluted terrestrial ecosystem. Zanzibar has very beautiful marine parks with many coral reefs and other water creatures, which are suitable for nonconsumptive tourist activities such as underwater photography, selective scuba diving using environmental techniques like buoyancy control, reef watching using glass-bottomed boats, and other sea sports.

The coral reefs cover approximately 218,596 km^2. The actual sizes of the reefs range from the narrowest on the western side to 1–2-km-wide on the east coast.

Nature trails have been established at Jozani, Masingini, Ngezi, Misali, and Chumbe. Spice tours arranged to the nature area and spice plots have proven successful, where tourists are guided to the field plots and plantations in the countryside to see (and taste) the various spices and medicinal and cosmetic plants and herbs. After the tour, tourists are able to relate the experience to food items on menus in restaurants and can even see the traditional cosmetics used by residents of the Old Stone Town. The meritorious islets surrounding Zanzibar deserve a special category for their beauty and attractiveness. These islets have terrestrial and marine environments. Chumbe, Misali, Mnemba, and Chapwani have been developed as resorts. Others are Bawe, Vundwe, and Fundo, which have potential but have not yet been developed.

The Case Study: Jozani Forest Reserve

The Jozani Forest Reserve is 35 km southeast of Zanzibar Town. It is a 33,000-ha area that was established as a reserve in 1945. This is the largest terrestrial area of natural vegetation on the island.

Its history dates back to the 1930s when a saw mill was erected by a private company. Taking advantage of lack of control, exploitation of the forest was extensive. Realizing its importance, the government acquired land in 1948 and the exploitation was stopped in 1965. It is surrounded by six community villages: Jozani, Pete, Unguja Ukuu, Charawe, Ukongoroni, and Cheju.

Since its establishment, Jozani Forest Reserve had been managed by the government through the Forest Department. In 1995 the Commission of Natural Resources, a wing of the Ministry of Agriculture, Livestock and Natural Resources, started to manage Jozani Forest in partnership with CARE Tanzania with financial support from the government of Austria. The Jozani Chwaka Bay Conservation Project (JCBCP) was created, aiming to (JCBCP, 1997):

- assist the government of Zanzibar in the creation, development, and management of Jozani Forest and Chwaka Bay mangrove nature conservation area;
- improve the local economy and living conditions of the surrounding communities through ecotourism and the establishment of wise use of resources in support areas to Jozani through community management initiatives;
- create awareness of the importance of conserving natural resources through extension on site.

This joint management has brought a new impetus to the Forest Reserve as a number of changes improved the status of Jozani Forest, including widening of the boundaries, infrastructure, management plan, ecotourism project program, awareness, training, and community participation.

Visitors Profile and Revenue Generation

Records of the visitation to Jozani Forest show a tremendous increase in the number of visitors since 1990, at an average growth of 50% each year (Table 11.2). Apart from domestic visitors, mostly school children, women's groups, and residents of Dar es Salaam, the majority of visitors come from abroad.

The 1997 figures (Table 11.3) show that the largest numbers of visitors are from Europe (Italy, U. K., Germany, France, Sweden, Belgium, and Denmark) followed by Tanzania, America, other Africa, Australia, Asia, and the rest of the world. The large number of Italian visitors is probably due to the fact that there are a number of Italian hotels on the east coast whose clients stop over at Jozani on their way to the East.

Table 11.2. Visitor Arrivals to Jozani Forest Reserve: 1990–97

	1990	1991	1992	1993	1994	1995	1996	1997
No. of visitors	116	279	600	1,623	3,641	6,191	12,793	17,360
Growth (%)	—	58%	54%	63%	55%	41%	52%	26%

Source. Jozani Forest Reserve (1998).

The distribution of visitors, however, follows the tourist season of Zanzibar, with the largest numbers in August and smallest in March. In 1997 there were 17,360 visitors, which produced US$63,612 collected as entry fees alone. This encompasses entry fees to the Board Walk, which increased fees from US$3 to US$10 per person. Another US$307 was collected through a donation box. The box is intended for the community conservation activities.

Ecotourism Attractions

Jozani Forest has much to offer ecotourists and nature-based visitors whose major motivations are enhancement of experience, increase of knowledge, familiarization, education, or otherwise. Three major ecosystems are restricted to one area—terrestrial, intertidal, and marine—where each has its own peculiarities.

The terrestrial ecosystem consists of high forest with both indigenous and exotic species of flora and fauna. A 2-km Nature Trail has been completed, passing through the ground water forest in the heart of coral dry evergreen forest zone. All major species along the trail are marked by numbers for further references. Some of these species are rare, endemic, or semiendemic. During a guided tour at each point the guide explains the nature of the plant, history, social/cultural importance, and its relation to the ecosystem. Some of the common plants along the trail are red mahogany (*Calophyllum inophyllum*), oil palm (*Eleais guineensis*), woody lianas (*Todalia* sp.), strangler fig (*Ficus natalensis*), raffia palm (*Raphia farnifera*), wild date palm (*Phoenix relinate*), and wild cardomon (*Fromomun hugustiphia*).

In 1975 Robin (JCBCP, 1998) found 33 plant species of ground water forest and underwater species in an area of 130 ha of land. In 1991 Ruffo (JCBCP, 1998) identified 98 forest species in 500 ha, excluding hubs and undergrowth.

The Forest is also home to fauna species. The red colobus monkey is an endemic species to Jozani (Figure 11.3). Its population has increased to some extent over the last 10-year period due to hunting restrictions, from a mere few hundred to an estimated total number of over 2,000 currently residing in the Forest and the surrounding area. The animals live in the coast fringes, coral shrubs, and mangrove swamps. Red colobus monkeys are very social and are found in groups of families of up to 30 animals of different age and sex. Feed-

Table:11.3. Visitor Arrivals to Jozani Forest Reserve by Origin:1997

	Europe	America	Australia	Asia	Tanzania	Other
No. of visitors	13,277	1,037	521	312	1,610	603
Percent	76%	6%	3%	1.8%	9.3%	3.5%
Rank	1	3	5	6	2	4

Source: JCBCP (1998).

Figure 11.3. Red colobus monkey.

ing on fig, leaf shoots, and unripe fruits they are sometimes a nuisance to farmers because they cause damage to crops.

The rare and threatened Zanzibar leopard lives at Jozani. Its population has been reduced to a only a few due to illegal killing of the leopard elsewhere and it now can only survive at Jozani Forest Reserve. Other animals include sun squirrels, elephant shrews, mangooses, adder duikers, and hyraxes. In 1972 Ruffo (JCBCP, 1998) found 95 butterfly species of which 9 are endemic and 26 semiendemic. There are also about 43 species of birds recorded to take shelter in the Forest.

A newly completed Mangrove Trail is another attraction of Jozani. The mangrove is nicknamed "forest in the sea." A horseshoe-shaped Board Walk 1 km long was built jointly by the Commission of Nature Resources, JCBCP, and residents of Pete village.

In Zanzibar there are approximately 18,000 ha of mangrove forest and Jozani is one of the areas designated for conservation. Along the trail three out of nine species of mangrove recorded in Zanzibar can be observed during the walk. Small creatures of the intertidal zone can be seen, such as crustaceans, molluscs, crabs, and prawns. To complete the entire Board Walk, including watching intertidal creatures at the stream and a 5-minute rest at the extension takes approximately 45 minutes (Figure 11.4).

Management of Jozani

Since 1995 Jozani Forest Reserve has been jointly managed by the Commission for Natural Resources, JCBCP, and Pete community. In reviewing its management objectives and in preparation of its tourism plan, Jozani Forest Reserve specified its main objectives (JCBCP, 1998):

• Maintain a high standard of services, keep facilities, trails, attractions, and permanent information displays in good condition, and ensure a continuous supply of take-home

Figure 11.4. Board Walk in Jozani Forest Reserve.

interpretative materials.
- Assure the generation of sufficient revenues to support tourism-related activities in addition to those aimed at preserving the integrity of Jozani Forest Reserve and generate a fund for the benefit of the local community.
- Increase the standard of work performance of Jozani-based staff.
- Safeguard the welfare of Jozani's red colobus monkey population, with particular attention paid to habituated groups.

Jozani Forest Reserve has been suffering from poor facilities and services, lack of control, and the fact that money generated as entry fees, instead of being reinvested, went directly to the treasurer. But if desired goals are achieved, the facilities and services will improve, monkeys will be safeguarded, and the local community will be fully involved.

A number of tasks were set, each intended to enable management to attain one of its objectives. The visitor center and educational and information centers were built, toilets facilities were improved, and parking areas and driver's post were built. Other tasks included: production of promotional and publicity materials, guidelines, record keeping, training guides, and encouraging village residents to produce quality handicrafts.

Currently the manager of Jozani Forest Reserve is answerable to the Commission for Nature Resources, JCBCP, and liaisons with the Pete community.

Experience elsewhere in the world shows that negative impact to the Reserve could result if care is not taken to ensure carrying capacity is not exceeded. Management has a number of options to choose from to maintain resources and ensure sustainability. One option would be to stop visitation to the monkeys, or to restrict visitation to the morning or afternoon only.

Another would be to issue a certain number of permits to individual tour operators, but not restrict independent travelers, or to limit visitor groups to 10 people at one viewing. Also, raising entry fees to US$10 per person might cut down the number of visitors.

The impact of some of these options is very difficult to assess, because they also depend on other intangible elements. For example, reduction of the visitation to a minimum does not necessarily ensure safety of the monkeys and the ecosystem, because one visitor with unsociable behavior might be more harmful than 10 caring and environmentally conscious visitors.

Management did in fact raise the entry fee to US$10, hoping that to at least cut down the number of visitors while other options are being worked out. In 1993, in the Amboseli District (Weaver, 1998b, p. 123), entry fees to the national parks were raised from US$5 to US$20, but that did not reduce the tourist influx.

Community Participation and Benefit Sharing

Jozani Forest Reserve is surrounded by six villages. Residents of the villages depend to a large extent on the forest as a source of building materials, firewood, farming, hunting, fishing, and for other social activities. Some residents own plots of land but, due to the colobus monkey population explosion, the animals are now harming their crops. Also, the village residents sometimes have to stop using their plots in order to conform to the conservation guidelines.

Realizing that conservation of this nature is more effective where local people are fully involved, the Jozani Forest Reserve adopted several programs to ensure that local residents are at the center of the project. All villages are represented in various committees. The Steering Committee of JCBCP has three of its members from the village community. The committee oversees the project and advises the Commission of Nature Resources accordingly. The Tourism Plan was discussed and approved by Chwaka, Charawe, Cheju, Pete, and Ukongoroni before it was sent to other organizations for comments and approval.

Recently, local village experts in wildlife were included in research to determine whether or not the leopard, which is believed to be approaching extinction, still exists. The research, led by two South African experts, Christ and Tilde, found no live leopard in the Forest, only 6-month-old feces. In fact, the leopard's existence in Zanzibar is fictitious in the eyes of the younger generation, although village elders insist otherwise.

Jozani Forest Reserve creates both temporary and permanent jobs for the village residents. The Board Walk at Jozani was funded by the government of the Netherlands and CARE Tanzania, supervised by the Commission for Natural Resources, but it was the residents of Pete village who provided labor for construction. The Jozani Forest Reserve and JCBCP employ 12 forest officers, 13 forest guides and guards, and 7 administrative staff. However, for high managerial and other posts it is difficult to employ local residents because most of them lack necessary qualifications and training.

In 1996 five members of the Village Advisory Committees attended a 1-week study tour in Tanga on mainland Tanzania to observe, discuss, and learn various aspects relating to coastal management and mangrove conservation.

The village Advisory Committee constructed two gates at Paje and Charawe Roads to restrict illegal cutting of poles. Several poachers were caught and poles were confiscated. In this instance there were 72 scores of building poles and 29 scores of coral and mangrove forest. Now regular patrols are conducted to help decrease this illegal activity.

The village Advisory Committee advised Jozani to place temporary sanctions on Charawe after it was found out the villagers were conducting illegal cutting of red mahogany. As a result Charawe was fined.

The local community around the Reserve uses the facilities mainly for educational purposes. In 1997 Kitogani, Chwaka, and Kinyasini school children participated in a study tour and the same was organized by Sunni Madras. In the same year 140 residents from seven villages visited the Reserve.

The school children of Unguja Ukuu and Kitogani had a drama competition, with conservation as a theme. Seven hundred educational leaflets were published and distributed to the village, and another 450 information booklets were published for tourists.

A study conducted by Young (1997) in July 1997 on living standards and sources of income pointed out that for Jozani Forest Reserve to remain for future generations the forest must benefit the community by providing revenue, particularly from ecotourism.

To avoid conflict and misapplication of revenue from different activities, Jozani Forest Reserve has a distribution mechanism that assures each beneficiary obtains its share. Revenue from entry fees is directly appropriated by the treasurer, the Forest Reserve, and Pete village. The revenue from the donation box goes to the Community Development Fund, and money from sales of postcards, booklets, maps, and guides goes to the local community. In 1997 US$5,970 was allocated to the Advisory Committee as a grant, another US$5,075 was allocated to the seven villages surrounding the Reserve, and US$747 was spent for administration (JCBCP, 1998).

Future Prospects of Ecotourism in Zanzibar

The future of ecotourism in Zanzibar depends on both domestic and international factors. Internationally, ecotourism is becoming more popular as people become more aware and conscious of the need for a more environmentally friendly developmental approach.

Changing attitudes and taste among international traders and nongovernmental organizations becoming more aggressive and powerful in environmental issues indicate a positive response to ecotourism.

In Zanzibar's struggle to search for an appropriate form of tourism, massive development is not recommended due to its small size and fragility of the ecosystems. The importance of conserving and sustaining its natural and cultural heritage, involving the community in conservation efforts, and ensuring resources are not exploited cannot be underestimated. In this context, ecotourism gives hope towards that end.

Currently ecotourism is mostly based on a variety of spices, marine habitats, and the protected areas, such as Chumbe, Misali, Masingini, Jozani, and Ngezi. Some of these attractions are also for other types of tourists.

The case of Jozani Forest Reserve can serve as a model for other ecotourism development in Zanzibar. Although Jozani generates revenue in different ways, its primary objective is to make tourism and other activities contribute directly to conservation and to the livelihood of the community.

Chapter 12

Tourism and Conservation: The Application of Economic Policy Instruments to Wildlife Tourism in Zimbabwe

M. Thea Sinclair and Alan Pack

Summary

Zimbabwe's CAMPFIRE program exemplifies the way in which economic policy instruments can be used to increase the economic returns from wildlife tourism, thereby promoting income and employment generation in rural areas and supporting wildlife conservation. The program aims to give local communities ownership and control of the wildlife within their domain and to ensure them a return from the use of such resources, in the form of cash and/or community projects. Charges, quotas, and regulations, applied to wildlife viewing and hunting tourism, are the instruments used to facilitate this objective. Foreign donors' provision of financial support for the program illustrates the way in which the option or existence value of wildlife can be financed from external sources. Although the CAMPFIRE program has been welcomed in some areas of Zimbabwe, it has been less successful in areas where the economic returns from the program have been relatively low or unequally distributed.

Key words: Economic policy instruments; Wildlife tourism; Conservation; CAMPFIRE

Introduction

Zimbabwe is a prime example of a country whose comparative advantage in tourism lies in its natural resources. Its variety of climate, along with such spectacular features as the Victoria Falls, plains, highlands, and granite hills, compensates for the lack of beaches and relative scarcity of urban tourism attractions. Wildlife, in particular, has proved to be a key source of tourist interest. With wildlife viewing or hunting as their main objective, tourists have ventured into rural areas of the country, usually under the auspices of a safari organizer. Wildlife tourism has been one of the few sources of increasing income and employment for the population of these areas. In other respects, their economic context is one of poverty and instability, owing to the severe droughts that periodically devastate crop output. Low economic growth at the national level, combined with unemployment, inflation, and balance of payments deficits, has severely limited the amount of assistance provided by central government.

One of the most interesting wildlife-based tourism initiatives to have been introduced in rural areas in Zimbabwe is the Communal Areas Management Program for Indigenous Resources or CAMPFIRE program. The program is innovative in ensuring that wildlife, which is not normally valued within a market context, is assigned a monetary value (e.g., in the form of hunting fees). Other policy instruments, such as quotas and regulations, are also used with the objective of obtaining an economic return from wildlife. The program is unusual in attempting to assign the control of natural resources, together with much of the income from them, to the local community. However, the hunting component of the program has proved controversial and the distribution of income has created tensions in some communities.

This chapter will consider the ways in which economic policy instruments have been applied to wildlife tourism in Zimbabwe under the CAMPFIRE program, and will examine some of the strengths and limitations of this community approach to tourism. The economic context for the program will be outlined in the next section of the chapter, in order to illustrate the range of economic problems that has confronted Zimbabwe in recent years. The following section will consider the growth and nature of tourism in the country, including the concentration of demand among a small number of nationalities. The concepts of sustainable development, sustainable tourism, and market failure will then be discussed, prior to examination of the economic methods that can be used to value natural resources and the associated policy instruments that can be applied, notably prices, quotas, taxes, subsidies, and regulations. The next section will consider the development of the CAMPFIRE program, indicating the ways in which economic instruments have been utilized within the program and demonstrating the case for applying economic methods to wildlife tourism. The contribution and difficulties associated with wildlife tourism development under the program will be discussed in the final section and a number of implications and proposals will be suggested.

The Economic Context

Both economic and tourism development in Zimbabwe have been closely related to political events in the country. Following the Unilateral Declaration of Independence of 1965, the economy grew strongly, the average of annual growth rates of real gross domestic product (GDP) approximating 6% between 1967 and 1974 (World Bank, 1980-97). However, the subsequent oil price rises and the upsurge of the independence movement were accompanied by considerably lower rates of growth, of 2% during most of the 1980s and under 2% during the first half of the 1990s. The population increased by an average of 3.1% between 1980 and the mid-1990s.

The government's ability to counter low living standards was limited owing, in part, to heavy debt repayments, amounting to around 23% of the budget and 30% of export earnings in the mid-1990s. Although the rate of inflation declined from 45% at the beginning of the decade to 23% in 1995, the unemployment rate for the same year was over 33%, compared with 10% at independence. The country was thus faced with the problems of high unemployment, low per capita income, and an unsustainable budget deficit. Severe droughts in the mid-1990s worsened the plight of the rural population and there were recurrent demands for land resettlement policies and indigenization.

Zimbabwe's external relations were dominated by the Economic and Structural Adjustment Program, which commenced in 1991. It was an outward-looking development strategy that favored policies of "liberalization" of the exchange rate and international trade. In line with traditional International Monetary Fund (IMF) and World Bank policy recommendations, many restrictions on the exchange rate, international trade, and foreign investment in the country were lifted. A unified floating (market-determined) exchange rate regime was introduced, import quotas were abolished, and, by 1995, exporters were allowed to retain all of their foreign currency earnings and foreign investors to remit up to 100% of their profits. These measures, along with the privatization of some state enterprises, stimulated increases in foreign capital inflows in the form of both portfolio and direct investment. Production rose and, by 1996, the country's balance of payments on merchandise trade was in surplus (Central Statistical Office, 1978–98). However, the history of trade deficits and ongoing debt repayments precluded significant expansion of the economy, so living standards remained low and unemployment high. It was in this context that the growth of international tourism was welcomed as a means of generating foreign currency earnings, income, and employment.

International Tourism in Zimbabwe

During the 1970s and 1980s, the growth of tourism in Zimbabwe was dominated by the independence movement and the subsequent internal unrest of 1982–87. Although the number of international tourist arrivals was as high as 368,000 in 1972, numbers had plummeted to 79,000 by 1979. It was not until the attainment of independence in 1980 and, subsequently, the more peaceful conditions of the second half of the decade that arrivals again started to rise significantly. Zimbabwe continued to increase in popularity during the 1990s, as is shown in Figure 12.1, and by 1996 the number of tourist arrivals in the country (net of tourists in transit) exceeded 1.5 million, the fourth largest figure in Africa, following South Africa, Tunisia, and Morocco.

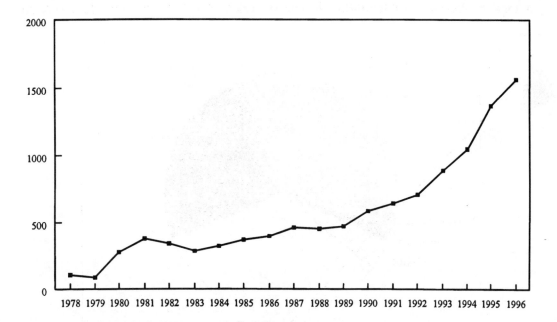

Figure 12.1. Tourist arrivals in Zimbabwe (thousands). Total arrivals minus arrivals in transit. Source: Central Statistical Office (1978–98), WTO (1998c).

Large numbers of foreign tourists in Zimbabwe come from South Africa, which accounted for 45% of total arrivals in 1980 and 33% in 1996. Many South Africans come to Zimbabwe to visit friends and relatives, while visitors from Zambia, which accounted for 26% of arrivals in 1996, often engage in cross-border purchases. An additional 10% of arrivals came from Mozambique. Hence, tourism in Zimbabwe is characterized by a high level of concentration in terms of origin countries, as illustrated in Figure 12.2. Other major origin countries were the U.K. and Ireland, with 4% of arrivals, Germany with 2%, and the U.S. and Canada with 2%. However, the length of stay of tourists from Western Europe has been double that of visitors from Africa, averaging 10 days for Europeans compared with 5 days for Africans at the beginning of the 1990s. The key problem in terms of the length of stay is its decreasing duration over time, from an average of 11 nights in 1980 to less than 5 nights in 1995.

Most of the tourists who arrive in Zimbabwe, around 86% in 1995, come for the purpose of a holiday rather than business (Central Statistical Office, 1996). The country's favorable climate ensures that neither holiday nor business tourism is characterized by a severe degree of seasonality, with the exception of the peak in holiday arrivals during the Christmas period. Many tourists are relatively young, around half being under 35 years of age. Preferred holiday destinations outside Harare are concentrated in the northern region of the country, notably Lake Kariba, Hwange National Park, and the geographically proximate Victoria Falls. However, the huge popularity of the Victoria Falls, with approaching 20% of total overnight stays in 1995, is posing an increasing threat to the environmental sustainability of the country's most important tourist attraction.

Foreign currency receipts from tourism and travel, measured in real U.S. dollars, moved broadly in line with the growth of arrivals, as illustrated by Figures 12.1 and 12.3. Expenditure on tourism abroad by Zimbabwean residents was more unstable, increasing between 1978 and 1980 but, with the onset of recession, declining until 1986 and, with the exception of 1991–93, increasing during the late 1980s and the 1990s. The country attained a surplus on its tourism balance in 1991 and tourism contributed a rapid increase in foreign currency earnings during the ensuing years, as is shown in Figure 12.3. Foreign

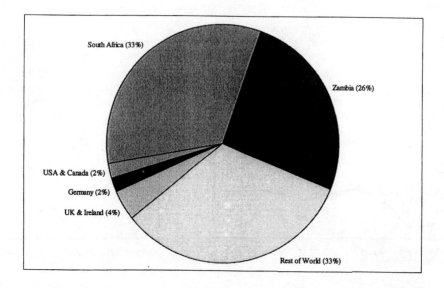

Figure 12.2. Tourist arrivals by origin: 1996. Source: WTO (1998c).

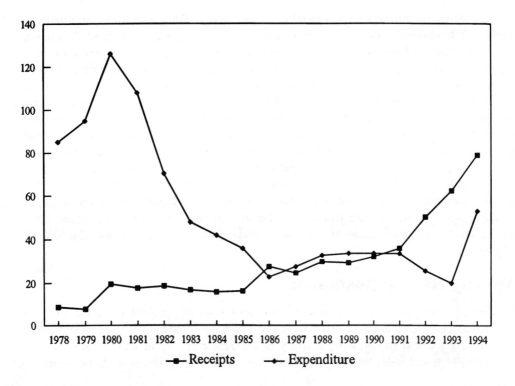

Figure 12.3. Tourism receipts and expenditures (real US$ million). Source: International Monetary Fund (1979–97a).

currency receipts derive predominantly from tourists from the U.S., with 35% of the total, South Africa with 12%, and the U.K. with 11%. Average daily receipts per capita have been similar for U.K. and South African tourists, but considerably higher for Americans. As in other developing countries, tourism provides a high share of export earnings (Sinclair, 1998), attaining 10% of total receipts from goods and services in 1995, compared with the respective shares of around 20% for exports of tobacco and 20% for gold and ferrochrome. Overall, tourism was one of the fastest growing sectors in the economy during the 1990s. By 1995, receipts from international tourism, including passenger fares, accounted for 3.7% of the GDP and receipts from domestic tourism for 0.9% of the GDP, compared with shares of 1.7% and 0.9% in 1990 (Travel and Tourism Intelligence, 1997). The level of employment generated by the tourism sector rose from 40.5 thousand in 1990 to 83.4 thousand in 1995, accounting for 7% of national employment, compared with mining's share of around 5% of both GDP and employment.

Well over half of foreign visitors arrive by road from neighboring African countries and there is a good road infrastructure within Zimbabwe itself. Increasing accessibility by air is also available to the generally higher expenditure tourists who come on long-haul flights. The more liberalized policy towards air transport, which was implemented during the 1990s, stimulated more flights to and from the country by a range of international airlines including Air France, American Airlines, KLM, Lufthansa, Swissair, South African Airways, and Qantas. The state airline, Air Zimbabwe, provides both international flights and flights to a wide range of domestic destinations, thereby capturing considerable revenue from internal tourism travel.

The supply of tourist accommodation has grown steadily over time, as illustrated in Figure 12.4, which also demonstrates a clear excess of supply over demand. Foreign direct investment in the hotel accommodation sector, up to a maximum 70% foreign share, was encouraged by the Zimbabwe Investment Centre during the Economic and Structural Adjustment Program of the 1990s. Although domestic firms own most of the tourist accommodation in the country, major international hotel chains are increasing their participation in the sector; for example, Holiday Inn, Intercontinental, and Sheraton provide high category accommodation in Harare and at Victoria Falls. There is also good availability of middle category and budget accommodation as well as safari camps, many of which cater for high-expenditure tourists, promoting income generation in relatively poor rural areas. Safari tourism provides a monetary return from Zimbabwe's abundant wildlife and other natural resources. This contrasts with the common view that natural resources are, intrinsically, public goods that are freely available and not subject to market forces. The economic methods that can be used to value natural resources will be discussed in the following section.

Valuing Natural Resources

Greater tourist use of the natural environment, not only in Zimbabwe but on a worldwide scale, can have adverse effects on the ecosystem, inhibiting species reproduction and posing a threat to the sustainability of the resources upon which tourism is based (Cater, 1994; Roe, Leader-Williams, & Dalal-Clayton, 1997). On the other hand, tourism pro-

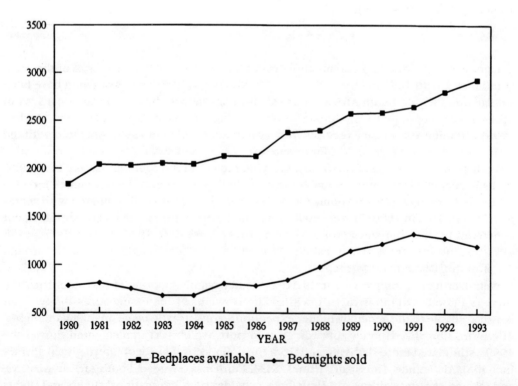

Figure 12.4. Hotel occupancy in Zimbabwe (thousands). Source: Original data compiled by Research and Planning Department, Zimbabwe Tourist Development Corporation, Harare (1994).

vides revenue that can be used to assist resource conservation. Thus, an area's abundance in natural resources and potential for natural resource-based tourism may be of short-term or long-term duration, depending upon whether the resources are used sustainably.

The term sustainable development and, analogously, sustainable tourism development, encompasses two approaches. The weak approach to sustainable development involves the maintenance of the total stock of natural and human-made resources and permits the substitution of the latter for the former. In contrast, the strong approach does not permit substitution, ensuring that natural resources are not depleted (D. W. Pearce & Turner, 1990). Thus, a strong approach to sustainable tourism development would require the maintenance of the total stock of natural resources. In practice, the weak approach has prevailed (Beioley, 1995; Global Environment Management Initiative, 1992; Hemming, 1993; Welford & Goudson, 1993).

One of the main causes of natural resource depletion is the public good nature of many of these resources (Clark, 1973; V. L. Smith, 1968). Access to the resources is often free and unconstrained, permitting tourist incursions that sometimes exceed the carrying capacity of the resources. The social costs and benefits associated with the use of the resources frequently differ from the private costs and benefits owing to the existence of "externalities," such as environmental degradation stemming from excessive use of the resources (Hanley & Spash, 1993; Sinclair & Stabler, 1997). In this case, there is said to be market failure, owing to the unpriced effects of the resource use. Even in the case when a price is paid for access to natural resources, the price only takes account of individuals' preferences insofar as they are reflected in the ability to pay, which is, in turn, dependent upon the underlying distribution of income and wealth. Hence, the preferences of the poor and of future generations are attributed a low or zero weighting and their ability to benefit from the resources is constrained.

As one of the main reasons for the excessive use of natural resources is their free availability, the attribution of an explicit monetary value to them could constitute a step towards eliminating their overexploitation. The total economic value of natural resources consists of two components: use value and nonuse value. Use value is the direct and indirect value that the resources provide to those who use them. Nonuse value consists of option value, which is the value that is attributed to the possibility of using the resources in the future, and existence value, which is the value individuals place on the continued existence of the resources, irrespective of any intention of using them.

Three main methods have been applied to estimate the value of natural resources. The first is the hedonic pricing method (Garrod & Willis, 1991; Rosen, 1974; Sinclair, Clewer, & Pack, 1990), which estimates the unpriced characteristics of goods and services (e.g., the natural resource component of a safari holiday). A major problem with this method is that it only takes account of the value of natural resources insofar as they are included within the total holiday price and, therefore, may result in undervaluation of the resources. The second method is the travel cost method (Clawson & Knetsch, 1966; A. J. M. Harrison & Stabler, 1981; Loomis, Creel, & Park, 1991), which uses the cost of travel to the tourism site as an estimate of the value of the resources at the site. However, the assumption that travel cost is an adequate measure of the value of natural resources is not always valid and the method lacks a strong theoretical underpinning. The third method is the contingent valuation method (Brookshire, Eubanks, & Randall, 1983; Garrod, Willis, & Saunders, 1994; Hanley, 1988; Lockwood, Loomis, & DeLacy, 1993; R. C. Mitchell & Carson, 1989; Willis, 1989), which involves questioning tourists about their willingness to pay for natural resources. The problem is that tourists' responses to questions about the amounts that they would be willing to pay may differ from the amounts that they would actually pay, if required to do so.

In spite of the limitations of the above and other methods for valuing natural resources (Bateman, 1993; Bateman & Turner, 1993; Sinclair & Stabler, 1997), their application has the important advantage of drawing attention to the key role that such resources play in attracting tourists and to the high value that many tourists attribute to them. For example, the application of the travel cost and contingent valuation methods to the case of safari tourism in Kenya indicated the high amounts that tourists are willing to pay for elephant viewing (G. Brown & Henry, 1989). It also strengthens the case for using resources sustainably because, without them, tourism demand, foreign currency earnings, local income, and employment would fall. Hence, it is useful to consider the range of instruments that policy-makers can implement when attempting to obtain ongoing monetary returns from natural resources.

Relevant policy instruments fall into three main categories. The first is price-based instruments, which include prices and charges, taxes, ongoing subsidies, or one-off grants. For example, charges are levied for admission to some national parks or reserves, taxes are imposed on overnight stays in tourist accommodation or on air departures, and subsidies or grants may be allocated to landowners who make environmentally attractive property available to the wider public. The second category may be termed quasi-market instruments and includes quotas, marketable licenses, and permits. These attempt to exercise some control over the numbers of tourists who have access to natural resources and may be complemented by the use of price-based instruments in order to provide a source of revenue. The third category is regulations, which impose direct controls over access to and/or use of resources. Regulations have the advantage of transparency but require an effective organizational structure for implementation. Support from the local community is also necessary if regulations are to be credible and operate successfully. Different combinations of policy instruments may be implemented to suit specific circumstances. The combination of policy instruments and community involvement that was applied in Zimbabwe's innovative CAMPFIRE program will now be considered.

The CAMPFIRE Program

Like other aspects of tourism development in Zimbabwe, the CAMPFIRE program is rooted in the political history of the country. During colonial rule of African countries, policy towards wildlife involved designating huge tracts of land as national parks and reserves, to be controlled by central government. Although the policy succeeded in preserving the countries' abundance in natural resources, it had considerable adverse effects on the rural population, increasing problems of animal encroachment on surrounding areas and decreasing the total amount of land available for crop cultivation and domestic livestock. Not surprisingly, many of the inhabitants of rural areas developed a hostile attitude towards conservation policy, unmitigated by their economic context of poverty and the general absence of alternative forms of employment.

More recently, several significant developments in conservation policy have occurred. The first was the 1960 Wildlife Conservation Act, which gave commercial farmers greater control over wildlife on their land and enabled them to obtain increasing monetary returns from it. This was followed by the 1975 Parks and Wildlife Act, which gave farmers complete control over wildlife on commercial farming land, subject to its sustainable use and with the exception of a few protected species. The underlying assumption, consistent with the theoretical arguments of the previous section, was that wildlife would receive greater protection if attributed a monetary value. The policy approximately doubled the area of private land used for wildlife ranching, to around 8% of the total area of Zimbabwe in 1990, compared with 13% for national parks and safari areas (Cumming, 1990). However, it was clear that increasing demand for wildlife was required alongside the growing supply from commercial ranches. It was also clear that the inhabitants of communal lands, covering 42% of the country and 50% of the population, had little incentive to promote wildlife conservation, as the control of the wildlife was retained by central government and local people obtained little economic benefit from it. Tourism appeared to provide an answer to both problems (McIvor, 1994), but before it could be promoted successfully in communal areas, the appropriate administrative mechanisms had to be established.

The prerequisite for increased incentives for wildlife conservation was deemed to be greater ownership and control of wildlife at the local level. The first steps towards this aim were undertaken via Operation Windfall in 1978-80, which aimed to distribute income generated by a wildlife culling program to district councils for expenditure on local projects (Barbier, 1992). This was followed, in 1982, by an Amendment to the Parks and Wildlife Act, which gave district councils control over wildlife on the land under their jurisdiction. Thus, district councils, which are responsible for poor communal lands, had been granted rights over wildlife similar to those of the commercial farmers on more productive, privately owned land.

The CAMPFIRE program, announced in 1984 and officially initiated in 1989, was developing alongside the administrative changes that were occurring at the district level. The program aimed to transfer the ownership and management of natural resources from the national government to local communities, thereby converting open access resources, which were subject to overexploitation, to common property with locally determined rights of access and exclusion (Thomas, 1995). The assumption was that local people would support wildlife conservation if they were involved in the process of wildlife management and benefited from it. The aim of the Wild Life Department, as stated within its guidelines for the program, was that each member of the local population would belong to a "producer community," which would receive a return of at least 50% of the district council's income from natural resources, notably wildlife, in the area covered by the community. The return would take the form of cash and/or community projects and the choice concerning the nature of the return was to be taken by the producer community. The communities were to be small, consisting of around 100-200 households who, in addition to managing the wildlife itself, would be responsible for grazing, forestry, and water resource use.

The CAMPFIRE program started in northwest Zimbabwe, in the Guruve and Nyaminyami districts, and subsequently spread to other areas of the country (Barbier, 1992). By 1995, over 250,000 people were involved in the program, which covers around two thirds of all rural districts in Zimbabwe, bringing one third of the country under communal or privately owned wildlife conservation. The main instruments used to ensure that wildlife provides a monetary return in communal areas are regulations, charges, and quotas, which are used in the context of wildlife viewing and hunting tourism. Regulations prohibiting poaching have been imposed, the idea being that these will be supported and made effective by producer communities who gain from tourists' use of the resources. Decisions about the quotas of different species to be made available for hunting are made at the local level, in consultation with the Department of National Parks and Wildlife Management and the World Wide Fund for Nature. Safari operators, sometimes in partnership with local people, submit tenders for wildlife quotas for periods of 3-5 years. High fees are charged for trophy hunting (Bond, 1994) (e.g., $10,000 for an elephant in 1997). The additional charge for tourist accommodation in particularly scenic locations can amount to $800 per day, part of which is received by the district council in the form of rent.

The district council levies a 15% tax on the total income obtained from wildlife resources and is also permitted to retain up to 35% for costs incurred due to wildlife management. A share of the remaining income obtained from CAMPFIRE is distributed to local people (39% in the early 1990s), although the precise shares vary between different areas. The income is distributed either as individual cash payments or in the form of additional infrastructure, including improved water provision, school facilities, and medical care. Local people also obtain income from wildlife culling and meat sales, which contributed around 4% of total income from wildlife tourism in the early 1990s. By far the largest share of income comes from hunting, which accounted for over 80% in the same period.

The results of the CAMPFIRE program have been mixed. The use of economic policy instruments within the program has clearly demonstrated that wildlife has a high monetary value and that hunters, in particular, are willing to pay high fees for large animals. The imposition of quotas, along with effective antipoaching regulations, appears to have ensured the sustainability of animal populations and the numbers of some species (e.g., elephants) have increased. However, additional revenue could be obtained by more flexible implementation of hunting fees and the use of an increased share of the annual culling quota for hunting purposes. For example, some elephants inflict a particularly high level of damage on crops and people during the rainy season. Lower fees for tourist hunting of problem elephants during this period would provide additional income to local communities who would otherwise shoot the elephants themselves, foregoing the income that could be obtained from them (R. Taylor, 1995).

Overall, the CAMPFIRE program has not been self-financing but has remained dependent upon subsidies from abroad. It may be argued that the program has become an example of the use of transfers from overseas to finance the option or existence value of wildlife. However, the continued disbursement of such transfers has been challenged by antihunting lobbies, notably the Humane Society of the U.S., which is opposed to hunting on ethical grounds. Supporters of the program pose the counterarguments that regulated hunting contributes to conservation, decreases illegal poaching, and is compatible with rising populations of hunted species, in addition to providing employment and income that sustain the human populations of poor areas. Nonetheless, over the long run, the economic returns from wildlife viewing may exceed those from hunting (Roe et al., 1997). Some local people have already entered joint venture partnerships with private sector operators in order to obtain increasing income from "nonconsumptive" wildlife viewing tourism, which can be made compatible with "consumptive" hunting tourism via zoning regulations (R. Taylor, 1995).

The attitudes of local people to the CAMPFIRE program have varied between and within different areas. Although the inhabitants of areas with low human population densities have benefited from considerable increases in income per capita, the returns in more densely populated areas have tended to be relatively low. Income from the program also varies from year to year and, in some districts, decreases in per capita returns during a year of low tourism demand have resulted in discontent, compounded by disagreements over the distribution of the revenue. The aim of cooperative decision-making has not always been upheld as, in some areas, small groups have taken control of revenue allocation without wider consultation.

Conclusions

Zimbabwe's economic problems are not untypical of those of the wider region to which it belongs. During the past three decades, sub-Saharan Africa has experienced, on average, zero per capita growth, the lowest in the world, accompanied by high levels of unemployment and poor life expectancy (Easterly, 1996), and it is only since 1995 that significant growth has occurred. The positive contribution that tourism has made to Zimbabwe, particularly during the 1990s, has been one of the few bright spots within this gloomy scenario. Tourism has become one of the foremost sources of foreign currency earnings and has brought about large increases in income and employment. Moreover, the additional income that tourism provides has helped to finance the increases in human and physical capital that underpin economic growth (van der Ploeg & Tang, 1994).

The CAMPFIRE program exemplifies both the policy instruments that can be used if tourism is to make a long-term contribution to the economy and the effects that it can bring about. It is clear that developing countries can obtain a considerable monetary return from their natural resources and ensure the sustainability of the resources themselves if policy instruments, including quotas, fees, and regulations, are used effectively. The income obtained from tourism can be used to promote improvements in human and physical capital, as illustrated by the expenditure of CAMPFIRE income on schools and medical services, local grinding mills, tractors, roads, and communications. Furthermore, some Zimbabwean villagers have started to build and manage tourist accommodation themselves, thereby obtaining an additional source of income, and other African countries, including Botswana, Malawi, and Zambia, are introducing similar programs (Hess, 1997).

However, tourism is not without its problems. As a means of increasing per capita income, the CAMPFIRE program has proved considerably more successful in some areas than others. Disquiet concerning the program has occurred among some communities in more densely populated areas as per capita cash receipts from tourism have not only been relatively low but have also fluctuated over time, frustrating the overoptimistic expectations of many members of the rural population. District councils in many areas have disbursed less than 50% of the income from wildlife to producer communities. The communities themselves are characterized by an unequal distribution of power so that many members of the community have little involvement in the program and some receive few benefits from it (Hasler, 1995). Notable examples are migrant settlers who are not allocated income from CAMPFIRE, as well as women, who have little involvement in the program or control over cash that is distributed to male heads of households (Bird & Metcalfe, 1995; Nabane, 1995). The associated problem is that without general support from the local community, the long-term future of the program is at risk. The implication is that the distribution of the returns from the CAMPFIRE program should be generally acceptable, providing all members of the community with returns that exceed the social costs the program entails.

Further solutions to such problems include increasing and stabilizing the income that is available for local distribution by means of raising and diversifying tourism demand. However, individual tourism enterprises in Zimbabwe have limited financial resources and expertise in marketing, and the national organization responsible for tourism marketing, along with training, licensing, and grading tourism establishments, has experienced a number of problems. When it was established in 1984, the Zimbabwe Tourist Development Corporation lacked a clear definition and prioritization of its objectives, in particular a clear policy towards the tourism sector. As a parastatal, it lacked the force of government ministries and the resources and expertise necessary for formulating a tourism plan. Its activities were also insufficiently coordinated with those of related government bodies and with those of the private sector, its budget was inadequate, and changes in its leadership were common.

In an attempt to overcome these difficulties during the 1990s, the Zimbabwe Tourism Authority was made responsible for marketing and related activities. However, the coordinating body for the private sector, the Zimbabwe Council for Tourism, had insufficient resources to pay qualified staff to formulate and organize effective strategies for tourism development. Moreover, the Economic and Structural Adjustment Program, which determined the overall economic context during the period, provided virtually no guidance for tourism development and also functioned within the context of an unreconstructed political regime with established interests. The consequence was that the tourism sector has lacked an effective institutional and organizational context and a number of the policies that were implemented resulted in confusion among travel agents, tour operators and tourists themselves (Kaufman, 1992). One example is the different hotel accommodation prices that are supposed to be charged to domestic and foreign tourists (Economist Intelligence Unit, 1992). These have acted as a deterrent to some African tourists and impeded the flexibility of price setting, which is necessary to attract early and late bookings by tour operators and travel agents. Thus, increasing efficiency in the institutional framework for tourism policy formulation and implementation would be beneficial.

Policies towards the development of tourism, along with other sectors of Zimbabwe's economy, should be formulated and implemented, taking account of the wider regional context (Dieke, 1995). Zimbabwe is a member of the Common Market for Eastern and Southern Africa (COMESA), the Regional Tourism Organisation of Southern Africa (RETOSA), and the Southern Africa Development Community (SADC). The latter was established in 1980 and also includes Angola, Botswana, Lesotho, Malawi, Mozambique, Namibia, South Africa, Swaziland, Tanzania, and Zambia. The dominant member of the SADC group is South Africa, which accounts for over 75% of regional GDP compared with Zimbabwe's 3% share. South Africa is already the most important market for international tourism in Zimbabwe, and tourism demand has increased along with rising income in South Africa. Conversely, Zimbabwe's high level of dependence on the South African market means that periods of economic recession in its dominant neighbor are likely to bring about notable decreases in tourism demand. These could have significant adverse effects on Zimbabwe if unaccompanied by rising demand from other origins. South Africa also poses a challenge as a potential competitor to Zimbabwe, both in terms of its growing attraction as a destination for international tourists and as a supplier of the inputs that tourists consume.

This challenge is not insurmountable, as economic theory indicates. Countries that are members of trade blocs can benefit from trade creation by supplying products that are differentiated, in terms of their characteristics and quality, from those of fellow members. Thus, by taking advantage of its distinctive features, Zimbabwe can supply types of tourism, as well as products consumed by tourists, that fill specific niches in the market and that may, in addition, be complementary to those supplied by South Africa, Zambia, and other countries in the region. Natural resource-based tourism is one such case, constituting a broad category that encompasses a variety of tourism types. There is considerable scope for the development of a wider variety of sustainable tourism in different regions of the country and, given the improvements in air accessibility to Zimbabwe, for increasing tourism demand over time. The development of types of tourism such as wildlife viewing, canoeing, white water rafting, trekking, riding, painting, and sculpture would decrease the country's dependence on tourism revenue from hunting, the future of which is uncertain. It would also ensure that a wider range of resources in communal lands is used to benefit the local population. A national institutional and organizational structure providing a sound basis for such developments is clearly necessary. In this respect, cross-country research on the advantages and disadvantages of the structures that are in place elsewhere, as well as on alternative types of natural resource-based tourism, could provide useful guidance not only for Zimbabwe but also for the range of countries attempting to develop tourism sustainably. At the same time, Zimbabwe provides the rest of the world with important insights into the economic policies and structural arrangements that can enable local communities to benefit from their natural resources.

PART III

INSTITUTIONAL STRUCTURES AND STRATEGIC POLICIES

Chapter 13

Institutional Support for Tourism Development in Africa

Erik Holm-Petersen

Summary

Institutional capacity forms a central issue in developing the basic frame for economic development. However, in the Sub-Saharan Africa region severe lack of capacity with respect to general economic management as well as specific management skills within the tourism sector has formed a strong barrier to growth. In general terms, most of the countries have not had the capacity to utilize the tourism development aid provided in the past. Although the African countries have remarkable possibilities for tourism development, few countries have thus been able to utilize this growth potential. The lack of institutional capacity combined with a general lack of understanding among tourism policy-makers has furthermore resulted in a low priority of the tourism sector.

Understanding of the role of the private and public tourism sectors and understanding of the need for integrated planning involving focus on sustainable natural resources, as well as involvement of communities and local entrepreneurs in the tourism development, are prerequisites for setting an optimal tourism development strategy. Awareness creation through politically high profiled regional collaboration can in this respect form one of the means to be used by the tourism sector. Consequently, collaboration within tourism has been established in southern and western Africa and is being developed in eastern Africa.

Tourism development projects, including tourism master plan projects, received donor support in the past. In most cases, however, the effects of this planning work were limited and in recent years donors have changed their support pattern to incorporate a more strategic and comprehensive approach with a clear implementation orientation. In order to get full benefit of this approach, projects have incorporated a strong element of institutional capacity building and increasingly more funds have been made available for institutional support.

Recent trends in the attitudes of African tourism policy-makers, although reluctantly, as well as the policies of donor agencies, thus point at a much more structured and focused development strategy in the future. This strategy will be based on power sharing between the private and public sectors, increased privatization efforts, and a joint sector approach combining tourism and natural resources.

Key words: Institutional support; Tourism development; Nongovernment organizations; Community involvement; Regional cooperation; Bilateral and multilateral donor organizations; Integrated planning; Roles of private and public sectors; Sustainability; Participation of local entrepreneurs; Aid effectiveness; Ecotourism; Integrated program approach; Institutional changes; Capacity building; Political awareness creation; Holistic approach; Donor coordination; Privatization

Introduction

Tourism is recognized worldwide as a strong growth sector (WTO, 1997a) and the international tourism industry forms an economic sector of crucial importance for the world economy, as well as the economy of individual countries. Although being endowed with the basic natural attractions for development of tourism, the majority of the poor African countries, needing the tourism potential more than most other countries to be a basis of economic growth, are generally outside this mainstream development. Tourism has in many of these countries not taken off. As can be seen in the following, the lack of institutional capacity is one of the key factors causing this state of affairs.

Aid to Africa has increased tremendously over the years. African countries receive aid from a vast number of bilateral and multilateral organizations, as well as aid from nongovernmental organizations (NGOs). However, even with this massive influx of aid and technical assistance, it has not been possible in most African countries to generate the needed economic activities to foster sufficient economic growth to alleviate poverty (van de Walle & Johnstone, 1996). Four critical deficiencies have been identified to explain the lack of overall effect of aid to Africa, namely: lack of recipient ownership, poor coordination of aid, inability to cover recurrent costs, and the proliferation of stand-alone projects.

The core problems causing inefficiency in development efforts are, according to the above source, considered to be formed by a combination of the deficiencies in the overall aid management performed by donors and the lack of managerial and organizational capacities in the African countries. Economic growth is not considered to be due to effective public institutions. But an effective public sector combined with political stability provides the framework for enabling the private sector to successfully develop economic activities, a finding that can be widely supported by experience from Asia.

Consequently, the development of institutional capacity forms a central issue in developing the basis and frame for economic activities. The need for institutional capacity building covers a wide spectrum of activities, including planning capabilities, an efficient financial sector, provision of statistical data and information, and skills and professionalism of the labor force required to address the needs of a modern economy (Moore, 1994).

The importance of institutional capabilities leads to a general recognition of the need for focus on institutional building within development aid, as lack of institutional capacity results in noneffective use of scarce resources and decreases the ability to absorb project-specific aid activities. The World Bank (1998a) addresses this particular issue stating: "For human welfare to be advanced, the state's capability—defined as the ability to undertake and promote collective actions efficiently—must be increased" (p. 3). This basic statement is then transferred into a two-part strategy consisting of "Matching the state's role to its capability" and "raise state capability by reinvigorating public institutions" (p. 3). In the Annual Report for 1997 (World Bank, 1998b), the bank states "Sub-Saharan Africa's severe lack of capacity in economic management and related areas is well documented and may be the missing ingredient in the region's development" (p. 45).

The objectives of this chapter are to identify the importance of institutional support, to explore the past trend in the support available to African countries within tourism, and, based on an analysis of the key parameters, to identify the role of institutional support within the future development of Africa's tourism.

However, prior to dealing with these subjects it is essential to define the analytic framework in the context of: the situation within tourism; the tourism product base—protection of natural resources; and community involvement in tourism and wildlife.

The Situation Within Tourism

A key parameter for defining the institutional support to the tourism sector is to understand the roles of the private and public sectors and to foresee the potential conflicts between these two sectors.

The Public Tourism Sector

Tourism involves a large number of value chains, as tourism activities are interlinked with numerous activities within most of the other economic sectors. Although the private sector normally performs the role of developing the business part of tourism development, the public sector plays a crucial role for the overall development and performance of the sector (WTO, 1994). It is thus the public sector that takes care of:

- immigration and customs regulations;
- infrastructure (airports, roads, electricity, communication, water, sewerage);
- control of environmental, social, and cultural aspects of tourism;
- investment policies and incentives (import regulations, tax laws);
- trade regulations (company registration, licensing, building regulations, etc.);
- training of human resources (overall education, hotel schools, and business management training).

In addition, the public sector normally operates a National Tourism Organization (NTO) with a budget for the overall marketing and promotion of the country. Governments also define tourism and aviation policies and set the framework for private sector operations (Wheatcroft, 1994). Finally, governments are normally the custodians of the natural resources in the form of national parks, reserves, and other protected areas. Private sector-owned and -operated reserves and parks only play a significant role within few African countries. As a consequence, government policies and resource allocations with respect to development, operation, and maintenance of national parks and reserves are crucial factors for the development of the main attraction for tourism, namely the flora and fauna.

Without the wildlife and the spectacular natural attractions such as the Okavango Delta in Botswana, Victoria Falls on the border between Zimbabwe and Zambia, Table Mountain in South Africa, the Serengeti in Tanzania, just to mention a few of these World Heritage sites, there would be very limited tourism to Africa. The private and public sectors in Africa therefore need each other in order to develop tourism into a strong economic sector. It is this symbiotic need for collaboration and the need for an integrated and holistic approach to developing the full potential of the sector that, if unfulfilled, tends to create general obstacles for tourism development in many African countries.

Understanding at the government level of the specific needs of the tourism sector and its potential for creating economic development is the first requirement. In particular, it is necessary for governments to understand how tourism can support the national conservation policy with respect to cultural and natural resources and how tourism can be used to distribute economic activities to the village level. Without understanding of the economic value of the natural resources, very limited tourism development can take place.

The prerequisite is thus to form a development policy taking these issues into consideration and to provide a strategic framework for policy implementation. The next step is to transform policies and strategies into specific actions. Without institutional capacity to formulate and implement the policies, governments cannot initiate developments. Therefore, the creation of technically, financially, and politically strong government institutions within tourism and environment/wildlife is necessary to ensure full utilization of the sector's development potential.

In order to ensure this full utilization, it is necessary that governments realize the need for collaboration with the private sector.

The Private Tourism Sector

While the need for public sector institutional support is widely recognized, the similar need for the private sector is much less in focus.

In developed societies with a high level of education, a high local and national spending power, a well-developed transport, infrastructure, and communication network, and an experienced private tourism sector, the general entrepreneurial skills, the competition, and the availability of a range of financial resources ensure a healthy tourism development. However, in the case of most African countries lacking these general resources, the private tourism sector is mostly also weak and fragmented.

Development of tourism in the industrialized countries is often based on leisure products developed for local, regional, or national consumption and then marketed internationally. A very good example of this system can be seen in South Africa, where wildlife tourism (e.g., to Krüger National Park), the wine route, the garden route, etc., were tourism products demanded by the national consumers, but with the political changes the same products were widely and very successfully offered to the international market. The point is that a local demand forms the financial basis for development of sustainable tourism. Also, the experience and know-how gained through local market orientation is crucial in the internationalization process.

Poor African countries, however, are faced with a very different situation. The social and economic structures and, consequently, the local consumption and social and economic behavior are very different from those of the industrialized countries. Because the international tourism business to a large extent is geared towards moving visitors from the developed to the undeveloped part of the world, indigenous local developers have only to a limited extent been able to be successfully involved in the development of tourism businesses aiming at the international market. Tourism has therefore traditionally been considered "a white man's business for white people."

The existing bottlenecks causing the lack of participation of indigenous investors are becoming more and more pronounced because product technology, marketing sophistication, and consumer protection measures in the international markets are getting more and more outspoken within international tourism. The barrier to cross for new entrepreneurs in developing countries seems almost insurmountable.

The results of this situation are reflected in the tourism development pattern in several African countries, and it forms the root cause of the negative political attitude to the private tourism sector among policy-makers.

First of all, the national private tourism sector is often dominated by strong international investors and stakeholders. Second, only limited national and even less local indigenous participation in the sector is found. Third, tourism has not been considered a priority sector; the political commitment to tourism is often very limited and consequently public funds are not devoted to the sector. Finally, because of the above factors, the private tourism sector has been fragmented and it has been difficult to establish strong national tourism associations to represent the interests of major private stakeholders, such as accommodation establishments, car rental companies, restaurants, tourist shops, and tour companies, not to speak of local associations. Tourism establishments have to a large extent focused on their own operations rather than the interests of the sector.

The combination of low public sector interest with private sector fragmentation and lack of commitment forms one of the key reasons for a situation where tourism development potentials have not been utilized.

To move away from this often deadlock situation, it is necessary not only to undertake public sector institutional building, as described above, but it is equally important to strengthen the private sector institutions and to support general efforts to ensure as wide a participation as possible in the development of the sector.

The Tourism Product Base: Protection of Natural Resources

A high population growth, combined with a low level of technical and financial skills within the agricultural sector, where traditional methods are still highly in use, has resulted in a need for new land. This need has been combined with a move away from communal use of land to "private plots," and a more intensive land use system has been introduced.

The wide open spaces have in this process to a still larger extent been transformed into small plots behind fences. The role of wildlife has been changed from being a natural and integrated part of land utilization to being a problem for crop production. As a result, more and more land has been depleted of freely moving wildlife and the wildlife left has been confined to protected areas. As said by Dr. Western, the Director for Kenya Wildlife Service, we are moving towards creating mega zoos for the wildlife.

However, even within national parks, the protection of the game is still problematic. The declining numbers of rhinos, elephants, and gorillas are obvious examples of what has happened. The subject of sustainable conservation is widely debated (Western & Wright, 1994) but a clear way ahead has not been defined. However, it is recognized that utilization of the economic value of the natural resources is necessary for protecting the resource for the future. Therefore, changes in the institutions working with conservation towards being "business oriented" and towards understanding and accepting the obvious link between tourism and conservation are of crucial importance.

This management-oriented approach should include a very open policy involving the private tourism sector, the communities adjoining the protected areas, and the public in general. This involvement should include definition of ways and means to obtain direct benefits for stakeholders as well as defining strategies for long-term sustainable use of the natural resources.

Community Involvement in Tourism and Wildlife

Traditionally, in most African countries national parks and protected areas were created by the governments with limited involvement of the private sectors. Land was taken away from communities and people were resettled to provide areas protected for the sake of biodiversity. Conservation measures were therefore considered to be in conflict with the interests of the communities. The change in the approach to conservation, combined with the increased understanding of the economic value of the natural resources for tourism purposes, has initiated a new development.

The private sector has moved into conservation partly through creation of private sector conservancies on farm land (transferring farm land into private game farms) and partly through involving communities in wildlife conservation in buffer zones adjoining the protected areas. The possibilities of private sector ownership of game and creation of direct economic income from the game through tourism have changed the overall conservation approach. The process of introduction of new strategic concepts has only been possible through legislative changes combined with institutional changes within management of national parks. In addition, it has been necessary to create an institutional basis at the community level in order to enable the communities to play their role in the sustainable management of natural resources.

Trends in Institutional Support

Institutional support to the tourism sector has gradually changed with the improved understanding of the parameters for sustainable development. However, it is important to analyze this process of change to improve future institutional support.

The Historical Context

Africa's particular endowment with wildlife and natural scenery formed an early basis for tourism development. Spearheading the mass tourism development in the 1960s and 1970s were Murchsion Falls and Queen Elisabeth National Park in Uganda, Victoria Falls in Zimbabwe, the traditional safaris products of Kenya, and the beaches of Mozambique as a playground for tourists from Zimbabwe and South Africa. At that time the developments were generally spearheaded by private sector operators supported by the national park administration trained by the past colonial administration.

In order to initiate tourism development in other African countries, so-called tourism master plans were developed for most countries south of Sahara. For instance Hoff & Overgaard produced a tourism master plan for Ghana in the early 1970s financed by the Danish International Development Assistance (DANIDA). The trend in that period was that all countries should have master plans, including countries such as Rwanda and Burundi— plans that never materialized and were to a large extent collecting dust on the shelves of the national tourism offices. However, other plans were particularly useful, for instance, the planning framework for the development of Diani Beach south of Mombasa in Kenya, which today forms one of the key tourist areas of Kenya.

The master plan work was supported by a wide number of bilateral donors, as well as through UNDP-supported WTO projects. Generally, plans were orientated towards matching the national attractions formed by the flora, fauna, and scenic beauty with the international market demand. Institutional building in a wider sense did not form a core part of the work undertaken, but often the public sector was designated to have a central role within training of tourism staff, transport of tourists by the national carriers, development and operation of accommodation facilities, and marketing organizations. Consequently, a number of parastatals were established during that period.

Because of the need for skilled human resources within the tourism sector, the master plans often identified the need for staff training, and the development of hotel schools was a standard part of the master plans. Consequently, a number of hotel schools, often supported by technical assistance from the International Labor Organization/United Nations Development Program (ILO/UNDP) or bilateral donors, such as Swiss assistance, were established. Hotel schools were thus developed in Kenya (Utali), Zimbabwe (Bulawayo), Uganda (Fairview), and Mozambique (Andalucia), just to mention some of the initiatives taken.

The plans likewise identified the importance of marketing, and governments therefore established public sector marketing organizations, often named national tourism boards. Likewise, government initiatives were taken to provide tourism facilities and government-owned and -operated hotels were widespread in most African countries. Facilities were mainly developed in national parks, but government-owned prestige luxury hotels were also constructed in capitals and main cities. Scarce financial resources were allocated for the development of prestige projects. and the operations, often under expensive foreign management, continued to drain the public resources for years.

The development strategy had a strong public sector focus combined with technical support from the donor community for specific issues. Very limited emphasis was given to the private sector and, although the public sector was in focus, institutional building as such did not play a central role.

A period of widespread civil wars and political instability in some of the African countries, combined with general mismanagement within the public sector, resulted in a virtual collapse of most of the public sector initiatives in the tourism sector. As a consequence, tourism in Africa suffered. Developments were taking place, not because of, but despite, government efforts.

The negative development occurred on almost all levels but could most seriously be found with respect to:

- depletion of the natural resource base through mismanagement of the resources, increased population pressure on the land, and poaching;
- depletion of the human resource base in the public sector resulting in very poor performance of public services;
- a downward spiral in performance of the public sector-owned and -operated facilities;
- complete lack of resources to undertake marketing activities;
- deterioration of the infrastructure.

Under these circumstances the private sector tried to develop tourism with limited government input, and on the basis of private sector initiatives success stories can be recorded in countries like Kenya, Zimbabwe, and Botswana.

The Current Situation

The trends described above were leading tourism in most of the African countries into an increasingly difficult situation. However, during the 1980s and 1990s there was a change of direction. Internal factors such as political changes combined with improved economic stabilization paved the way for new developments. In some cases the economies were totally restructured from a plan economy to a market economy and in most cases economies were made more open. However, also external factors played a role in the changing situation as donors took new initiatives and adopted new approaches. Some of the important external related factors are listed in the following.

Focus on Management of the Natural Resources

Major donors such as the World Bank and the European Union (EU) recognized that without efforts to protect the environment, the natural resources would be depleted with strong negative environmental results and with major negative implications for income generation through tourism. This recognition came as a result of a growing general consensus on the need for a sustainable development defined by the World Commission on Environment and Development, also named the Brundtland Commission, in their report *Our Common Future* as "development that meets the needs of the present without compromising the ability of future generations to meet their own needs" (World Commission on Environment and Development, 1987, p. 20). The report formed a breakthrough in a new approach to development planning and the work has later been followed by several new initiatives within environment and development.

As a consequence of this change in focus, the World Bank- and EU-supported national park and protection area development plans and actions were given stronger emphasis.

Numerous project examples exist, but good examples are the International Development Association's (IDA) project on the Institutional Capacity Building for Protected Areas Management and Sustainable Use (ICB-PAMSU) program in Uganda, the EU-funded Zambia Wildlife Authority project in Zambia, the World Bank-funded Kenya Wildlife Service project in Kenya, and a number of projects in Tanzania, Zimbabwe, and Botswana. All these projects are aiming at sustainability of the management of natural resources through:

- Training of the management staff and bringing in a new type of managerial staff in order to improve overall management. The area includes organizational and financial management.
- Provision of new equipment and facilities to boost morale and provide the basis for improving the managerial and operational functions, including antipoaching activities.
- Improvement of technical skills, including research programs.
- Park utilization plans, including park management plans.
- Improved infrastructure to make the parks more accessible.
- Involvement of the communities in the management of natural resources and ensuring that benefits of the resources are given to communities.
- Focusing on commercial activities aiming at financial self-sustainability.

A successful implementation of the above strategies will often depend upon tourism as a key to creation of income and commercial activities within the national parks as well as the adjoining communities. Without income from tourism, protection of natural resources is seldom financially viable and the protection cannot be long-term sustainable.

The concept of linking protection of the environment to community development and further to tourism activities is gaining widespread support, not only from the multinational donors mentioned above but also from a wide number of bilateral donors and NGOs. For instance, the World Wildlife Fund (WWF), the World Conservation Union (IUCN), Deutsche Gesellschaft für Technische Zusammenarbeit (GTZ), Swedish International Development Cooperation Agency (SIDA), and USAID have initiated, separately or jointly, a number of projects in Africa within the above-mentioned field.

A direct focus of this strategy is building up of the capacity of the institutions dealing with management and operation of the national natural resources.

Focus on Community Participation

Donors and, in particular, NGOs are well aware of the need for involving local communities in the development of tourism and management of the natural resources. Numerous projects are found in this field, such as the CAMPFIRE (Communal Areas Management Programme for Indigenous Resources) project in Zimbabwe, the protection of gorillas in Uganda, the Living in a Finite Environment (LIFE) program in Namibia, and the Community Wildlife Service in Kenya, just to mention a few well-known examples. The work undertaken underlines the need for a long-term donor involvement in the community development, including support of institutional capacity building, project management training, and coordination with other stakeholders (Western & Wright, 1994).

Focus on the Private Sector

The private sector support contains components on all levels. Most donor organizations provide specific programs to support the private sector. While donors and NGOs undertake assistance on the community level, international lending organizations such as the International Finance Corporation (IFC) supported by the Africa Project Development Facility (APDF) provide finance and financial guidance to commercial tourism projects. Also, the UNDP and bilateral private sector programs are aiming at private sector support.

The private sector focus has a particular element of assistance to indigenous entrepreneurs. Examples are a World Bank-supported project in Zimbabwe, and the UNDP assistance in Uganda to Uganda Tourism Association under the private sector program.

Reduction of the Role of the Public Sector

Governments are not capable of successful operation of financially viable tourism facilities and services. Based on recognition of this fact, governments in Africa have generally undergone a privatization process where accommodation facilities and services, including in some cases the national carrier, have been privatized. This trend has given a boost to the tourism sector and has provided a basis for development of a much healthier sector.

Focus on Integrated and Sustainable Tourism Programs

Previously, the available bilateral as well as the UNDP resources were only sufficient to fund the production of a master plan, which on average would cost between US$0.5 and 1 million depending on the comprehensiveness of the study, or to support a specific and short-term activity, but resources were generally insufficient to support the institutional building capacity of the private and public sectors within tourism in the country, not to mention the actual implementation of the planning work. The integrated program approach involving long-term commitments and provision of necessary resources (programs can easily run for at least 2–3 years involving grants in the range of US$3–5 million), however, came into existence through the Fourth Lomé Convention ("Lomé IV Convention," 1996) providing provisions related to four main areas of sector support: human resources and institutional development, product development, market development, research and information. Furthermore, a joint declaration between the ACP countries places strong emphasis on trade and service activities aiming at general economic development.

EU-funded tourism programs aiming at all or most of the above-mentioned activities including institutional building are at present in existence or under development in Uganda, Tanzania, Kenya, Mozambique, Zambia, Namibia, Zimbabwe, Senegal, and Botswana.

These programs aim at an overall and sustainable development of tourism in the countries involved. Although the projects are generally linked to the public sectors, they aim at developing a better understanding between the private and public sectors, as well as a political understanding of the importance of giving power and influence to the private sector as part of the development process. The general approach is to ensure that the public sector only plays the roles previously outlined in the sections above, while the private sector plays the roles related to commercial operations in general. This means that governments should give a specific development mandate to the private sector.

Fostering of Regional Cooperation

As part of Lomé IV, the EU has supported development of regional tourism organizations within the ACP countries. The formation of regional tourism institutions has been an important part of the EU overall tourism development strategy within the ACP countries. The regional tourism organizations created are in particular focusing on tourism marketing and promotion; but the regional programs also include product development, support to an improved information base (tourism statistics), and training issues. Major programs were first initiated in the Caribbean, followed by the South Pacific, and finally followed by assistance to the SADC countries. In 1995 EU thus supported the initial steps to form a regional tourism organization consisting of the former Southern Africa Development Coordination Conference (SADCC) countries and South Africa. After a series of regional workshops the Regional Tourism Organisation of Southern Africa (RETOSA) came into being. Although all the countries involved agreed to the establishment of RETOSA in 1996, the organization only became operational by 1997 due to internal power discussions between the private and public sectors. While Lesotho originally had the tourism portfolio for the SADCC countries, Mauritius took over the portfolio when it joined SADC.

The eastern African countries were at a sideline of this development, although Tanzania is a member of RETOSA. The strong development of tourism to southern Africa, with very high growth rates experienced in Republic of South Africa and Zimbabwe and also partly in Namibia, combined with the formation of RETOSA, increased the competition faced by eastern Africa. Tourism development efforts initiated at the national level through assistance from EU, the World Bank, and UNDP have therefore been followed by initiatives through British aid (ODA) to support the creation of a regional tourism setup for eastern Africa.

Also West Africa has moved into regional cooperation, at least with tourism marketing, and the Economic Community of West African States (ECOWAS) has been supported by EU in this respect.

Types of Institutional Support

As can be seen from the above, support for the African tourism sector contains a whole spectrum of initiatives, including technical issues such as formulation of training programs, production of marketing material, participation in tourism fairs, purchase of computers, and formulation of integrated national tourism plans. However, in order to ensure long-term sustainability, the programs also focus on building up the institutional capacity. The institutional capacity building projects contain a large number of facets, such as:

- Reorganization of central institutions working with tourism issues (tourism ministries, tourism boards, national parks boards, statistical departments working with tourism statistics, and tourism training institutions).
- Training of staff in the central institutions, either through attachment of international advisors and consultants or through training abroad of the staff.
- Prrovision of equipment to support the institutional efficiency.
- Formulation of strategies and policies through definition of new legislation, white papers, etc., aiming at a clear definition of the roles of the private and public tourism sectors and aiming at enforcing improved collaboration between the two sectors. Furthermore, an important subject has been to ensure long-term financial sources direct or channeled from the tourism sector to the national institutions working with training and marketing/promotion, to reduce the institutional dependence on the ministries of finance.
- Development of regional tourism institutions to facilitate tourism development in the member countries and to undertake regional tourism marketing and promotion.
- Assistance to community participation in tourism through specific community-related projects but also through development of community institutions to support the development.
- Strengthening of the private tourism sector, in particular indigenous entrepreneurs involved in tourism development.

Future Possibilities

Deriving from the past experience, a path for the future content of institutional support for the tourism sector can be outlined.

General Observations

African governments are faced with numerous resource problems within all sectors, but particularly the health and education sectors require a major proportion of the existing resources. Consequently, resources available for tourism and wildlife are limited. It is under these circumstances of paramount importance that the private tourism sector mandate is clearly defined and that the role of the sector is enhanced. Furthermore, it is important that financial systems are created to channel resources from tourism to public sector institutions to supplement direct public sector contributions.

Redistributing the roles of the private and public sectors and setting up new financial sources for the long-term support of public sector institutions form key steps towards a revival of the tourism development efforts. To achieve this, new legislative measures and new political understanding are required. Political awareness creation is thus a key instrument in ensuring the required changes.

In most cases this change does not take place without involvement and assistance from the international donor community. Institutional changes and institutional building are thus very important elements in the overall strategy of change. The time of piecemeal support for specific technical issues has passed (it may come back when the new institutions have been developed).

Integration of development efforts within the tourism and environmental sectors forms another important issue. In some countries tourism and wildlife are dealt with by the same ministries, but in other cases two different ministries are involved. In some African countries "culture" is dealt with by a third ministry, increasing the need for coordination.

The involvement of donors and, in particular, the commitment made by EU, UNDP, and the World Bank towards long-term development of tourism and wildlife sectors indicate the increasing understanding of the importance of long-term involvement and coordination. This has already had a positive effect on the tourism development of the countries in the region. If this long-term commitment is continued and the coordination of the two sectors further enhanced, tourism to Africa south of Sahara is likely to change in the coming years.

Obstacles to the Development

The positive expectations for the future are faced with grave difficulties.

Depletion of the Natural Resources

Efficient management of the natural resources, including development of sustainable sources of income for planning and protection through donor assistance, is required to keep Africa as a tourism destination of the future. The integration of tourism and wildlife planning must be enhanced, not only on the national level, but in particular on the regional and local levels. Therefore, decentralization and institutional building on these levels form the key to development. If this process is not initiated, it is likely that the wildlife resources will be depleted and Africa's attraction as a tourist destination (except for some small specific locations) will diminish.

Community Involvement

Spreading of the economic benefits of tourism and involving communities in tourism development and protection of wildlife are essential for the long-term survival of the sector. Donor support and, in particular, NGO support to communities, combined with an overall strategy giving communities a particular role, constitute the way forward. Failure to understand the importance of this subject will provide a long-term obstacle to development.

Participation of Local Entrepreneurs

The international focus on ecotourism should be used to refocus Africa's tourism to the local level involving to a larger extent communities and local entrepreneurs. Without this decentralization of tourism, local participation cannot be achieved and tourism will not form the growth sector of the future.

Redistribution of Roles

Governments of Africa have to some extent looked at tourism as a new form of colonialism. Consequently, governments have not been keen to give power to private tourism sectors that, to a large extent, were seen as dominated by nonindigeneous entrepreneurs. However, the sector cannot develop if this political attitude towards the sector prevails. Governments must reconsider their position, reducing the public role to the essential issues of setting the framework for development. This new understanding of the distribution of roles should make it possible for private/public sector tourism boards to be dominated by the private sector and should also provide new financial means to undertake activities within marketing and training.

The Role of the Donor Community

Continued and enhanced donor support for an integrated and coordinated development of the sector is at the present stage crucial for moving the sector ahead. Because of the fragmentation of the private industry and because of the general lack of political willingness, combined with limited financial resources to assist the development, tourism to Africa needs outside assistance to move ahead. Effective sector support aimed at achieving set goals will require efficient government institutions. Consequently, institutional capacity building will form a strong element in the donor program design.

Aid Effectiveness

Donors and NGOs are at present making a vast amount of resources available toward institutional building, not only within the tourism sector, but also within other sectors of the economy. The technical assistance provided by the donors is at present only monitored occasionally. Because of the magnitude of resources involved, it is expected that donors will gradually place more emphasis on control of the effectiveness of the resources spent. Output quality will thus come into focus. As it is difficult to measure the outcome quality of institutional support projects, donors will have to give more emphasis to project preparation. Also coordination of projects among donors is essential. Setting up of coordination committees for integrated sector development programs would constitute a step forward. In setting up institutional development projects, donors can furthermore ensure a strong focus on the essential processes and components, as described in this chapter. A holistic and integrated approach will be necessary for the results to be positive. In this context the most crucial factor will be to ensure the political commitment to the process of change, as described throughout this chapter.

Conclusion

Sub-Saharan Africa's general lack of tourism development is not caused by the lack of potential. The core problem has been to identify why the wanted tourism development has not taken place. Findings strongly indicate that the severe lack of economic management and institutional capacity, as also stated by the World Bank, forms the missing ingredient.

The region has, over the years, been provided with a considerable amount of assistance with respect to developing the tourism sector. However, if the aid has not had the envisaged effects, it is largely due to the following key factors:

- lack of institutional capacity;

- lack of political commitment;
- discrepancies in the technical approach.

It has been found that institutional capacity building must form part of a comprehensive tourism development program and that the program must be wide enough to incorporate protection of the natural resources in the form of sustainable tourism products, as well as participation of local entrepreneurs and communities.

A joint holistic donor approach with donors coordinating the various components into a comprehensive tourism development strategy is required. The integrated tourism development programs developed by the EU under Lomé IV have given a new dimension to this approach within tourism. The World Bank works on a similar approach with respect to protection of the natural resources in a number of African countries. A combination and integration of the programs undertaken by these two key donor agencies could provide the new basis for adopting the necessary holistic approach to sustainable tourism development and could bring institutional capacity building within natural resources and tourism closer to each other.

Tourism policy-makers in Africa must first of all realize that the aim is not to get as much donor assistance as possible (getting aid has been a target in itself) but that the aid must be coordinated and targeted. Policy-makers must therefore adopt an integrated approach and demand donors to form part of a comprehensive development strategy.

Second, political commitment to tourism and commitment to building up the institutional capacity must be prerequisites as part of the development strategy. This commitment should be measured in the form of tourism legislation, tourism policy documents or white papers, and budgetary commitments.

Finally, tourism policy-makers must understand the need for collaboration with the private sector and must be ready to hand over power, resources, and activities to the private sector, where the private sector is found to be the best implementing body.

With all these components in place and through donor assistance programs to support the tourism institutions, tourism in Africa can form a strong economic locomotive in development of the region.

Chapter 14

Tourism and the Transatlantic Slave Trade: Some Issues and Reflections

Nathan K. Austin

Summary

Interest in heritage as a tourism attraction is growing worldwide. This is because of the perceived importance of such an attraction in enhancing economic and social development. A number of African countries have also joined on this bandwagon and, with assistance from the World Tourism Organization (WTO) and the United Nations Educational, Scientific and Cultural Organization (UNESCO), have initiated measures to revisit and preserve the events of the transatlantic slave trade as heritage tourism products. However, there is a need to exercise considerable care in the development and utilization of such events for tourism development purposes considering the sensitive impact that such events may have on black Africa and also on black–white race relations. Thus, this chapter argues that these events may raise ethical and other such related questions that, in the main, might be considered incompatible with the traditional leisure-oriented image of tourism. Furthermore, issues of differing perspectives on authenticity and objectivity are also difficult to resolve. Similarly, it is worth noting also that an understanding of visitor emotions and the need for the "education" of potential visitors, hosts, and project planners about the current relevance of the history of the slave trade will be most beneficial to its utilization in tourism. Relevant policy initiatives should place importance on the symbolism and essence of the current relevance of the history of the trade to black Africa. Finally, the success of the development of tourism in Africa within this milieu and the need for a total visitor experience would require a coordinated and cooperative effort, if the potential benefits of bringing the people of black African descent together for their mutual benefit is to be realized.

Key words: Transatlantic slave trade; Race; Black Africa; Diaspora; Tourism; Emotions; Visitors; Presentation; Interpretation

Introduction

The relationship between tourism and heritage has been recognized ("Heritage and Tourism," 1996; Prentice, 1993). As used here, "heritage" refers to both physical and intangible things of value, of society's past creation and/or inheritance, which have been passed on to the present generation. Key components of heritage might include historical sites or buildings (e.g., forts and castles), or cultural heritage (e.g., local handicrafts, norms), or still others (e.g., transport museums, shrines, etc.). In tourism terms, their importance stems from the fact that they are attractions, which are often promoted as heritage products for tourist "consumption." If properly managed, in presentation and interpretation terms, they can offer excellent opportunities to create economic benefits for the host destinations.

Thus, in Africa, as elsewhere in the developed and developing worlds, there is also a growing interest in heritage tourism, as reflected in the 1995 Cairo Declaration (Economic Commission for Africa [ECA], 1996b). The Declaration, which was adopted under the aegis of the World Tourism Organization (WTO), committed African leaders to support the United Nations Educational, Scientific and Cultural Organization (UNESCO) and other international interest groups and agencies in their attempt to identify and preserve for posterity a number of World Heritage sites. One such initiative was the "Silk Route Project" for the former Eastern European countries and, in the African context, the "Slave Route Project" (WTO, 1997d). In relation to the latter, it was expected that the development of the "Slave Route Project" would enhance the promotion of cultural and thus heritage tourism as part of Africa's economic development strategies.

However, there is concern that the utilization of the historical events of the transatlantic slave trade in tourism development may evoke ethical and other questions. There are many reasons for this, not the least being the sensitivity associated with the trade. Some critics would argue that the "Slave Route Project," as presently conceived, is perhaps a poignant reminder, albeit painfully, of "man's inhumanity to man." There are, of course, other issues (e.g., required intergovernmental cooperation, host reception, interpretation and presentation including marketing, particularly relating to data and artefact, overall authenticity and relevancy, etc.); these issues merit further consideration.

This chapter considers these issues, given the importance of tourism in global, regional, and national economies. The chapter also argues that there is a need to balance economic benefits that such heritage products can engender against the inevitable emotions, problems, and difficulties stemming from the interchange so that tourism does not become a particular handicap. Before considering the above issues, however, it seems reasonable to provide a brief historical context of the transatlantic trade and to assess its implications for Africa.

The Transatlantic Slave Trade

While human exploitation had existed in Africa before the advent of contact with Europe (Lovejoy, 1981), the trade in black Africans across the Atlantic beginning in the 16th century represented a new form of enslavement characterized by brutality and based on race. Until 1860, when the slave trade was formally abolished, the trade in Africans was part of the triangular trade between Africa, Europe, and the New World (Sallie, 1994). In its simplest form, the slave trade involved the shipment of textiles, jewels, knives, kettles, sheets, mirrors, and guns from Europe to Africa for the acquisition of captives, who were then shipped to the New World in return for sugar, tobacco, and cotton for the European markets. Curtin (1971) suggests that some 10 million unfortunate black Africans were landed on the shores of America as slaves during the trade. However, it is often argued that an assessment of the real magnitude of black African lives affected should include those who survived as slaves in the New World and those who lost their lives as a result of the violent process of capture, inhumane "storage" of human cargo at the coastal fortifications, and subsequent appalling conditions of shipment across the Atlantic.

Africans then saw other Africans who did not belong to their kinship or tribal group-ing as outsiders. It was therefore possible for the rulers and the military and trading elite, aided by the widespread supply of European firearms and driven by the desire for other imported items, to engage in the capture of "outsiders" into servitude (Obadina, 1998). European financiers also provided the substantial and high-risk capital required for slave trading expeditions from Europe (Inikori, 1982). These contributed significantly to the pursuit of the enslavement of one another to the point where it became, to a large extent, an act of survival for many African states of the time (Rodney, 1989). African ruling classes and the elite thus played an active role in the supply of captives for the trade.

Once in the Americas, the captive became a slave for life under a sophisticated and legally sanctioned system of racial oppression (Allen, 1994). This view is also shared by Temperly (1996), who argued that "the most oppressive [of] regimes as measured by the degree of power wielded by owners and the lack of protection afforded bondsmen" (p. 145). The slaves and their early descendants suffered segregation and the denial of eco-nomic means (A. H. Jenkins, 1995), designations of lower caste status, discrimination, in-timidation, and disfranchisement (Button, 1989; Philipp, 1994). Today, the descendants of those African slaves survive as nationals of countries scattered across the Americas, where many of them continue to suffer subtle forms of racial oppression (Allen, 1994; Hacker, 1992; Sigelman & Welch, 1991).

Consequences for Africa

The event of the transatlantic slave trade is the major social experience that has since shaped the destiny of all the people of black African descent. While independent Africa has created its fair share of the catastrophes that plague its people, the trade in its people remains the dominant factor explaining the socioeconomic situation of black people.

Sallie (1994) argues that the slave trade is a fundamental factor in the disparity in eco-nomic status between Europe and Africa. Inikori (1982) and Rodney (1989) explain fur-ther that the African continent lost to the slave trade the prime of its labor force aged between 15 and 35, at a time when productive activity on the continent was heavily de-pendent on human labor. The continent was left with a declining and mature labor force and was denied the natural compelling pressures of population growth and its generally consequent positive benefits of increasing ingenuity, economic adventure, and increased production. Although there was exchange implicit in the slave trade, the exchange was largely for the purposes of survival and the pursuit of warfare rather than a production-oriented exchange. The existence of the slave trade, thus, retarded the development of a commodity exchange market, which is essential for economic growth.

From a social development perspective, the African continent was a theater of constant conflict and warfare. This destabilized the social order, creating a situation that encour-aged frequent warfare (Inikori, 1982). A general feeling of social insecurity reigned (Rodney, 1989), adding to the significance of the lack of any productive activity. The slave trade decimated and weakened the continent, preparing the grounds for subsequent coloniza-tion, which, through the massive exploitation of its mineral and forest resources, contrib-uted to the socioeconomic underdevelopment of black Africa.

The most important and singularly dominant legacy of the transatlantic slave trade, how-ever, is how the rest of the world has since related to the black people of African descent. The presumed racial inferiority of the black race, which became ingrained in the world community primarily as a result of the trade in black people, continues to define political, economic, and social relations between peoples of black African descent and the rest of the world (A. H. Jenkins, 1995). The issue is not that of individual esteem or achievement but that of belonging to a race at birth that is socioeconomically alienated and disadvantaged. Whether one's ancestry is in part or fully of black African origin, the presumed derogatory designation and social stigma remains. Being black today is not only determined by the color of the skin but by one's black African ancestry. It is this singular overriding racial legacy and its link to the transatlantic slave trade that presents, arguably, a unique opportunity for the development of tourism in sub-Saharan Africa.

Opportunities for Development in Tourism

Bound together not as a "pure" race but as a group of people who share common historical and social experiences, struggles, and origin (Hecht, Collier, & Ribeau, 1993; Isaacs, 1964), people of black African descent, through their dispersion outside their homeland, share a collective identity and destiny that is centered on Africa. For those in the diaspora, an identification with the origins of the transatlantic slave trade and with Africa as the ancestral "home" is increasingly being perceived as the missing link in their quest to find their roots and to understand their collective sociohistorical experience, an act that is considered necessary for their self-realization (Bruner, 1996).

As a result, African-Americans in particular have been visiting sites associated with the events of the slave trade. For example, in 1990, by conservative estimates, a total of only 609 African-Americans visited the Cape Coast Castle, Ghana—a preserved former slave castle. The level of visitation of African-Americans to the site had risen to an estimated 2,617 by 1994 (N. K. Austin, 1997). Though these numbers are relatively small, its significance lies in the potential market of millions of people in the diaspora with African ancestry, especially in the Americas, the Pacific, and the Caribbean regions. For Africa, with its generally deteriorating economies, it is the growing significance of tourism in terms of employment, foreign currency earnings, and the unique position it occupies as the destination where the beginning of those historic events took place that is most beneficial. Furthermore, as noted, the WTO and UNESCO, recognizing the economic and social dimensions of the tragic events of the slave trade, have combined their efforts in the development of the "Slave Routes Project." The project intends to study the deep-rooted causes and methods used in the transatlantic slave trade, identify, restore, and promote sites, buildings, and places associated with it, through tourism development (WTO, 1997d). The international dimension of the project gives prominence to the development, confirming its relevancy and assures its successful execution, with regard to planning. However, for these opportunities to be favorably exploited, a number of major difficulties need to be overcome, especially as a result of the emotional sensitivity of the history of the transatlantic slave trade. These issues are the subject of the following section.

Issues of Concern

As noted, there are many "areas of concern," mainly relating to the utilization of the events of the transatlantic slave trade in tourism development. They include, for instance, the question of presentation and interpretation of the events, among others. Each issue area is identified and briefly analyzed below.

Ethical Presentation and Interpretation

The utilization of the historic events of the trade in tourism has to contend with the ethical dilemma relating to the sensitivity of those events to the descendants of black

African slaves and its potential encouragement of racism amongst black people, towards whites. In addition, it has to overcome the difficulties of different and often racially biased perception of what constitutes objectivity and authenticity in the presentation and interpretation of data and exhibits associated with the events of the trade (N. K. Austin, 1997). Depending on how it is presented and interpreted, it could create an even wider rift between blacks and whites.

Leisure Orientation

The events associated with the trade do not fit too well within the current leisure-oriented image of tourism. Visitor sites, for example, generally described as tourist/heritage/cultural attractions or sites, assume a leisure orientation, at least in part, for the visitor. Thus, their management allows for the provision of varying degrees of fun and leisurely orientation. However, for many visitors, including those whose ancestors were directly involved in the trade, visitation to a site or exhibit associated with the events of the trade is not likely to be leisure oriented. The difficulty therefore lies in the management of the needs of a continuum of different visitor groups, from the "serious" to the "frivolous" (Pfafenberger, 1983).

Differing Visitor Expectation and Desires

The needs of visitors, as determined by their expectations and desires of the site or exhibit, have the potential for causing dissatisfaction where visitor experience is not perceived to match those expectations and desires. As a result, management of such sites and exhibits may be required, for example, to provide avenues for different learning experiences for visitors. But therein also lies the development of multivariate views and perceptions of the site/exhibit, which has the potential for the "continued attraction of visitors with different and often contradictory expectations" (Austin, 1997, p. 169) and desires. Management decisions made in this regard ultimately determine who visits the site or exhibit and thus its viability.

Relations Between Africa and the African Diaspora

It has been observed that some black people of African descent living outside the continent of Africa do not regard themselves as having very much in common with Africa. Such views are confirmed by several authors (Bruner, 1996; Gilroy, 1993), who have variously claimed alleged feelings of "outsider status" experienced by Americans of African descent on visits to Africa and the declining relevance of Africa to blacks in the diaspora. The reasons for this state of deliberate or unintentional nonidentification with black Africa and its people by a section of those of the African diaspora are varied. They are due, in part, to the long period of separation from Africa and its culture and the fact that Africans in the diaspora have developed a new "distinct" culture in their "new home." Another contributory factor is the painful reality that Africa has undergone an entirely different and unpleasant evolutionary growth. From the early days of contact with Europe, Africa has suffered the detrimental trade in its labor force, the foreign dominance of colonialism, the hopeless dependency period of neo-colonialism, through to its current marginalized socioeconomic status in the world community. Many Africans in the diaspora are therefore grateful not to be a part of this immensely disadvantaged position of the continent. For others, an association with Africa implies an identification with the consequences of the transatlantic slave trade, which they claim portrays and underlines an existing perception of powerlessness of Africans in the diaspora and which does not add positively to their efforts at the total liberation of the black man (Hooks, 1990).

The Essence of the Visit

How ordinary Africans, as the destination hosts, see and relate to the African diaspora in particular and how project organizers view those undertaking the visit, whether as "tourists," "visitors," "pilgrims," or even "foreigners," is of major importance. Africans in the diaspora on visits to the African continent see themselves as "coming home." This feeling of "coming home" and the reconnection with the land of their fathers represents the essence of the visit. In reality, most are received as strangers (Bruner, 1996) and treated as such by the hosts. Furthermore, for most of the African countries involved, the priority of the development of the events of the transatlantic slave trade in tourism is the potential economic gain. The challenge is the need to refocus the priority on the essence of the "visit."

Intergovernmental Cooperation

The routes of the trade are spread across several contemporary national boundaries. Therefore, as envisaged by the WTO and UNESCO, the process of creating a total experience for the visitor will require a great deal of intergovernmental planning and cooperation, in the actual development, utilization, and promotion of the "slave routes." The possibility of individual countries developing perceived unique aspects of their heritage, which are of relevance to the trade, irrespective of what other countries within the same region are doing, could result in an undifferentiated and unconnected visitor experience.

Marketing the Sensitive

It is highly probable that the sensitivity of the events of the transatlantic slave trade would interfere with the efficient and effective marketing of the development in tourism. Marketing decisions relating to issues such as target markets, market viability, and extent of communication, among others, may be moderated by the emotional sentiments of visitors, political influence, and the persuasion of other stakeholders. For example, it is currently argued that the nature of museums, relative to their role in tourism for the purposes of visitation, is such that general marketing principles and objectives such as revenue generation cannot be applied to them without significant modification (Bradford, 1994). Similarly, the nature and purpose of the development of the events of the transatlantic slave trade in tourism may require some modification in the application of the general concepts of marketing to it. The reason is that it has social implications, which transcend the traditional economic success criteria of efficient and effective marketing.

Some Reflections

On the basis of the analysis described, it is possible to prompt a number of reflections.

A Subjective Perspective

The potential for the inappropriate utilization of the historic events of the trade in tourism development is real. However, its development in Africa represents a unique opportunity for bringing those events of the past to the present generation in its natural setting. Moreover, all accounts and/or presentation of historical events are subjective even when not so intended. Therefore, it is difficult if not impossible to devise, in the strictest sense of the word, an objective and authentic presentation of those historic events.

Those events are of such emotional significance and contention for different groups of people that their presentation and interpretation in tourism development will always be accompanied by inherent problems of differing perspectives. Often issues underlying visitor-held emotional postures will be reflective of larger societal considerations, such as the existing economic disparity between Africa and Europe. Thus, such attempts at presentation and interpretation will always be contested by interest groups, experts, racial groupings, etc., irrespective of the approach taken.

As already mentioned, efforts to incorporate the differing views will often result in the depiction of a multivariate picture of what those events represent. They will in turn contribute to the continued attraction of visitors with different and often contradictory expectations, which may have to be satisfactorily met over time, with ever-increasing multiplicity of fudged presentations, interpretation, and other visitor facilities, which will in turn determine subsequent visitor types. It is untenable, in the long run, for such a historic event of strong emotional significance to different and often opposing groups of people to be portrayed in its historical totality irrespective of those strong emotions. Rather, the presentation and interpretation should reflect factual accuracy but from a subjective perspective, portraying the uniqueness of those events in an enlightening and constructive manner. Furthermore, as a result of the sensitive nature of the events of the trade to various groups, intergroup conflicts are inevitable at sites and other presentations associated with it. These conflicts over time may shape the future market and the viability of the tourism development. Management effort, therefore, must seek to identify, understand, and manage these conflicts.

The Learning Environment

Visitors to a site or some other form of presentation that is connected to these historic events, as described, will generally undertake such visitation with a strong desire to learn about those events of the past (N. K. Austin, 1997). This desire to learn will differ with respect to the level and nature of site-related information required by visitors. In all social endeavors the responsiveness and flexibility of any learning environment in line with the needs of those desiring to learn within that environment is a major contributory factor to the success or failure of the learning experience. The portrayal of the historic events of the transatlantic slave trade in tourism development, as an environment for learning, should not be any different. While being mindful of the problems of multiple presentations, the development of differentiated tour routes and the incorporation of physical simulations, for example, will help satisfy the needs of different groups of visitors. Visitor management would require considerable skill in the areas of physical and psychological separation of visitors with different emotional attachments. This calls for the ability to institute measures that have the potential of encouraging the visitor through the selection of presentational formats, facilities, and services that best fit the level of emotional attachment they hold. For example, previsit promotional literature would clearly explain what the site stands for and the various services provided within it, with an indication of the nature and level of emotional content.

Need for Communication and Dialogue

The concerns of both visitors and other stakeholders over issues of restoration and preservation are best resolved through management attention to communication with its "public," willingness to listen to their views, and cooperation with them. Developmental programs relating to such sensitive issues ought to be open to discussion and, as and when decisions are made, they should be communicated to interested parties. Particularly, the relevant details of restoration and preservation works, such as what is being done, why it is being done, together with assurances over management attention to issues of authenticity and objectivity, should be regularly communicated. These can take the form of information available at the presentation site as well as regular public relations exercises.

Incompatibility of the Leisure Orientation

There is an urgent need for an understanding that while the events of the trade may be employed in the development of tourism, potential visitors are not likely to be of a leisurely orientation. Moreover, to associate it with a leisure orientation is a potential route to the trivialization of the significance of the symbolism of the presentation. As discussed previously, it adds to the problems of visitor management through the attraction of the "uninformed" visitor in particular. It may also cause site staff to loose sight of what the site is about, or to encourage the demonstration of inappropriate site behavior on the part of both visitors and site staff. It is suggested that presentation, interpretation, the provision of support facilities such as a "quiet room" for reflection, the training of staff in dealing with visitors, and the general education of the host population as a whole should all be focused on the emotional sensitivity of the events associated with the trade.

Opportunities for Improved Racial Relations

From an ethical perspective it may be argued that the chances for improved racial relations are best served by the avoidance of dwelling on painful racial issues of the past. Alternatively, the portrayal of those historical events gives both blacks and whites an opportunity to come to terms with slavery and thus a better chance at getting over its consequences. For good relations to take hold between two social groups, one of whom has felt and still feels aggrieved, the first step is for both groups to come to terms with the presumed causes of those negative relations. This is a role that the portrayal of the events of the transatlantic slave trade in tourism is well placed to serve. As already discussed, the problem lies not with the desirability of the portrayal of the events of the trade in the development of tourism, but with how it is managed.

Black African Descent: Its Importance

Though some black Africans in the diaspora have made economic strides, together with the economically disadvantaged black African in the diaspora, they still must cope with racially based socioeconomic constraints that have made them anxious and created a desire for a means of change in the collective black liberation struggle (Hooks, 1990). Thus, for many Africans in the diaspora, the search for an understanding of their collective socioeconomic situation and the longing for a positive change remain as strong as ever. Thirty-four years ago, Isaacs (1964), addressing the question of "Negro American" identity, discussed the potential of the larger "Afro-American" community spread across the Americas, the Caribbean, and the Pacific islands. The wisdom offered was that, black people recognizing fully their common cultural and historical background under European slavery is the route to a complete resolution of the identity problem of the "Negro American." Thus, being of African descent has been the most dominant factor in their collective sociopolitical and economic experience. Although citizens of different contemporary nations, their collective survival and well-being depends on that realization. The exploration of the events of the slave trade, through tourism in the continent of Africa, serves as the unique recognizing medium for Africans in the diaspora to relate to their collective sociohistorical experience. The essential task of this tourism development must be to link the relevance of the historical experience to the present socioeconomic status of the black African, both in Africa and in the diaspora. Thus, site presentation and interpretation, as well as interactions with the host community, should extend beyond establishing historical facts into areas of practical cooperation, which can help resolve some of the socioeconomic problems faced by peoples of black African descent.

Balancing Economic and Social Objectives

The clarity of the mission statement of management in implementing a practical and balanced design of cooperative economic and social objectives and subsequent marketing effort is a necessary initial step in the presentation of the events of the trade in tourism. The reason is that the social significance of those historic events underpins the economic viability of the development in tourism. Other issues, such as complementary packaging of tour products between countries, which offers the visitor the experience of the total enslavement process of the transatlantic slave trade as it occurred on the continent of Africa, and the cost barrier of Africa's regulated air travel market, need to be resolved. There is also the need for increased professionalism in the dealings of African tour agencies and national tourism boards with overseas tour operators. Areas requiring improvements include tour package development and pricing, timely and accurate provision of required travel-related information, actual on-site tour handling, and an understanding of visitor preferences, motivation, behavior, and emotions and their effects on visitor expectations and desires.

Reeducation From an African-Centered Perspective

Finally, the success of the development of those historic events in tourism requires a massive reeducation of many Africans and Africans in the diaspora. It is within the context of a heightened perception of the socioeconomic experience of people of black African descent from an African-centered perspective that the events of the transatlantic slave trade will continue to be of utmost importance.

Conclusion

This chapter has addressed the justifiable concerns with regard to the utilization of the highly sensitive and "live" history of the transatlantic slave trade in tourism development. In doing so, the chapter has attempted to clarify the major implication of the development, for the realization, understanding, and improvement in the collective socioeconomic situation of people of black African descent and its potential impact on global racial relations, besides the more obvious economic gain for ailing African economies.

The key observations made, which include the nonleisure orientation of the utilization of the events of the slave trade in tourism, the racially biased perception of those events, the need for awareness education of potential visitors, host communities, and tourism planners, and the potential "healing" role for black–white relations, offer a number of policy initiatives for tourism planners.

These initiatives should revolve around the need to incorporate and place greater emphasis on the symbolism and essence underlying African diaspora visitation to sites associated with the events of the slave trade and linkages to the present collective circumstance of people of black African descent. Also, it ought to be realized that even though visitation to heritage sites will usually have a socializing and leisure-oriented component, the heritage under consideration and its current relevance to people of black African descent give it a role that is not compatible with tourist visitation in general. Finally, because of the widespread nature of the events of the transatlantic slave trade on the continent as a whole, a total picture and visitor experience cannot arise from individual and uncoordinated efforts among the nations of Africa. It should rather be viewed as a continental endeavor, thereby giving greater meaning to its more useful role of bringing the people of black African descent together for their mutual benefit.

Chapter 15

Regional Cooperation and Tourism Development in Africa

Victor B. Teye

Summary

   Regional economic cooperation provides significant opportunities for individual countries to expand their resource base, increase investment potential, and implement marketing strategies, among other things, in pursuit of general economic development. Either directly or indirectly, the tourism sector can derive significant benefits from regional cooperation arrangements. Over the last decade, developing regions have made significant efforts to achieve greater degree of regional economic integration and cooperation. Some of these regional groupings include The Association of South East Asian Nations (ASEAN) and Mercosur in Latin America. These initiatives have coincided with either new or reinforced regional integration policies and institutions in the industrialized countries, such as the treaty and expansion of the European Union (EU) and the establishment of the North American Free Trade Area (NAFTA). While both the EU and NAFTA objectives include the gradual integration of selected developing countries in North–South cooperation, developing countries are placing greater emphasis on regional cooperation among themselves at two South–South levels. The first is interregional cooperation among different regions in the developing world, while the second is intraregional cooperation among proximate countries in the same broad geographical region. This chapter describes efforts at intraregional economic cooperation in Africa, and examines the Southern Africa Development Community (SADC) as a model approach to tourism planning, development, and management at subregional levels.

Key words: Regional cooperation; Integration; Tourism; Development; Southern Africa Development Community

Introduction

   Regionalism has been described as cooperation and integration among proximate states that share a sense of their own individual inadequacy in dealing with problems of security and welfare (Renninger, 1979). Development of tourism at the regional level means that the different states in a particular geographical region will cooperate and integrate "their attractions, capital, infrastructure, natural and human resources to serve the needs of the domestic and international (inter-regional and intra-regional) tourism sectors" (Teye, 1991, p. 288). This cooperative approach in Africa is important for a number of reasons. First, the Africa tourism region, occupying about 11,692,878 square miles (30,284,587 km²) is endowed with physical tourism resources that include a vast array of relief forms, topography, fauna, flora, maritime, and aquatic resources. Second, each country in the five sub-Sahara African region (excluding North Africa) is a long-haul destination relative to the tourist-generating regions of Europe, North America, and Asia. Third, there is substantial subregional travel and tourism at the intraregional level. Indeed, for most African countries, neighboring countries, particularly those sharing common borders, constitute their largest international tourism markets. Consequently, the large size of Africa, the diversity of its tourism resources, its locational disadvantages, and the importance of its various subregional tourism markets provide some of the incentives for regional cooperation. A group of countries acting as a unit is better able to educate the marketing intermediaries (tour operators and travel agents) in the tourist-generating countries in order to overcome some of the negative perceptions and images of Africa, a major problem hindering efforts to promote and market sub-Sahara Africa (Nyaruwata, 1986). Similarly, a group of countries acting in concert has better leverage to protect their interests in dealing with institutions such as Tourism Transnational Corporations (TTCs), which play a critical role in the tourism development process.

This chapter examines efforts at regional cooperation in Africa with a focus on its relevance to the tourism industry. It begins with a review of the rational for regional cooperation in tourism, then it examines attempts at regional cooperation in the postindependence period. The discussion then describes regional cooperation among southern African states in the area of tourism, which can serve as a model for other regions in the rest of Africa.

International Tourism in Africa

International tourism arrivals and receipts in 1996 was about at 23.3 million and $8.7 billion, respectively, for Africa (WTO, 1998c). Table 15.1 shows the relative position of the top 20 tourism revenue earners in Africa in 1997. In global terms, the total figures represent a mere 3.8% of the 613 million arrivals and an even smaller 1.9% of the $444 billion for international tourism. Furthermore, the proportions have remained almost at these levels for more than a decade. A noticeable characteristic is the concentration of the industry in just a few countries. For example, South Africa, Tunisia, and Morocco received 55.4% of all arrivals in 1997 (WTO, 1998c) and, as further indicated in Table 15.1, as much as 57.6% of revenue of international tourists to Africa in 1997. The WTO Commission for Africa has observed that "international tourism in Africa has also been held back by the lack of infrastructure investment, chronic transportation shortages, the restricted promotion and marketing budgets, and the absence of political support in some countries of the region" (WTO, 1997c, p. 20). Most, if not all, of these obstacles can be reduced or even eliminated through a regional approach to tourism development.

Benefits of Regional Tourism Cooperation

An increasing trend in international tourism is the desire of tourists to visit more than one destination on a trip, especially to a long-haul tourist region. In the case of destinations in developing regions of Asia, Africa, and South America, a substantial segment of visitors from the main tourist-generating regions of North America and Western Europe prefer visiting a number of countries on a single trip. Multiple tourism destination development, which allows the creation of regional tours and multinational circuits, is only one element of regional cooperation in tourism development. Others include:

- joint promotion and marketing;
- tourism facilitation, including liberalization policies for passport and visa requirements;

- currency regulation, immigration, and customs controls;
- collection of uniform tourism statistics;
- investment incentives and regulations for local and foreign investors;
- transportation system policies for landing rights, charter flights, and overland international crossing;
- standardization and regional classification of tourism facilities;
- coordination of health and medical requirements;
- conservation and preservation programs for natural, historical, and cultural resources;
- personnel and manpower training;
- foreign assistance (aid) programs;
- international representation on foreign markets.

In the case of African countries, some of the above considerations are so central to tourism development that they require bilateral and multilateral cooperation. Malaria and cholera outbreaks, for example, can spread quickly across international boundaries. Hence, international tourism arrivals to a whole region could decline dramatically and devastate tourism and related industries. Wildlife poaching has been a major problem threatening the tourism industries of east, central, and southern Africa. It was estimated, for example, in the mid-1980s that the elephant population in the Central African Republic had dwindled from 160,000 to only 10,000 in about two decades. The problem is also serious in several countries in east, central, and southern Africa such as Uganda, Rwanda, Mozambique, and Angola where military activities in

Table 15.1. Top 20 Tourism Earners in Africa (1997) International Tourism Receipts (excluding transport)

Rank 1990	Rank 1997	Country	Receipts (US$ million)	% of Total
2	1	South Africa	2,297	26.3
3	2	Tunisia	1,540	17.6
1	3	Morocco	1,200	13.7
5	4	Mauritius	504	5.8
4	5	Kenya	502	5.7
11	6	Tanzania	360	4.1
—	7	Reunion	273	3.1
10	8	Ghana	266	3.0
13	9	Zimbabwe	250	2.9
9	10	Namibia	210	2.4
8	11	Botswana	181	2.1
6	12	Senegal	160	1.8
7	13	Seychelles	122	1.4
33	14	Uganda	103	1.2
16	15	Cote D'Ivoire	88	1.0
24	16	Nigeria	86	1.0
—	17	Eritrea	75	0.9
19	18	Madagascar	67	0.8
18	19	Zambia	65	0.7
15	20	Cameroon	39	0.4
		Total 1–20	8,388	96.0
		Total Africa	8,742	100.0

Source: WTO (1998c).

the form of protracted liberation wars, civil wars, and military governments have proliferated firearms, making it easy for poachers to go on the rampage. The long and unsecured borders of some of these countries require institutionalized cooperative arrangements with neighboring countries to deal with the complex problems of poaching. For example, Zambia shares open borders through isolated regions with eight countries (Malawi, Mozambique, Zimbabwe, Botswana, Namibia, Angola, Zaire, and Tanzania), none of which can solve its poaching problems alone. In this regard, Abdel-Wahab (1974) provides another reason for regional cooperation by pointing out that:

> As political tension in one country tends to affect tourism to the whole region, it is logical that close tourist cooperation between countries forming one tourism region should be worked out . . . tourist attractions in those countries should be made to complement rather than to compete with each other. (p. 43)

Commenting on the joint development of the East Africa tourist product for the North American market more than two decades ago, Popovic (1972) observes that:

> A stay on a beach at the end of a charter flight, with a short visit to a game park or the nearest city, will hardly appeal to American tourists. When they depart on a trip overseas they are likely to visit a range of countries and stay in each only a few days, visiting only the main highlights. This should be kept in mind when planning facilities and programmes. (p. 25)

Today, this travel pattern is no longer characteristic of the North American travel market alone. Hence, a common theme that runs through the tourism plans of most developing countries is the recognition of the need for multiple-destination programs that involve regional cooperation. It is important to note additional implications of regional cooperation at two levels: government and individual (Dieke, 1998). The need at the government level is to utilize local resources as inputs in the development of general and tourism-specific infrastructure, as well as the operation of tourism facilities for the various market segments. Implicit in this consideration is the role of governments in directing and supporting private sector efforts of tourism enterprises in this endeavor. At the individual level, there is the need for concerted efforts to direct the different market segments (leisure, business, visiting friends and relatives) to "consume" local products in order to increase the benefits of tourism while reducing negative impacts, such as those attributable to the environmental bubble, where visitors have only fleeting contact with the African tourism product.

Regional Cooperation Efforts in Africa

The recognition and acceptance of the idea and ideals of regional cooperation preceded independence of most African countries from colonial rule. Central to the establishment of the Organization of African Unity (OAU) was the ultimate goal of both continental political and economic unity under the vision and influence of the Pan-African integrationists. The new African states were faced with the task of attaining sustainable economic development in restricted and uneconomic domestic markets in what could rightly be classified as several ministates. They were desperately limited by capital and skilled manpower, having survived prior to independence through direct economic links with their metropolitan colonialist governments, which provided financial and technical assistance. At the First and Second Conference of African Heads of States in April 1958 and June 1960, respectively, the independent states formally proposed economic cooperation as a strategy for economic transformation. Then at the Third Conference of African Heads of States in May 1963 to inaugurate the OAU, economic cooperation was not only endorsed, but was recognized as a development concept and was included in the principles and objectives of the organization. At four subsequent OAU meetings in 1970, 1973, 1977, and 1979, implementation guidelines were established. The ultimate objective was to establish an African Economic Community in five successive stages starting at the subregional levels. The stages involved the establishment of Preferential Trade Area, Free Trade Area, Customs Union, Common Market, and Community.

As a result of these continental initiatives, as well as others at the subregional and intercontinental level, more than 200 regional cooperation organizations have been established in the past 40 years in Africa. These were considered, in many instances, as vital foundation and pillars for eventual continental economic integration. A major milestone was reached at the Second Extraordinary Session of the Assembly of Heads of States and Governments in April 1980 held in Lagos, Nigeria. The implementation guidelines that had been established in the 1970s were incorporated into an operational plan. This became known as the Lagos Plan of Action, in which members agreed on the establishment of subregional economic communities by the 1990s. With respect to the actual implementation of the plan, a Regional Continental Community was to be established by the year 2000. The timetable called for the following areas of economic cooperation in the 1980s:

- Strengthen the existing regional economic communities and establish other economic groupings in subregions where they did not exit, so as to cover the whole continent (central Africa, eastern Africa and southern Africa, West Africa and North Africa).
- Strengthen sectoral integration at the subregional level effectively, particularly in the fields of trade, agriculture, transport and communications, industry, and energy.
- Promote coordination and harmonization among the existing and future economic groupings for a gradual establishment of an African common market.

During the decade of the 1990s the strategy focused on two major areas. The first involved taking steps for further sectoral integration in each subregion, with particular emphasis on the harmonization of strategies, policies, and economic development plans, as well as promotion of joint projects. This strategy also included harmonization of financial and monetary policies. The second strategy area involved measures to effect the establishment of an African common market and other steps that would lead to the attainment of the aims and objectives of the African Economic Community.

The 28th OAU Summit in June 1991 acknowledged the difficulties in achieving the targets, and postponed by 35 years the date for the eventual establishment of the African Economic Community to the year 2035. A new and more gradual timetable was established to achieve a community status over a 34-year period divided into six stages as follows:

- strengthening of the existing subregional communities over a 5-year period;
- stabilization of fiscal regimes applied to intrasubregional trade to last 8 years;
- establishment of a free trade area at the level of each subregional economic grouping would take 10 years;
- coordination and harmonization of tariff and nontariff regimes between the subregional economic grouping in 2 years;
- establishing of an African Common Market in a 4-year period;
- establishment of the African Economic Community in 5 years.

Nomvete (1993) has identified some of the interrelated problems that have delayed or frustrated regional cooperation of Africa to include

parochialism; lack of grassroots support; dearth of local private businessmen and skills; excessive external dependency of African countries; transport problems; policy-induced problems; problems inherent in co-operation arrangements; multiplicity of organizations;

political factors; the relative stagnancy of African economies and the international economic environment. (p. 51)

These are the major obstacles and challenges that need to be overcome in order to achieve continental-wide regional cooperation and eventual integration. From the new gradualist approach, it appears that the original advocates for cooperation were either too optimistic or underestimated the obstacles. Langhamner (1993) argues that Africa has never succeeded in having three fundamental conditions that are central to the successful realization of regional cooperation. The conditions that must ideally exist simultaneously are sustained political stability and commitment, steady growth of the national economy at a desirable rate, and absence of a major subregional economic disparity. Clearly, most African economies have deteriorated or stagnated in the last 10–20 years and have had to resort to such painful measures as structural adjustments, currency devaluations, raised interest rates, and divestiture of state-owned enterprises.

These problems and challenges notwithstanding, a number of cooperative institutions presently exist at the subregional levels. These include the Economic Community of West African States (ECOWAS) established in 1975; West Africa Economic Community (CEAO) founded in 1974; Economic Community of Central African States (ECCAS), which came into being in 1983; and the Preferential Trade Area for Eastern and Southern African States (PTA), which was set up in 1981. There have also been recent efforts at reviving the former East African Economic Community (EAEC), which broke up in 1979. It was considered the most viable regional cooperative institution. It also had important tourism components. For example, it coordinated several regional programs and institutions, including railways, harbors, telecommunications, airline, and common currency (Delupes, 1969). A key component of the community was a regional tourism industry that facilitated the establishment of a number of tourist circuits within the common borders of the three countries of Kenya, Uganda, and Tanzania.

While specific tourism development projects or activities are marginal to the mission of most of the existing cooperative institutions, two points should be noted here. First, regional cooperation in the field of tourism has received widespread acceptance in the last 15 years. For instance, the Niamey Conference on "Intra-African Cooperation in Tourism" (Economic Commission for Africa [ECA], 1986) highlighted the economic and social consequences of Africa's overdependence on foreign markets, and the need to diversify with more promotional efforts at the domestic and intraregional markets. Since then, the ECA and the WTO commission for Africa have played ongoing important roles in sensitizing African tourism ministries and agencies, as well as the tourism private sector, about the need to move toward greater regional cooperation. Second, given the intersectoral nature of the tourism industry, the sector tends to benefit from other more specific activities, particularly in the areas of infrastructure development, such as transport, telecommunication, energy, and water resources. In some instances, projects are specific to tourism. For example, a proposal for regional and rural development approved by the CEAO in 1984 included "development of regional tourism, setting up of a shipping line, regional transport plan, and a programme of scientific research" ("A World Survey," 1987, p. 190).

Currently, the southern African region has evolved the most important regional cooperative organization with specific sectoral areas that include tourism. This chapter now examines the Southern Africa Development Community (SADC) organization, and its activities that can become a model for regional cooperation in Africa for greater realization of the continent's tourism potential.

The Southern Africa Development Community

The Southern Africa Development Conference (SADCC) was formally established in 1980 and became the SADC in 1992. However, there were several initiatives over quite a period of time before its establishment became a reality. The first major conference was held at Arusha, Tanzania, in 1979 to harmonize development plans and to reduce the region's economic dependence on South Africa. The nine original SADCC member countries included Angola, Botswana, Lesotho, Malawi, Mozambique, Swaziland, Tanzania, Zambia, and Zimbabwe. In 1980, a regional economic summit conference was held in Lusaka, Zambia, where the Lusaka Declaration was approved. This was a statement of strategy entitled "Southern Africa: Towards Economic Liberation." The 1980 summit conference also established a program of action that assigned specific studies and tasks to member governments. There were 10 sectoral commissions located in each member country (two commissions were in Maseru, Lesotho), two of which were directly related to tourism. These were the Tourism Sectoral Commission located in Lesotho, and the Southern Africa Transport and Communications Commission with its headquarters in Maputo, Mozambique. A secretariat administered SADCC's activities; however, there were three levels of coordinated involvement above the secretariat level. First was the annual summit meeting, which was attended by heads of states and governments or their representatives. The second was the council of ministers, which met at least twice a year, in addition to special meetings held to coordinate regional policy in any of the 10 sectoral areas. The third was the annual conference of SADCC's international cooperating partners (donor governments and international agencies) to review progress in the various sectors of the organization's program and to present new projects requiring assistance.

The main focus of SADCC's projects was transport because it was regarded as the most important sector to be developed, on the grounds that, as the Lusaka Declaration noted:

> the dominance of the Republic of South Africa has been reinforced by its transportation system. Without the establishment of an adequate regional transport and communication system, other areas of cooperation become impractical. (SADCC, 1981)

The organization's priority was the improvement of road and railway services to the coastal member countries, particularly Mozambique and Tanzania, so that the land-locked member countries could transport their exports and imports to bypass South African ports. These developments also had positive impact on road and rail passenger services in the region. Some transport projects had direct tourism benefits. For example, civil aviation projects included the construction of a new airport, which began in 1984 at Maseru, Lesotho, as well as improvements of major airports in Mozambique, Swaziland, Zambia, and Zimbabwe. There were also programs on the joint use of maintenance facilities, on regional air worthiness certification and aviation legislation, and on navigational aids. Initially tourism development projects had a low priority. However, as in the case of transport projects, both direct and indirect benefits to tourism were substantial. For instance, sectoral projects for manpower development, wildlife, energy, forestry, and industrial development each had both direct and indirect impact on tourism in the region. The significance of tourism in southern Africa can be seen from Table 15.2. The region received 30.5% of Africa's total tourist arrivals and 31.7% of tourism receipts in 1997. It should be pointed out that Malawi, Mauritius, Mozambique, Tanzania, Zambia, and Zimbabwe are for WTO statistical purposes part of eastern Africa, while Angola is part of middle Africa. When these seven SADC countries are included, the size of the southern African tourism industry is clearly substantial, making it the dominant tourism region in Africa.

Unlike any other regional cooperation institutions in Africa, SADC established a Tourism Sector in 1984, which underscored the importance of tourism to each member country (Table 15.3), as well as their interdependence on each other's markets. In August 1994, South Africa became the eleventh member of SADC and gave further impetus to the cooperative endeavors of tourism development. In that year it recorded 3.66 million arrivals and a corresponding $2.2 billion (Table 15.3). Given its geographical size and diversity, level of economic (including tour-

Table 15.2. Tourism Trends in Africa by Subregions 1994 and 1997

Region	Tourist Arrivals (000) 1997	% of Total Africa 1994	% of Total Africa 1997	Tourism Receipts (US $ million) 1997	% of Total Africa 1994	% of Total Africa 1997
Eastern	5,541	20.7	23.8	2,390	24.5	27.3
Middle	328	1.6	1.4	78	1.1	0.9
Northern	8,077	42.9	34.7	2,768	39.2	31.7
Southern	7,102	26.6	30.5	2,745	26.7	31.4
Western	2,243	8.1	9.6	761	8.5	8.7
Total	23,291	100.0	100.0	8,742	100.0	100.0

Northern Africa: Algeria, Morocco, Sudan, and Tunisia. Southern Africa: Botswana, Lesotho, Namibia, South Africa, and Swaziland. Malawi, Mauritius, Mozambique, Tanzania, Zambia, and Zimbabwe are included in Eastern Africa. Angola is part of Middle Africa.
Source: WTO (1998c).

ism) development, a relatively high per capita income of its population, and its position as a regional gateway, South Africa has, since its admittance into SADC, assumed a leading role in the development of a strong regional tourism industry.

Table 15.4 shows the importance of South Africa as a regional tourism destination. It is also the leading market for individual destinations in the southern Africa region, particularly Zimbabwe, Botswana, Swaziland, and Mauritius. For example, of the 1.56 million tourists who visited Zimbabwe in 1996, nearly 512,00 or about 32.7% were from South Africa (WTO, 1997c).

Within SADC's tourism sector, two other organizations that existed were the Tourism Coordination Unit and the Southern Africa Regional Tourism Council (SARTOC). At the 1994 Consultative Conference of SADC in Botswana, the Tourism Sector outlined its tourism strategy for the region as follows:

- greater utilization of the local resource base, including the diversification and improvement of the region's tourist product;
- development of appropriate infrastructure;
- superstructure and related tourism amenities in the rural areas;

Table 15.3. Tourist Arrivals and Receipts in Selected SADC Countries: 1994 and 1997

Country	Arrivals (000) 1994	Arrivals (000) 1997	% of 1997 Total	US$ Million 1994	US$ Million 1997	% of 1997 Total
Angola	11	8	0.1	13	9	0.2
Botswana	625	728	7.2	124	181	4.6
Lesotho	97	112	1.1	17	20	0.5
Mauritius	401	536	5.3	357	504	12.8
Namibia	326	410	4.0	220	210	5.3
South Africa	3,669	5,530	54.4	1,424	2,297	58.4
Swaziland	336	322	3.2	33	37	0.9
Tanzania	250	350	3.4	192	360	9.2
Zambia	141	278	2.7	43	65	1.7
Zimbabwe	1,105	1,894	18.6	125	250	6.4
Total	6,961	10,168	100.0	2,548	3,933	100.0

Source: WTO (1998c).

- ensuring proper planning of tourist projects through closer liaison with other sectors of SADC;
- promotion and encouragement of intraregional travel and initiation of deliberate incentive programs by member states;
- ensuring proper production and dissemination of the region's promotional material;
- encouragement of selective tourism;
- training of professional and skilled personnel at all levels.

Broadly, the current Tourism Development Program comprises four components: Tourism Product Development, Tourism Research and Marketing, Tourism Service, and Human Resources Development and Training. Some of the key tourism projects are now briefly described.

Tourism Marketing

The objective of the International Distribution Network Project was to set up an efficient network of incoming wholesalers to program and package comprehensive regional multidestination tours; to sell these internationally and regionally and to handle incoming passenger flows. The following activities were undertaken:

- identification of suitable incoming wholesalers based on regional experience and international exposure and contacts;
- identification of suitable national offices for combining into regional cooperative marketing organizations;
- identification of weaknesses in the distribution sector in member states, and design and implement action of technical assistance programs;
- communicating with selected operators and drafting plans of operation;
- inspection of selected tourism products within the region;
- drafting of tour programs, itineraries, and costings;
- production of brochures;
- marketing and selling tours.

Intraregional Tourism Research

There are four main objectives of this project. The first objective is assessing the size, potential, and needs of the traditional (middle-high income) traveling public in the region. Second is to assess the needs and possibilities for lower income groups to take holiday travel. The third

Table 15.4. Significance of Regional Markets to South Africa: Tourist Arrivals by Main Markets

Origin/Markets	1995 (000)	1996 (000)	% of Total
Lesoto	1,054	1,147	23.2
Zimbabwe	724	736	14.9
Swaziland	647	671	13.6
Botswana	352	447	9.1
U.K.	244	244	4.9
Namibia	212	199	4.0
Germany	168	195	3.9
Mozambique	128	211	4.3
Other countries	959	1,094	22.1
Total	4,488	4,944	100.0

Source: WTO (1998c).

objective is identifying means of communicating and distributing the tourism product of the region to differing segments of the population. Fourth, the project is to identify product requirements and price levels appropriate to regional needs.

Classification of Hotels and Tourism Plant

To achieve uniform quality assurance throughout the southern Africa region, the objectives of this project are to design and implement a standard grading and classification system for hotels and other accommodation establishments and other operators. The aim is also to achieve uniformity of service standards throughout the region. Additionally, this program is to ensure acceptable international standards of service and relevant value-for-money at all tourism plants in operation.

Harmonization and Standardization of Tourism Statistics

This project aims to design and implement a homogeneous data collection system in the region. In this regard, a guide derived from the various data-gathering methods was designed by the sector, with a view to having it adopted for reference purposes by all member states.

Hotel and Tourism Training

SADC recognized that the existing hotel and tourism training institutions and facilities in the region were inadequate, and could only cater for lower level personnel. At the same time, high cost of training middle and senior management abroad was seen as prohibitive, hence the urgent need to strengthen existing local institutions to cater for the training needs of the tourism sector. The aims of the project, therefore, are threefold. First, to introduce training schemes and upgrade facilities for the tourism industry. Second, to ensure a steady supply of skilled manpower to the industry. Third, to improve standards of service throughout the region, particularly in less developed areas.

The description above covers only a few of tourism-specific projects in the SADC region. Others that are equally important include Women in Tourism Development, Train-the-Trainer, and Tourism Market Research on Long-Haul Markets. In April 1996, a new organization, Regional Tourism Organization for Southern Africa (RETOSA), was established to replace SARTOC. The new organization, which is based in Pretoria, South Africa, will guide the regional cooperative approaches to tourism promotion and marketing in SADC, which now consists of 14 member countries. In its short period of existence, it has undertaken several key initiatives including hosting a workshop on regional investment issues with the World Bank's Multi-lateral Guarantee Investment Agency (MIGA), and a workshop on the 5-year Regional Tourism Marketing Plan in July 1997. One key challenge facing SADC, which RETOSA would have to deal with, is how to position the southern African tourism region firmly in the long-haul European and North American marketplace but in such a way that it distinguishes the diversity of the regional product so that each member state is not disadvantaged. This is especially important given actual or perceived dominance of South Africa. This problem in the first place derives from the "substitution" of South Africa, the country, for southern Africa, the region. Secondly, South Africa has in the past and continues to market itself as a "World in One Country." These issues notwithstanding, the opportunities for regional cooperation for tourism development in SADC, spearheaded by RETOSA, are tremendous and the real challenge is how to maximize these to the mutual benefit of all member countries.

Conclusion

This chapter has examined efforts to establish regional economic cooperation groups as a step toward a continental African integrated market. While there have been setbacks in meeting the desired objectives on schedule, a review of some of SADC's tourism sector activities indicates that viable benefits can accrue from a regional cooperation strategy that identifies tourism as a specific sector with peculiar characteristics and needs. The present program of the SADC tourism sector is designed to provide a product that meets the demands of the various market segments. But more importantly, it has been developed in the context of national and regional socioeconomic development objectives, in order to produce a number of outcomes. The first is to ensure the viability and profitability of the industry. The second is to maximize tourism's contribution to regional development through foreign exchange earnings, employment creation, human resources development, and rural development. The third outcome is ensuring conservation of tourist attractions, preservation of culture and environment, as well as retention of foreign exchange, and, finally, to promote maximum use of local materials in construction and other tourist operations.

Admittedly, each African region faces peculiar opportunities and challenges. SADC was established originally to reduce reliance on Apartheid South Africa, "a common enemy." Political changes in southern Africa, and in South Africa in particular, increased the momentum for regional cooperation and strategies to generate viable results. West Africa, for example, has its political peculiarities of Francophone and Anglophone "division." The biggest obstacle has been regional political instability. Sustained political stability in itself, and the growth in tourism that it facilitates and eventually fosters, are both important elements in the recognition of the role that tourism can play in economic development, first at the national level, and eventually at the regional level. Even then, the process is evolutionary. In the case of SADC the initial tourism programs were based on a project-by-project planning approach, which resulted in a set of projects that did not closely reflect the priorities of the sector. It therefore became necessary to adopt a more coordinated sectoral planning approach. In this respect, a draft 5-year development strategy for the tourism sector was completed and, once approved by council, formed the basis for formulating a well-coordinated regional tourism development program.

Chapter 16

RETOSA and Tourism Development Cooperation in Southern Africa

Shepherd Nyaruwata

Summary

There has been a global trend to create regional tourism cooperation organizations in recent years (e.g., in the Caribbean and Asian regions, among others). In one sense, this development might be seen as a response to the growing world competition, coupled with the effects of globalization. The obvious advantages of this situation will be not only to ease travel and enhance investment but also to aggressively put the particular region in the tourism spotlight. The establishment of RETOSA (Regional Tourism Organization of Southern Africa) in 1995, involving 14 countries of Southern African Development Community (SADC), reflects this phenomenon. The primary aim was to market and promote the SADC region in partnership with the public and private sectors of the member countries of the region. This chapter examines, within the context of RETOSA, the importance that the SADC member states attach to regional cooperation as a means of achieving sustainable tourism development in southern Africa, and offers some perspectives on future direction of the organization. Despite the short period it has been in existence, RETOSA has demonstrated the usefulness of pooling resources together and approaching the generating markets as a single holiday destination. For example, joint promotional activities have already been undertaken with principals in the region's primary markets. Given the commitment that the member states have shown toward the organization and the growing involvement of the private sector to RETOSA-driven promotional activities, the organization has the potential of growing into a sound and viable promotional tourism organ of southern Africa.

Key words: Southern African Development Community (SADC); Regional Tourism Organization of Southern Africa (RETOSA); Tourist attractions; Institutional framework; Private and public sectors; Marketing and promotions; Tour operators; Travel media

Introduction

The trend in regional groupings that developed during the last two decades saw the formation of the Southern African Development Coordination Conference (SADCC) in southern Africa in 1980. The organization was finally transformed into the Southern African

Development Community (SADC) in 1992, with membership drawn from 14 countries of the region (Table 16.1).

For a number of reasons, the region has not been able to utilize fully its tourism potential. First, a lack of political unity during and after decolonization forced each country to develop independently its own tourism sector. Second, the differences in levels of economic development in each member state resulted in tourism being accorded at best a very low priority and at worst not being recognized at all. Third, the protracted wars of liberalization that occurred in the region, as well as the civil wars that some of the countries experienced after attaining independence, created an environment that was not very conducive to the sustainable growth of a tourism industry. Finally, the political ideology of the majority of the postindependence governments encouraged direct state participation in those areas of the economy that are usually the domain of the private sector. The overall result, which also applied to the tourism sector, has been a limited development of a vibrant private sector. Increased global competition forced member states of the region to realize that marketing and promoting themselves as tourist destinations in world markets would not yield meaningful results. Given the formal existence of SADC as a regional organization, it was realized that the establishment of a regional organization to spearhead tourism promotion and development would be the first prerequisite if the region is to compete meaningfully in the global tourism market. Against this background the Regional Tourism Organization of Southern Africa (RETOSA) was finally established in 1995 with the mandate of coordinating the marketing and promotion of southern Africa.

This chapter examines, within the context of RETOSA, the importance that SADC member states attach to regional cooperation as a means of achieving sustainable tourism development in southern Africa. First, the chapter presents a profile of the region and considers the development problems facing the area. Second, it considers the reasons for regional tourism cooperation and discusses potential bottlenecks. The chapter also assesses RETOSA's work programs, and offers some perspectives on future direction of the organization.

Table 16.1. Background to Southern Africa

Country	Area (km²)	Population (million)	GNP per Capita (US$, 1996)
Angola	1,247 (m)	11.6	340
Botswana	585,000	1.6	3,020
Democratic Republic of Congo	2,267,600	47.4	120
Lesotho	30,355	2.1	670
Malawi	118,484	11	180
Mauritius	1,865	1.2	3,690
Mozambique	799,380	17	67
Namibia	824,268	1.6	2,080
The Seychelles	433	0.77	6,960
South Africa	1,223,201	42	3,140
Swaziland	17,000	0.9	1,170
Tanzania	945,000	28.3	130
Zambia	752,614	9.3	430
Zimbabwe	390,757	11	620

Sources: SADC (1997, pp. 1.2–12.3) and WTO (1998c, p. 118).

Southern Africa Development Cooperation

Profile and Problems

As can be seen (Table 16.1), southern Africa comprises 14 countries that have major differences in terms of land mass, population size, and levels of economic and social development. One might also add to this characterization that these countries have had different colonial experiences with different consequences for the region, at least in tourism cooperation terms. For instance, the small countries are often apprehensive of their relationship with other member states, fearing that their interests will be overshadowed by those of the bigger members of the regional grouping. Related to this apprehension of being overshadowed is the perceived loss of independence, as well as national identity, as the cases of the former Senegambia Confederation and the East Africa Community demonstrate (Dieke, 1998). On the other hand, the bigger or more "successful" countries in the association might often feel that working with the less successful countries will dilute their efforts in the marketplace and retard the growth of their tourism sector.

Given these fears, it was logical that the SADC members had to take the issues on board during the formation of RETOSA because of their potential to undermine regional tourism cooperation (Hoof & Overgaard, 1995, pp. 4-5). In consequence, as Poon (1996, pp. 4-6) has usefully summarized, some of the key issues that helped SADC countries to adopt a regional approach to tourism development are as follows:

- a weak regional marketing and promotional base and lack of regional identity in the markets;
- a narrow product base;
- overdependency on a few markets;
- overexploitation of key resources;
- inadequate infrastructure;
- cumbersome immigration and customs regulations;
- inadequate human resource;
- cumbersome investment policies.

While on one hand these problems are themselves obstacles to cooperation, on the other it is important to mention that, from the viewpoint of tourism, southern Africa is a small player in the global tourism industry. As such, the implication is that the future of tourism to the region depends on full regional cooperation. Each issue of relevance to this chapter is considered below.

Need for Tourism Cooperation in Southern Africa

Despite the perceived costs of cooperation discussed above, there are often compelling reasons that force countries to appreciate the logic of working together in a regional framework. In the case of southern Africa, several other factors are particularly pertinent, starting with marketing.

Marketing

It was realized that the marketing of the region was weak, unfocused, and uncoordinated. Most of the money that was being spent on marketing and promotion by the individual countries and companies was not being optimally utilized because efforts were not pooled together for maximum impact in the marketplace. There was also the question of the growth in the complexity of the characteristics of the current tourism market about which many writers have noted more generally (Holloway & Robinson, 1995; Payne, 1993). For example, the travel motivations of any standard socioeconomic group in a given market, like Germany, Japan, or Britain, now vary widely depending on the specific conditions of each household. In relation to southern Africa, there is therefore no single country in the region that has the technical expertise and the financial capability to effectively penetrate these market segments. However, by acting together, the region will have a viable base it can use to access the various market segments in the different generating markets of the world.

At present 65% of tourist arrivals to the member states are from the region. The overdependency on a few markets is further aggravated by the fact that each of the countries of the region relies heavily on the former colonial powers as source areas for their overseas customers. Recent developments in the region (e.g., weakening of the South Africa rand) have painfully demonstrated the dangers of overdependency on a few markets. The region is only able to address this and similar types of problems when it is working together as one destination.

Southern African countries are located fairly far away from the main tourist-generating countries of Europe, North America, and Japan. Generally airfares to the region are high and hence the total cost of a holiday to any of the countries of southern Africa is high. The holiday packages offered by each individual country give the potential of a narrow product base and are therefore not competitive, especially given the cost of airfares to the region. However, when the multiple attractions of the various countries of the region are combined and promoted in a set of multidestination holiday packages, they become a viable competitive choice for potential travelers. This has been one of the major compelling factors that has persuaded the countries of the region to develop and promote their tourism through the umbrella organization, RETOSA.

Product Base

Southern Africa is endowed with a wide variety of natural and man-made tourist attractions. The region's product range includes the renown national parks of Tanzania, Zambia, Zimbabwe, Botswana, and South Africa with highlights like the Serengeti in Tanzania, the Kruger in South Africa, and Okovango Delta in Botswana, the "sun, sea, and sand" of Mauritius, Namibia, Mozambique, Angola, Tanzania, the Seychelles, and South Africa, and the unique world scenic attractions like Victoria Falls in Zambia and Zimbabwe. In addition, the region's abundance of cultural diversity ranging from those of Swaziland, Lesotho, Malawi, and Mozambique to those of Namibia, Tanzania, and South Africa helps to add value to the overall attractiveness of the region in the market place.

Overexploitation of Key Resources

Related to the issue of product base has been the overexploitation of the key attractions in each of the member states (e.g., as mentioned, the Victoria Falls in Zimbabwe and Zambia, Kruger National Park and Cape Town in South Africa, the Serengeti in Tanzania, and the Okovango Delta in Botswana). The decision to work together as one destination has meant that pressure could be released from the key attractions of each country and hence ensure the long-term sustainable use of these resources.

Cumbersome Immigration and Customs Regulations

For a long time, nationals of southern Africa have had to obtain visas to visit other countries in the region. International tourists have also had to apply for visas from each country on the itineraries to the region. Besides the costs of the visas the potential tourists have had to endure the delays that are encountered in obtaining the visas from the embassies of the various countries. It gradually dawned on the region's member states that for them to benefit from the forecast growth in tourism during the next decade and beyond, it will be essential to put into place regulations that facilitate the freer movements of persons in the region.

Cumbersome Investment Policies

The increasing interest being shown by international investors in the region has also shown the individual countries the bargaining strength of international hotel and tour operating chains. The member states have now realized that their own strength lies in developing common investment policies and regulations, which they can use as a block when dealing with powerful potential investors to the region.

Miscellaneous Factors

Given the persistent problems that the traditional sectors of industry have been experiencing during the past years, falling prices of minerals, a contracting manufacturing sector, and an unstable agricultural sector that has had to cope with highly inconsistent weather patterns, the tourism sector is perceived as one of the few key industries that will act as an engine for growth for the region in the next millennium.

Davidson (1993) has generally articulated other reasons why regions are pinning their hopes for economic growth and expansion on tourism in the coming decades, including:

- it has enormous potential for employment creation in both the urban and rural areas;
- it is amenable to participation by small-scale operators, including rural communities;
- it has a strong potential for stimulating the growth of other industries in the region because of its high intersectoral linkages;
- it is a direct earner of foreign currency—a commodity that is in short supply in the majority of member states;
- the region possesses a large wealth of unexploited potential in the sector.

Tourism Policies and Institutional Framework

Figure 16.1 shows an organizational structure of SADC with distinct areas of responsibility and relationships. In the context of this chapter, there are two aspects of the structure that are of interest. The first is the tourism coordination unit (TCU) and the other is RETOSA. Created within the Ministry of Tourism and Leisure in Mauritius, the TCU is responsible for the overall coordination of tourism development policy of SADC. This therefore implies that the TCU is responsible for interfacing with all the member countries in the region with a view to streamlining all policy matters that directly or indirectly affect tourism in southern Africa. Other areas of its responsibility are visa issues, cross-border matters pertaining to the movement of tourist vehicles, and security of tourists. Still other tasks include tourist taxes, human resource development, and the needs of the industry, airline policies, and such like matters.

On the other hand, as noted, RETOSA is SADC's marketing and promotion arm and has its headquarters in Johannesburg in South Africa. Figure 16.1 shows not only the respective place of RETOSA and TCU within the SADC structure but also how both organizations are linked vis-à-vis other members of the SADC. First, in a number of instances the policy initiatives taken by the TCU would have resulted from advice from RETOSA, which would have foreseen or realized the negative impact of the issue on the marketing efforts of the region. Second, the board of directors of RETOSA is made up of two members from each

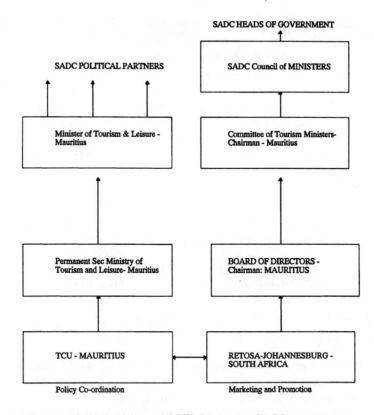

Figure 16.1. Position of RETOSA in the SACD structures.

country, one representing the private sector and the other representing the public sector. The composition helps to bring together the key players in the region's industry, with the result that the programs undertaken by the organization are reflective of the perceived needs of both the private and public sector stakeholders. With this background the rest of the chapter now proceeds to examine in detail the significance of RETOSA vis-à-vis SADC regional arrangements for tourism as reflected in its work programs.

Role and Functions of RETOSA

Reference has been made to the mandate given to RETOSA as the official SADC body authorized to create a concrete destination identity in the tourism market for the region to compete effectively. Furthermore, as a regional body, it is to combine the varied public, private, and community tourism interests into a focused and objective organization better able to respond on issues of "global" common interest or concern. In these respects, the main aims of RETOSA as stated in its Charter (RETOSA, 1996, p. 2) are:

- to market and promote the region in close cooperation with the national tourist organizations and the private sector;
- to facilitate, encourage, and assist in the development of tourism in the region;
- to encourage the involvement of rural communities in the tourism industry.

On a general level, such aims may appear simplistic. However, on reflection they do mask as much as they reveal, particularly relating to RETOSA's remit. What therefore may be implied from the above is that RETOSA has a broad brief that includes the following:

- RETOSA is to be a proactive organization in order for it to serve the interest of the region effectively.
- It will seek to consolidate current generating source markets (particularly Western Europe, North America) while simultaneously exploring new or less well known markets especially in Eastern Europe, etc. These twin roles will require that RETOSA should work closely with the many national tourism organizations and the private sector in the SADC area and also the major tourist "trigger" markets outside.
- Underpinning all this is the need for RETOSA to have a strong lobbying role both in southern Africa and beyond in order to enhance sustainable tourism to the area.

Program of Work

Given the above scenario as described, RETOSA has proceeded to draw up a Five-Year Business Plan of 1997/98 to 2002 (RETOSA, 1998), whose objectives will guide its activities. The broad outline of the Plan is set out as:

- to increase the volume of business to the region;
- to motivate broader intraregional product programming in the target market;
- to increase the awareness of the travel trade in source markets of the region's multi-faceted products;
- to increase consumer awareness and motivation in southern Africa of the benefits of leisure travel in the region;
- to develop and sustain a mutually beneficial relationship with suppliers in the region's markets;
- to identify and develop market niches for the region;
- to identify additional funding sources for the organization's marketing and promotional programs.

In pursuant of the above, RETOSA has also set itself a number of specific targets to be achieved within the plan period (e.g., increasing the region's market share of tourist arrivals from the 1997 figure of 1.6% to between 2% and 3% by the end of the plan period). The overall thrust of the business plan's objectives is to build a clear destination identity for southern Africa utilizing the resources available in the region as well as those of overseas partners with holiday programs to the region through "smart partnership." While there are several problems still facing the region, as discussed above, the various measures being undertaken by the member states to address these issues will lead to the creation of an environment that is conducive to the attainment of the business plan objectives. For example, all member states have agreed to use their overseas offices to distribute regional tourist information, and the private sector in the region has responded positively to co-funding of the first regional tourist directory with RETOSA.

Since its inception in 1997, the organization has undertaken a number of activities within the region and overseas that were aimed at establishing a sound foundation for its future operational activities. First, a well-focused communication program targeted at the key stakeholders in the industry in the region was undertaken. This entailed, among other things, holding meetings with industry and public sector executives in the various member states, participating in regional tourism fairs, and publishing and circulating the organization's newsletter. These activities were aimed at creating an awareness of the existence of the organization. They also offered an opportunity to explain the aims and objectives of the organization and at the same time build industry's confidence on the organization.

Second, a number of interviews were held with both the trade and consumer media within the region. The communication through the media was aimed at increasing the trade's as well as the general public's awareness of the activities of the organization.

Third, negotiations were undertaken with a number of tour operator associations and individual tour operators in the region's primary markets. These discussions were aimed at developing concrete plans for jointly promoting southern Africa in the source markets.

Finally, contacts were made with the region's cooperating partners utilizing the appropriate SADC structures with a view to securing additional funding for the organizations' operational programs.

An Assessment of Work Program

It is pertinent to note that the above activities and the rest of the promotional programs that were undertaken during the organization's first year were able to generate a significant awareness in the industry of the existence of RETOSA and what it stands for. For example, over 40 press articles were generated in both the travel trade and consumer media in the region and overseas ("Making Southern Africa Work," 1998; "RETOSA Ready for Action," 1997; "RETOSA Recognises the Operators," 1998; "SADC Leaders Scrutinise RETOSA Charter," 1997). From another perspective it can be said that the activities were able to begin to address the issue of adding value to what individual countries and companies are doing in marketing and promoting themselves. For instance, joint promotional programs were undertaken with tour operating associations in Britain and Germany. The benefits that the region will reap from sustaining this approach in marketing itself are immense: stretching of budgets, greater media and promotional buying power, faster growth of awareness of the region's products in the marketplace, and strong possibilities of expansion of holiday packages by both new operators and those that traditionally sell southern Africa.

However, the experience of the first year also brought to the fore challenges that the organization has to address in the years ahead. On the one hand, there is an understandable skepticism within certain sections of the private sector in the region. The organization needs to deliver concrete results from which the private sector can perceive direct benefits. This will assist in increasing its credibility within the industry. On the other hand, the taking off of the organization has created high expectations, some of them to unrealistic levels, in the key stakeholders in the region for it to improve the overall performance of the region in the markets. It will be essential for the organization to set out realistic targets that all the stakeholders will agree to and use as a basis for evaluating the organization's performance. This approach will go a long way in preventing the development of a crisis of expectation that in the medium and long term would hinder the implementation of a properly structured marketing and promotional program for the region.

Development Resources

The regional approach to economic development has led to infrastructure developments that have a direct positive impact on the overall development of tourism. For example, multilateral arrangements between South Africa, Mozambique, and Namibia, and between Botswana, Namibia, Zimbabwe, and Zambia, have resulted in the construction of major highways linking these countries, and these developments have facilitated the easier movement of tourists between and among the countries involved.

At a macro-level, southern Africa is developing an infrastructure that is capable of meeting the needs of a growing tourist industry. For example, while there were 21 international airlines flying into Johannesburg in 1991, these had increased to 48 in 1994 and by the first quarter of 1998 the number had grown to 54 (author's personal communication with the airports company of South Africa). Further, a number of international hotel groups have either expanded their operations or have located in the region during the past 5 years. These include the Holiday Inn, the ITT Sheraton, the Intercontinental, the Hilton, the Best Western, the Days Inn Group, Novotel, the Hyatt, and Summit International Hotels. However, at the micro-level there are evident bottlenecks that need to be addressed at both country and regional levels (e.g., inadequate trained manpower, overexploitation of a few attractions leading to ecological threats, and international air access bottlenecks).

Visa

In order to address the problem of visa difficulty, the region has now developed two protocols: a tourism protocol and another on the free movement of people. Both protocols, which are still under discussion by the member states, have the ultimate objective of creating a single visa for visitors to the region and removing restrictions on the movement of nationals of the region and nonnationals alike.

The logical outcome of all this is that the trends in tourism development to the region during the last few years show that the pull factors of southern Africa are currently stronger than the negative factors. For instance, in 1995 the region received a total of about 8.7 million tourist arrivals, in 1996 the figure increased to 9.7 million, and by 1997 the figure had reached 9.9 million (WTO, 1997c, 1998c).

Investment

A large number of projects are currently being undertaken in the various member states and several are on the drawing board. The increase in investment in tourism has been encouraged by the constant growth of the industry in recent years as well as the development of investor-friendly policies in several member states. For example, the adoption of privatization policies in countries like Zambia, Tanzania, Malawi, and Mozambique has helped to attract foreign investment in the tourism sector. In order for the current positive trend in the overall growth of the industry to be sustained, it is essential for the region to compete effectively in the source markets. This will ensure that investors are able to get reasonable returns on their funds on the projects they have embarked upon in southern Africa.

Conclusion

Southern Africa is currently positioned to experience a steady growth within the tourism sector. There are a number of key factors that are contributing to this positive development. First, the political stability that has slowly evolved in the region since the beginning of this decade is now being consolidated. The area's image as an investment destination has markedly improved. Tour operators and other industry players in the tourist source markets are therefore inclined now than before to promote holidays to the region.

Second, the multiple enlightened investment policies that several governments are implementing—privatization, gradual opening up of the skies, creation of special development areas, etc.—assist in increasing a more investor-friendly environment, which will act as a major incentive for the private sector to increase and expand its activities in the tourism sector.

Third, the governments of the region are in the process of putting into place regional policies that are geared at facilitating interstate movement of people. For example, once the tourism protocol has been finalized and rectified by all member states it will mean that cross-border movements of clients by tour operators will become smoother and faster than they are at present. In the long term there is the strong possibility of the concept of the "univisa" becoming a reality in the region. Visitors to the region will need to acquire only a single visa, which will enable them to visit any SADC member state during a single tour to the region.

Fourth, the current growth of the long-haul market segment means that destinations like southern Africa have a major opportunity to increase their market share if they adopt a properly focused approach to their marketing and promotional programs. Related to growth of the long-haul market is the increasing significance of the special interest markets [e.g., meetings, incentives, conferences and exhibitions (MICE), sports, ecotourism, and cultural tourism], which southern Africa is in a position to cater for adequately.

While the above factors augur well for a sustained growth of the tourism sector in southern Africa, it is important for the region to address effectively those factors that are likely to hinder its competitiveness in the global markets. For example, parochial interests of certain institutions of member states need to be properly addressed so that they do not dilute the unitary promotional approach of the region.

In most cases adoption of common policies by any grouping of countries often takes a long time. The SADC region is no exception to this observation. This therefore means that the member states have to put forth concerted efforts in coordinating themselves if the proposed protocols and the related policies are to become a reality in the short term or at least in the medium term. Failure to do so will remove a key element in the creation of an enabling environment that is conducive to the growth of the tourism industry.

It was noted above that there is a certain level of skepticism on the part of the private sector with regard to the ability of RETOSA to carry out programs that will meaningfully add value to their own efforts in the market place. It is important for RETOSA to communicate continuously with the industry, fully involve it in its activities, and produce tangible results in the short term to establish full credibility within the industry. Once this is achieved it will be easier for both the private and public sectors to pool their resources together to market and promote the region in the various source areas of the world.

Given the political will of the region to market and promote itself as one destination and the business opportunities that are brought about by a buoyant tourism industry, RETOSA is in a unique position where it will have to implement programs that are geared at achieving the vision of the region. At the same time, it needs to ensure the involvement of all the stakeholders in the industry in its activities in order to build trust and confidence between the various players from both the public and private sectors. This will hopefully, in the end, create a feeling of ownership to the programs being implemented, a singleness of purpose and sense of oneness as a destination, which are key ingredients to the successful implementation of any regional tourism promotional plan.

Chapter 17

Open Africa: An African NGO Tourism Initiative

Noel N. de Villiers

Summary

Can a strategic catalyst galvanize Africa around a vision of single-minded purpose aimed at optimizing the benefits of tourism in conjunction with protecting its nature and cultural heritage? Open Africa is engaged in an initiative to do so, and this chapter reports on its progress to date. Drawing on Africa's strengths, essentially what Open Africa is doing is to set a systemized process in motion, aligned to coincide with perceived global trends in tourism and the energy generated by the African Renaissance theme. Probably unprecedented in history in terms of its scope, the success or otherwise of the initiative will depend on its popular appeal.

Open Africa is a not-for-profit registered organization. Its trustees and advisors are all eminent leaders in their fields, who see the role of Open Africa as being that of a strategic think tank rather than transactional. Although the initiative was founded with a clear end picture in mind—to optimize Africa's tourism potential in a manner that will nourish and restore its resource base—no guidelines exist on how to set about changing the paradigms of an entire continent. Initially simply to articulate what was in mind proved hugely challenging, and then to steadily build a strategy and devise an enabling system meant starting with a clean sheet of paper with each new step taken. Nor is this an academic exercise. Despite several of Open Africa's trustees and many of its supporters being scientists and academics, its founding was based on experience and intuition rather than research. Blind faith borne out of a love for and belief in Africa was also a factor.

Key words: Open Africa; Nongovernmental organization; Global yearnings; Africa's strengths; Afrikatourism; Roots and routes; Cape to Cairo networking; Values and principles; Community participation; Branding and marketing

Introduction

Africa has both a huge desire and a vast potential for tourism, but a catalytic force is needed if this potential is to be realized. Few disagree that tourism could create many jobs on the continent, probably faster and at less cost than any other economic activity. There are few discussions about development that do not include often dramatic statements about how tourism could alter the continent's fortunes for the better. Generally, the argument goes that this is possible provided the poor image and negative perceptions surrounding Africa can be improved. Sometimes reference is made to this also being provided tourism's development does not follow the usual world trends. The reason for this is that, given the sensitivity of Africa's "product" and the commercial inexperience of its rural communities, inappropriate tourism could result in an exchange of hedonism for heritage.

There is a sense that while the advantages in maximizing the benefits of tourism are recognized, efforts to do so are haphazard. This is not surprising. Governments are not well equipped to find a path between the opportunities and threats in tourism. In Africa, as elsewhere, government departments are structured around the traditional sectors of the global economy. This mold is not ideally suited to tourism. Experience proves that tourism's multisectoral impacts defy strategic optimization through compartmentalization within a single ministry. In any event, tourism ministries are usually more focused on marketing than planning.

Nor can private sector businesses be expected to do more for tourism than will sustain them directly. They furthermore have differing vested interests. This, and the wide spectrum of their inputs and financial resources, militates against the mounting of a coordinated industry initiative to plan and promote tourism.

Aid agencies like the World Bank and European Union do support tourism-related projects, but usually sporadically and not according to an overall plan or strategy. Thus, if tourism becomes a "new generation" industry for Africa in the 21st century, in which it holds sway over a prominent niche specific to its circumstances and characteristics, this will not happen solely for reasons of government or outside intervention. Nor is it likely to happen by chance. Only the emergence of a galvanizing force from within the spirit of Africa itself could bring about the sense of single-minded purpose to achieve this.

The success rate of socioeconomic uplifting endeavors in Africa through the traditional sectors of the world economy is questionable. Other than for isolated pockets of progress, the continent is insufficiently competitive and has too great a backlog in skills and training to enable the radical improvement in its prospects needed to avoid the situation from worsening. This worsening situation is also impacting on conservation, which in Africa means it is threatening what are arguably the continent's greatest assets. You cannot say to a man whose children are starving that he must worry about butterflies.

Paradoxically though, saving the butterflies could be what saves both the man and his child. There is a connection between these two imperatives that suggests Africa could, within a relatively short time, emerge from poverty and debt into a dawn of progress and prosperity, while simultaneously leading the world in developing a new Earth ethic. The coincidence of tourism's phenomenal rise and growth potential, with the global environmental crisis and the consequent emphasis it has placed on all things natural, provides Africa with a propitiously unique opportunity to establish itself as the 21st century haven for nature-interactive tourism.

This is the background that gave rise to the establishment of Open Africa in 1993. The only nongovernment organization (NGO) devoted exclusively to tourism development transcontinentally in Africa, its founding was inspired by South Africa's emancipation. The events leading up to 1994 gave rise to what has since and is ever more popularly being referred to as an African Renaissance, the spirit of which creates the ideal climate for what many people have always believed, which is that Africa's greatest potential is in sustainable tourism.

Initially and broadly speaking, Open Africa had the rather vaguely articulated mission to elevate African values, pride, and prosperity—based on respectful, restorative, sustainable, and profitable use of the unique qualities of Africa's human and natural environment. Since then it has narrowed this down to a specific vision, coupled to a method of accomplishing that vision.

Open Africa's success will depend on the extent to which its concepts are adopted, but whether an NGO or any such structure can make a difference in harnessing tourism's potential transcontinentally is still an open question. No such precedents exist. There are many NGOs operative in conservation and community upliftment, which connects with tourism, but few if any (other than marketing cooperatives) are engaged in initiatives to strategically enhance tourism's potential.

Tourism in Africa

The history of tourism in Africa started with the Ernest Hemingway-inspired and at that time grossly exploitative hunting expeditions. Slowly it graduated from that to sightseeing and mostly vehicle-bound animal photo-safaris, into an ever greater though still minuscule (by world standards) interest in the continent's magnificent natural splendors, both land and marine based. Recently, this interest has expanded to include Africa's place in the history of humankind—in its cultural heritage, paleolithic, archeologic, and artistic. Emerging as a factor in this has been the spirit of Africa, its ancient wisdom, traditions, and values. Both roots and routes are featuring as ever stronger attractors to tourists who in a sense could be described better as pilgrims to this, the mystique-filled land of their ultimate ancestors.

The pilgrim label is not fanciful, as anyone who has spent a night in the African bush will confirm. Asked once about this strange sensation, where it is as if some weight falls off one's shoulders and one becomes enveloped in peacefulness upon treading Africa's soil, well-known conservationist Dr. Ian Player answered that it was easy to explain. With utter conviction, yet quiet simplicity, he replied, "It is because your soul recognizes that it has come home" (personal communication with the author, 1992).

Latest WTO's data (1998c) suggest that Africa has only a 2% share of the over 500 million market of people moving around the world annually as tourists. By the year 2006, just 8 years from now (at the time of writing), this figure will have more than doubled to number 1 billion. Despite Africa's lowly market share, tourism already accounts for 16.5 million jobs on the continent. So if the 2% could be doubled to 4%, which off such a low base should not be too difficult, then quadrupled, Africa could in a relatively short time be catapulted from its perceived basket case status to quite the opposite.

Tourism's projected growth has been demographically determined and is not simply an extrapolation of present trends. Reams of data support the projections, but suffice it to say that whereas 100,000 years ago there were only about 10,000 people living on earth, it took 99,800 years to reach 1 billion. By 1930 world population had increased to 2 billion, by 1960 to 3 billion, by 1975 to 4 billion, by 1987 to 5 billion, by about 1998 to 6 billion. People have always traveled; the only difference is that there are so many more who are now doing so.

The key question is, where are the billion tourists going to go, and why should a greater proportion of them visit Africa? Many will by then have "done" Europe several times. The Far East has attractions, and so does South America and many other places. Noticeably, however, as soon as destinations become popular, they invariably and almost instantly get invaded by denominators of sameness that subject them all to an aura of banal commonality. The Big Mac you find at Disneyland is the same as the one you find in Paris or wherever, as are the experiences and forms of entertainment on offer. This causes fashionable destinations to go into decline quite quickly.

But whether or not the popularity of overcrowded destinations diminishes, more significant is something else that is happening. This is changing things anyway.

Human Compulsion

Wherever one looks these days, a tremendous yearning is evident within humanity to reconnect with the Earth. Signs of this phenomenon are everywhere; one cannot switch on the television (TV), read a book or magazine, listen to the radio, or scan a newspaper without coming across them. Even ecotourism is a manifestation of this yearning, and if you think about it, it is relatively easy to explain.

For all the time that humanity has existed, our survival has been intrinsically intertwined with nature in a dependency mode that demanded eternal respect. This mode remained constant from the very beginning—until just 300 years ago, when Isaac Newton and others came along and said this was no longer necessary. They postulated that nature is linear, mathematically determinable—that it can be manipulated and controlled, and that in effect nothing (or very little) is animate. Put simplistically, what Newton did was to set the world on course for industrialization, which had many advantages, but simultaneously started a process of severing the umbilical cord between humanity and its ultimate mother, the Earth.

Great advances were made, but at great expense. Putting aside the environmental damage and other imbalances, such as the widening of the gap between the rich and poor, what happened and is happening is that people in especially the advanced nations are shriveling up inside, their spirits are pining—*they are starved of the sustenance not of food for their stomachs, but of food for their souls.*

The 300 years during which this alienation has been occurring sounds like a long time. To the living it sounds like eternity, but measured against the time span of humanity's historical background, it is as nothing—merely a blip on the screen. It is like sending your child on a 2-minute errand to the shop to buy bread, but he returns with a lollipop instead. The lollipop is nice, but you have to go back for the bread, for the family cannot survive on lollipops.

Similarly, humanity is now returning to the food for its soul, and that food is the food of Africa.

As the birthplace of humankind, this is where all culture began; Africa is where the relationship between humans and their natural surroundings is still alive. Covering one quarter of the earth's land surface, Africa is where in the history of the world the least number of species extinction has occurred; where the greatest variety of species exist; and where the roots of humans in their present form can be traced back to fossilized footprints lodged in the sand less than 100 km from Cape Town.

Rick Gore, the senior assistant editor of *National Geographic*, who wrote up the story of the finding of these footprints, ended the article with the following words, echoing the yearning to reconnect:

> We cover the prints with sand and head back down the beach. I turn and conjure a parting image of that lone figure standing atop the dune, hair blowing in the breeze, dark skin aglow in the sunset. In my mind she will forever be Eve. I know that's romantic, but I'm a modern human, and I need my symbols and stories to make sense of this world. I imagine her taking that first step down the dune. It's a small and tentative step, latent with curiosity, and 117 000 years later we still don't know where it will ultimately lead. (Gore, 1997, p. 92)

True that we do not know where it will lead. But what we do know is that seldom can anything be predicted with such certainty as the acceleration of the environmental crisis on the one hand (concomitant with a steady withering of our spirits), in tandem with increased global competitiveness as China and other countries with huge production capacities improve their industrial outputs on the other. If the global market is toughly competitive now, imagine what it is going to be like in 30 years' time. And, if what is happening to the environment today is evoking the sort of yearnings for the reconciliation with nature presently being evidenced, think what proportions they will have reached by then.

The Law of Supply and Demand

What has all this got to do with any potential for tourism-induced prosperity in Africa? Primarily it has to do with the law of supply and demand.

If the above scenario is even only half right, then shortly, within the next few years, a huge proportion of the world's biggest market is going to be seeking what is becoming one of the world's rarest products: wilderness. Africa in all its vastness is a wilderness preserve of extraordinary proportions.

Many of tourism's features are ideally suited to Africa's circumstances. For a largely unindustrialized continent the prospect of importing customers is infinitely more attractive than the proposition of trying to catch up with the globe's export markets. Tourists bring themselves to the product instead of the product having to be distributed to them, and then, moreover, pay cash for what they experience and leave the "product" behind for resale over and over again. Furthermore, most of Africa's tourist attractions are in the rural areas, which is also where job creation needs are greatest.

The essential qualities of flair, friendliness, hospitality, and charisma, the essence of what is needed for a healthy tourism industry, are all indigenous traits of Africa. And because people usually excel in doing what they like doing best, it makes sense for Africa to build on these, its strengths.

Open Africa

The mystique of Africa has aroused the curiosity of travelers since early times. For this and other reasons, Open Africa took the view from the outset that Africa itself is the trump card in the tourism potential of its component parts. To avoid imposing or intruding upon the sovereignty of individual states, this approach obliged the initiative to be a pull and not a push action, there for those who believe in it to subscribe to of their own free will.

Open Africa's first output was to proclaim the vision that *Africa can turn its nature and cultural resources into one of the most valuable products on Earth*. Whatever is rare is valuable, so the vision is easy to explain, but it was aimed at more than just the principle of supply and demand. This can best be illustrated by quoting an extract from what was written to President Nelson Mandela prior to asking him to be the patron of Open Africa:

> There are a number of coinciding factors providing a unique opportunity for Africa at this time. These are: the global environmental crisis, which is likely to remain a feature now for as long as the planet continues to support life; a yearning especially among people in the advanced nations to reconnect with their spiritual roots and with nature; the fact that Africa is custodian of the widest variety of the world's natural splendours; and the fact that this is the birthplace of humankind.
>
> Synchronized with these is the phenomenon that tourism has become the biggest and the fastest-growing economic sector in the world. Collectively these factors combined with our climatic conditions, the beauty of our landscapes, and the hospitality and natural charisma of our people, could put Africa at the forefront of a new generation industry of mammoth proportions in the 21st century.

> People need to have a star upon which to hitch their wagon, something t
> yet Africa has never had any kind of vision of hope. To turn the splendou   . our
> natural and cultural heritage into one of the most valuable product on Earth is such
> a vision. It is one to which all can subscribe, because it has benefits for all. Whether
> old or young, rich or poor, black or white, male or female, everybody stands to ben-
> efit from pursuing this goal. It is something with which to capture the imagination
> not only of Africa, but of the entire world. It is a means of restoring and nurturing
> African pride.
> It is our view Mr Mandela that you could inspire the sense of single-minded purpose
> that would make this happen. (Personal letter to President Mandela, 1996)

President Mandela accepted the patronage of Open Africa without hesitation.

As the vehicle through which to realize the vision, Open Africa then proposed the reinvention of tourism in an Africa-appropriate format, under the branding *Afrikatourism* and
based on the twin principles of sustainability and community participation. This proposal
was also multifaceted. Bearing in mind that tourism and even ecotourism is highly competitive globally, and that ordinary tourism can and often does disrupt and destroy places
and environments equally as fast as it raises them up, Africa must necessarily design a
mode of tourism specific to its product and circumstances. In South Africa, for example, a
new White Paper on tourism embraces many concepts relating to the reinvention of tourism in an African mode, in what it calls Responsible Tourism; only, the suggestion here is to
give it an African branding, Afrikatourism, exclusive to this continent, its circumstances,
and its product. This product, Open Africa proclaims, is potentially superior to what the
rest of the world is calling ecotourism.

Initially there was some resistance to the concept of Afrikatourism. Why reinvent the
wheel, some said; while others felt the perceptions of Africa were too negative to allow for
such a branding. But already it has received such strong support that Pretoria University
has established a Centre for Afrikatourism Studies and several government agencies are
commissioning research into its application as a development tool. Despite a limited budget with which to create awareness of the concept, already many operators are allying
themselves with the principles of Afrikatourism, and interest from all over Africa is constantly intensifying.

The next step was the conceptualization of what has become known as the *African
Dream*, to link the splendors of Africa in a continuous network of Afrikatourism Routes
from the Cape to Cairo. Route networking is the easiest way of planning and the most
effective way of selling tourism, while it also has many benefits for tourists.

Africa has 136 million hectares of proclaimed protected areas—in total an area half the
size of India (McNealy, Harrison, & Dingwall, 1994). In addition to this there are hundreds
if not thousands of conservancies and game farms, plus vast areas of wilderness that are
not agriculturally exploitable, like deserts, swamps, and forests. Besides these areas, some
of which are already or can be linked contiguously, there are a myriad of fossil, sacred, and
heritage sites of extraordinary interest, more often than not situated within magnificent
natural surroundings.

The Cape to Cairo concept proved easy to grasp and led to the development of a project
to implement it through innovative use of leading edge technology on the Internet. A Web
site featuring a map of Africa has been designed (www.openafrica.org), on which details
of participants in the African Dream will be entered according to their exact geographical
coordinates. The project has three primary objectives:

- To stimulate the development of Afrikatourism Routes, both new and existing.
- To gather information on Afrikatourism resources.

- To disseminate information on Afrikatourism to potential participants and consumers.

Presently, one nodal model of Afrikatourism Routes covering the Western Cape is being mapped. Once completed, this model will be made available to other areas wishing to participate in the project. The process of forming a route or converting an existing one to embrace the principles of Afrikatourism is facilitated by extension officers who spend time in the field explaining the concepts of Afrikatourism and the project to tourism operators and communities. Simultaneous to spreading the word about Afrikatourism, valuable information on the tourism sector is gathered this way. Each route and each participant is accurately mapped by using Global Positioning System (GPS) instrumentation, so that the information gathered is of a spatial nature coordinated with the needs of planning and other relevant bodies.

With game parks and protected areas as the beacons between which they stretch, for Afrikatourism Routes to be meaningful they must each have at least one outstanding feature around which their attractions can be developed. The only criteria for participation in the project, which is free of charge, is adherence to the values and principles of Afrikatourism. These, quite simply, entail utilizing resources sustainably in a manner that embraces community participation.

Web site viewers will be able to zoom in on areas that interest them and see the routes that have been mapped. Each route, in turn, will display background information covering its features and characteristics, together with a list of participants and their contact details.

Thus, corridors of tourism development will become a reality, visibly snaking their way across the continent in what will hopefully become an infectious initiative. The African Dream could become the biggest transcontinental project ever undertaken. Despite this, it will be relatively easy to accomplish. Its socioeconomic benefits, through job creation, through serving as an information source to tourists, and as a database for planning, will be many. It contains the motivational elements that will stimulate Africa to take a new look at itself, to recognize the tremendous wealth in its heritage, and to protect that heritage. It will inspire the universal question, "what are *you* doing to bring us one step closer to the dream?" This is a question that can be posed by anyone—government departments, officials, corporations, airlines, municipalities, artists, politicians, and housewives—to anyone. It is a calling to which all Africa's people will want to answer—a compulsive, spontaneous response to the beat of Africa's distant drum. It will serve the interests of conservation better than even legislation could, for anyone whose actions detract from the dream will have to account to the public for their behavior.

It also means the industry will be easier to manage, but, what about violence, crime, and a lack of infrastructure?

Violence and tourism are incompatible. Africa is perceived to be extremely violent, even though violence is endemic in few countries on this continent by comparison with the rest of the world. Nevertheless, perceptions are very difficult to change. But in this case a network of tourism routes will probably do more than anything else could to improve Africa's image.

Crime is a city problem, no different in Africa than elsewhere, and tourists better than anyone already know that. Governments are aware of this too and are especially sensitive about protecting tourists, which is an effective incentive to them to combat this scourge. Meanwhile, it is a fact that rural Africa, which is where most of its splendors are situated, is virtually crime free.

Infrastructure is not as much of a problem as it is made out to be. People visit places to experience them as they are and in Africa this means primarily to interact with nature, which allows for innovative creativity in providing facilities. Several game parks, for example, have tented accommodation that attracts the same revenue as do five-star hotel rooms that cost 20 times as much to erect. Disneyland is amazing, but does not compare with the African night sky; Europe is full of art galleries, but here we have prehistoric paintings in caves stretching over thousands of kilometers from one end of the continent to the other; there are orchestras in all the major cities of the world, but here musicality is a part of the rhythm of life of every African village. It is not that Africa is better, but that it is different, and what we need to do is to become aware ourselves of the value of that difference and to turn it into an asset for others to appreciate.

Following on the vision, Afrikatourism, the Cape to Cairo concept, and the African Dream Project, Open Africa has introduced an icon to serve as a logo for Afrikatourism, and as a symbol of everything that is excellent in Africa (Figure 17.1). This footprint image has especially been based on the fossilized footprints found near Cape Town, having in mind also that to feel a place, the best way of doing so is through your feet; that in terms of continuity there is nothing more contiguous than footsteps; and that everything Afrikatourism embraces has to do with getting one step closer to the dream.

But the icon is meant to convey more than that. It is a symbol—a symbol of hope. The significance of symbols is that they make you feel "something" without being specific about what that something is.

Instead of analyzing it reductively, which is what articulation demands, the intention is that it should be amplified imaginatively, from the "what is" to the "what could be" scenario. Divined out of the many and great but unrecognized strengths of Africa, this footprint and what it symbolizes in terms of Afrikatourism and the African renaissance is beyond the reach of verbal expression, for its meaning is in what it inspires, arouses, stimulates, and initiates in the minds and hearts of those who believe in it.

As a symbol, what the footprint implies is there to be molded in the minds of its adherents, stretched, pulled, pushed, and experimented with—like a tune to which one can dance, a kite to fly, a song to sing; flexible, pliable, and unfettered, it should never be reduced to absolutes in terms of words or explanations. This way, what it embraces can be "owned" by anyone who is proud to be African.

Appealing as is the idealism and emotion it evokes, Open Africa's initiative will succeed or fail according to the extent to which ownership of it is taken over at the operational level by tourism industry participants, NGOs, and governments. Conservationists generally embrace the principles and are leading the way in applying them, which is also influ-

Figure 17.1. Footprint icon of Open Africa.

encing NGOs at community level to do the same. Although this is significant, ultimately it is going to be profit opportunities in the private sector that makes the difference. If entrepreneurs make money out of Afrikatourism and in so doing create jobs, governments are also certain to provide their support.

Key to inspiring entrepreneurship are the intermediate public/private promotional bodies like publicity associations and tourism boards. These usually underfunded organizations are invariably staffed by highly motivated and enthusiastic people, despite the considerable obstacles they face in achieving their goals. If the concept of Afrikatourism Routes is embraced by them as an enabling opportunity to focus and coordinate their initiatives, half the battle will be won. Once that happens, the benefits of target marketing will flow through, while simultaneously enhancing the prospects for seamless cooperation between areas without disturbing their sovereignty. Thus, liaison with these intermediaries is the next critical step for Open Africa.

Although its trustees have no ambition for Open Africa to exist beyond its usefulness as a strategic catalyst, until then its own sustainability must be ensured. The founding of the initiative was enabled financially through Africa's leading petroleum company, Engen. This they justified by contextualizing their main corporate responsibility thrust, job creation, with their commercial aim to sell more fuel. Everything to do with tourism has a fuel component. Following this principle, of contextualizing corporate responsibility and commercial goals, Open Africa is now drawing more corporate entities into what is being called a Team Africa alliance. There are few forms of enterprise that do not benefit through a vibrant tourism sector, and while alliance members gain from using the footprint icon as a marketing tool, their use of it in turn gives more exposure to Afrikatourism and provides Open Africa with a source of revenue.

Conclusion

Open Africa can be summed up in a sentence. It is a vision to which all Africa's people can subscribe, coupled with an Africa-exclusive niche, branding, and enabling system that aims to link the continent's splendors through networked Afrikatourism Routes from the Cape to Cairo.

Considering the complexity of tourism, its perceived intangibility, and the fact that Africa comprises more than 50 countries, will this make a difference?

It is too early to tell whether Afrikatourism will take root as intended, though the early signs are positive. If it does, the next threshold will be how readily Afrikatourism Routes develop and whether the concept becomes infectious. In some places "the route concept" is already well established and successful, the Wine Route near Cape Town being an outstanding example.

The route concept offers extraordinary opportunities for innovation and variety. Besides following significant features and characteristics, which Africa is blessed with in vast quantity, they can be based on any of many modes of transport. With safaris already a distinctively African form of exploration, historic, rail, river, sea, horseback, hiking, balloon, bicycle, ox wagon, and even elephant-borne routes can be added to the conventional means of travel by road and air. Further innovations are invited in the nature of routes themselves, some of which could be thousands of kilometers long (say a Rift Valley Route), and others no more than a few hundred meters through a marketplace, for example.

Much will depend on attitude, and attitudinally Africa is presently in an excitingly dynamic phase. The words renewal, revival, and renaissance are in the air, which is the ideal climate in which to enlist common allegiance and support for something in which people can genuinely believe—a message with a promise around which they can be united in a common cause. Open Africa's message is such a message.

Chapter 18

African Tourism Training and Education: Hits and Misses

Roger Doswell

Summary

This chapter takes a generalized approach to Africa, drawing on the examples of a wide variety of countries from across the continent. In this it has attempted to construct an aggregate of African experience. Although Africa is diverse and countries are not the same, there is value in constructing this kind of general picture. It provides insight into the successes, failures, and omissions—the hits and misses—and we can compare and assess any country's experience against the rule. The chapter discusses the tendency to irrelevance and cultural bias in many past initiatives, and the influence exercised by the aid donors. Public sector administration is also discussed, together with the reasons why certain courses of action are simply inappropriate or unworkable. The chapter goes on to describe Africa's training hits and misses and partial hits and misses. It then summarizes the types of training needs, the distinct levels of skill, and the right kinds of institutional approach. The chapter concludes by outlining an African approach to tourism vocational education and training.

Key words: Hits and misses; Partial hits and misses; Irrelevance; Cultural bias; Public sector administration; Employment information system; National training plans and strategies; Employable skills; Occupational skill standards; National curriculum; Testing and certification; Opportunities; Attitudes; Expectations; Needs; Entry-level requirements; In-service training; Multinationals; Fast food; Mobile units; Distance learning; Regional collaboration; Levels of responsibility and skill; The institutional approach; National committee or council; Vocational teachers; Support network; Public awareness

Contemporary Africa and Tourism Education and Training

Vocational education and training covers the development of a people's capacity: the teaching of specific skills and knowledge; the process of preparing and helping them to be able to perform jobs to given standards. In Africa, where the development of previously unknown industries and services created a sudden and immense need for new skills and knowledge, it is especially challenging.

To say that an industry knows what it needs can be a false generalization. Some enterprises know; others do not. Training institutions should sometimes follow the lead given by industry; sometimes they should take the lead themselves.

- Generally one can follow the lead of the more professional companies (these include the multinationals). They usually have sound marketing, well-developed products, up-to-date technology, and sound training programs. These companies tend to show the way. They are usually the first to support the activities of a training institution, using its services and employing its graduates.
- However, other companies may have poor standards. They do not know how they are deficient or what they need. In such cases, the training institutions should take the lead—setting standards and providing relevant training. Unaware of their problems, many enterprises do not recognize the value of training. "We're very experienced," they say, "we don't need training."

From another standpoint, students leaving a full-time course may be trained but need to acquire experience. Doing the job will develop confidence and polish skills. Effective training needs a partnership between the industry (selected enterprises) and the training institutions—each supports the other in providing the right mixture of theory, practice, and experience.

Irrelevance and Cultural Bias

There are three sets of criteria that should govern the development of operational standards:

- Best practice and common principles in satisfying safety, hygiene, cleanliness, upkeep, and many customer care requirements. These represent international norms; they apply in any country.
- Culturally determined practices that reflect the whole feel and way of life of the country in question. These are practices that may vary from country to country. For example, in a Western context good service may mean placing food onto the customer's plate. In another culture it may be normal to allow customers to place food onto their own plates.
- The satisfaction of market expectations: the likes and dislikes of particular customers.

Multinational hotel and tourism companies tend to follow best practice in all their operations. They may also mix Western and local practice, meeting international customer expectations while incorporating local features. For example, multinationals may operate international style food and beverage outlets as well as restaurants or bars with local styles and themes.

Both bilateral and multilateral aid programs have funded and flavored many technical assistance projects with European-focused values. However, all such aid agencies have tended to acknowledge the importance of cultural differences. For example, in 1976 the International Labor Organization pointed out that, "each training structure reflects a different national philosophy in training young people for a trade, springing from its own human (ethnographic even) social, historical, political, and economic background. These differences are of course not confined to countries with a long-established tourism tradition and they are even more marked in developing countries" (International Labor Organization, 1976, pp. 2–3).

However, Western vocational teachers often failed to introduce local elements into their courses. They used curriculum from home without adapting the content (e.g., menus, recipes, and service techniques). The belief that this was right was often deeply rooted in a teacher's values. There was often an attitude of superiority and "we know best." Mostly Europeans, such people have never doubted themselves or questioned the relevance of their teaching.

Courses not only ignored local commodities, supplies, and culinary and hospitality traditions, but also disregarded the rest of the country's cultural fabric. Ali Mazrui points out the case of universities, "In most African countries the institution of the university itself is one large piece of Western culture transmitted to an alien country" (Mazrui, 1990, p. 200). Perhaps this could not be otherwise, given the newness of the institutions and the need, at the time, to recruit teachers from abroad. Teachers bring their particular values and mindset with them.

Even so, aid agencies have made little effort to prepare their technical experts for international assignments in any formal way. They have not tried to teach the teachers about the local culture, to sensitize them to the underlying values, and to show them how to adapt standards to the local needs and realities.

In this regard the key issue is always relevance. The International Labor Organization (1976) has also indicated that, "Taking into account the inertia and resistance to change which usually affect institutional training structures, the models offered by countries with a long established tourism tradition cannot always be said to be well suited to present hotel and tourism conditions and patterns" (p. 2). Talking about Jamaica, Rex Nettleford pointed out back in 1970 that it was vital that the University of the West Indies satisfy "the needs of the territories it was designed to serve" (Nettleford, 1970).

However, when there are no local teachers international agencies supply foreign personnel. "Let's send a team in," they say. Even when briefed and well prepared these personnel may still come heavily laden with irrelevant material and concepts. Also, their African counterparts may pick up, and hold to, some of the same inappropriate ideas. The result is that Africa has often imported obsolescence, irrelevance, and resistance to change.

The answer to this situation is well recognized. It has been better in the long run to send people out to study than to bring people in to teach. This enables Africa to develop its own cadres of experts and technical teachers. However, to bring them home again needs a stimulating and stable environment, good conditions, and competitive salaries. When these Africans return home, they develop others and work their own miracles. However, Africans sometimes stay where they are—they do not come home and so foreigners take their place.

For example, an African may accept an offer of US$60,000 annually to leave Africa and teach in the U.S. An international agency hires a foreigner to replace him, also for an annual salary of $60,000. The African cannot earn $60,000 if he stays at home, while the foreign teacher replacing him may never be offered $60,000 to work in the U.S. This seems one of life's absurd contradictions, to be overcome only through Africa's economic growth and development.

Imported standards and curriculum should always be adapted to local culture and circumstances. However, in an increasingly globalized environment there is more sharing, more technology transference, and a greater convergence in systems and standards than ever before. The Internet can now access information quickly and openly. An explosion in technical publishing has also thrown vast quantities of information into the public domain. More chances now exist to search out and adapt the best of international experience and benchmarking. Hence, the zeitgeist cliché "think globally and act locally."

Public Sector Administration

Tourism training should be the subject of a public and private sector partnership. Forces join together under public sector coordination to provide training for all types and levels of need.

In this sense, one can judge governments:

- by what they want to do and can do;
- by what they decide not to do;
- by what they recognize that they cannot do.

The private sector and general public tend to expect too much of governments. On the other hand, governments do well to understand their own limitations and where they need to improve.

What makes a hit or miss, or an initiative that only partially hits or misses, is usually a complex question. Something was either right, partially right, or wrong given the particular characteristics, timing, constraints, and capacity of the administration responsible. The following 13 points are typical of the problems encountered:

- The circumstances were different from those supposed. The solution didn't work.
- Needs were not researched. Wrong courses of action resulted.
- Political priorities were misplaced. The idea was desirable but unworkable.
- The timing was wrong. The idea might have succeeded but conflicting activities deflected support.
- Consultation was absent. Not enough people knew.
- Involvement was absent. Not enough people participated.
- The resources were inadequate. There were insufficient funds, people, and know-how.
- The administrative capacity was deficient. The organization and people responsible were unable to cope with the demands.
- People didn't respond. Cultural values and social criteria made them think differently.
- The idea just didn't work. It didn't fit with the country's beliefs, rhythms, patterns, and ways of doing things.
- The policy and power relationships changed. There was no continuity of approach from either the government or the private sector or both.
- External aid agencies followed their own ideas; after they quit there was no follow-up. Local capacity and involvement were absent.
- Nobody believed strongly enough. There was no will to succeed; not enough determination, not enough desire.

The existence of the right conditions is critical to the success of a thing. Trying to create these conditions is the first priority, but sometimes a government is blocked by profound differences or difficulties. It can stumble into unworkable courses of action: "we tried—but I don't know, we just couldn't."

Hits and Misses

This section is descriptive only, identifying many of the training situations, successes, and predicaments currently or recently found around Africa. The "Hits and Misses" has been used to highlight the rights and wrong. However, most things do not fall neatly into a particular category. A "hit" is seldom a complete hit and is usually best described as a partial hit; in turn, a partial hit can also be described as a partial miss. Most happenings might best be described as partial hits and misses. For example, some things are either done well or only relatively well done, or partially, or badly, or not at all. Countries are poorly advised or wrongly copy another country's mistaken solutions. And sometimes resources are not used to the best advantage.

Like development itself, the hits and misses are often random by nature. There is little structure or strategic thinking. However, there is always some training that occurs even at the most elementary on-the-job level. And there is no training, however sketchy or misguided, that does not bring some benefit.

Hits

- **Attempts made to establish a comprehensive national training plan or strategy.** One has tried to identify all current and future training needs, by occupation, level of skill, subsector, and location. This is a hit. However, the training provided responds to some but not all of the needs. One has achieved part of a strategy but not a complete strategy.
- **Training institutions now exist where none existed before.** One has established tourism training institutions and centers. Even when aimed at the wrong objectives, mismanaged and underfunded, they still exist. Alternative funding, a different or enlarged role, and revised objectives can probably revitalize them.
- **Tourism training has sometimes helped to absorb people in need.** One may have identified and addressed significant retraining needs (e.g., among the combatants engaged in civil wars).
- **Supervisory and management courses have been a good way to start.** Industry has often supported supervisory and management courses. Training should always start from the top; only trained supervisors can train their own staff. This type of training also brings recognition and status, acting as an advertisement for other programs.
- **Training that has concentrated on employable skills.** In many cases courses have quite rightly concentrated on the development of employable skills (courses clearly based on job-related skills, e.g., separate modular courses for hotel reception, housekeeping, food preparation, and restaurant service). Students can go on, after a year of basic skills in one area, to acquire skills and knowledge in another area. They can also go on to study an area in greater depth, at the intermediate and advanced levels. Governments do well to create a system of accreditation, standards, testing, and certification, encouraging enterprises to operate their own training programs within a common framework.
- **Too many management diploma courses for new entrants.** In other cases, countries have introduced full-time management diploma courses for school dropouts. Some of these courses, with something of everything, teach too much too shallowly. It is not easy to find employment for insufficiently skilled graduates.
- **Multinationals have made a significant contribution.** As already noted, the presence of multinational hotel and tourism enterprises has brought many good training systems with well-prepared trainers and training materials. Multinationals tend to demonstrate soundly developed standards and procedures, and generate a large number of well-trained personnel.
- **Fast food outlets have also helped.** Internationally, franchised fast food outlets have made a notable contribution to training. They have both taught and demonstrated sound cleanliness and hygiene, workplace discipline, and courteous service.
- **Mobile units have spread training.** Training institutions can wrongly concentrate courses and programs in one place only. Mobile training teams take training to the various regions of a country—to wherever it is needed.

- **Distance learning has also spread training**. Distance learning has opened up new possibilities for various workers. Well-produced training material multiplies the training impact.

Partial Hits and Misses

- **Opportunities for regional collaboration**. Africa has seen considerable collaboration between countries. However, opportunities remain for the tourism training institutions to exchange more information on standards, curriculum, and teaching material. This takes full advantage of "best practices" distilled from the continent's collective experience. However, one sometimes finds the attitude, "We don't want to copy other countries. We want to develop something ourselves." Any approach should be adapted to local circumstances but one can always learn from others. It is a fitting axiom that, "there is always another country somewhere that is doing it better than you."
- **Curricula that have been developed but without occupational skill standards**. Curricula without standards are like journeys without destinations. Institutions have often failed to prepare and agree upon occupational skill standards with the industry, before drawing up the corresponding curriculum. These standards, agreed upon by industry, ensure that curricula have clear objectives that match the needs.
- **In-service training programs may represent isolated and uncoordinated initiatives**. There may be in-service training courses found in only a few businesses. In these, widely different standards exist and there is no uniform system of certification.
- **Situations where there is no testing and certification available for existing workers**. Few attempts have been made to accredit prior experience and learning with opportunities for existing workers (who have learned on the job) to brush up their skills and knowledge, take a test, and obtain the appropriate certification. This denies them recognition and a way to structure and advance their careers. Also, because there is a correlation between standards, training, and quality, the sector cannot assess accurately its relative strengths and shortcomings. Nor can it link training standards and staff competence to any licensing and classification of hotels, restaurants, and other establishments.
- **Training schemes are seldom aimed at women**. Improved training and career prospects for women should act as major criteria in the development of training initiatives.
- **Skills training that has taken too long**. Skills training has often been too long (e.g., a basic housekeeping course that takes a year). With well-developed teaching methods and materials, training can be quicker.
- **Training institutions, once established, often deteriorate rapidly**. Some training institutions, once established, have continued to operate with relative success. Others have had difficulty in maintaining their installations and equipment, in keeping their teaching staff, and in funding their training programs. Once a training establishment starts to deteriorate in this manner it loses credibility.
- **Teachers leave to work in the industry**. Qualified and experienced vocational teachers may be head-hunted by the industry. Offered better salaries and conditions, they leave their training posts. Government-run institutions are only competitive when their personnel are given comparable salaries and career prospects.
- **Teachers get out of date**. Some teachers who remain possess insufficient industrial experience and have difficulties in keeping up to date. This makes them lack credibility. Exchange schemes and periods of industrial attachment can help to overcome this problem.

- **Courses are often padded with content of a general educational nature.** Curricula sometimes include large chunks of general educational subjects, ideologically or politically focused. This encroaches on the vocational training content and there is less time available to achieve the targeted levels of job knowledge and skills. Educational authorities may also force tertiary-level vocational training institutions to spend valuable time filling in the gaps left by an inefficient secondary school system.
- **Vocational training objectives should be focused.** In relation to the last point, there is often the tendency to look at general education and vocational training as one process. To some extent this is right. However, training should focus on its objective—to enable a person to get a job, do it effectively, and earn a living.

Misses

- **A reactive rather than active stance.** Many countries deal with aid donors in a passive way: "Let them make us a proposal and then we'll see." It is better to take the approach, "Let's make them a proposal." This forces people to think out their needs and what they should ask for. There is a difference between getting what one needs and getting what one is given.
- **A lack of employment information.** Sometimes, no accurate data exist on the profile and characteristics of the existing labor force, or on future staffing and training needs.
- **Training institutions run by the public sector.** Training institutions have been run by different government agencies, sometimes the Ministry of Labor, sometimes the Ministry of Education, and sometimes the Ministry of Tourism, either alone or working in collaboration. However, "fighting for territory" between one or all of these parties has often served no purpose other than wasting time and resources.
- **Training has not triggered development.** Training has responded to development. It has not been used to trigger development. Training for personnel in small enterprises, community development projects, and family-run businesses may well trigger the creation of new projects, or business extensions and expansion. In this case, all new proposals must be shown to be feasible. These projects, to be successful, need specific marketing programs (through perhaps a marketing cooperative). Projects should be initiated not only because they are desirable but because they are feasible.
- **Too much emphasis has been placed on the public sector role.** The private sector has often neglected training while the government's training role has been exaggerated.
- **Governments' attempts to fund training have tended to be ineffective.** Various ways of funding tourism training, through training levies on total wages or tourism taxes on hotel and restaurant revenues, have met with little success. These types of taxes are difficult to collect in a consistent and equitable way. They may also be difficult to disburse in a fair and effective manner. Worse, sometimes they have not been used for their intended purpose but swallowed up wholly or partly into the general revenue.
- **The private sector does not have confidence in public sector initiatives.** In many countries the African private sector has had little confidence in government-operated training institutions, preferring to rely on its own (often mediocre) on-the-job training programs.
- **Parts of the private sector do not support training.** In addition to the point above, the African private sector may not believe in formal in-service training programs and certification. "It wastes working time, adds to costs, fills the heads of the workers with

the wrong ideas," businessmen say, "Staff get too full of themselves and start to ask for better conditions, shorter hours and more pay!"

- **Training in secondary schools overlooked**. Hotel and tourism training has often been overlooked at the secondary school level. Secondary schools may not be vocationally oriented and, if they are, may not include hotel and tourism subjects. Such schools may be ideally located, in the vicinity of areas of tourism development, to introduce basic entry-level courses. It is often cheaper and more timely to train in these secondary schools than in tertiary-level technical training institutions.

- **Entry-level requirements too high**. Educational entry requirements for courses are sometimes too high. They may exclude important and needy sections of society. This is particularly true for basic/entry-level courses.

- **There have been few work-based supervisory and management training schemes**. Industry-wide supervisory and management certificate and diploma schemes can be introduced for skilled workers, supervisors, and middle management personnel. Based on core subjects and electives, they can recognize a wide range of short courses, seminars, workshops, and other part-time training activities. Personnel can accumulate credits over a period of time in a flexible way. Such schemes create opportunities for existing personnel who may not have had the chance to attend college or institutionally based full-time courses.

- **No formal entry-level in-service training schemes**. One has ignored formal entry-level in-service training in some types of establishments. However, new entrants have learned by working on the job, and although most are not well trained they have become experienced workers. As noted, they could now undertake a refresher course and go through the testing and certification procedures.

- **There is an excess of university graduates**. Countries may often have an excess of university graduates in a variety of disciplines. With few appropriate job and career opportunities they join the unemployed. However, if the needs exist, conversion courses can bring such persons into the hotel and tourism field.

- **Student attitudes and expectations**. Vocational education and training not geared to employment realities can develop false expectations. Just as university education may not match job opportunities, tourism education and training may not fit with an industry's needs. This can occur not only in terms of skills, but also in student attitudes.

- **No multiskilled training for small enterprises**. For the more modest small enterprises, restaurants, and guest houses, the skills included in curriculum are too specialized (e.g., cook, food service, housekeeping, and front office). Staff need simple skills in two or more of these specializations.

- **Few new skills for the owners and managers of existing small enterprises**. While many countries have developed full-time management education for school dropouts, few have succeeded in upgrading the skills of the owners and managers of small tourism enterprises.

- **Training opportunities favor the children of the urban elite**. Institutionally based full-time courses for school leavers usually have an entry requirement of senior high school certificate or equivalent. Such courses are often management oriented, leading to the award of diplomas or degrees. They may be government subsidized and/or require the payment of fees. As a result, one finds the following characteristics:

  — students are the children of the middle and upper middle classes drawn from the urban areas;
  — these students will only consider careers in international class hotels or travel agencies, of which there are few;

— they will not work in small enterprises, unless they are owned by their families;
— students are often put off by the hours and working conditions in hotels, and prefer to work in banks, insurance, retailing, and other service subsectors. They see the hotel and tourism course as a passport to this kind of career.

- **Skills become part of a rigid hierarchy.** One tends to place the skills and knowledge that pertain to the management and operation of tourism enterprises on a ladder, climbing from low-level to high-level requirements. This ladder tends to become too fixed. While some people are at the top and some people are at the bottom, the system should be open and adaptive. It should allow for free movement based on job skills and performance. Many countries have created a rigid hierarchy with no linkages or movement between the different levels. People tend to be locked into particular jobs for their lifetimes with no opportunity to grow and advance.

Training Needs

A part of the problem of "misses" may be caused by the failure of tourism development plans. They may miss a number of potential initiatives, particularly those a little outside the mainstream markets. An example is the special interest market segments, which seek alternative tourism possibilities, covering distinctive cultural, natural, and ecotourism experiences. The following supply-led breakdown of types of tourism enterprises indicates these options; each type of enterprise will then create a particular set of training needs.

Types of Enterprise

- **Community-based projects.** Tourism at the local community level offers opportunities for the development of marketable small projects. These can be built through collective action and neighborhood collaboration. Training can stimulate locally based initiatives, and create sustainable livelihoods. Village tourism represents one example of a community-based project of this kind.
- **Small and micro tourism enterprises.** Tourism offers many possibilities for small or micro initiatives: for example, running small guesthouses or restaurants, handicraft kiosks or food stalls, offering beach services such as manicures or massages, and selling fresh fruit or beverages on the beach. These may be organized through local community initiatives or various types of self-employment or cooperative schemes.
- **Family-type projects.** Family-type projects may consist of any of the above small projects. They are of the type to engage the whole family in the enterprise. For example, a small family-run guesthouse may not only represent a feasible business in itself but diversify the accommodation supply in an attractive and compelling manner.
- **Supporting small enterprises in related sectors.** Tourism offers a chance to develop various kinds of supporting services (e.g., in agriculture and fisheries, supplying hotels and restaurants with fresh produce and fish). There may be other market gardening possibilities such as the production of flowers, and room and table displays and decorations, or similarly, in providing, for example, laundry and dry cleaning services, or in printing brochures, in-house and promotional material.
- **Medium-sized tourism enterprises.** Medium-sized tourism enterprises are likely to employ 30 persons or more. The scale of their operations usually requires management and occupational specialization.
- **Large local private or government-run enterprises.** Depending on the country, there are some large locally owned and operated private companies. Most government companies have now been privatized.

- **Large chain-operated and/or -owned units.** As already noted, these tend to act as the leaders of the industry, employing modern management techniques and up-to-date technology.

In his opening address to the UN seminar on economic restructuring and social policy, Rafeeuddin Ahmed pointed out that,

> Poverty cannot be reduced without economic growth, and economic growth cannot take place when millions are still trapped in poverty. The poor are key economic players, and their importance must not be overlooked. Economic growth must therefore be based on the mobilisation of the poor's resources and abilities, and on their access to key assets of production. It should empower people not marginalize them. Poverty reduction must not only be seen as an end in itself but as a means for achieving sustained economic growth. (Ahmed, 1995)

Tourism can do something to alleviate poverty. In particular, the earnings from small, locally based tourism enterprises may ripple through a whole community; small inputs can bring big impacts with training providing both the ideas and the skills.

Levels of Responsibility and Skill

The distinctive levels of skill and responsibility found in tourism enterprises are well described (Doswell, 1978). There are differences between types of hotel, restaurant, and tourism businesses, but the same five levels can be summarized as shown in Table 18.1.

Job competence is normally based on a combination of technical, social, and personal skills. These differ in mix and complexity according to each job. Jobs may be either less or more skilled. No job is completely unskilled, and less skilled is always a more appropriate term than semiskilled. The major hotel occupations (front office clerk, housemaid or room attendant, waiter or waitress, and cook), for example, normally require intermediate-level skills. However, new entrants (hired after technical training at school or college) are less skilled—at basic or entry level. They need to gain experience, add new knowledge and skills, and advance to intermediate level. Depending on vacancies, some intermediate-level staff may then advance to supervisory level.

Systems should be flexible, respond to people's potential, and encourage them to advance from one level to another. They should be helped to choose a training option to suit their needs, and counseled accordingly.

The Institutional Approach

A particular activity left on its own is unlikely to continue. Funds run out, people pass on, needs change, interest wanes, and the activity dies away. There is nothing to anchor it, no guaranteed succession, no permanent secretariat, no organizational continuity. The activity is not slotted into a policy framework, headquartered somewhere, and given a building. It is not institutionalized.

An institution needs an organization to run it, one that can modify and develop itself according to changing needs and circumstances. An institution fulfills a continuing role. People may come and go, the objectives and activities may change, but the institution goes on.

An institution can also provide the focus for industry-wide training, help to coordinate and supervise agreed standards, and generate the necessary curriculum and teaching material. An institution can create the nucleus of a total training system. It can act as an accreditation body for other centers and programs, administrating the corresponding testing and certification.

Table 18.1. Levels of Skill and Responsibility in Tourism Enterprises

Chief Executive Officers and Deputy Chief Executive Officers. Plus the corporate functional specialists: Financial Comptroller/Treasurer, Marketing Director, Operations Director and, alternatively, Owner/Managers	This level is more entrepreneurial than managerial in the operational sense. It involves the development of corporate policies and strategies, the mobilization and deployment of resources, and the assessment of risks and opportunities.
General Manager and Deputy General Manager. Plus the senior marketing, operational and financial managers or specialists	This covers management at the unit level, with the achievement of the agreed objectives, sales targets, and planned profits. This may include freedom to manage the unit, promote it, and deploy its resources to the best advantage (depending on the degree of empowerment).
Middle management. Department heads.	This level covers the achievement of objectives at a functional or departmental level, translating them into specific monthly, weekly, and daily work plans and schedules. Responsibilities and tasks are covered by job descriptions and skill standards.
Skilled staff	This level covers the objectives specified in the departmental work plans and schedules described above. Personnel also fulfill responsibilities in accordance with job descriptions and occupational standards.
Basic, first level, or entry level and junior operative staff	The basic level covers the fulfillment of specific tasks spelled out by supervisors, and included in job descriptions and skill standards.

Indeed, to provide the necessary leadership and coordination, institutions do not have to undertake all the training themselves. W. Arthur Lewis, in his classic book on development planning (Lewis, 1966), judges that, "A vast multiplication of the facilities for technical training requires priority in every development plan. These need not always be institutional; facilities for apprenticeship and in-service training are just as important" (p. 105).

A key training institution should not be centripetal by nature, drawing its activities to itself, narrowing down and limiting its scope, shutting itself off from the industry it serves. Rather, it has to be centrifugal in its actions, spinning off activities, reaching outwards to spread its influence, covering all needs wherever they occur.

A Vocational Education and Training Strategy and System

The following eight components integrate to form an African training structure and strategy—a total system. However, everything can keep changing, get out of balance, or fall away. Or, with innovation and new ideas, it can get better. A system has to be held together and kept up to date. It has to advance.

- A labor force and training needs information system is important. It monitors the profile and characteristics of the current and future labor force, and identifies the precise training needs of the existing staff and the new entrants to the sector.

- A national committee or council brings together representatives of all the public and private sector interests involved with tourism education and training. This committee or council should deal with all training needs, in all parts of the country, at all levels of skill for all occupations. It should agree on the standards and objectives for each of these. The committee or council should monitor, and advise on, all aspects of training needs, and the schemes, programs, and centers developed to respond to them.
- A cadre of well-qualified and experienced local vocational teachers is essential. However, only attractive opportunities and rewards keep vocational teachers in teaching. To stay, the best ones need a chance to reach out beyond their training institutions. Teachers can help industry; as well as training staff they can make studies, tackle projects, and solve problems. This allows teachers to build their careers, expand their reputations, and augment their earnings. Industry provides teachers with recognition; it bestows prestige and rewards them.
- A training standards, curriculum, materials, and methods information system is also essential. It assures a constant inflow of information, drawn from the Internet and other sources.
- In support of the previous objective one builds a support network establishing formal links with a range of training institutions in various parts of Africa and the world at large. This should include participation in various international associations and organizations active in tourism education and training, and facilitation of international recognition and accreditation of the country's own programs and certification.
- A human resources development strategy describes how each training need will be met. The strategy responds to identified needs and should cover all skill levels. It covers all preemployment institutionally based training (university or equivalent, technical colleges of different categories, and vocational secondary or high schools). It also covers work-based or in-service training at all levels, including various kinds of short, recycling, and upgrading courses.
- Lead training institutions act as hubs in a country-wide network of programs. They can maintain employment information systems and research needs, develop standards and curriculum, accredit other centers and programs, act as testing centers, develop trainers (through "train-the-trainer" courses) and vocational teachers, advise on teaching methods and materials, and field mobile training teams. As noted, to institutionalize does not mean to freeze. The institution goes on constructing the network, keeping it open and flexible, able to respond quickly to a wide variety of needs.
- Public awareness programs are an important part of the system. In Africa they have often been overlooked or only partially organized. They are aimed at four main areas (Doswell, 1997): first, informing people about the positive aspects of tourism; second, ensuring that people are consulted and involved in decisions about tourism development; third, helping them to take advantage of the opportunities offered by tourism; and last, explaining the characteristics of inbound tourists. This lack of knowledge of tourism often gives rise to social, political, and economic discontent, which sours relationships between tourists and the host communities. One aims training programs at all occupations in direct contact with tourists (e.g., hotel, tourist accommodation, restaurant, bar and catering staff, shop assistants, taxi drivers, travel and airline staff, rental car, and currency exchange services).

A country develops its own comprehensive tourism vocational education and training system as described above. It develops it as a home-grown initiative drawing on international experience and expertise. In this sense, the concluding word goes to President Issaias

Afewerki of Eritrea. He combines relevant and globally available information—the learning-from-elsewhere with a do-it-yourself approach. He is quoted as saying,

> We are not rich; we do not have many resources; we are affected by things we cannot control. But we prefer to face our problems ourselves. If you teach someone to fish, instead of giving him fish, then he has a sustainable future. . . . This is difficult for people; it takes a long time. . . . But in the long term, success can only come from inside us. ("Africa Rising," 1998, p. 69)

Chapter 19

Tourism and Land Tenure in Sub-Saharan Africa: The Expansion of the Modern Space Economy

David B. Weaver

Summary

   To date, there has been little explicit focus on the issue of tenure in the tourism litera-ture. Within the context of modernization dynamics, this chapter examines the relation-ships between tenure and tourism in a variety of sub-Saharan spatial contexts. Dominant metropolitan areas and surrounding modern hinterlands possess relatively sophisticated tourism sectors, especially in southern Africa, while the dominantly communal lands of the transitional/traditional space economy participate only marginally in this sector. Pro-tected areas, despite their wilderness-like quality, may be perceived as a special type of modern space increasingly mobilized to provide ecotourism-type experiences. The com-munal lands/protected area interface is identified as a zone of tourism-based tension be-tween the modern and traditional space economies.

Key words: Teure; Protected areas; Communal land; Modernization

> Landholding is at the center of the confluence. Nothing evokes more varied sym-bolic connotations or more intricate legal philosophies. Nothing excites deeper pas-sions or gives rise to more bloodshed than do disagreements about territory, bound-aries, or access to land resources. (Shipton, 1994, p. 347)

Introduction

   Although control over land and other resources is obviously a critical factor in influenc-ing patterns of tourism development, there has been little explicit focus upon tenure is-sues in the tourism literature (D. Pearce, 1989). This holds true for sub-Saharan Africa, even though questions of land and resource ownership have featured prominently in investiga-tions of other sectors, such as agriculture, and in the overall regional development litera-ture (e.g., Shipton, 1994). The neglect of tenure in the sub-Saharan tourism literature owes largely to the relatively low profile of tourism in most of the region (in marked contrast to agriculture), and to the subsequent paucity of research in virtually all aspects of the re-gional tourism industry. While a small number of idiosyncratic tenure-focused tourism studies have been produced, the particular contribution of this chapter is to identify and discuss the broader regional and subregional patterns and trends. The first section examines these trends from the context of a modernization/developmental paradigm. The categories derived from this exercise are then used in the subsequent section to describe and discuss the implications of these patterns for resource use in general, and for the tourism industry specifically.

Modernization and Tenure Patterns in the Sub-Saharan Space Economy

Modernization

Despite the current focus on the nebulous phenomenon of "globalization," the modernization paradigm remains a convenient and relevant framework for understanding changing structures and patterns of tenure within sub-Saharan Africa and elsewhere. As a comprehensive historical process, modernization is defined by Eisenstadt (1966) as

> the process of change towards those types of social, economic and political systems that have developed in Western Europe and North America from the seventeenth century to the nineteenth and then have spread to other European countries and in the nineteenth and twentieth centuries to the South American, Asian and African continent. (p. 1)

Modern space economies, in this framework, are gradually supplanting *premodern* or *traditional* space economies through the diffusion of "Western" capital, technology, and sociopolitical systems. With regard to tenure, structures that are essentially communal gradually give way to systems based upon principles of private ownership, with public participation, through government, tolerated in at least some arenas.

Whether this transition is a positive or negative process is a matter of interpretation, long debated in the development literature by two competing perspectives. Modernization theorists and their neoclassical allies, on one hand, have associated modernization with gradual improvements in quality of life. Communal tenure arrangements, as with other attributes of the traditional space economy, are seen as anachronistic impediments to economic and social development (Firmin-Sellers, 1995). Advocates of Dependency and World Systems theory, in contrast, have equated modernization with the subjugation and subsequent incorporation of viable traditional societies into an exploitative world capitalist economy, in which they serve as dependent "peripheries" supplying cheap labor and goods to the privileged "core." "Rich" and "poor" segments of society, effectively, are both outcomes of the same process. Although this peripheralization process is often presented as a dichotomy between oppressed indigenous peoples and white oppressors, Cheru (1992) points out that the indigenous elite within newly independent African states have often perpetuated and accelerated the modernization process in their own narrow interests. In either case, the issue of tenure, as cited in Shipton's opening quote, is especially sensitive, given its connotations of power and resource control.

The Modern/Traditional Continuum

References to discrete stages such as "traditional" and "modern" are misleading insofar as the modernization process is continuous in nature. The extremes are represented in areas such as the Witwatersrand and in parts of the Kalahari Desert, respectively, but elements of *both* tradition and modernity are evident within most areas of sub-Saharan Africa. Whether a particular area is considered traditional or modern is often thus a question of degree. With regard to tenure, this logic tends to hold true in the more northerly regions of the sub-Sahara, with "pure" communal arrangements gradually giving way, along a modernization continuum, to the private/public dichotomy associated with modern space economies. In such southern countries as South Africa, Zimbabwe, and Namibia, however, hard lines of demarcation were imposed and enforced by the political fiat of minority regimes to separate areas of extensive European settlement from "native" areas. Despite the attainment of majority rule in this subregion, these tenure dichotomies continue to persist as artifacts of the apartheid era. Figures 19.1 and 19.2, respectively, represent hypothetical models of the "southern" and "northern" sub-Saharan states, indicating patterns of modernization discussed in the following sections. States such as Kenya are intermediate between the two variations. Neither variation, however, accounts for anomalies such as Ethiopia, where a traditional feudal structure was supplanted by a Marxist state, or countries such as Tanzania during periods of experimentation associated with policies of "African Socialism."

For both scenarios, a basic distance–decay relationship is apparent, with several distortions as noted. At the core of the modern space economy are *dominant urban centers*, where the characteristics of modernization are best expressed. Such centers function as international gateways and foci for the administration, transportation, manufacturing, and tertiary activity (e.g., finance, retailing) of the state. In the southern variation, dominance may be shared by several urban areas (e.g., Johannesburg, Capetown, and Durban in South Africa), while urban primacy, or single-city dominance, is more characteristic of the northern variation. Northern primary cities also have a greater tendency to display characteristics of dualism, wherein the modern urban space economy coexists with a parallel informal sector. Spatially, this is most visible in the extensive shantytowns of the urban periphery (O'Connor, 1983). Informal (e.g., "squatters' rights") tenure arrangements are charac-

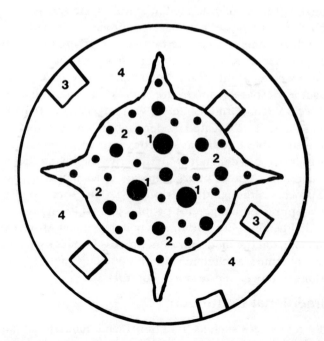

Figure 19.1. Sub-Saharan space economy: southern variation. (1–3) Modern space economy: 1) dominant metropolitan areas (private ownership, some public); 2) modern hinterland (private ownership, some public); 3) modernization exclaves (public ownership). (4) Transitional/ traditional space economy (communal ownership, some private).

teristic of the shantytowns, while the modernized portion of the urban area is dominated by formal private or government control over land.

Extending outward from the dominant urban center is the spatially extensive *modern hinterland,* which is occupied by commercial, privately owned farmlands and other primary sector land uses integrated into the national and global economy. This area provides a high level of services and goods to its inhabitants through a hierarchy of central places. As the state modernizes, this hinterland expands both through contagious diffusion (i.e., an outward extension of the concentric circles) and hierarchical diffusion (i.e., through the growth of lower level urban centers connected by transportation corridors to the main body of the hinterland. This latter form of diffusion is one form of distortion that modifies the "pure" distance–decay relationship. The modern hinterland of sub-Saharan Africa is best articulated in the southern variation of the model, with extensive and clearly demarcated European settlement areas having been established in South Africa, and to a lesser extent, within Zimbabwe and Namibia (Weaver & Elliott, 1996). In the northern variation, the modern hinterland is less articulated in part because of the absence of a European settlement area. Kenya, Zambia, Angola, and Mozambique are intermediate, having had more ephemeral and now residual phases of European settlement. In all cases, the modern hinterlands combine with the dominant urban centers and "modernization exclaves" (see below) to comprise the modern space economy.

Given the rapid pace and deep penetration of the modernization process, it is appropriate to identify a *transitional/traditional space economy,* adjacent to the modern hinterland, in which characteristics of the modern and the traditional are both encountered. Following the distance–decay logic, attributes of modernization tend to dominate near the modern hinterland, while traditional characteristics continue to hold sway in the more

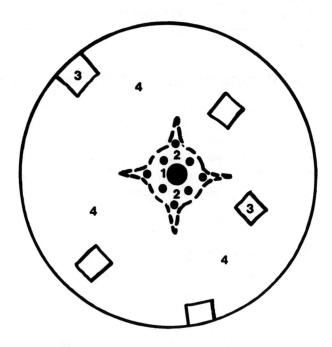

Figure 19.2. Sub-Saharan space economy: northern variation. (1–3) Modern space economy: 1) dominant metropolitan area (private ownership, some public, some informal); 2) modern hinterland (private ownership, some public); 3) modernization exclaves (public ownership). (4) Transitional/traditional space economy (communal ownership, some private).

peripheral regions of the state. Subsistence-based forms of agriculture such as shifting cultivation, nomadic herding, and hunting/gathering, accordingly, have been modified in varying degrees by an increasing level of commercialization, while communal tenure patterns are experiencing widespread distortion and erosion through the intrusion of titling arrangements (Shipton, 1994). Nevertheless, lands falling under the communal rubric are still extensive. For example, it is estimated that 90% of Ghana remains under such land tenure arrangements (Appiah-Opoku & Mulamoottil, 1997). As suggested earlier, the southern variation tends to possess sharp boundaries between the private and communal lands as a residual of colonial rule (evident also in the intermediate states), resulting in somewhat more inertia as to the transformation of these areas into private tenure dispensations. Northern boundaries, on the other hand, are more flexible and interdigitized, indicating a more complex pattern of tenure.

A second major distortion to this model is the presence of imposed *modernization exclaves* within the transitional/traditional space economies. These may assume several forms, including mining or other resource-based settlements, military sites, and protected areas. The latter are particularly important, with national parks and other highly protected spaces (e.g., IUCN categories I–V) constituting about 125 million hectares, or 4.6% of sub-Saharan Africa, in 1993 (World Resources Institute, 1994). Some of these, however, are located within the modern space economy, and do not fall under the exclave rubric. Because these areas tend to be spatially extensive and can be created almost instantly, the establishment of protected areas has contributed significantly to the rapid expansion of the modern space economy. Moreover, because the desired environment of protected areas is a relatively "natural" physical environment, their establishment usually involves the expropriation of truly traditional landscapes. An additional characteristic that pertains to both the northern and southern models, and that has significant implications for resource access and tourism (see below), is the existence of sharp lines of demarcation between the protected areas (i.e., the modern space economy) and the communal areas (i.e., the transitional/traditional space economy).

Implications for Resource Use and Tourism

The modernization process, accompanied by changes in tenure arrangements and in the relationships among the various zones, has resulted in significant changes to patterns of resource use within sub-Saharan Africa, and has subsequently been a major factor influencing patterns of regional tourism development and relevant policy and management considerations. The following sections examine both resource use and tourism in the context of each individual zone described above. Given the residual nature of the true traditional space economy, the latter is considered concurrently with the transitional space economy.

The Dominant Urban Center

Dominant urban centers in sub-Saharan Africa, fundamentally, are the foci of their respective national tourism industries, as they are with other tertiary sector activities. Distinct and complementary patterns of involvement are associated with the private and public sectors, respectively, as in any modern space economy. Tenure-wise, government tends to own gateway facilities and functions associated with international seaports and airports, while the private sector usually controls the accommodation sector, with higher levels of expatriate participation among larger scale hotels. In most of the sub-Sahara, these dominant cities possess a virtual monopoly on business tourism and gateway traffic. More complex is the situation in South Africa, where a mature urban hierarchy accommo-

ʿdates three major metropolitan centers (i.e., Johannesburg–Pretoria, Capetown, Durban) that collectively account for 71% of all bed-nights sold to foreign tourists in 1993 (TTI). Where a dominant city is coastally located (not indicated in Figures 19.1 or 19.2), this high level of tourism concentration may be elevated by the availability of 3S-type (sea, sand, and sun) opportunities within the metropolitan area. Aside from the issue of dominance in tourism, two tenure-related issues with political and management implications are the minimal participation of the informal urban sector (aside from guesthouse-type accommodations and anomalies such as "township tours" in South Africa), and the continuing primary role of minority (i.e., white and Asian) and expatriate private interests.

The Modern Hinterland

Where the transition to a modern space economy has occurred outside of the major metropolitan areas, the natural environment has been largely supplanted by a relatively stable pattern of plantations, commercial ranches, and smaller scale farms, all indicating the economic integration of such lands into broader national and global economies. Scattered throughout such areas are remnant natural habitats protected under public and, less commonly, private auspices. The modern hinterland accounts for most of the remaining tourism industry not concentrated in the dominant metropolitan city, just as it accommodates most of the remaining commercial sector in general. This is most apparent in the European settlement modern hinterlands of southern Africa, where geographical concentrations of wealth are accompanied by racial disparities in the control of this wealth. Whites, for example, control an estimated 80% of the Zimbabwe's private enterprise, and a similar portion of its large-scale commercial farming, despite constituting only 1% of the national population (Meldrum, 1995). Similarly, about 4,000 farmers of European descent control the commercial agriculture sector in Namibia (Weaver & Elliott, 1996).

An analysis of tourism within the modern hinterland of southern Africa reveals concentrations of activity within several distinct spaces. First, nonmetropolitan urban areas offer local and regional attractions, while providing accommodation and other services for domestic tourists in transit. Second, a select number of accessible and high-profile protected areas (e.g., Kruger in South Africa, Victoria Falls in Zimbabwe, and Etosha in Namibia) accommodate large volumes of domestic and international visitation, with some spillover effect accruing to nearby urban areas. A variation of this space involves the growing provision of private game reserves established on commercial farm properties and augmented by vacation farm or B&B-type accommodation. Namibia, for example, had 47 "guest farms" in the early 1990s, accounting for significant portion of that country's accommodation inventory (Shackley, 1993). South Africa's former Transvaal province alone possessed 450 private nature reserves during the same period, while tourism opportunities were made available at many of the country's 8,000–9,000 private farms where at least a portion of the resident livestock consists of wild species (V. Butler, 1995). In Zimbabwe, groups of ranchers have combined to form "conservatories" to manage free-ranging wildlife that had been privatized in a controversial attempt to restore the state's wildlife stocks and to provide a viable alternative to cattle ranching in dry land regions (Hess, 1997). The third type of space entails coastal resorts that provide 3S-type opportunities in suitable locales. In all three instances, a substantial international clientele is augmented by a large domestic market of predominantly European descent, apartheid-era legislation such as the Group Areas Act and the Separate Amenities Act serving to effectively eliminate blacks from participation in the domestic tourism scene (Mkhize, 1994).

The general pattern of tourism activity in the modern hinterlands of the northern model is comparatively simple, owing to the constraints posed by the incipient character of this zone, the small domestic tourist market, and the comparative paucity of international stayover arrivals. One major exception to this pattern, however, is found in the emerging coastal resorts of Kenya, The Gambia, and the island-states of Seychelles and Mauritius.

Modernization Exclaves: Protected Areas

The following discussion focuses upon protected areas, as the other types of outpost mentioned earlier have little if any influence on tourism patterns and trends. Like their counterparts adjacent to or within the modern space economy, protected area exclaves are paradoxical in a number of intriguing ways. First of all, insofar as they represent the desire of a prosperous developed society to preserve, for aesthetic and environmental-related reasons, the remnant natural habitats that have not been requisitioned and radically modified to facilitate economic growth, they are a quintessential feature of the modernization process. However, the visual appearance of the protected area landscape is anything but modern, with park managers usually seeking to minimize any human influences, and thus preserve the area in a "natural" condition. Hence, whereas modernization implies change, progress, and spatial development, the protected areas are intended to be fundamentally unchanged and undeveloped. It is also paradoxical in that this same static quality is the major force responsible for the increased integration of remote protected areas into the national and global economies, with the experience of wild and semiwild environments being in demand among the mainly city-based tourist market. Concurrent to this integration, increased visitation levels can of course serve to distort the environmental qualities that attract visitors in the first instance.

In the face of increased competition for resources in the sub-Sahara, it will be the realized and potential revenues from tourism, rather than any environmental considerations per se, that will justify the continued existence of most protected areas. In the case of privately controlled protected areas, located almost exclusively in the modern hinterland of Zimbabwe or South Africa, the incentive of substantial long-term "private benefits" (i.e., profit) compels their owners to employ sustainable management techniques. However, public protected areas at best provide diffuse "social" benefits for the citizens of the state as a whole. In this much more prevalent scenario, individual citizens or segments of government do not anticipate tangible benefits from the parks for themselves, and thus have little incentive to allocate the effort and resources necessary for their sustainable management (Dixon & Sherman, 1990). This situation contributes in no small part to the chronic problems associated with tourism that characterize public protected areas in the sub-Sahara as well as in other parts of the less developed world (Weaver, 1998b). These include the inadequate provision and training of park staff, lack of controls over visitor numbers and activities, lack of integrated management plans for individual parks or park systems, and the presence of irresponsible private operators and other service providers who optimize their private benefits without concern for the environmental integrity of their behavior (a "tragedy of the commons" situation). Central to all of these problems is a lack of resource allocation. Although approximately 70% of Kenya's international tourist traffic cite natural attractions as the primary reason for visiting that country (Japan International Cooperation Agency, 1994), only US$7 million of the US$350 million in earnings from international tourism was reinvested in the national protected area network in 1987 (Olindo, 1991). The result, in the absence of appropriate remedial measures stemming from a greater appreciation of the growing linkage between international tourism and protected areas, is likely to be a proliferation of Amboseli-type scenarios, entailing unregulated visitor increases and widespread environmental deterioration (Weaver, 1998b).

MODERN

Transitional/Traditional Space Economy

The issue of resource competition is highly relevant to the communal land residents of the traditional and transitional space economies, and particularly to those communities whose activity space is situated adjacent to the protected areas. This section will therefore elaborate the discussion of protected areas contained in the previous subsection. However, before pursuing this relationship in greater detail, an overview of resource allocation and tourism in these modernizing landscapes is in order. With respect to both variables, the situation in the southern model may be appropriately summarized as one of extreme disparity relative to the modern space economy. The continuing dominance of a small white farming community over the commercial agricultural sector of Zimbabwe, for example, has been noted earlier. However, this is made even more apparent when contrasted against the presence of 7 million blacks (or more than two thirds of the national population) within the overcrowded and impoverished Communal Areas (Meldrum, 1995). Such extreme disparities also apply especially to Namibia (Weaver & Elliott, 1996) and South Africa.

With the recent collapse of all minority-controlled governments in southern Africa, the problems of unresolved land reform and inequitable access to resources have resurfaced as highly explosive political and social issues. This discontent presently focuses upon agriculture, but could increasingly involve tourism as the latter grows in importance, particularly in park-adjacent regions. As a whole, the communal areas of southern Africa and the remainder of the sub-Sahara are virtually negligible as venues for tourist activity or accommodation, the one notable exception being the establishment of recreational complexes such as Sun City in the now defunct bantustans of South Africa (Rogerson, 1990). Inadequate services and facilities in large part account for this paucity, but to these structural shortcomings must be added at least four additional factors. First, increased government rhetoric as to the need for integrating these marginal areas into the national space economy is not frequently matched by tangible government action. For example, Namibian government policies of "national reconciliation" and an open investment climate are serving to reinforce rather than dissipate existing tourism-related (and other) inequities (Weaver & Elliott, 1996). There is also a tendency to allocate scarce funds to areas in the modern hinterland that already possess some degree of development and therefore require fewer inputs to achieve tangible results.

Second, communal structures of tenure, while theoretically amenable to "community-based" tourism scenarios (Murphy, 1985), are not attractive to private tourism investors, who prefer the long-term stability and control offered by formal private property arrangements. In communal situations, disputes about property inevitably emerge as communal conflicts, with more far-reaching and dangerous implications than evident in ownership disputes between individuals (Agbese, 1996). Given these criticisms, it is ironic that the gradual intrusion of private ownership options has also been dissuasive to some investors by contributing to a climate of uncertainty and confusion as to the "rules of the game" for resource control.

Third, impoverished local communities themselves lack the capital and expertise to embark upon tourism-related enterprises, often becoming dependent upon external sources of funding to sustain their operations. This is in stark contrast to the European-descended farmers of southern Africa's modern hinterland, who have access to the organizations, resources, and services that facilitate the exploitation of tourism opportunities.

A fourth major problem, serving in particular to reduce the potential of the communal lands for nature-based tourism, is widespread environmental deterioration. Several factors in combination are culpable for this development, including overcrowding, poverty, foreign debt burdens, the lack of democracy (Mabogunje, 1995), and the removal of land from traditional tenure arrangements during the modernization process. Concerning the population level, persistently high total fertility rates result in high levels of net natural increase despite migration to urban areas, reaching, for example, 3.5% per annum in the communal areas of Namibia (Wilkin, 1989). Ensuing problems of predatory cultivation, overgrazing, deforestation, and poor irrigation practices are exacerbated by the erosion, through nationalization or privatization initiatives, of traditional communal tenure systems widely regarded as having been conducive to the long-term sustainable use of the environment (Kaoneka & Solberg, 1994; Mabogunje, 1995; Solbrig & Young, 1992). The evidence for such a linkage is extensive. For example, the gradual replacement of communal tenure structures by individual property structures in Nigeria resulted in the "privatization" of biotic resources, and subsequently in hunting and gathering abuses brought on by the elimination of traditional regulations and taboos (Osemeobo, 1993). In Burkina Faso, the breakdown of communal arrangements through land reform during the 1980s resulted in massive land clearances and predatory farming practices as communities reacted to government slogans that land should only belong to those engaged in its cultivation (Stamm, 1994). In Cote d'Ivoire, logging concessions and farmland expansion, facilitated by privatization of property, is cited as a major factor in the reduction of the country's forest cover from 12 million ha in 1960 to just 1.5 million ha in 1985 (Cheru, 1992). The combination of population increase and land contraction is effectively illustrated by the Maasai, who experienced an untenable fivefold increase in population density between the beginning of colonial rule and 1961, as their lands decreased from 200,000 to 93,000 km^2 in 1961, while their population increased from 45,000 to 117,000 (Nyamwange, 1994). Wildlife populations, not unexpectedly, have been negatively impacted by the disruption of habitat in the above examples, and it is sometimes even the case (as in Namibia, Weaver & Elliott, 1996) that private lands within the modern space economy accommodate far more large mammals than the communal areas, despite their high level of habitat modification.

Another vehicle for communal land contraction, and hence increased resource scarcities and environmental degradation, has involved the alienation of land for the establishment of protected areas. As noted above, the preservationist mandate of formally designated protected areas precludes or at best discourages most forms of traditional resource utilization. Communities deprived of their traditional supportive lands are naturally resentful of the loss, especially when the subsequent nonuse of those lands for hunting, herding, etc., is at best perceived as nonsensical, and at worst, genocidal. Compounding the sensitivity of the issue is the fact that much of the sub-Saharan protected area network is an artifact of colonial-era native and land use policies. Certain parks, such as Kruger National Park, can be seen as buffer zones designed to serve various geopolitical objectives of colonial governments, while others, more commonly, were blatant attempts to appropriate additional lands from the indigenous majority, and incidentally, as in Kenya, to provide for the recreational needs of the local white elite (Akama, 1996). In many cases, the often insensitive alienation of indigenous land has persisted as postcolonial policy, as with the Ik people of Uganda, and the Maasai (see above) and Hadza of Tanzania, who have experienced relocation to make way for game reserves, national parks, and other economic development schemes (Hitchcock, 1993). In the Mid-Boteti region of Botswana, the expansion of the protected area for game management has been identified as a major factor in the deterioration of the local natural environment (Vanderpost, 1995). But whether established as the result of colonial or postcolonial policy, some of these parks, as discussed above, have emerged as major venues for ecotourism-type pursuits, leading to either the exacerbation or amelioration of the resource scarcity/resentment nexus, depending on the circumstances.

Positive and Negative Aspects of Protected Areas: Communal Land Interactions in Tourism

An extensive literature has emerged on the tourism-based relationships between protected areas and adjacent indigenous communities, but this should not obfuscate the fact that the actual number of individuals so impacted represents a minute, albeit high-profile, portion of the total sub-Saharan communal land population. Scrutiny of these relationships, however, is justified on several grounds, including the continuing expansion of protected area networks, of the tourist trade within those networks, and of resident populations in adjacent areas. Furthermore, local conflicts over resource access may erupt into politically charged issues of national scope, having consequences that can reverberate in a negative way throughout the broader tourism industry. Finally, proximity to protected areas, at least in the foreseeable future, represents the best opportunity for the residents of the traditional and transitional space economies to participate in the tourism industry. Investigation of the relevant case studies, therefore, allows for the identification of associated problems that may be encountered, and of solutions that could be implemented, as the tourism interface between the two spaces continues to expand.

Local attitudes toward tourism in many cases are initially prejudiced by the above-mentioned resentments that accompany the alienation of traditional land for protected areas, to the extent that tourism is associated with these venues. Such prejudices are likely to be reinforced, and resultant antitourism actions taken, when locals perceive few if any direct benefits from tourism to compensate for the reduced access to other resources, or when locals see themselves as having little influence over the sector. In the sub-Saharan context, Akama (1996) states generally that "rural communities surrounding protected natural areas have little or no influence on decision making or the institutions of wildlife conservation and tourist management" (p. 571). There are, however, some exceptions to this pattern, as noted below, but even in cases where there is local participation in tourism, issues of inequity still persist within some communities, a problem again tied into the issue of tenure. Recent developments in the Maasai lands of Kenya are instructive. The constriction of communal lands through alienation and increased privatization has jeopardized the pastoral lifestyle and forced local communities to pursue supplementary alternatives such as tourism and commercial agriculture. Accordingly, some Maasai elders have leased land, to which they have laid claim, to operators of safari camps in the vicinity of protected areas, thereby reaping most of the resultant economic benefits. According to Berger (1996):

> Protected area managers and the tour industry have tended to overlook the rights and needs of the Maasai community as a whole. Their activities concentrate power and wealth in the hands of a minority who have easy access to opportunities for investment. This has tended to undermine communal social security, increasing inequity between families and groups. Socio-cultural and economic marginalization of the majority is creating conflict, and this has the potential to fuel political upheaval, to which tourism is particularly vulnerable. (p. 183)

A genuine "community-based" tourism industry, therefore, is not automatically attained in the context of a communal tenure situation.

For those who do not benefit from tourism or lack any influence in its management, there is little evidence to date of direct action against tourists or the tourist industry.

However, there is little doubt that tourism has been indirectly (and probably in most cases unintentionally) affected by local actions relative to wildlife and other natural resources. Prominent among these is the killing of species attractive to tourists, but regarded as a nuisance by locals due to their association with livestock predation, the spread of disease, and crop damage. Antagonistic attitudes by locals toward certain types of wildlife have been reported in a wide variety of settings, including Saiwa Swamp National Park in Kenya (Ogutu, 1997), the Mid-Boteti region of Botswana (Vanderpost, 1995), Tanzania (Newmark, Manyanza, Gamassa, & Sariko, 1994), and Hwange National Park in Zimbabwe (Potts et al., 1996). In an area of Swaziland where locals cited few personal benefits from an adjacent conservation area, about one half of the surveyed residents expressed sympathy or support for poachers, and most believed that the protected area should be disbanded if it interfered with development initiatives that created local jobs (Hackel, 1990).

The overall picture, then, is of impoverished local communities that, apart from some members of the local elite in some communities, do not receive significant benefits from tourism and do not share in the decision-making process. There is, however, at least some evidence of tourism-related initiatives that are beneficial to both local communities (as a whole) and protected areas. Several of these, again, are located within the Maasai lands of Kenya and Tanzania. Initiatives such as the Imbirikani and Kuku Group Ranches involve a combination of livestock rearing and ecotourism-type enterprises operated along communal management principles, and augmented by the leasing of communal land for small tourist lodges (Berger, 1996). In addition, indigenously controlled conservation groups such as the Ol Choro Oirouia Wildlife Association have been established in communities near Amboseli National Park to collect user fees from tourists using their dispersal lands. Preliminary assessment of such groups suggests significant success both financially and in curtailing the activities of poachers, because the tourists are attracted in large part by the available wildlife resources (Sindiga, 1995). Facilitating such initiatives are revenue-sharing mechanisms introduced by the Kenyan government after 1990 to replace unsuccessful compensation-based programs (Sindiga, 1995). Associated policies include the preferential treatment of local communities in the provision of goods and services to the tourist industry, and the establishment of a locally managed trust fund to accommodate fees levied on visitors to game lodges. Resulting funds are to provide local services such as schools, hospitals, and cattle dips. Implementation in some communities has resulted in significant revenue flows, and the local county council, which includes the Maasai Mara NR, is reputed to be the wealthiest in Kenya largely as a result of these receipts (Herliczek, 1996). However, problems are also apparent in this revised strategy, including unrealistic local expectations, internal political conflict (Christ, 1994), and additional evidence of disproportionate benefits accruing to the local elite (Akama, 1996).

Innovative initiatives are not confined to Kenya. Over 50 Integrated Conservation and Development Projects (ICDPs) have been implemented in 20 sub-Saharan countries with the broad mandate of facilitating both environmental protection and economic development (Alpert, 1996). Characteristically, ICDPs are tailored to the circumstances of each host community, and are theoretically based on "holistic" principles of interdependency between the human and natural environment, which is tantamount to adopting a median approach between unregulated development and strict protection. Tourism tends to occupy a prominent role in the ICDPs, involving efforts to channel gate receipts from nearby protected areas to local communities, to promote local enterprises involved with the sale of handicrafts, and to provide material incentives to locals in exchange for access to wildlife resources (Barrett & Arcese, 1995). A recent sample of five ICDPs in Cameroon, Rwanda, Kenya, and Zambia, however, revealed a number of problems, including continued resentment over the loss of customary lands within protected areas, an inordinately high level of dependency on external support, and inadequate revenue generation due to their small size. Doubt has also been expressed as to whether growing human populations can subsist over the long term on finite and inherently unstable wildlife resources (Barrett & Arcese, 1995). Contrasting evidence, however, is offered by the Londolozi Game Reserve in South Africa, a 17,000-ha area in the Sabi Sand Game Reserve adjacent to Kruger National Park. This highly successful ICDP, offering three lodges capable of accommodating 48 tourists, realized net profits of R2.32 million, 65% from foreign sources, and provided employment for 135 persons (Muller, 1997). The profitable mountain gorilla tourism initiative in the Bwindi-Impenetrable Forest of Uganda is also cited as a successful ICDP, although dependency upon foreign aid remains problematic (Nowak, 1995).

CAMPFIRE

Among the most controversial of the wildlife/tourism initiatives being implemented on communal lands adjacent to protected areas is Zimbabwe's CAMPFIRE (Communal Areas Management Programme for Indigenous Resources), which invests authority over natural resources in local governing bodies as an incentive for their sustainable management. Made possible by 1975 legislation (Parks and Wild Life Act) conferring custodianship of wildlife to land occupiers, CAMPFIRE's tourism component has become virtually synonymous with consumptive forms of wildlife utilization. District councils lease concessions to commercial hunt operators, who return a portion of their earned income to those councils for disbursement as cash dividends, or for infrastructural development. Between 1989 and 1992, 90% of all CAMPFIRE income in Zimbabwe came from sport hunting, while all other forms of tourism accounted for only 1%. In part, this skewed pattern owes to the short-term leasing arrangements allowed under Zimbabwe's communal land legislation, which dissuades the more capital-intensive photo-safari operators (Potts et al., 1996).

With its emphasis on hunting, CAMPFIRE represents a rather glaring deviation from the more widespread regional trend toward nonconsumptive, ecotourism-type scenarios (Weaver, 1998b). However, this is not to imply that such options cannot be sustainable, or that their economic impact is negligible. Eighteen percent of Zimbabwe's territory currently participates in CAMPFIRE, and 80,000 residents received $900,000 in case dividends in 1995, representing a 5% increase in the average annual income of those participants. Concurrently, it is argued that only about 1% of the country's elephants is killed each year, while the species population is expanding by 5–7% per annum due to the concomitant decline in poaching activity. The elephant population has, as a result, actually increased from 52,000 in 1989 to 74,750 in 1995 (Sugal, 1997). A recent survey in Tsholotsho communal district, adjacent to Hwange NP, revealed that 84% of household heads believed that CAMPFIRE had increased the value of wildlife (Potts et al., 1996), thus helping to overcome prior perceptions of trophy animals as symbols of oppression. As adjacent protected areas essentially function as wildlife reservoirs for the participating communities, such positive evaluations may also extend to the parks as well. One former Zimbabwean National Parks scientist has suggested that the popularity of CAMPFIRE owes to its success in synthesizing the Western tradition of private ownership and the African tradition of community-level self-government (cited in Hess, 1997). Despite criticisms about its consumptive emphasis, dependence on foreign aid, and the exclusion of wildlife-poor districts, similar initiatives have been inaugurated in Zambia, Malawi, and Botswana, which now have about 150 controlled hunting areas in communal areas (Hess, 1997).

The success of the various consumptive and nonconsumptive tourism initiatives described above is in large part attributable to a community's ability to achieve the modern/

traditional synthesis described above by Hess, wherein a combination of net private (e.g., individual payments) and social benefit (e.g., village infrastructure) is obtained from local wildlife resources. Of course, various external factors, such as facilitating government legislation (as in Zimbabwe), sympathetic governments (as in South Africa), the availability of start-up funding, the presence of tourist-attractive wildlife, and proximity to popular protected areas, are also vital in this success, as demonstrated by the case studies. In spatial terms, these programs in essence involve the creation of transitional buffer zones, where the interests of both areas are taken into consideration, in preference to sharp and conflict-conducive boundary lines between the "hard-core" communal lands and the protected areas (i.e., the traditional and modern space economies).

Conclusions

The most significant tourism pattern evident in the sub-Sahara with respect to the modernization/tenure equation is the glaring disparity between the modern and transitional/traditional space economies, evident in both the southern and northern variations of the sub-Saharan modernization space economy model. Large metropolitan areas are clearly the focal point of national tourism industries, but tourism has also infiltrated to a greater or lesser extent into the modern hinterland. This is particularly true for the southern African countries where an extensive hinterland emerged as a consequence of European settlement and political control, and where the descendents of these same settlers constitute a significant pool of domestic tourists. Associated tenure dispensations include privately owned (especially in the case of accommodations and some private protected areas) and government-controlled land (public protected areas, gateways). Of particular interest are the outlying public protected areas, which, while peripheral in location and appearance, are fundamentally products of the modernization process. These are becoming increasingly important as tourism venues, and accordingly, as vectors for the further penetration of modernization impulses.

In contrast, traditional and transitional areas throughout sub-Saharan Africa are notable for their paucity of tourism activity. The one major exception to this generalization, in addition to the Sun City-type developments in South Africa, is the successful participation of some park-adjacent communities, especially in parts of Kenya and Zimbabwe. These have managed to attain a functionally effective balance or synthesis between traditional and modern modes of tenure and operation, in the process achieving both private and social benefits. Unfortunately, such efforts, while well publicized, represent and benefit only a miniscule proportion of residents in the traditional and transitional space economy, and mask the situations where tourism/wildlife/community relationships remain far less harmonious. Within most of traditional and transitional areas, however, tourism in the foreseeable future is all but precluded due to the existence of a negative rather than positive synthesis. In essence, these areas are trapped between the "pure" traditional and the modern space economies, being disadvantaged on one hand by the failure so far to attain the latter, and on the other by the erosion of the environmentally and socially sustainable adaptations of the former. Accordingly, they are neither modern enough to accommodate a viable commercial tourism sector (as in the modern hinterland) nor are their physical environments "natural" enough (and, increasingly, socially and culturally viable enough) to sustain a community-based, ecotourism-type sector. In terms of its implications for political stability and the broader development process, it is not unreasonable to suggest that the inequitable distribution of activity between the modern and traditional/transitional space economies is one of the most serious challenges facing the contemporary sub-Saharan tourism industry. For some modernization theorists, the situation may be interpreted as an issue of incomplete transition that will be rectified by the passage of time and the inexorable diffusion of the modernization process. For some dependency theorists, however, the current situation may represent the "normal" equilibrium that is to be expected as a consequence of the same forces. Further complicating the debate is the existence of southern and northern variations of the modernization model. Because of its persistent racial component, sharper spatial/tenure divides, and more developed tourism industry, it is the southern states that will likely first experience tourism-related unrest; in contrast, the northern situation is still too incipient to make any extrapolations with respect to the tourism industry.

Chapter 20

Tourism and Foreign Investment in Africa[1]

Desmond Omotayo Brown

Summary

This chapter argues that, despite the touristic attractiveness of Africa as a tourist destination, foreign tourism investment flows to the continent are relatively low, when compared to other developing regions of the world. This is due, in part, to higher perceived risk levels by potential investors. The various types of perceived risk factors (impediments) are analyzed, in addition to the market entry strategies employed by the few investors. Some incentives to increase the flow of foreign investment are discussed.

Key words: Foreign investment; Africa; Tourism; Economic development; Political risk; Impediments; Image; Culture

Introduction

World tourism is increasingly gaining an appreciable share of international trade. Before the 1970s, the majority of African countries benefited very little from the fast growing international tourism. In the 1990s, however, like many other regions, Africa has witnessed tourism expansion over the past few decades from 3 million international arrivals in 1970 to 15 million is 1997.

Although most tourism activity is concentrated in developed countries, developing countries and transitional economies (many of which are in Africa) have a potentially strong role to play in this area, and they are gaining market share quite rapidly. The WTO's statistics indicate that international tourism grew fastest in developing countries in terms of both arrivals and receipts. In a recent study by the International Hotel Association, an estimated $6.5 billion was spent on tourism-related activities in Africa in 1997. Industry gross output for travel and tourism in the continent has been estimated at over $40 billion annually, with the sector accounting for 1 in 10 jobs. The majority of these visitors were tourists who were attracted to the continent by the various species of birds, animals, and other wildlife, cultural dances, unusual geographic formations, participation in game hunting and fishing, and, above all, the enjoyment of unpolluted beaches and tropical sunshine (Filani, 1975). Given these favorable circumstances, it is ironic to note that one of the most critical factors affecting the pace of tourism development is investment. The two main sectors most frequently requiring significant amounts of capital investment are tourism-related infrastructure (traditionally a responsibility of the public sector), and investment in superstructure (which is mostly a private sector activity). In this vein, tourism is one of the few industries that require significant public/ private sector partnership and coordination (Multilateral Investment Guarantee Agency, 1997).

The Problem

Given the above discussion, foreign investment in tourism-related superstructure is relatively very low, compared to other developing regions of the world. The share of long-term private capital—defined as the sum of private loans (bank loans plus bond finance), portfolio equity flows, and foreign direct investment—supporting tourism development is lower, as a percentage of GNP, than that of any other tourism destination in the world. African countries with established tourist industries have the need for more capital investment in new or existing tourist accommodation, infrastructure, and services. Those countries that have little or no established tourist industries are considering the possibilities of tourism development. Why has Africa been left out?

This chapter argues that investors perceive the risks to be higher in Africa than in other regions and that they face greater impediments in identifying and exploiting profitable opportunities than elsewhere. It reviews some of the impediments African countries face in attracting foreign investment in general and concludes by highlighting some international efforts that have been made during the last 20 years to attract foreign tourism investment in Africa. Specifically, the chapter examines the following:

- firms' motivation to invest abroad;
- the potential benefits of foreign tourism investment to Africa;
- the attractiveness of Africa as a tourist destination for foreign investment;
- foreign direct investment in tourism;
- general market entry strategies of foreign investors;
- trends in market entry strategies in Africa;
- some international incentives to attract foreign investment to Africa during the past 20 years.

Why Firms Invest Abroad

Along with profitability, foreign firms invest abroad to seek growth as yardsticks for measuring success among firms in an industry. For example, results of a 1989 survey of 433 chief executive officers (CEOs) in the U.S., Canada, Japan, and the Pacific Rim nations indicate that about 50% of CEOs think that expanding abroad is crucial to the success of their organization (Anders, 1989). Thus, substantial increases in domestic market shares often come with geographic expansion of sales and service operations. Clearly, then, potential investors abroad engage in developing what they perceive as the "right" business format when considering international expansion. In doing so, they must deal with several major concerns that are crucial to international success. These include matching strategies to environments, creating the correct structures globally and locally, properly diagnosing important environmental threats and opportunities, and effectively dealing with cultural diversity (Olsen & Merna, 1993).

The Potential Benefits of Foreign
Tourism Investment for Africa

The potential benefits of tourism development for local communities in Africa include training, employment, income, health services, transportation, and recreational facilities. Tourism can also help improve educational standards and, if properly managed, bring new life to the culture and crafts of people while preserving the cultural heritage of local populations. Additionally, the following have been cited in the tourism literature as general reasons why governments seek to adopt and develop a strategy of international tourism as an export industry:

- The creation of a favorable impact upon employment in the country (e.g., new jobs in hotels, travel agencies, government, handicraft industries, etc.). An increase in urbanization through the continuous growth of construction and renovation of tourist facilities.
- Helps increase the governments' earnings of foreign currency, which developing countries badly need for bridging or reducing their deficits in balance of payments, thus fostering the development of their national economies.
- Acts as a channel for redistribution of wealth by redistributing capital between developed and developing countries.
- Accelerating the multiplier effect within the economies of a country and regions.
- The stimulation of output and employment.
- The stimulation of domestic investment.
- The stimulation of foreign exchange.

Africa's Touristic Attractiveness for Foreign Investment

Africa is a continent of more than 50 countries with about 520 million or more inhabitants. In economic and human terms, this region is considered by most strategic business analysts as "too important to ignore" (J. E. Austin & Kohn, 1990). With the growing importance of international competition, global strategy has recently emerged as a popular concept among managers of many international tourism firms. O. D. Brown (1996) has empirically established the touristic attractiveness of African destinations as a profit center for international tourism investment. His research revealed that profits in Africa appear to be derived from the continents' natural factors [climate (42.5%), flora and fauna (51.2%), lush vegetation (52.4%), natural, undisturbed beaches (42.9%)] (Table 20.1). Moreover, respondents seemed to give depth and breadth to cultural/outdoor factors such as open-air activities (51.2%), historic sites and monuments (42.1%), variety of ethnic customs to observe (46.8%), and opportunity to participate in local tribal life (41.65%) as well. These findings suggest that travel destinations in Africa generally reflect the feelings, beliefs, and opinions of international tourists as offering touristic attributes that may be unmatched in providing satisfaction in terms of unspoiled beauty and unique experiences.

Impediments to Foreign Direct Tourism
Investment in Africa

A recent survey of travel intermediaries and tourism destination marketing organizations that do business in Africa revealed that the perceived risk deterring foreign investment in Africa appears to be higher in many African countries than in any other region of the world (O. D. Brown, 1996). These are due to:

Table 20.1. Frequencies of U.S.-Based Travel Intermediaries' Perceptions of Touristic Attractiveness on Profits in Africa

Attractiveness Item	Scale (%)					Mean Score	SD
	1	2	3	4	5		
Multiple physical tourism resources	2.4	3.9	11.8	40.2	41.7	4.2	0.943
Africa's unique geographic position astride the equator	5.6	9.6	23.2	36.8	24.8	3.7	1.12
Favorable climate attractive to U.S. tourists	3.1	7.1	17.3	42.5	29.9	3.9	1.02
Very attractive scenery & landscape	0.8	1.7	3.1	41.7	54.3	4.5	0.641
Diverse array of flora, fauna, & aquatic resources	0.8	1.9	7.9	51.2	40.2	4.3	0.649
Clean, plentiful, & undisturbed natural beaches	2.4	7.1	23.8	42.9	23.8	3.8	0.968
Plenty of open air activities	1.6	3.9	13.4	51.2	29.9	4.3	0.858
Opportunity to participate in hunting safaris	14.3	6.3	16.7	32.5	30.2	3.6	1.40
Plenty of lush vegetation	0.8	3.2	14.3	52.4	29.4	4.6	0.797
Abundance of wildlife	1.8	2.4	8.7	38.6	50.4	4.4	0.743
Plenty of historic sites & monuments	0.8	4.8	13.5	42.1	38.9	4.1	0.880
Interesting tribal life	1.7	2.4	13.6	40.0	44.0	4.3	0.782
Variety of ethnic customs to observe	1.1	4.0	10.3	46.8	38.9	4.2	0.783
Vast array of towns to visit & shop	1.6	6.3	17.5	41.3	33.3	4.0	0.955
Opportunity to participate in local tribal life	0.8	4.8	25.6	41.6	27.2	3.9	0.887

Respondents utilized a 5-point Likert-type scale to indicate their degree of agreement or disagreement with respect to selected items as follows: 1 = strongly disagree; 2 = disagree; 3 = neutral; 4 = agree; 5 = strongly agree.
Source: O. D. Brown (1996).

- economic environment;
- political risk factors;
- limited size of domestic markets;
- poor or deteriorating tourism infrastructure;
- lack of domestic tourism planning and promotion;
- lack or low level of skills and general technological capabilities;
- poor image abroad;
- inconsistent government tourism policies and burdensome regulations;
- cultural barriers (i.e., the social systems).

Economic Environment

A key factor that cannot be ignored in attracting foreign direct investment is that fundamental differences do exist in the nature of the business environment in Africa, which varies considerably from that of the home country of potential foreign investors. For example, a recent survey of 450 U.S.-based tourism professionals and prospective investors who have actually visited the continent revealed the following as perceived characteristics of the business environment in Africa (O. D. Brown, 2000):

- slow responses to phone/fax messages;
- inability of local officials/contacts to get questions answered and poor follow-through, which hinge upon business decisions;
- unenforceable verbal contracts;
- outdated land tenure systems, which do not convey title to land;
- unreliable postal systems;
- erratic airline schedules;
- irregularity of flights to many countries in Africa;
- harassment and corruption at customs check and immigration checkpoints;
- black market currencies and currency instability.

These factors, further aggravated by balance-of-payment issues, can have decisive influences on the opportunities and barriers of foreign investment. In addition, there are problems of inadequate and efficient institutional and financial infrastructures such as banking and other financial institutions. In many cases, large structural fiscal deficits, erratic monetary and exchange rate policies, and weak financial systems have contributed toward high variable inflation and interest rates. Because tourism is an extremely fragile and volatile industry, these factors have worsened the general investment climate.

Political Risk Factors

Political stability is one of the essential prerequisites for attracting international tourists and foreign investment to a destination. It is important not only for the development of the infrastructure that is required for tourism, but also because of the pivotal role that images play in tourism marketing and promotion (Hall, 1994). Thus, it is a fundamental precondition to the successful establishment of a tourist industry.

A considerable number of writings have illustrated the kinds of events or situations related to political risk. A review of the general literature suggests that there are numerous illustrations of political risk events. For example, events such as expropriation, war, labor conflict, foreign exchange control, production quotas, and import/export restrictions have been reported by Brewer (1981), Bunn and Mustafaoglu (1978), Lax (1983), Overholt (1982), Robock (1983), and Teye (1988). The group of African countries affected by these circumstances seems to continue to grow. For example, during the 1970s and 1980s, Zambia, Zimbabwe, Mozambique, and Namibia served as examples of countries that were involved in national liberation wars. During the 1980s and mid-1990s, Liberia, Sierra Leone, Rwanda, Somalia, Sudan, Angola, Chad, Eritrea, and Ethiopia have been involved in prolonged periods of conflict at one point or another. Furthermore, strikes and protests as a result of unpaid wages and stipends or against economic policies occurred in about a dozen countries in 1992 (Economic Commission for Africa, 1993).

Limited Size of Domestic Markets

Markets in Africa are typically relatively small. Further, most African economies have an average GDP of $3.4 billion (or $311 per capita) (UNCTAD, 1994). Annual GNP growth (excluding South Africa) averaged 2.3% during 1983–89 and 1.4% during 1990–95, compared with 3.8% and 5.1% for all other developing countries (excluding the former Soviet Union) during these periods (World Bank, 1996). Although many attempts have been made to address this limitation [e.g., the creation of regional groupings through regional integration such as Economic Community of West Africa States (ECOWAS), Southern African

Development Community (SADC)], some of these groupings have either collapsed or proven to be ineffective in terms of increasing intraregional tourism trade promotion.

Poor or Deteriorating Tourism Infrastructure

In many African countries, tourism development is hampered by poor, institutional, and, in many cases deteriorating physical (especially telecommunication and transportation) human infrastructure, and the lack of capital to improve it. Issues such as primitive conditions at some airports, inadequate or poor local ground transportation, unreliability of local postal services, etc., have been empirically documented as impediments to lack of tourism investment and large-scale promotion to Africa (O. D. Brown, 2000).

Lack of Domestic Tourism Planning and Promotion

Planning for international tourism appears to dominate any consideration of domestic tourism planning in many African countries. The WTO has defined a domestic tourist as:

Any person residing within a country, irrespective of nationality, traveling to a place within this country other than his usual residence for a period of not less than 24 hours or one night for a purpose other than the exercise of a remunerated activity in the place visited. The motives for such travel may be:

1. Leisure (recreation, holidays, health, studies, religion, sports);
2. Businesses, family, mission, meeting.

Although domestic tourism exists in Africa, it is not usually quantified, hence its economic impact in not fully known because it is not fully developed as an industry. However, its nurturing and development should be given top priority in developing countries' national planning because it has the advantage of not being susceptible to the same levels of fluctuations as international tourism. Additionally, if developed appropriately, it can help to provide a more experienced workforce for later servicing high-volume and more demanding international tourism.

Lack or Low Level of Skills and General Technological Capabilities

A frequently discussed issue about tourism's operational success in Africa is the unavailability of sufficient suitable labor. However, a very small percentage of national tourism bureaus' budgets are being spent on vocational and technical training to meet the needs of the tourist industry. Tourism is a highly service-oriented industry. One reason for this deficit is the low level of importance placed on the service sector by most developing countries. Services for profit have traditionally been viewed as less desirable than manufacturing (McKee & Tisdell, 1990). Like most service activities, the final product is somewhat intangible. By and large, tourist facilities in many African countries exist to service the needs of vacationers from wealthier countries. Thus, if countries elect to entice foreign tourism investors, they should expect to provide a minimum amount of service comparable to international standards. Some of the prevalent service-related issues that need discussion, attention, and action in many African countries can be generally categorized under *lack of training*. Some specific issues include: unfriendliness to tourists, inability to answer questions and give directions, demanding bribes at customs and immigration points, difficulties in obtaining visas to visit, etc. (O. D. Brown, 2000).

Poor Image Abroad

It has long been recognized that destinations' image have a profound impact on the host nation. Africa as a continent has a negative image (Ankomah & Crompton, 1990). Teye

(1988) posits that among a host of interrelated factors responsible for the limited development of Africa's tourism potential, the continent's poor image abroad is of great significance. Ahmed (1991) argues that the effects of negative images on tourism are detrimental. Tourists on vacation desire to escape the mundane, the pressures of office, and the chores of the home. Based on the current image of civil strife, and other political instability factors in many African countries, foreign investors might be hesitant to invest in tourism facilities. This makes promoting the subregion of Africa very difficult. This can have decisive influences on the opportunities and barriers of foreign investment. Furthermore, this difficulty is compounded by the fact that most countries in Africa wishing to promote tourism are handicapped by meager financial resources to undertake any meaningful dissemination of information to counter the negative images abroad (Ankomah & Crompton, 1990).

Inconsistent Government Tourism Policies and Burdensome Regulations

Planning for tourism occurs in a number of forms (development, infrastructure, promotion, and marketing), structures (different government organizations), and scales (international, national, regional, local, and sectoral) (Hall, 1994).

A major obstacle to tourism investment in Africa is a lack of coordinated or unified government policy for tourism planning. Because planning is rarely dedicated towards tourism, the industry tends to be fragmented. Some effects of this are: inconsistency in policy, corruption among government officials, lack of long-term vision, lack of, or poor, tourism promotion, and unreliability of tourist services in general.

Cultural Factors

Cultural distance between the home and target country is another concern to investors in the international marketplace. Olsen and Merna (1993) have suggested that, in general, a business environment can be perceptual. Being perceptual, it will be defined differently from individual to individual, and even those definitions will vary as a function of past experiences and training. In discussing culture and value systems in Africa, therefore, foreign investors scrutinize the various cultural variables existing within the business environment in order to understand their managerial significance relevant to their business intentions. Thus, finding the appropriate local partner is crucial to the success of investment in a target country. When the cultural values differ significantly, investors often encounter a high cost of information acquisition (Root, 1987).

Market Entry Strategies of Foreign Tourism Investors

In order to ensure their international growth objectives, foreign tourism firms tend to employ a variety or combination of entry growth strategies. Six major strategies have been cited in the literature by Tse and Olsen (1991), which are:

- strategic alliances,
- franchising,
- market segmentation,
- joint ventures,
- acquisition,
- management contracts.

Among these, the most widely used in many developing countries are joint ventures and franchising. These will be briefly discussed.

Joint Ventures

This concept was introduced as an expansion strategy for hotel investment in Communist countries by Root (1987). It was defined as an Industrial Cooperation Agreement (ICA). Conceptually, it is a contractual or equity relationship between a Western company and a government enterprise in Communist countries. Usually, the foreign investor provides the technical and management expertise, while the country partner (usually the government) provides the land, labor, and other raw materials. Such agreements allow foreign firms to sell equipment and other products to their partners (Root, 1987).

Franchising

Franchising is a form of licensing in which a company (franchisor) licenses a business system as well as other property rights to an independent company or person (franchisee). A management contract gives an enterprise the right to manage the day-to-day operations of an enterprise in a foreign target country. Rather than equity ownership, companies provide technical advice, preopening assistance, management service, and marketing support in return for a fee (Tse & West, 1992).

Current Market Entry Strategy Trends in Africa

Historically, during the 1970s and early 1980s, the incidence of nonequity, low-equity investment, or both reflected many governments' preferences. The underlying motivation for this position was the increased stake that many governments had in developing the corporate sectors of their economies. Hence, the prevalence of nationalization, indigenization, and mandatory joint ventures in many African economies.

Ironically, in the 1990s, however, with the increasing environmental complexity and cultural differences in African markets, these forms of entry tend to suit the interests of most foreign investors. This is especially true for tourism investments—especially in the case of hotel development. For example, a recent study reported that there has been a steady increase in the number of luxury-class hotels built in Africa in recent years. The major players in this effort have been Sheraton, Hilton, Intercontinental, and the French Accor chain, together with Hong Kong interests in Mauritius. However, the involvement of these chains has mostly been in the form of management contracts, reflecting nonequity or low-equity associations, the sole purpose of which is to reduce risk. This phenomenon also applies to other tourism-related business (e.g., fast food, car rental services) (Cockroft & Riddell, 1991).

Some Incentives to Increase Foreign Investment in Africa

The view that international tourism is a primary means for Third World development is gaining strength. Evidence of this can be seen from the fact that United Nations Educational and Scientific Organization (UNESCO), WTO, IMF, and the World Bank now encourage it. They view it from an economic and social development perspective—foster economic growth, improve human living standards, promote intercultural understanding, and nurture world peace. These and other organizations are slowly realizing that while Africa's many difficulties are well documented, the extent to which they are of Africa's own making has generated substantial disagreement among various quarters. To address this and similar development issues, various efforts have been made by both international financial institutions and African regional groupings to provide and offer incentives for sustained growth and foreign direct investment opportunities in the continent. Some of these are outlined below:

- The Investment Marketing Services Department (IMS) of the Multilateral Investment Guarantee Agency (MIGA) acts as a principal instrument for providing foreign direct investment and dissemination on investment opportunities in tourism to developing and transitional economies. Further, this department has a number of programs aimed at assisting governments and businesses in developing countries to understand the tourism development process. Issues considered crucial in the tourism development process, which are central to MIGA, include:
  - tourism market trends;
  - tourism-related investment trends;
  - infrastructure development;
  - superstructure development;
  - project financing;
  - economic valuation of projects;
  - creation of attractive investment climate.
- SADC, comprising 14 governments of the region, working together on economic development, especially in tourism investment growth. During his recent (1998) visit to the region, President Clinton acknowledged that potential and proposed the Africa Opportunity Act to fund trade and economic development.
- In 1992, The Debt For Development Coalition, Inc. (DDC), a U.S profit organization based in Washington, DC, brought together four leading U.S. not-for-profit institutions involved in international development, environmental and cultural survival activities to assist the government of Ghana in a tourism development project in its central region. The four institutions are: the Midwest Consortium for International Activities (MUCIA), the Smithsonian Institution, Conservation International, and the U.S. Committee of the International Council on Monuments and Sites. The consortium will assist Ghana in studies of the park's resources, planning and construction of park facilities, training of park scientific and management staff, the marketing of the park and the development of the interpretive/educational programs for visitors. The U.S. Agency for International Development will provide $5 million for DDC to purchase and block currency to cancel intercompany debt, generating benefits of about 300%. According to the DDC, plans are under way to embark on similar projects in Kenya, Nigeria, and other sub-Saharan African countries in the foreseeable future. The bulk of such investment, which for the most part will be private, may eventually come from multinational corporations of the developed world.
- In February 1990, Ghana held an investment promotion conference, emphasizing the need for stimulating private direct investment in that country. Ten countries, including the U.S. and five West European countries, attended the conference.
- At the end of 1990, Togo was the first of a number of sub-Saharan African countries to operate private duty-free export processing zones (EPZs), which are essentially industrial parks that use resources of private export firms to manufacture and export products. These zones are expected to stimulate domestic economic growth, and are being guided by OPIC and the U.S. Agency for International Development.
- In September 1989, the Overseas Private Corporation (OPIC), a sustaining, U.S. government-owned agency, in collaboration with a select group of major U.S. corporations, created a $30 million diversified investment Africa Growth Fund. The fund is designed to provide foreign currency equity to U.S. companies interested in medium- to long-term investments in Africa. As of March 1990, 40 investment proposals were being considered by the fund (C. B. Pratt, 1991).

- In December of 1989, the Fourth European Economic Community (EEC) trade and aid treaty (Lomé IV, 1990–2000) for 68 African, Caribbean, and Pacific countries was signed. This treaty serves as an instrument for the promotion and protection of direct investment.
- In April of 1988, MIGA, a World Bank affiliate, was established, to provide private investors who are signatories to the MIGA charter guarantees against expropriation, currency inconvertibility, and losses from civil disturbances in developing countries.
- In 1987, some 31 business members of the African Business Roundtable visited the U.S. and held meetings with corporate executives. The objectives of the meetings were to acquaint U.S. investors with untapped business opportunities in Africa in an effort to improve Africa's business image and to promote U.S. private investment in the continent.
- In December 1985, for example, the Committee on African Development Strategies, a group of 42 U.S. citizens, released a 12-point recommendation, the "Compact for African Development," which outlined how U.S. policy can best support the development of the continent.
- In 1983, a bilateral investment treaty was signed between Senegal and the U.S., and was approved by the U.S. Congress in 1988. This treaty confers a most favored nation status to U.S. investors in Senegal, establishes free transfers of capital and profits, and provides eligibility for OPIC insurance against currency in convertibility and investment expropriation.

Discussion

Few alternatives for economic development besides tourism in Africa exist today. Despite the handicaps outlined above, some countries in the region are attracting private capital flows. Their efforts to adopt outward-looking policies and establish stable macroeconomic environments are beginning to pay off, hence the growing number of tourism policy formulation taking place in the continent. Most African countries now have agencies or organizations that perform the planning and policy formulation at the highest level of government in order to protect the long-range social and economic well-being of their countries. This is particularly true in East African countries, where government policies on tourism have been pronounced. Uganda, Tanzania, and Kenya, for example, have effective tourist organizations responsible for the planning and development of the tourism industry. In Cameroon, Sierra Leone, Ghana, and The Gambia in West Africa, there are government ministries responsible for tourism at the cabinet level of government.

With foreign tourism firms' control of technology and knowledge through successful operation of chains, more effective competition for such resources through ownership of equity, management contracts, franchise arrangements, or leasing arrangements in the future is predictable. This implies that although some companies have their properties scattered throughout the world and dramatic investment shifts have taken place from the U.S. to countries like Japan, Great Britain, Canada, Hong Kong, India, etc., the notion of global competition has not yet fully taken hold. More countries in Africa will be included in the foreseeable future. This suggests that there are tremendous opportunities in these countries that are still untapped.

Second, due to the increasing quest for free trade and liberalized markets, and the present international economic situation, foreign tourism investors and African countries need each other. With the steady increases in international travel, tourism, and trade, a strategy used by hotel chains is to follow their clients to international destinations. The chains' desire is to develop and exploit brand loyalty through familiarity of brand name and service and international reservation systems. Furthermore, the governments of less developed nations are less ideological in the 1990s and beyond than they were in the 1970s (Chaudhuri, 1988). Harden (1990) suggests that "many African leaders have stopped blaming their problems on the legacy of colonialism" (p. 53). As a result, an increasing number of countries are admitting that foreign industrial interests are crucial to their development strategies, and are developing congenial and liberal policy environments to foster business cooperation (C. B. Pratt, 1991). With the emergence of political stability and the inevitable end to the various civil, political, border, and ethnic conflicts, increased visitation and foreign direct investment in tourism projects seems destined for African countries. Some important contributory factors to this increased visitation include economic and ethnic/cultural linkages, and improvement in transport and communications.

Finally, with the continent's population increase to 500 million in the 1990s and beyond, and projected to double in about 20 years, "Africa cannot be forever ignored by foreign investors" (Ankomah, 1990).

Conclusion

This chapter has argued that Africa south of the Sahara is a region that is genuinely unique in its scenic and cultural attractions and flora and fauna. However, it is handicapped by factors in the economic environment: political risk factors; limited size of domestic markets; poor or deteriorating tourism infrastructure; lack of domestic tourism planning and promotion; lack or low level of skills and general technological capabilities; poor image abroad; inconsistent government tourism policies; and burdensome regulations and cultural barriers in its social systems. As a consequence, foreign investment in tourism-related superstructure is relatively very low compared to other developing regions of the world.

Within such generalities, however, there are many qualifications to be made. Some countries are doing better than others in terms of attracting foreign tourism investment. For example, Kenya, with its well-established reputation, could either attract more foreign investment or decline, depending on government policy and political stability, while South Africa seems to be poised, in the short run, to attract increased foreign investment.

Note

[1]Tourism, as used in this chapter, includes railroads, airlines, automobile rental companies, hotels, restaurants, food and beverage producers, travel agencies, communications firms, museums, souvenir makers, and various forms of entertainment and other tourism-related superstructure. Africa as a reference point in this chapter refers to south of the Sahara.

Chapter 21

Community Participation in Tourism in Africa

Laud A. Dei

Summary

In this chapter the word community is used to describe a group of any size whose members reside in a specific locality and have a historical heritage. In Africa such groups are headed by village heads, chiefs, and kings, and they are the owners of the land. Tourism alters the nature of politics and may initiate conflicts when governments impose tourism development without consultation. For these reasons, the opportunities for the control of tourism must be in the hands of the indigenous people and tourism should be community driven. A model of consensus is proposed to ensure that indigenous culture is not "commoditized" and that conflicts are reduced.

Key words: Community; Social exchange; Sustainable tourism; Social carrying capacity; Ecotourism; Cultural inertia; Poaching; Nature sanctuaries; Agrotourism; Cultural villages; Consensus model of planning

Introduction

"Community" is a word that lacks precise meaning. *The New Oxford Dictionary of English* (Pearsall, 1998) defines it variously as a group of people "living together in one place" or "having a religion, race, profession, or other particular characteristic in common" (p. 371). The group can also be "the people of a district or country considered collectively, especially in the context of social values and responsibilities" or still "a body of nations or states unified by common [economic] interests." Perhaps what these four definitions imply is the idea of an organized body or group of people in the same locality sharing common characteristics, which might include economic, political, social, and other interests.

As used in this chapter, the term refers to a group of any size whose members reside in a specific and historical locality. For administrative purposes and for convenience, politically created units or settler groups shall constitute a community. Thanks to the multiscale interpretation and interlinkage of the term "community," the spatial impact of national policies and individual development can be traced throughout a nation. But reference shall be made to special communities that offer common or similar tourism products. The Kikuyu and Luo of Kenya, the Akans and Ewes of Ghana, and the Basawa (Bushmen) of

Botswana are some typical examples of ethnic-based communities in Africa. Still others include the Igbo and the Yoruba of the southeastern and southwestern areas of Nigeria, respectively. Such communities might be described as clans or tribes headed by traditional rulers (e.g., chiefs and kings) or family heads.

Interest in community-based participation in tourism development has been growing in recent years (Murphy, 1985; Tosun, 1998; Tosun & Jenkins, 1998). Proponents of this strategy have argued that community involvement will help create entrepreneurial opportunities for locals and will help engage them in developmental decision-making. It will also ensure that tourism development engenders benefits to the residents of the tourist area and is not disruptive to their lives, particularly relating to the sociocultural and environmental consequences usually associated with tourism. In this sense, community participation will create good host–guest neighborliness. Community policy is also important for sustaining the tourism sector for the benefit of both foreign tourists and native residents, not just for today but also tomorrow. It needs to be stated, however, that there are barriers to the community approach to tourism development, be they at an operational, structural, or even cultural level (Tosun, 1998, pp. 83–93). In consequence, questions of how to overcome the barriers and how to encourage participation become relevant.

This chapter addresses these issues and details the case for and against community involvement in tourism development planning. By way of illustration, the chapter then focuses on Ghana, probably the "best community practice" case in tourism in nonsettler Africa, and to some extent on Zimbabwe. Furthermore, the analysis critiques the issues raised earlier in the introduction, and proposes a model with guidelines for tourism planning based on achieving broader rural participation in the sector (Laban, 1995).

Rationale of the Community Concept

To further the points made in the introduction, it is worth stating that the land tenure system in Africa is such that there are three types of community land: land owned absolutely by a group of people or individuals; clan or family land; "stool" or "skin" land. The concept of "stool" land is peculiar to southern Ghana and that of "skin" to the north of Ghana. There is no firm legal definition of a "stool," but there are statutory legal definitions of "stool" lands. Forest Ordinance regards as "stool" land, all lands that are at the disposal of any native community. They are usually ancestral lands, which belong to communities. In Africa tourism development encroaches on common property. For this reason many African countries recognize the need for community involvement in tourism.

The degree of tourism development in a community affects the perception of the local community. A well-developed tourism region that creates jobs and offers social facilities to the local community is seen positively as a blessing to the local people. If, however, tourism is developed at the expense of other needed benefits, the community will resent its presence.

Distance from place of residence to tourists areas determines the frequency of contact of local communities with tourists. The higher the frequency of contact the more irritated the local community becomes if the general economic conditions of a community do not improve and if there is not enough public education to inform the community about the benefits to be derived if they were to support and be involved in the industry.

Liu, Sheldon, and Var (1987) observe balanced perceptions of impacts by communities with a longer history of links with tourists. In other words, perceptions of impacts are related to level of tourism development (Perdue, Long, & Aller, 1987). On the other hand, entrepreneurs are always positive about tourism compared to other groups (Pizam, 1978; Thomason, Crompton, & Kamp, (1979).

Tourism generates employment, which must benefit communities that live close to the tourism facility. Pizam (1978) sees a positive relationship between employment in and support for tourism and associates economic dependency on tourism with more positive perceptions of tourism. Adherents to this concept include Husbands (1989), Perdue et al. (1987), Mansfield (1992), Madrigal (1993), Glasson (1994), and Lankford and Howard (1994).

Location factors play a major role in how communities perceive tourism. As distance from place of residence to tourist areas increases, communities are less positive about tourism (Belisle & Hoy, (1980). However, Keogh (1990) observes that people living closer to a tourism facility see more negative impacts from tourism.

A relevant factor in the African tourism development scene is political self-identification. Snepenger and Johnson (1991) see residents with conservative political views being more negative about tourism than those with moderate or liberal views.

The level of awareness in the form of advertisement or public relations is relevant to the level of attachment of a community to a tourism facility. Residents of a community with a public relations campaign are more positive about tourism than those not exposed to a public relations campaign. This poses a major problem in many parts of Africa if modern public relations techniques or advertisements are used. The role of the local chief and his linguist is very crucial here in information dissemination.

In the final analysis attitudes toward tourism follow some kind of equity or social exchange function (Lankford & Howard, 1994; Perdue et al., 1987). Madrigal (1993) describes social exchange theory as providing an economic-like analysis of interaction that focuses on the exchange and mutual dispensation of rewards and costs between actors. The underlying assumption of exchange is that actors behave in a way that maximizes the rewards and minimizes the costs they experience. This presupposes that communities must benefit from tourism facilities located in their localities.

The concept is consistent with African traditional forms of governance and administration. African land tenure system makes room for community participation and thus protects the local community or the individual from exploitation. The traditional Ghanaian concepts of *abusa, nnoboa, akwanbo, susu,* and others elsewhere in Africa are all community oriented.

Abusa is a word that means tripartite division. An *abusa* laborer is a man who is employed by a farmer to look after one or more of his farms and who is rewarded with a one-third share of the farm produce. They are often loosely called caretakers. *Nnoboa* means collective preparation of land for farming; it is rotational and involves two or more farmers. *Akwanbo* is communal work on roads and paths; it takes place normally before annual festivals. *Susu* is an indigenous banking system involving individuals and small communities; proceeds are paid on rotational basis to individuals at an agreed interval.

Community-based tourism provides the necessary conditions for sustainable tourism, which Lane (1991) defines as "satisfying jobs without dominating the local economy. It must not abuse the natural environment and should be architecturally respectable. . . . The benefits of tourism should be diffused through many communities, not concentrated on a narrow coastal strip or scenic valley" (p. 1).

Sustainable tourism is linked to an ecologically sustainable development (ESD) framework (Brundtland, 1987). This framework is worldwide and is used to highlight key issues in managing economic growth and change with reference to tourism development. In some countries the Brundtland report has been translated into natural goals, policies, and more detailed principles (J. A. Pearce, 1980).

Formalized tourism development in some parts of Africa has a short history. Exceptions are South Africa, Zimbabwe, Kenya, and some Maghreb countries (e.g., Tunisia). Since Ghana's independence in 1957, a few international standard hotels and facilities have been provided or are in the process of being completed. Tourism attractions in Africa include national parks, nature reserves, slave castles, waterfalls, authentic African culture, and tropical flora and fauna. Large amounts of international and domestic development funds have been used to sensitize the national and the international community to the attractions of Africa, which has for a long time remained on the periphery of the tourism industry.

The truth is that very soon the major international donors will phase out their support for this industry. Africa will then rely mainly on internal resources and domestic funds to maintain its tourism industry. Investment in the industry is currently very substantial and considerable funding must be continued to protect and sustain the investment.

In the light of this background, this chapter questions the sustainability of some current policies and practices of governments. By focusing attention on the development of a community tourism product, it is believed that several past research and planning weaknesses may be rectified. The importance of community survival in a permanent home in which to live, work, and play is the central point of this chapter, notwithstanding the community's tourism potential.

Direct or indirect linkages between state and village appear to considerably limit possibilities of local effort. The conclusion that community participation in management is more successful when the state has fewer serious involvements in local administration seems justifiable. The current attempts by African governments to decentralize will transfer competencies to lower administrative levels or to local communities. This is when NGOs appear on the scene to enhance community efforts from a participatory point of view.

Community participation is strongly influenced by ethnic and cultural factors. But policies concerning ethnic and cultural tourism are much more contentious and controversial than for other types of tourism, mainly because the resource itself is the people who have their own views and could participate in the policy-making process. Tourism alters the nature of politics and may initiate conflicts when governments impose tourism development without consultation. Thus, the opportunities for the control of tourism must be in the hands of the indigenous people or communities living close to the tourism facility, and that tourism should be community driven. However, it is necessary that there must be some input of policies and legislation from governments to enable this to happen. The latter should not imply commoditization of a community's culture; such a move leads to a reduction in its authenticity.

A planning challenge in tourism is to ensure that present minor irritations do not blossom into issues that could threaten a community's sociocultural objectives and viability as a destination. One possible solution is to influence national tourist policy so that the flow to each particular region is optional—neither too high nor too low—and to convince the policy-makers that beyond a certain level further increases are counterproductive. The limits of local tolerance for tourism may be described as a social carrying capacity; exceeding this threshold will have detrimental effects on the industry, because an unfriendly atmosphere will reduce a destination's attractiveness (Murphy, 1985).

There must be greater involvement of local community in the development of local tourism. This will permit a greater degree of local control over the direction of tourism development and ensure the use of local resources will increase employment and economic benefits to the community. Where residents have the impression that tourism is in the hands of outsiders, in the form of big companies and hotel chains, local people feel more alienated from the industry.

Hence, tourism planning in Africa must not be "top down." Local communities must be treated as resources and must benefit from the proceeds of such resources. Opportunities must be provided to obtain broad-based community participation in tourist events and activities. It should not be forgotten that it is the residents' home that is being put on display and the residents who must act as hosts, whether or not they are directly involved with the industry.

Social carrying capacity guidelines seek to balance community aspirations with the type and pace of tourism development undertaken. Local involvement is seen as one way of controlling the pace of development, integrating tourism with other activities and producing more individualistic tourist products. By emphasizing the individual character of a destination, tourism can become a vital force against the worldwide homogenization of culture.

Case Studies: Ghana and Zimbabwe

Van den Breemer, Drijver, and Venema (1995) identified nine case studies of community participation projects in Africa. These are located in Chad, Cameroon, Mali, and Zimbabwe. Reviewed are cases from Ghana and Zimbabwe, two countries that offer contrasting biomes: the tropical rainforest and the tropical grassland. The flora and fauna of both countries are quite different but both countries experience or have experienced community antagonism in one form or the other. On other hand, it appears Ghana has a lot to learn from the Zimbabwean CAMPFIRE experience (R. B. Martin, 1992). Another justification for choosing Ghana and Zimbabwe is that both countries represent the two major vegetation zones of Africa and therefore solutions to problems of one can easily be replicated in areas of similar vegetation cover.

The major findings in the two case studies are that:

- wildlife is recognized by the local communities as useful in the promotion of tourism;
- tourism contributes to rural development;
- in Zimbabwe the local community is more involved in wildlife conservation than in Ghana.

CAMPFIRE Project, Zimbabwe

The CAMPFIRE (the Communal Areas Management Programme for Indigenous Resources) project in Zimbabwe involves the utilization of wildlife resources and management by communities living in a wildlife area. It is known as the CAMPFIRE program (R. B. Martin, 1992). It is an example of the utilitarian approach in conservation. It has two major aspects:

- it uses wildlife as an economic resource through promotion of tourism;
- it returns income from the resource to communities living with wildlife.

Thus, it aims to contribute to rural development and also to change attitudes towards wildlife and therefore to conservation resources. The combination of conservation and use of wildlife resources has long been seen as a strange mix, but increasingly it is being recognized that a regulated use of nature and its products has at least two advantages for conservation programs.

In Africa, the creation of a national park of a resource reserve means the curtailment of legal access to wildlife and the deprivation of the best agricultural land. This certainly contributes to a general attitude towards wildlife, which then is seen as a nuisance and a threat to people and crops. The community sees wildlife and the reserve as a rightful communal resource to which access was unjustly restricted by an intruder. In many communal areas in African countries, though legally a no-access resource, wildlife use for subsistence hunting or "poaching" has been approved by the community as "a defiant gesture" against a powerful intruder.

Ghana Wildlife Society (GWS)

The role of Ghana Wildlife Society in community-oriented ecotourism is vividly described by Owusu (1996). The society was first formed in the early 1970s. It became dormant but was revived in 1991 by the SAVE, the Seashore Birds Project—Ghana (SSPB-G).

The society is committed to reaching out to people wherever they are to educate them on environmental and wildlife issues. It therefore carries out regular visits to schools and communities using talks, films, and slide shows, symposia, durbars, and campaigns to get conservation messages to the people.

The society engages in the development of community-based ecotourism through its wide membership and a wide coverage of the country through its wildlife clubs, club leaders, education coordinators, and community conservation education officers. This asset is being exploited to work with communities living in the vicinity of potential tourist sites, offering training in nature interpretation and other aspects of ecotourism.

The society has also encouraged the development of marine turtle conservation strategy for Ghana. The strategy advocated is community based. The coastal people are the key stakeholders in the marine turtle as a resource. It is therefore in their interest that the resource is not extirpated. It is also imperative to have their support, cooperation, and participation in any strategy to conserve turtles in Ghana. The strategy advocated seeks to forge a partnership between the local communities, the Ghana Wildlife Society as an NGO, and governmental agencies concerned with conservation of Ghana's natural resources, such as the Wildlife Department.

In relation to the Kakum National Park project in Ghana, Quaye (1996) sees that the best way to save the tropical forests is by associating the forest people with their management. Summing up this view, Ryan (1995) states that:

> A movement to protect forests which starts from the local peoples has more opportunity of maintaining the necessary flexibility. Any action from outside that attempts to restrict the use of forest against the will of those living there is doomed to failure, as may be seen from the deterioration of many national parks in the tropics. If the forests are to remain ecologically stable, it is essential that the requirements of the inhabitants be respected. (p. 3, quoted in Quaye, 1996)

Quaye observes that the Kakum National park (KNP) project has taken cognisance of this view and has taken steps to work in harmony with the communities through education, involvement, and, most importantly, by providing alternative sources of income.

In conclusion, Quaye notes that cultural inertia plays a major role in maintaining traditional indigenous knowledge and how such knowledge is applied in conservation practices. In some ethnic groups the ritualized control of forest resources, through periodic prohibitions rooted in ancestral customs, is still a frequent practice that affects the harvesting of particular plants or hunting of particular animals. This constitutes elements of species and genetic conservation; such communities should be encouraged to play a more active role in forest management.

Dei (1997a, 1997b) has similar views on Kakum National Park. The park covers an area of 356 km². It is underlain by Birrimian rocks of gneisses and schists and is located on both Fante and Assin Attandanso lands. It protects the watershed of the Kakum river system. All these give to the park a strong physical unity in terms of lithology, climate, and flora and fauna of the equatorial biome.

Underlying the uniform physical environment are cracks in human relations between park officials and local communities and among local communities of differing ethnic origin. Research carried out in the five villages, Mfuom, Gyaware, Abrafo-Odumasi, Afiaso, and Mesomago, by the Department of Geography and Tourism, University of Cape Coast, indicates a simmering discontent among the local population. The major actors in this are the Fantes and the Assins. The minor actors are the different ethnic groups (the stranger farmers) that have set up villages around the park. Both groups have different perceptions about the benefits of the park. Both groups see the park as an encroachment on their farmlands but the former feel embittered about their nonparticipation in the running of the park, particularly the Assins. Before the creation of the park in 1989, the area covered by the park played a very remarkable role in the life of the people. There was much human activity within the forest because it served as an economic shelter for the local communities. Farming was the principal economic venture. The forest served as hunting grounds for grasscutters, duikers, antelopes, and many other animals. It also provided raw materials in the form of canes, wood, and hides for local craftsmen.

The creation of the park meant also the creation of a new environment and possibly a new economic order and discipline. It resulted in shrinkage in cultivable land, hunting grounds, access to medicinal herbs and other forest products.

The objectives of the study were:

- to determine human activities before and after the creation of the park;
- the determine perception of the park by the local community;
- to determine the involvement of the communities in the management of the park;
- the determine the socioeconomic benefits to the people since the creation of the park;
- to anticipate problems and opportunities in the future for the community.

Domestication of game animals was suggested to reduce poaching, but the strong craving for bushmeat is an expensive culinary taste very detrimental to the survival of animal life in the park. To educate the population to domesticate game animals will therefore not solve the problem. Because the majority of the settlers are literate, the introduction of a new type of domesticated animals on a large scale, like chicken, rabbits, goats, sheep, and even pigs (for the Christians), may help solve the problem. It is interesting to note that about 66.6% of settlers are Christians while 33.4% are Moslems. It is estimated that with the imposition of the ban on Kakum Reserve, about 88% of the inhabitants now feed on fish. Most settlers agree that the creation of the park has affected business activities.

Because a significantly portion of the communities are literate, they see the relevance of the park for the following reasons:

- to protect the environemnt (6.66%);
- to conserve the environment for future generations (30%);
- for infrastructure development (16.6%);
- for tourism (18.33%);
- for employment (8.33%);
- other reasons (20%).

A major significant and indispensable fact about tourism and sociocultural and socioeconomic consequences is that there can be no tourism without cultural change (Table 21.1C, D, and E). In plain words, if a government or a state does not want to be affected by the results of the industry then the new venture has to be abolished. This, however, does not appear to be so in Ghana. Individual respondents were equally divided as to the benefits to be derived from the park (Table 21.1C). The entire community, however, believes that the park will be beneficial to them. Further, they have no apprehensions about the decline in moral values or conflict of interest, even though 66.67% are not involved in park activities.

Table 21.1. Villagers' Perceptions Following Park Establishment

	Percentages		
	Yes	No	Indifferent
A. Effect of park on business activities	75	25	
B. Response to ban on human activities	75	8.33	16.67
C. Benefits from the park	50	58.33	
Individual benefits	50	33.33	
Community benefits		8.33	
D. Decline in social and moral values	33.33	66.67	
E. Conflict of interest	16.67	83.33	
F. Involved in park activities	33.33	66.67	

The local community believes strongly that the creation of the park would not have any negative impact on their culture. It remains to be seen whether this will continue to be so with time. It is, however, a feeling that can be utilized to encourage cultural practices among the varying ethnic groups as part of a package for participation in the running of the park. In a multiethnic or multitribal society, as the one in the park area, multicultural activities could be encouraged for the enjoyment of both the local community and the visitor.

From Table 21.2 it is clear that communities living around the park benefit from some kind of economic ventures related to the environment. Such ventures could operate both within and outside the park. With restrictions imposed on the park, it is assumed that the communities operate outside the park. Note the significance of herbs for traditional medicine and the use of forest products for roofing.

As shown in Table 21.3, the majority of the people support the creation of the Park and its use for conservation purposes. However, they are not happy about the destruction of their farms by wild animals that stray outside the park and their nonparticipation in the management of the park. They agree, however, that they have been compensated financially for the release of their lands.

Table 21.4 shows a firm commitment by the community not to hunt within the park; however, they will hunt outside the park. A point was strongly made that any animal that strays outside the park would be considered as an enemy and would be shot. It is significant to state that bushmeat (or meat from game) is a delicacy among Ghanaians. This observation is significant in any attempt to plan for wildlife conservation in the park. With time the animal population in the park will increase and there will be several cases of

Table 21.2. Economic Activities and Other Benefits Derived by Communities Living Around the Park (%)

Village	Rope & Pole		Thatch Collection		Collection Harvesting		Addition of Herbs Income	
	Yes	No	Yes	No	Yes	No	Yes	No
Mfoum	7	93	8.2	91.8	70	30	63.2	36.8
Gyaware	96.7	3.5	99.0	1.0	92.6	7.4	76.2	23.8
Abrafo-Odumasi	6.8	93.2	4.8	95.2	66.3	33.7	69.1	30.9
Afiaso	98.2	1.8	98.2	1.8	97.8	8.2	75.3	24.7
Mesomago	98.9	1.1	98.9	1.1	93.3	6.7	78.2	21.8

Table 21.3. Reaction of Local Communities to Issues Related to the Creation of the Park (%)

	Destruction of Farms by Wild Animals Compensation		Release of Land and Compensation		Support for Conservation and Parks		Participation in Park's Management		
	Yes	No	Yes	No	Yes	No	Yes	No	Indiff.
Mfoum	78.2	21.8	88.6	11.4	95.8	4.2		88.04	11.6
Gyaware	79.3	20.7	89.3	10.7	96.7	3.3		90.61	9.4
Abrafo-Odumasi	97.3	20.8	88.4	11.6	98.2	1.8		94.03	5.7
Afiaso	78.5	21.5	90.3	9.7	94.3	5.7		86.09	13.1
Mesomago	77.21	22.8	89.2	10.8	89.6	10.4		96.21	3.8

trespassing and eventual death of such animals. This will bring friction between the local community and park administrators. Domestication of game animals, as is being suggested, will maintain the acquired taste for game meat, thus encouraging poaching when meat from domesticated game is no longer available.

With the creation of the park more and more people will visit this rural environment. This will obviously affect residents' cost of living. The few cases of price change shown in Table 12.5 are indications of what is expected in the future. It is anticipated that the change will have an impact on the lifestyle of the local community. The impact will be positive if local participation in the administration of the park leads to income-generating activities that will increase the purchasing power and therefore residents' standard of living.

National parks, protected nature sanctuaries, water protection areas, etc., are natural resources. Though the objective of conservation is inherent in the definitions of these concepts, utilization is also a concern. Perhaps one of the answers to effective park management may be found in the introduction of agrotourism, a new concept in ecotourism. Unlike the old tourism of the 1950s, 1960s, 1970s, and 1980s, agrotourism is the tourism of the future and is characterized by flexibility, segmentation, and more authentic tourism experiences.

Agrotourism

Hohnholz (1994) and Dei (1997b) advocate the concept of agrotourism in the solution of problems arising from noncommunity-oriented tourism. Agrotourism is tourism that

Table 21.4. Views on Hunting Within and Outside the Park (%)

	Age 10–29		Age 30–49		Age >50	
	Yes	Indifferent	Yes	Indifferent	Yes	Indifferent
Mfuom	96.0	4.0	98.0	2.0	94.0	6.0
Gyaware	94.2	5.8	97.0	3.0	97.2	2.8
Abrafo-Odumasi	90.8	9.2	96.0	4.0	98.6	1.4
Afiaso	96.0	4.0	96.1	3.9	97.9	2.1
Mesomago	98.0	2.0	94.0	6.0	96.4	3.6

Note: Yes indicates willingness to hunt outside the park. No means nobody will hunt within the park.

Table 21.5. Effects of Park on Prices of Some Forest Products (in Cedis)

Product	Unit Price Before Park	Unit Price After Park
Grasscutter (average size)	1,500	3,300
Cane (average length)	15	50
Maxwell-Duiker (average size)	2,000	4,500
Thatch (one piece)	15	450
Pestle	50	450
Cane basket	100	550

places emphasis on marketing rural products to the tourist who finds this merchandise exotic, traditional, romantic, or different from his usual way of life, while making sure that the environment is conserved.

For Kakum National Park a strategy for an integrated rural development involving the local communities is suggested. Kakum Park region is multiethnic or multitribal and this variety must be exploited as an incentive for tourism. Each village or small town is proud of its cultural inheritance and would want tourists to participate in their festivities, be they religious or secular. It is suggested that the famous "concert parties" be revived and introduced at village levels and that tourists be urged to participate. This is already being done in Accra. The idea is to revive a feeling among the people in the park for their own tradition and to display this inheritance for their own delight and that of the tourist.

Tourists could participate in traditional hunting, fishing, and farming, basket-weaving, cocoa farming, etc. The sometimes quite low social prestige of fishermen and farmers could be improved through tourist participation. Tourists would gain an impression of the hard work of the villagers as well as a sense of adventure and of the exciting and beautiful experiences in village life. Cultural villages with modern facilities should be set up to encourage tourists to live in rural areas and participate in the real Ghanaian village life, where *Ananse* stories could be told in simple but comfortable theaters. Such villages should have modern shopping centers managed by village tour operators. This would enhance capacity building of local craft industries. The idea is to develop a more distinct tourism of Kakum image and identity, leading to development of Kakum's unique identity and image in the international arena. To further achieve the above objectives, it is suggested that hotel consortiums be built along the coast, with one overnight stay possibly in the park. Another suggestion would be to have bungalows in a village run like the bungalows in the wildlife reserves. This would encourage the settlers of the park area to revive their traditional dances and costumes, which they could display at village museums. Such traditional ceremonies could be much more exotic and refreshing than a dinner dance or a cultural show in a five-star hotel.

Creating a tourist-oriented national park can mean interfering in the traditional way of life for nearby community residents, but it can also offer the chance of reviving lost traditional practices, and for some areas it can open up avenues in improved agricultural methods that concentrate first of all on tourism. Tourism invents culture in the sense that it represents the living world of others. Agrotourism makes the national park an authentic living history museum for education, adventure, and pleasure.

An effective control of a national park should be community participation oriented in the form of decision-making on issues of security. It should also mean developing an enterprising economic environment around the park through education and financial assistance. In extreme cases, environmental "spies" or "whistle-blowers" could be employed from among the local population. Two major communities are targeted generally for Africa.

Coastal-Based Tourism Communities

Coastal communities specialize in beach resorts, and heritage and cultural tourism. By the nature of their geographical location they can be sensitized to realize their potential in the tourism industry. These are the areas where Europeans first came into contact with Africans. Architectural remnants and relics of cultural behavior may still be seen in these areas. Examples of such communities are found along the coasts of Senegal, Côte d'Ivoire, Ghana, Benin, Tanzania, Kenya, etc.

The traditional beach resort consists of three land use zones:

- A specialized beachfront zone of tourist amenities and big hotels. Shops tend to open in the tourist season and cater solely for leisure shopping.
- The seafront trading zone is known as the Recreational Business District (RBD).
- A commercial core, situated just behind the RBD, with nonrecreational shops, offices, and services such as banks. This is the Central Business District.

Young (1973) and Smith (1992) observe that resorts go through various recognizable stages of land use change, from when the first tourists arrive at an undeveloped beach resort. The stages start with a small coastal fishing or farming settlement with no tourism at all.

At stage 2 second homes appear followed by the first commercial tourist accommodation. By stage 4 tourism is established and beginning to trigger off changes in the host community. In Stage 5 tourism expands until the Recreational Business District is established. These stages may differ from place to place but in reality change happens gradually and continually rather than in sudden steps. However, some planned resorts may start at one of the stages and be scattered along a particular stretch of coastline. These separate tourist resorts are sometimes known as tourist "enclaves."

The impacts of the changes in the nature of the coast resorts and their associated tourists may cause the host community some concern. The changes may be cultural, social, economic, or physical. The scale and nature of the tourism facility will determine the level of the impact. At some point sections of the community may exert pressure for stricter policies for land use and landscape control (e.g., land use zoning, control of high-rise development in prime sites, traffic management schemes). Local groups may also urge policies to constrain the negative social and cultural impacts of tourism on the community.

Nature-Based Tourism Communities

Nature-based tourism is found around game parks and forest reserves in Africa. Such reserves are found in Ghana, Côte d'Ivoire, South Africa, Zimbabwe, Kenya, Tanzania, and Botswana, among others.

The natural environment is used for nature-based tourism. It involves traveling to places for activities and experiences that are dependent on nature. Solitude is an essential part of the wilderness experience in nature tourism. In Africa, as has been noted, the land or the environment belongs to the people. Any development on a piece of land encroaches on land belonging to an individual, a stool, skin, or family. The land tenure system is such that there are three types of community land: land owned absolutely by a group of people or individuals; clan or family land; stool or skin land.

With the gradual demise of the colonial system of centralized administration and its gradual replacement by a decentralization characterized by district governments, the stage is now set for community participation in rural tourism. Under the old system the direction of change of the forest or grassland was prescribed by imported models, as seen in the setup of Game and Wildlife Departments of many African countries. In this discussion the concept of "pioneer space" is advanced to bridge the "implementation gap" between tourism policy and effective results with district governments playing the pioneer roles. District capacity building in rural tourism development and sustainability must be accepted and encouraged. The "pioneer space" needs to be created in each district and must be administered by the community itself. The concept could be utilized to deal with land disputes under a modified system of conflict resolution with greater community consultations and less recourse to the courts.

The "pioneer space" system will fulfill several policy-oriented objectives:

- Create an environment in which village-based resources, both human and physical, could be utilized for indigenously owned and operated tourism development. For example, the need for "Western" technical expertise, and costs, would be kept to a minimum.
- Support the capacity of the local community to obtain and retain control over the venture.
- Maintain a high degree of authenticity to enhance the sociocultural experience of the visitor.
- Protect the host community from adverse tourist ratios that could undermine village stability.
- Provide tourists with the protection afforded by existing legislation and regulations.
- Protect the investor and establish a system of loan repayments appropriate to the situation where some capital is required.
- Introduce a system of checks and balances to prevent unscrupulous people from taking advantage of the nonapplication of normal legislative and regulatory requirements.

The concept suggests that appropriate development would be small- scale, village-based tourism utilizing a limited range of intermediate technology. Such tourism by its nature would be "soft," culturally and environmentally oriented, with the emphasis on a traditional experience for the visitor. It would thus allow village life to continue with minimum disruption from the presence of visitors.

The Consensus Model of Planning With Communities

A model of consensus is proposed. Consensus eliminates the concept of "commoditization" often associated with external development of community property, which is based on two necessary conditions (Laban, 1995): that internal regime arrangements work successfully, and externally, that the community property is indeed property, defended against access by outsiders.

The model in Figure 21.1 is based on the Delphi technique (Green, Hunter, & Moore, 1990) and on the new political structure of Ghana (Ghana Ministry of Local Government, 1996). The technique underscores consensus while the new political administration of Ghana focuses on decentralization and allows grassroots participation in decision-making.

The old system of planning in most African countries has a number of drawbacks:

- It is insensitive to community aspirations and opportunities for local-level development initiatives.
- It inhibits integrated analysis synthesis and action, and represents a limited and partial approach to solving development problems.
- It hardly explores the interactive nature of development planning.

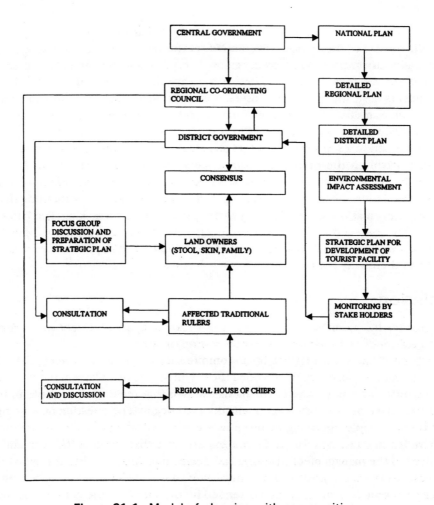

Figure 21.1. Model of planning with communities.

Under the old system the breakdown of community property management systems is usually described as having adverse effects on both social equity and ecological sustainability.

Public deliberations that come with community property management induce more monitoring of compliance to the social norms of sharing, greater consciousness of the future, or more moral weight being given to the future because the community, obviously, will live on even after the individual has died. Or, on a more down to earth level, community property may be more sustainable if its management tends to be regulated through older community members. Community property may be more sustainable because its management systems are usually old systems that would no longer have been there if they were not sustainable.

Against this background comes the new political system of community administration initiated by the Government of Ghana, which may be replicated in other parts of Africa. The new political system seeks to correct the inadequacies of the old administrative structure. It sees planning as a politico-technical dialogue and process and finds community participation as intersectoral and interdisciplinary collaboration involving continuous monitoring and evaluation to provide effective feedback.

Hence the model in Figure 21.1 advocates for top-down and bottom-up approaches to solutions involving communities. Governments at the various levels in the model have the right to plan tourism projects through regional and district governments in consultation with chiefs, subchiefs, and heads of families who are traditional owners of the land.

The model is basically based on consensus at every level. Hence, a tourism facility that develops from consensus is devoid of litigation and friction. It is thus a technique of judgmental forecasting that is very relevant to the peculiar African social set-up.

In this connection, each African country should devise a strategy for community participation in tourism on the basis of its own circumstances and needs. As has been stated earlier on, the Ghanaian model of grassroots administration may be studied by other African countries. This is because it provides policies and institutional structures that allow communities even at the lowest level to participate in decision-making. The latter allows tourism awareness even at the grassroots level, thus helping residents to appreciate the role of tourism in national development or of the benefits and improvements that tourism can make to their daily lives.

Conclusion

This chapter has examined some aspects of community involvement in tourism in Africa with reference to localities in two contrasting biomes.

It has been established that the local communities have come to accept the idea of tourism and nature conservation, provided these will bring improvement in their lifestyles. This is because the study done in Ghana has shown that most of the people in tourism-created areas have been affected economically and socially. The question now being asked is: why are the people not being involved in the administration of tourism facilities?

We have learned through this and other experiences that communities can and should be involved in the management planning and decision-making process. It is a fact that the local forest users have a great deal to contribute to our understanding of resources and resource problems. It is strongly recommended by an analysis of the consensus model that consultation is needed at every level in the planning and development of tourism facilities in Africa.

Author Note

Material for this chapter has been adopted from papers the author presented at two conferences sponsored by CEDECOM (Central Regional Development Commission, Cape Coast Ghana) at Cape Coast on 10 October 1997 and CI (Conservation International U.S.A.) at Coconut Grove Hotel, Elmina, Ghana, on 9–12 January 1996.

PART IV

FUTURE PERSPECTIVES

Chapter 22

Tourism and Africa's Long-Term Development Dynamics

Peter U. C. Dieke

Summary

This chapter details perspectives from various other chapters, draws together some of the salient policy issues facing Africa's tourism development, and concludes with a consideration of the way forward in the context of the necessary components of tourism development strategies for Africa in the new millennium. Important among them are:

- well-conceived and well-articulated but realistic tourism policy objectives;
- local involvement and control over tourism development;
- forging private–public sector partnerships for tourism development;
- raising gender awareness to enhance women's participation in the tourism sector;
- promoting regional tourism cooperation and integration;
- availability and allocation of appropriate resources (e.g., financial, human, product);
- developing equity in tourism benefits sharing;
- promoting community tourism awareness campaign;
- availability of appropriate legal framework for tourism;
- building image of a destination through a marketing and promotional campaign;
- expanding tourism entrepreneurial initiatives/investment opportunities.

Key words: Tourism policy objectives; Tourism community participation; Private–public partnership; Raising gender awareness; Tourism community awareness; Regional tourism cooperation and integration; Strategic resource allocation; Legal framework for tourism; Destination image building; Entrepreneurial initiative

Introduction

> ... developing tourism is not nearly as simple or as certain as most policymakers assume when tourism is adopted as a development strategy ... political needs often drive economic plans, sometimes with disastrous effects ... in other cases with mixed or even positive effects. . . . . (Richter, 1989, p. 180)

Such statements are at the heart of this volume. As international tourism is an intricate activity, it has important social and economic implications arising from its development, given the influence of economic and political actors in shaping the nature of the development. For this reason, it is useful to appreciate the wider social and other interrelated dynamics within which tourism development takes place. Of significance perhaps is the need to delineate a strategy framework to guide future development of the tourism sector as well as provide a reference point against which to evaluate the sector's success. A political economy approach to tourism development performs these tasks and further underscores one simple fact: the factors that facilitate or inhibit tourism development in Africa and indeed in the other less developed regional countries are not solely the easily recognized variables (e.g., amenities, attractions, and access) but also the intangible political, social, and historical forces.

Thus, the purpose of this final chapter is to determine, within the African context, whether the analysis in Chapter 1 is supported by the contributions from the other authors to (and perhaps others outside) this volume; to identify policy challenges confronting the tourism sector arising from the analysis; and finally, to use the synthesis to consider what might be the parameters for the future development of tourism in African countries as part of their economic development strategies.

Perspectives From the Chapters

In the first chapter, Peter Dieke introduces the broad issues of the volume, discusses the definitional issues, the historical, as well as the significance and the processes of, political economy of tourism development. Dieke examines the role of tourism in the development process and relates the synthesis to Africa's tourism development political economy setting. In identifying the underlying factors that influence tourism development in the region, Dieke discusses them as follows. First is a clear understanding that tourism development cannot meaningfully be analyzed in isolation from other components of society, history, economics, and polity. Second is that the formulation of tourism policies is based on an analysis of the market and also within the perspective of certain institutions and their modus operandi, taking into account the resources available in the countries and also the vested interests and opinions of various pressure groups. Third is that implementation of tourism policies depends on the responses of private or public institutions and individuals to those policies and the institutions through which those policies are to be implemented. Finally, institutions are important in defining tourism issues (e.g., distributional issues, environmental problems and concerns, and cultural matters), in mobilizing resources, in mediating interests, and in implementing tourism policy. The chapter concludes with an insight into the organization of the book.

From Chapter 1 the book is divided into four parts. Part I, on analytical prisms, contains four theory chapters, two of them within a comparative framework. It opens with Chapter 2 by Robert Poirier with a study on tourism in the African economic milieu. Poirier argues that research on tourism in the context of the political economy of Africa's development has been sparse, particularly as it relates to the question of tourism's impact in alleviating Africa's deepening economic woes. This chapter focuses its discussion on the vast potential of tourism as a major earner of foreign exchange but within the context of international and internal political economy. The role of IMF structural adjustment programs as a major engine driving tourism projects is examined, providing the international dimension of the chapter. The interaction of these external forces with the dynamics of intracontinental and African domestic politics provides the African political context of the essay. It is argued that tourism adoption has shown both positive and negative results in Africa, making a consensus for tourism as a policy tool difficult to achieve. The examination of these counterviews traces the manner in which countries have grappled with the potential for economic gain on the one hand and the social and environmental cost on the other hand. This chapter demonstrates that, with constrained resources available to African countries and uneven attractions for tourism, it will be impossible for the whole of the African countries to embark on a major expansion of tourism. Further limitations will come about as a result of structural adjustment pressures, political crises, and unstable democratization directions. Nevertheless, given the prospects of comparative advantage, privatization strategies, and integrated markets, it may well be feasible for many African countries to pursue tourism.

In Chapter 3, David Harrison pursues some of these issues by examining the social and cultural framework for tourism development in Africa. Harrison introduces a historical dimension to the debate, arguing that during the last decades of the 19th century and for much of the 20th century, tourism in Africa, especially where there were relatively large settler populations, was developed by colonialists for colonialists. In general, black Africans possessed neither the financial nor the cultural capital to compete with Europeans. Harrison goes on to argue that later, when mass tourism on an international scale developed, settler capital was joined by international capital, and this structure was one of the bequests of colonialism. The association of tourism in Africa with white colonialism led some Africans to oppose the tourism industry as another form of "underdevelopment." Another bequest of colonialism was the formation of several contradictory images of Africa, as the habitat of noble yet dangerous people, of noble yet dangerous animals, and similarly, as a series of beautiful but untamed landscapes. Such contradictions are reinforced in the West by current mass media coverage of Africa, which tends to portray the continent as prone to disease, poverty, and war, and tourism development is likely to be hampered as long as such images continue to dominate.

In Chapter 4, David Weaver surveys the political geography context for tourism development with a focus on southern Africa. His view is that the functional approach in political geography maintains that state power structures must constantly impose and reinforce a variety of "centripetal" (or state-enhancing) forces to offset the existence of various "centrifugal" (or state-eroding) forces. This chapter applies the functional approach to the tourism sector of southern Africa, emphasizing the central role of the Republic of South Africa. Weaver further suggests that during the Apartheid era, tourism was deliberately if tacitly employed as a centripetal tactic to generate revenue, attract potential immigrants, and, most importantly, to legitimize the "Homelands" while providing a convenient outlet for tourism products then illegal within South Africa itself. Concurrently, neighboring "casino states" such as Swaziland and Lesotho also attempted to capitalize on the demand for these activities. Tourism is also used as a centripetal force in post-Apartheid South Africa to assist in regional development and wealth redistribution strategies, and to promote the iconography of the new dominant ideology. However, tourism is also seen by some neighboring states as potential centrifugal force that promotes regional integration (and hence the weakening of state power) and facilitates the expansion of the South Africa sphere of influence.

Chapter 5 by Kit Jenkins provides comparative insights into the tourism policy formulation process in the southern African region. Jenkins's view is that most of the 14 countries comprising the Southern Africa Development Community (SADC) have attempted to formulate policies to guide the future development of the tourism sector. The approaches adopted have been very different, with some countries making an explicit policy statement and others incorporating policy intentions within broader tourism planning exercises. In most of the countries, with the exception of Angola, tourism is an important sector in the respective economies and is recognized as having potential to contribute to

general development objectives. A new feature of the policy formulation approach in southern African countries is the participation of the private sector into this process, and the
key role that the private sector will have in financing and in implementing future development. Jenkins further maintains that the change in the formulation process has been in the
respective roles of government and the private sector, leading to the development of a
partnership initiative. The contents of the various policy statements have areas of common concern (e.g., product development, marketing, funding, human resources). There is
an explicit preference to develop tourism within the existing sociocultural traditions and
with consideration of environmental quality standards. Implementation of policy is largely
reliant upon the existing institutional structures and with the extant legislation. Jenkins
then ends by suggesting that without appropriate changes in inadequate institutional structures and human resource capital building, implementation strategies will be frustrated.

Part II, on a small selection of six national-specific or area studies, starts with Chapter 6
by Edward Inskeep on planning sustainable tourism in Ghana. Inskeep postulates that
concepts of sustainable tourism have been refined in recent years and are now commonly
applied to all types of tourism development. The Integrated Tourism Development
Programme (ITDP) for Ghana represents a comprehensive planning approach to achieve
the sustainable development of international and domestic tourism, applying contemporary approaches to planning for sustainable tourism. Financed by the United Nations Development Programme UNDP) and Government of Ghana and executed by the World Tourism Organization (WTO), Inskeep states that the ITDP was implemented by the Ghana
Ministry of Tourism utilizing a team of international and national consultants working
closely with Ministry counterparts. The ITDP included national and regional planning, development programming, financial planning, project analysis, establishing a tourism information system, and other institutional improvements. The tourism policies and plans were
formulated within the framework of overall national development policy and planning.
Emphasis in the ITDP was given to developing a wide range of types of tourism based on
the resources available, spreading the benefits of tourism widely throughout the country,
consideration of economic, environmental, and sociocultural factors, involvement of all
stakeholders in the tourism planning process, developing community-based tourism
projects, and specifying implementation techniques. Achieving environmental protection
and historic and cultural heritage conservation objectives through tourism was a major
theme of the ITDP. Considerable effort was directed to facilitating financing of public and
private development projects. Training was an important element of the program in order
to enhance capabilities in both the public and private sectors of tourism. Providing the
institutional basis for effective development implementation and continuous tourism management was an essential aspect of the ITDP. Inskeep concludes by saying that many of the
approaches used in this program are applicable to other countries in Africa.

Similar issues emerge in Chapter 7, the subject of which is the planning of tourism in a
reconstructing economy of Eritrea. Peter Burns critically analyses conflicting advice on
the future development of tourism given to Eritrea, a country at the very start of its planning for tourism. The chapter commences with an examination of national development
planning processes. It identifies key issues including sociopolitical structures, participation, and the distribution of economic benefits. For tourism, it is argued that integration of
tourism policies into broader national development priorities is essential. The case of Eritrea
is an unusual one: a newly independent country with virtually no tourism infrastrucutre,
facilities, or technical knowledge. The main focus of the chapter is on two sets of advice
given to Eritrea at its first conference for the development of tourism held in 1993. Neither of these pieces of advice has the capacity to deliver equitable or sustainable develop-

ment in a way that reflects Eritrea's political ethos of democratic participation in decision-making. The chapter ends with the conclusion that a more effective way of planning must start with convincing tourism planners that there are alternative approaches that can and should integrate processes that such planners would presumably wish for their own countries, namely: participation, democracy, and pluralism.

In Chapter 8, Kit Jenkins examines the development of tourism in Namibia, beginning with a general background to this country before discussing the way tourism has developed and the nature and problems of tourism activity there. This is a geographically large country (824,000 km²) with a comparatively small population of 1.6 million people that became independent as a republic in March 1990. Historically it had been dominated in economic and political terms by its southern neighbor, the Republic of South Africa, to which it is closely associated through currency linkage and a customs union. Namibia, like many other countries in southern Africa, based its development strategy on agricultural and mineral resources. However, as early as 1992 government recognized that tourism could help to diversify the development strategy and consequently designated it a "priority sector." The government sought the help of the European Union to develop tourism. That organization, through its technical assistance programs, has since 1992 supported the tourism sector. Jenkins then assesses the progress that has been made in this process, examines the nature and impact of the provided technical assistance, and identifies the problems that have inhibited development. The author identifies these problems further as development issues that may have relevance to other developing countries seeking to define and implement a tourism development strategy.

A similar development slant on Kenya is pursued in Chapter 9 by Isaac Sindiga, beginning with facts and figures of the country's tourism sector. Tourism is the second highest foreign exchange earner (after coffee) and the sector contributes about 11% to Kenya's GDP according to the latest statistics. Sindiga discusses the origins and development of both wildlife and beach tourism in Kenya, analyzes the role of tourism in the economy, and outlines the challenges of the country's tourism industry at the entry of the 20th century and the prospects in the new millennium. His analysis shows that tourist numbers increased rapidly in the postindependence period as did investments in the industry. However, per capita real earnings in tourism have been declining over time. Further, contrary to popular belief tourism generates little employment and on average pays wages below the modern sector economy as a whole. Yet tourism is essential to raising the levels of income and developing certain remote areas of the country. In concluding, Sindiga further points out that government commitment to addressing the problems of the industry through repairing the damaged road infrastructure, ensuring peace and security, allocating more resources to security services, providing stable funding for Kenya Tourist Board (KTB), encouraging locally financed tourist hotel development through tax incentives, and comprehensive tourism planning could change the image of tourism and secure the place of this country as a competitive African destination.

In his study of tourism development in Botswana in Chapter 10, Adams Dambe Chilisa identifies and assesses the inherent problems facing the tourism sector in the country and considers their probable causes against a backdrop of a desired sustainable tourism development scenario. Chilisa also reviews government policies and institutional arrangements for tourism and argues that tourism policies in particular should be complementary and advocacy in nature, to reinforce the national development objectives. He then suggests that this approach should be incorporated into the country's tourism master plan, which seeks to address those issues taking into account the external and internal environments within which the tourism sector operates. Finally, the author offers future prospects.

In Chapter 11, Ahmada Khatib provides useful perspectives on the development of ecotourism in Zanzibar, an island region of Tanzania. Khatib points out that Zanzibar has recently embarked on tourism as a means to diversify its monocrop economy, mainly related to fishing, which has suffered from world economic recession in recent times. Given the island's fragile ecosystem, its small size, and the need for conservation of its cultural heritage, the island city-state is in the process of searching for an appropriate type of tourism. Ecotourism has been seen as one of the best options, which could at least minimize the problems associated with the other types of tourism. In consequence, ecotourism has been adopted as a "national" strategy option. Khatib further explores the Zanzibar experience with ecotourism by analyzing some policy issues arising from its development, and assesses the potential for its development. His argument is that there is a good potential in terms of attractions: both the conservation needs and promoting tourism as a business venture. Khatib makes a further suggestion that will enable this balance to be struck in the context of making the project self-financing: involvement of local community of the surrounding area, and making tourism directly contribute to the conservation and livelihood of the indigenous community.

A rather different kind of analysis forms the subject of Chapter 12. Thea Sinclair and Alan Pack focus on Zimbabwe's Communal Areas Management Programme for Indigenous Resources, or CAMPFIRE program, which they argue exemplifies the way in which economic policy instruments can be used to increase the economic returns from wildlife tourism, thereby promoting income and employment generation in rural areas and supporting wildlife conservation. The program aims to give local communities ownership and control of the wildlife within their domain and to ensure them a return from the use of such resources, in the form of cash and/or community projects. The authors suggest that charges, quotas, and regulations, applied to wildlife viewing and hunting tourism, are the instruments used to facilitate this objective. An additional view is that foreign donors' provision of financial support for the program illustrates the way in which the option or existence value of wildlife can be financed from external sources. Sinclair and Pack then conclude that although the CAMPFIRE program has been welcomed in some areas of Zimbabwe, it has been less successful in areas where the economic returns from the program have been relatively low or unequally distributed.

In Part III, containing nine chapters, the focus shifts to an examination of institutions, structures, and strategies: the centerpiece of tourism development dynamics. Part III begins with Chapter 13 by Erik Holm-Petersen, who points out that the development of institutional capacity forms a central issue in developing the basic framework for economic development. However, he maintains that in the sub-Saharan Africa region severe lack of capacity with respect to general economic management, as well as specific management skills within the tourism sector, has formed a strong barrier to growth. In general terms, the author believes that most of the countries have not had the capacity to utilize the tourism development aid provided in the past. Although the African countries have remarkable possibilities for tourism development, he believes that only a few countries have thus been able to utilize this growth potential. The lack of institutional capacity combined with a general lack of understanding among tourism policy-makers have furthermore resulted in a low priority of the tourism sector. Holm-Petersen argues that understanding of the role of the private and public sectors and understanding of the need for integrated planning involving focus on sustainable natural resources as well as involvement of communities and local entrepreneurs in the tourism development are prerequisites for setting an optimum tourism development strategy. Awareness creation through politically high-profiled regional collaboration can in this respect form one of the means to be used by the tourism sector. Consequently, collaboration within tourism has been established in southern and western Africa and is being developed in eastern Africa. Tourism development projects, including tourism master plan projects, received donor support in the past. In most cases, however, the effects of this planning work were limited, and donors have in recent years changed their support pattern to incorporate a more strategic and comprehensive approach with a clear implementation orientation. In order to get full benefit of this approach, projects have incorporated a strong element of institutional capacity building and increasingly more funds have been made available for institutional support. Recent trends in the attitudes of African policy-makers, although reluctantly, as well as the policies of donor agencies, thus point at a much more structured and focused development strategy in the future. This strategy will be based on power sharing between the private and public sectors, increased privatization efforts, and a joint sector approach combining tourism and natural resources.

In Chapter 14, Nathan Austin introduces a different type of institution— slavery and the slave trade—and reflects on the emotions surrounding the subject and its relationship to tourism. Austin views the recent global interest in heritage as part of tourism development strategy. This is because of the perceived importance of heritage attraction in enhancing economic and social development of host communities. The author claims that a number of African countries have also joined in this bandwagon and, with assistance from WTO and United Nations Educational, Scientific and Cultural Organization (UNESCO), have initiated measures to revisit and preserve the events of the transatlantic slave trade as heritage tourism products. However, there is a need to exercise considerable care in the development and utilization of such events for tourism development purposes considering the sensitive impact that such events may have on black Africa and also on black–white race relations. Thus, Austin argues that these events may raise ethical and other such related questions that, in the main, might be considered incompatible with the traditional leisure-oriented image of tourism. Furthermore, he points out that issues of differing perspectives on authenticity and objectivity are also difficult to resolve. Similarly, the author continues, it is worth noting also that an understanding of visitor emotions and the need for the "education" of potential visitors, hosts, and project planners about the current relevance of the history of the slave trade will be most beneficial to its utilization for tourism development. Relevant policy initiatives should place importance on the symbolism and essence of the current relevance of the history of the trade to black Africa. Within this milieu Austin indicates that the success of the development of tourism in Africa and the need for a total visitor experience would require a coordinated and cooperative effort, if the potential benefits of bringing together black people of African descent for their mutual benefit is to be realized.

Still on the subject of institutions, Chapter 15 by Victor Teye introduces a political dimension to the debate. Teye proposes that regional economic cooperation provides significant opportunities for individual countries in Africa to expand their resource base, increase investment potential, and implement marketing strategies, among other things, in pursuit of general economic development. He believes that, either directly or indirectly, the tourism sector can derive significant benefits from regional cooperation arrangements because of developments elsewhere. For instance, over the last decade, developing regions have made significant efforts to achieve greater degree of regional economic integration and cooperation. Some of these regional groupings include The Association of South East Asia (ASEAN) and Mercosur in Latin America. These initiatives have coincided with either new or reinforced regional integration policies and institutions in the industrialized countries, such as treaty and expansion of the European Union (EU) and the establishment of the North American Free Trade Area (NAFTA). While both the EU and NAFTA objectives include the gradual integration of selected developing countries of North–South cooperation, developing countries are placing greater emphasis on regional cooperation among themselves at two South–South levels. The first level is interregional cooperation among different regions in the developing world, while the second is intraregional cooperation among proximate countries in the same broad geographical region. Against this background Teye proceeds to describe efforts at intraregional economic cooperation in Africa, and examines the Southern Africa Development Community (SADC) as a model approach to tourism planning, development, and management at subregional levels.

In Chapter 16, Shepherd Nyaruwata expands on some of the above issues by analyzing the role of RETOSA (Regional Tourism Organization of Southern Africa) in Africa's tourism development cooperation initiatives. Nyaruwata makes the point that there has been a global trend to create regional tourism cooperations in recent years (e.g., in the Caribbean and Asian regions, among others). In one sense, these developments might be seen as a response to the growing world competition, coupled with the effects of globalization. The obvious advantages of this situation will be not only to ease travel and enhance investment but also to aggressively put the particular region in the tourism spotlight or map. The author cites an African example with the establishment of RETOSA in 1995, involving 14 countries of SADC as a reflection of this broad phenomenon. He suggests that the primary aim of RETOSA was to market and promote the SADC region in partnership with the public and private sectors of the member countries of the region. Nyaruwata further examines, within the context of RETOSA, the importance that the SADC member states attach to regional cooperation as a means of achieving sustainable tourism development in southern Africa, and then offers some perspectives on the future direction of the organization. Despite the short period that RETOSA has been in existence, it has demonstrated the usefulness of pooling resources together and approaching the generating markets with the idea that the region is a single holiday destination. He substantiates this claim by giving an example. Joint promotional activities have already been undertaken with principals in the region's primary markets. Nyaruwata believes that given the commitment that the member states have shown toward the organization and the growing involvement of the private sector to RETOSA-driven promotional activities, the organization has a potential of growing into a sound and viable promotional tourism organ of southern Africa.

In Chapter 17 Noel de Villiers writes about a tourism institutional arrangement of a different caliber: Open Africa, a nongovernmental organization. He starts by posing a question: Can a strategic catalyst galvanize Africa around a vision of single-minded purpose aimed at optimizing the benefits of tourism in conjunction with protecting its nature and cultural heritage? He addresses this question in the rest of the chapter by first providing some useful background to Open Africa, engaged in an initiative to do what this question is seeking an answer to, and then sketches its progress to date. Drawing on Africa's strengths, essentially what Open Africa is doing is to set a systemized process in motion, aligned to coincide with perceived global trends in tourism and the energy generated by the Africa Renaissance theme. Probably unprecedented in history in terms of its scope, the success or otherwise of the initiative will depend on its popular appeal. De Villiers provides further profile. Open Africa is a registered not-for-profit organization. Its trustees and advisors are all eminent leaders in their fields, who see the role of the organization as being that of a strategic think tank rather than transactional. Although the initiative was founded with a clear end picture in mind—to optimize Africa's tourism potential in a manner that will nourish and restore its resource base—no guidelines exist on how to set about changing the paradigms of an entire continent. Initially, simply to articulate what was in mind proved hugely challenging, and then to steadily build a strategy and devise an enabling system meant starting with a clean sheet of paper with each step taken. Nor is this an academic exercise. Despite several of Open Africa's trustees and many of its supporters being scientists and academics, its founding was based on experience and intuition rather than research. Blind faith borne out of love for and belief in Africa was also a factor.

Writing on African tourism training and education in Chapter 18, Roger Doswell takes a generalized approach to Africa, drawing on the examples of a wide variety of countries from across the continent. In this Doswell has attempted to construct an aggregate of African experience. Although Africa is diverse and countries are not the same, there is value in constructing this kind of general picture. It provides insight into the successes, failures, and omissions—the hits and misses—and we can compare and assess any country's experience against the rule. The chapter discusses the tendency to irrelevance and cultural bias in many past initiatives, and the influence exercised by the aid donors. Public sector administration is also discussed, together with the reasons why certain courses of action are simply inappropriate or unworkable. The chapter goes on to describe Africa's training hits and misses and partial hits and misses. It then summarizes the type of training needs, the distinct levels of skills, and the right kinds of institutional approach. The chapter concludes by outlining an African approach to tourism vocational education and training.

In his contribution in Chapter 19 on tourism and land tenure in sub-Saharan Africa, David Weaver claims that, to date, there has been little explicit focus on the issue of tenure in the tourism literature. Within the context of modernization dynamics, Weaver examines the relationship between tenure and tourism in a variety of sub-Saharan spatial contexts. The suggestion is that dominant metropolitan areas and surrounding modern hinterlands possess relatively sophisticated tourism sectors, especially in southern Africa, while the dominantly communal lands of the transitional/traditional space economy participate only marginally in this sector. Further, Weaver argues that protected areas, despite their wilderness-like quality, may be perceived as a special type of modern space increasingly mobilized to provide ecotourism-type tourism experiences. He concludes by identifying the community lands/protected area interface as a zone of tourism-based tension between the modern and traditional space economies.

In Chapter 20 Desmond Brown reviews the role of foreign investment in developing Africa's tourism resources. The chapter argues that, despite the attractiveness of Africa as a tourist destination, foreign tourism investment flow to the continent is relatively low when compared to other developing regions of the world. Brown offers some explanation for this, not least being the higher perceived risk levels by potential investors. He then goes on to analyze various perceived risk factors, in addition to the market entry strategies employed by a few of the investors. Finally, he discusses some incentive measures to increase the flow of foreign investment.

In Chapter 21, Laud Dei's discussion of tourism community participation describes the word "community" as referring to a group of any size whose members reside in a specific and historical heritage. He points out that in Africa such groups are headed by village heads, chiefs, and kings, and they are the owners of the land. His suggestion is that tourism alters the nature of politics and may initiate conflicts when governments impose tourism development without consultation. For these reasons the opportunities for the control of tourism must be in the hands of the indigenous people and tourism should be community driven. Dei concludes by proposing a model of consensus to ensure that indigenous culture is not "commoditized" and that conflicts are reduced.

Finally, in Part IV, which contains the concluding chapter, Peter Dieke details perspectives from the various chapters, draws together some of the salient policy issues facing

Africa's tourism development, and concludes with a consideration of the way forward in the context of the necessary components of tourism development strategies for Africa in the new millennium.

Economic Policy Challenges for Africa's Tourism Development

The contributions from the various authors have shown there are a number of policy challenges or issues facing tourism development in Africa that need to be tackled. The term "policy issues" is used in a generic sense, taking as a reference point the definition offered by Collier (1988, p. 1). In our context, the policy challenges are really defined by three elements: the *problems* arising from the development of tourism, the *processes* that generate them, and the policy *interventions* to solve them. This analysis will therefore attempt to show how these issues are relevant at the levels of the tourism industry and African governments. It is expected that the identification and examination of these matters will provide development guidelines for tourism in Africa in the next millennium.

Policy Issues for the Tourism Industry

The first of these is the need to delineate the relative roles of the private local and foreign tourism partners in development decisions in the continent. The decisions can be in the areas of investment, marketing, or even operating the tourism enterprise. The key issue for all concerned is to recognize that the development decisions made by them do have wider economic consequences for Africa. It is therefore imperative that investors recognize the implications of their actions in the overall interest of the long-run economic sustainability of the tourism sector.

The second major challenge is the need to develop human resources, particularly the indigenous personnel, to deliver quality services for tourists and to enhance general skills of the local workforce. Achieving these broad objectives will potentially encourage sound utilization of local suppliers and thus enhance not only their productivity but also intersectoral linkages. In this sense, the spin-off effect is obvious: foreign exchange will be retained locally and further income will be earned.

In the third place, there are problems facing the local tourism industry, which is dominated by a large number of small and medium-sized tourism enterprises (SMEs) (Othman, 1998). Although SMEs serve useful functions in tourism (e.g., the development of linkages, providing personal service, etc.), for most of them life is a daily struggle, with many of them operating at the margin of survival. They also lack the requisite experience to run tourism businesses along modern management principles; even the nature of tourism demand makes them uncompetitive as they are unable to capitalize on the economies-of-scale advantages. The real challenge is for them to develop marketing strategies, which would permit them to overcome some of these difficulties and thereby sell their products. Again, their limited resource base makes this objective hard to achieve.

Policy Issues for African Governments

The traditional role of government is to formulate policy for the tourism sector. Today the focus has changed because of changing priorities occasioned by development in the international tourism scene (e.g., the emergence of consumer interests). The challenge for national governments is to formulate policies for the tourism sector that best reflect the new thinking. Some important areas needing policy reorientation or refocusing are: consultation with local communities in the planning process; forging partnership with the private sector; liberal immigration regulations to facilitate free tourist movement; tourism infrastructure development policy to facilitate tourism development, for the benefit not just for tourism but the wider society. The last policy issue needs to be linked to devising viable and sensible options for financing tourism infrastructure. Other aspects of policy refocusing include entrepreneurial development initiatives, policies to enhance tourist length of stay, and policies to identify ways in which the benefits from tourism activity can be spread more evenly throughout society.

Future Agenda

To put the preceding analyses and the perspectives from the various contributors into a wider framework of an agenda for the 21st century, the view of Kofi Annan, the Secretary-General of the United Nations, on the African development challenge (which also includes tourism), is instructive:

> The basic strategy for achieving sustainable development through economic growth is now well established. The core components of the strategy include macroeconomic stability and a stable investment environment; integration into the international economy; a reliance on the private sector as the driving force for economic growth; long-term foreign direct investment, especially in support of export-oriented activities; adequate investment in human development areas such as health and education; a fair and reliable legal framework; and the maintenance of basic physical infrastructures. . . . Long-term success can be achieved only if African Governments have the political will not just to enact sound economic policies but also to persevere in their implementation until a solid economic foundation has been established. (cited in ECA, 1999b, p. 1)

As tourism is essentially an international economic activity, this section identifies and examines some of those elements of the strategy that are relevant to the long-term sustainable development of tourism in the African region. The following considerations are particularly striking because of their importance in shaping both a coordinated African tourism development policy in practice and enhancing conceptualization of the political economy of the process.

First, international tourism has come to stay for the foreseeable future and cannot casually be cast aside or treated less seriously than it deserves. The economic and other benefits (and negative benefits) accruing from its development are well recognized, both in the developed and developing world. Despite the mounting criticisms of the negative effects of tourism development, there is a groundswell of evidence that many African countries, encouraged by positive developments elsewhere, continue to pursue tourism promotion as part of their economic development strategies. Thus, tourism has now merited inclusion in national development plans of most African countries.

Second, as tourism develops and becomes intricate it will require strategic management of the process to maximize the benefits and contain or mitigate the negative impacts, in order to ensure that development conforms with national policy objectives. The development of the sector needs to be supported by large inflows of foreign resources (e.g., financial, personnel). Foreign involvement will obviously have wider repercussions for the decision-making sovereignty of the host government, thereby threatening the long-term sustainability of the sector. In other cases the role of government institutions and technocrats may not help advance the cause of tourism.

The third point is that tourism development cannot be separated from other facets of economy, society, and polity. Merely creating national, regional, and subregional institutions or planning bodies responsible for tourism is hollow in the absence of the political mandate and adequate resources to do their jobs. Here lie much of the difficulties with developing tourism in Africa; the result is ineffectual policies. This holds the key to future advances in tourism development in the region.

Fourth, in the same way that political support and sufficient resources hold the key to Africa's future tourism development, so too is the need to empower the African masses. This can be done in a variety of ways: by creating in them an awareness of the benefits of tourism; by allowing them access to entrepreneurial opportunities offered by tourism; by permitting women a role in the industry; and perhaps finally by giving them a sense of ownership in the sector. These are proactive measures and ones that negate the spirit of state capitalism and also gender inequality. African tourism policy strategies should aim to redress these deficiencies. It then means, as noted, that the existence of credible political commitment on the part of African governments is a *sine qua non* to the realization of such strategies. From this description it is clear that many chapters in this volume stress necessary tourism development strategies for Africa. Important among them are:

- well-conceived and well-articulated but realistic tourism policy objectives;
- local involvement and control over tourism development;
- forging private–public sector partnerships for tourism development;
- raising gender awareness to enhance women's participation in the tourism sector;
- promoting regional tourism cooperation and integration;
- availability and allocation of appropriate resources (e.g., financial, human, product);
- developing equity in tourism benefits sharing;
- promoting community tourism awareness campaign;
- availability of appropriate legal framework for tourism;
- building image of a destination through a marketing and promotional campaign;
- expanding tourism entrepreneurial initiatives/investment opportunities.

The implementation of such strategic objectives needs to be assessed against the backdrop of many imperatives: the bureaucratic environment within which tourism development takes place, in addition to the changing nature of national, regional, and international context. It also requires an understanding of the nature of state power apparatus, including of course the administrative system, as well as the economic, political interests and structures, and patronage systems. The response of the administrative agencies charged with tourism development will shape the environment in which these policy objectives are determined and implemented. In the final analysis, tourism development requires not only the formation of sound policies and decision-making mechanisms but also the development of appropriate institutional structures that are cohesive and are also seen to work in practice.

In summary, the above prognosis does not mean that all is lost in the African tourism development experience. Quite the reverse. It does mean that for the tourism sector in Africa to respond flexibly to changing realities in the international tourism market scene, the strategic development of the industry in the continent is paramount. This requires cooperation from all concerned—the tourism industry, the national governments, and indeed the international community—to make it happen, provided, of course, that the political will exists or can be created. In Africa (White & Bhatia, 1997) as in other parts of the globe, state capitalism has rolled back with dramatic though positive changes and results. There is no doubt that these developments will continue and tourism will, in the end, be the winner (Jenkins, 1994). The successes of many other destinations are a model for the late starters in Africa to copy. If they can do it, so too can we in Africa—a reflection of the counterpart syndrome—on the basis that safety and peace continue to prevail in the region.

Contributors

Nathan K. Austin is lecturer in the School of Management, Universiti Utara Malaysia, where he teaches Tourism Marketing and Research Methodology. He received his Ph.D. from the University of Strathclyde in 1997, and an M.Sc. in Tourism Marketing, University of Surrey in 1988. He also holds full membership of the Chartered Institute of Marketing, U.K. His main research interests are in heritage site management, tourist behavior, and visitor satisfaction.

Desmond Omotayo Brown holds a Ph.D. in Hospitality and Tourism Management from Virginia Polytechnic Institute & State University, an M.A. in Travel and Tourism Management from the George Washington University, as well as an M.B.A. in Hotel and Restaurant Administration from the University of New Haven. He is currently an assistant professor of hospitality and tourism at the University of Kentucky. He has had considerable industry management experience with various hotel chains, such as the Marriott, Holiday Inn, Ramada, and Hilton, as well as an airline and a tour company. His research and teaching interests include hospitality and tourism planning, development, finance, and marketing issues pertaining to Africa, where he has also done fieldwork. He has published about tourism in Africa in various journals including *Tourism Management, International Journal of Hospitality Management, Journal of Vacation Marketing, Journal of Travel Research*, and *Journal of Sustainable Tourism*.

Peter M. Burns is Chair of International Tourism and Development, School of Service Management, University of Brighton, U. K. His Ph.D. focused on the role of tourism master planning in national development. He holds master's degrees in Anthropology of Tourism and in Education. He acts as a consultant anthropologist to a number of international organizations (e.g., WTO, UNDP, EU, Asian Development Bank) specializing in tourism's human impacts. He has conducted and undertaken research in Yemen, Eritrea, Libya, the Pacific Islands, and Eastern Europe. His latest book, *An Introduction to Tourism and Anthropology*, was published by Routledge in 1999.

Adams Dambe Chilisa is Chief Executive of Fairground Holdings, a consulting company based in Gaborone, Botswana, specializing in the properties, conferences, and exhibitions business. A past executive committee member of the Hotel and Tourism Association of Botswana (HATAB), which is a private sector body that lobbies government support for favorable tourism legislation and policies, he now presides over this organization. Other former positions held included: senior manager with Tati Hotel, the Bosele Hotel, and President Hotel—all in Botswana. He also gained international experience working for Hilton International (Nairobi, Kenya), Moven-pic Restaurants (Switzerland), Novotel Group (France), and Trust Forte House (Heathrow, London, U.K.). A graduate of Kenya Utalii College, Mr. Chilisa also has a master's degree in Business Administration from Kensington University College, London, U.K. He has attended several management development programs at the University of Surrey (U.K.), Cornell University (U.S.), University of South Africa, Stellenbosch University (South Africa), as well as at other institutions. He constantly gives radio and television interviews in a number of countries, and makes presentations at international workshops on tourism in Botswana.

Noel N. de Villiers is founder of Avis in South Africa and an entrepreneur with 30 years of experience at chief executive level in a variety of tourism-related fields. An Africanist with a lifelong interest in conservation, he has always held the conviction that prosperity is within Africa's grasp through sustainable utilization of its sociocultural and nature resources. When political changes in this decade improved the climate for realizing these opportunities, he drew a group of like-minded people together to form what became The Open Africa Initiative.

Laud Alfred Dei, Ph.D., is Professor of Geomorphology at the University of Cape Coast, Ghana. He is the Dean, Faculty of Social Sciences and Director, University Consultancy Unit. His research interests are in the fields of costal geomorphology, beach tourism, and ecotourism with community participation. He has been involved in a number of ecotourism consultancies for Conservation International in connection with Kakum National Park in Cape Coast, Ghana.

Peter U. C. Dieke, Ph.D., is Senior Lecturer in Tourism & Director of Teaching at The Scottish Hotel School, University of Strathclyde, in Scotland, U.K. His teaching and research interests and activities are in international tourism development, tourism economics, and the formulation of tourism policies and development planning issues in developing countries. Specific regional interests are in Africa and the Mediterranean.

Roger Doswell is an international consultant in tourism planning and management, particularly in the field of human resources development. With an early background in hotel management he was Kobler Research Fellow and lecturer at the University of Surrey, U.K., in the 1960s. Moving back to industry, Mr. Doswell worked on hotel planning and development for Hotel Corporation of America, later Sonesta Hotels. He became a consultant within the framework of the United Nations and was tourism development adviser at the Caribbean Development Bank. He continued to work in the Caribbean on projects in both Cuba and the Dominican Republic. Mr. Doswell has also undertaken assignments in Iran, Iraq, Jordan, Saudi Arabia, and Syria, and in Ethiopia, Equatorial Guinea, Eritrea, Kenya, Nigeria, Zanzibar, and Zimbabwe. He has also worked on projects in Cambodia, Indonesia, Malaysia, and the South Pacific. Much of Mr. Doswell's project work has been aimed at developing a country's capacity to manage its tourism more effectively. He is the author of *Tourism—How Effective Management Makes the Difference*, published by Butterworth Heinemann in 1997.

David Harrison, Ph.D., studied sociology and social anthropology at the University of London. Subsequently he lectured in sociology at the University of Sussex, and in Nigeria, before becoming Coordinator of Tourism Studies at the University of the South Pacific in Fiji. In December 1998 he became Professor of Tourism, Culture and Development at the University of North London. Author of *The Sociology of Modernization and Development* (1988), editor of *Tourism and the Less Developed Countries* (1992), and joint editor with Briguglio, Butler, and Leal Filho of *Sustainable Tourism in Islands and Small States: Case Studies* (1997), Professor Harrison has written on the social and cultural impacts of tourism in the Caribbean, Eastern Europe, Southern Africa, and the South Pacific.

Erik Holm-Petersen has worked with tourism development in Africa for 26 years. His first project was a tourism master plan for Ghana in the early 1970s. The experience obtained through working with tourism development in Ghana was combined with research in The Gambia and the Seychelles, forming the basis for his Ph.D. thesis named Tourism and Development. The thesis was presented at the Copenhagen School of Business Management in 1975. Since then Dr. Holm-Petersen has worked as Consultant for Hoff & Overgaard/Carl Bro International, Denmark, with tourism development projects worldwide but with a concentration of projects in Sub-Saharan Africa. Countires worked in include, besides the above-mentioned three: Kenya, Uganda, Mozambique, Swaziland, Namibia, Zambia, Zimbabwe, and Rwanda. Dr. Holm-Petersen was responsible for establishing the Tourism Department of Hoff & Overgaard in 1972. For 26 years the Department has undertaken numerous consulting assignments within all aspects of tourism planning and development for the European Commission, the World Bank, Asia Development Bank, World Tourism Organization, and United Nations Development Program. Institutional building and integrated development planning have formed part of most assignments. Today Hoff & Overgaard is a member of the Carl Bro Group of Companies, which forms a multidisciplinary center of expertise employing over 2,100 technical experts worldwide.

Edward Inskeep is a consultant on tourism development planning based in San Diego, CA. He has carried out planning, research, and training projects in many countries for the World Bank, United Nations Development Program, and World Tourism Organization, as well as for several national governments. He has written numerous books, articles, technical reports, and conference papers on tourism planning, and is a member of the American Planning Association, American Institute of Certified Planners, Travel and Tourism Research Association, and The Ecotourism Society.

Kit Jenkins, Ph.D., is Professor of International Tourism at The Scottish Hotel School, University of Strathclyde. He has worked in over 45 developing countries and has teaching, research, and consultancy experience in Asia, Africa, Caribbean, and the Pacific areas. His main interest is in the formulation of tourism policies in developing countries.

Ahmada H. Khatib, Ph.D., is the Director of Marketing and Promotion in the Commission for Tourism, Zanzibar, Tanzania. Formerly, he was assistant head teacher in the Ministry of Education in Zanzibar. As a chairman of the Editorial Committee of the *Karibu Zanzibar Magazine*, he is active in writing feature articles not just for the periodical but also for others, including *Tanzania Daily*, *The Guardian*, and *The East African* newspapers. He is also founding Steering Committee member of the Zanzibar Ecotourism Association (ZEA). Dr. Khatib's academic background in island tourism originates from his doctoral research, which he completed at the University of Strathclyde, Scotland, in 1992. His current research interests focus also on small island tourism, conservation, and community participation.

Shepherd Nyaruwata is the Executive Director of the Regional Tourism Organization of Southern Africa (RETOSA), which is the organization responsible for the marketing and promotion of the 14 member states of Southern African Development Community (SADC). He has spent 15 years in the tourism industry during which time he has held positions of Director of Marketing of the then Zimbabwe Tourism Development Corporation, Manager, Research & Planning of the same organization, and Operations Manager of one of Zimbabwe's largest tour operating companies. Mr. Nyaruwata is a graduate of the University of Oxford where he read Geography and further obtained a graduate certificate in Education. He also holds an M.Sc. in Tourism from the University of Strathclyde in Scotland. Besides undertaking varied consultancy assignments in tourism he has also contributed to several publications in southern Africa and overseas on tourism marketing and development with special reference to Zimbabwe and southern Africa.

Alan Pack is Lecturer in Economics at the University of Kent. He is particularly interested in tourism modeling and forecasting, and has published articles and chapters on hedonic price modeling and tourism demand estimation and forecasting in Spain and the U.K. He has also completed reports on Tourism and Conservation for the Overseas Development Administration. He is currently undertaking research on foreign direct investment and economic growth.

Robert A. Poirier received his Ph.D. in Political Science from the University of Utah. He has been a faculty member at Northern Arizona University for more than 20 years and is a Professor in the Department of Political Science. He has specialized in issues of development in Middle East and North Africa, and has written extensively on tourism issues in Tunisia particularly, as well as general issues concerning the interface of political science and tourism research.

M. Thea Sinclair, Ph.D., an economist by background, is Professor of Economics of Travel and Tourism at the Christel DeHaan Tourism & Travel Research Institute, Nottingham Business School, University of Nottingham, U.K. She has published numerous articles and chapters on the economics of tourism and her books include *The Economics of Tourism, The Tourism Industry: An International Analysis* (with M. Stabler), and *Gender, Work and Tourism*. She has also completed studies for the Overseas Development Administration, the United Nations, and the World Bank.

Isaac Sindiga, Ph.D. (Syracuse University, Syracuse, NY), until his death in May 1999, was the Principal, Kisii College Campus, Egerton University, Kenya. He was on leave of absence from Moi University where he was Professor and former Head of the Department of Tourism, which he founded in 1992. He served on the editorial board of the *Annals of Tourism Research*.

Victor B. Teye, Ph.D., is Associate Professor of Tourism and Coordinator of the Travel and Tourism Program at Arizona State University in the U.S. He was a Fulbright Scholar in the Department of Geography and Tourism at the University of Cape Coast in Ghana from 1996 to 1998. He received his B.A. (Hons.) from the University of Ghana, and his M.A. and Ph.D. from the University of Manitoba in Canada. He was a Research Associate with the following: Institute of African Studies at the University of Zambia (1978), Institute for Statistical, Social and Economic Research (ISSER) at the University of Ghana (1979), and the Institute for Social and Economic Research at the University of Manitoba in Canada (1982). He spent 1983/84 with the University of Illinois at Urbana-Champaign as a Postdoctoral Fellow with the Regional Science and African Studies Programs. He then joined Arizona State University as a full-time faculty in 1984. He has presented research papers at several international conferences and has published in leading refereed tourism journals, including *Annals of Tourism Research, Tourism Management, Journal of Travel Research*, and *Tourism Recreation Research*. He has also served as a Tourism Consultant with the UNDP/ILO Hotel and Tourism Training Project in Ghana (1992), United States Agency for International Development (USAID) Mission in The Gambia (1994), and the Mid-Western University Consortium for International Activities (MUCIA) on the Natural Resource Conservation and Historic Restoration Project in Ghana (1994–1996).

David B. Weaver, Ph.D., has published numerous refereed articles and book chapters in the areas of tourism in peripheral areas, destination development, and ecotourism since receiving his Ph.D. in Geography from the University of Western Ontario in 1986. Dr. Weaver currently holds the position of Associate Professor in the School of Tourism and Hotel Management at Griffith University's Gold Coast campus in Australia. His new book, *Ecotourism in the Less Developed World*, was released in 1998.

Bibliography

Abdel-Wahab, S. (1974). *Elements of state policy on tourism with special emphasis on developing countries*. Turin, Italy: Italgratica.

Abraha, A. O. (1993). *Opening address*. Asmara: Ministry of Trade, Industry and Tourism.

Achebe, C. (1958). *Things fall apart*. London: Heinemann.

Adams, W. (1990). *Green development: Environment and sustainability in the Third World*. London: Routledge.

Adel, M. (1998). Starker partner für inter-conti. *Reiseburo Bulletin, 11*(6), 123.

Adventure World. (1996-97). *Africa from the Cape to Cairo: Group and independent holidays, 1996-97*. Sydney: Author.

Afigbo, A. E. (1972). *The warrant chiefs: Indirect rule in southeastern Nigeria, 1891-1929*. Harlow, Essex: Longman.

Afigbo, A. E., Ayandele, E. A., Gavin, R. J., Omer-Cooper, J. D., & Palmer, R. (1992). *The making of modern Africa: The 19th century* (Vol. 1). London: Longman.

Africa rising. (1998, March 30). *Time*, 69.

Agbese, P. (1996). Ethnic conflicts and hometown associations: An analysis of the experience of the Agila Development Association. *Africa Today, 43*, 139-156.

Ahmed, R. (1995). Opening Address in the Report on the United Nations Research Institute for Social Development (UNRISD) and the United Nations Development Programme (UNDP) seminar on *Economic restructuring and social policy*. New York.

Ahmed, Z. U. (1991). Marketing your community: Correcting a negative image. *Cornell Hotel and Restaurant Administration Quarterly, 31*(4), 24-29.

Akama, J. (1996). Western environmental values and nature-based tourism in Kenya. *Tourism Management, 17*, 567-574.

Akosah-Sarpong, K. (1990, March 5-11). Efforts to market Sierra Leone's natural beauty: From vision to reality. *West Africa, 3784*, 356-357.

Allen, T. W. (1994). *The invention of the white race: Racial oppression and social control*. London: Verson.

Alpert, P. (1996). Integrated conservation and development projects. *Bioscience, 46*, 845-863.

Ambrose, J. (1980). Land use and land management problems in Kenya. In T. Pinfold & G. Norcliffe (Eds.), *Development planning in Kenya: Essays on the planning process and policy issues* (pp. 101-117). Geographical monographs. Ontario, Canada: York University.

Amoa, B. D. (1986). *Tourism in Africa: Report on a regional consultation in Mombasa, Kenya*, December 16-20, 1985. Nairobi: Ecumenical Coalition on Third World Tourism (Africa Network).

Anders, G. (1989, September 22). Going global: Vision vs. reality. *The Wall Street Journal Reports: World Business*, p. R20.

Ankomah, B. (1990, February, 10-13). The 1990s: An African turning point. *African Business*.

Ankomah, P. K. (1991). Tourism skilled labor: The case of Sub-Saharan Africa. *Annals of Tourism Research, 18*, 433-442.

Ankomah, P. K., & Crompton, J. L. (1990). Unrealized tourism potential: The case of sub-Saharan Africa. *Tourism Management, 11*(3), 11-28.

Appiah-Opoku, S., & Mulamoottil, G. (1997). Indigenous institutions and environmental assessment: The case of Ghana. *Environmental Management, 21*(2), 159-171.

Ashton, E. A., & Patricia, S. (1994). *Local communities, and ecolodges: Preparation and planning*. Miami, FL: Sustainable Tourism and Natural Resources Development Services.

Attack devastates industry: Tourist spots around Egypt nearly empty. (1997, December 13). *Arizona Republic*, p. A28.

Austin, J. E., & Kohn, T. O. (1990). *Strategic management in developing countries: Case studies*.

New York: Free Press.

Austin, N. K. (1997). *The management of historical sites of emotional significance to the visitor: The case of the Cape Coast castle, Ghana.* Unpublished Ph.D. thesis, Strathclyde University, Glasgow.

A world survey (Vol. 1). (1987). London: Europa Publications.

Bachmann, P. (1988a). *Tourism in Kenya: A basic need for whom?* Frankfurt am Main: Peter Lang.

Bachmann, P. (1988b). The Maasai—choice of East African tourists—admired and ridiculed. In P. Rossel (Ed.), *Tourism: Manufacturing the exotic* (pp. 47-63), International Workshop for Indigenous Affairs (IWGIA), Copenhagen.

Bank of Namibia. (1996). *Annual report.* Windhoek: Author.

Baranizini, M. (1991). *A theory of wealth distribution and accumulation.* Oxford: Clarendon Press.

Barbier, E. B. (1992). Economics for the wilds. In T. M. Swanson & E. B. Barbier (Eds.), *Economics for the wilds. Wildlife, wildlands, diversity and development* (pp. 15-33). London: Earthscan.

Barrett, C., & Arcese, P. (1995). Are integrated conservation-development projects (ICDPs) sustainable? On the conservation of large mammals in Sub-Saharan Africa. *World Development, 23,* 1073-1084.

Bateman, I. J. (1993). Revealed preference methods. In R. K. Turner (Ed.), *Sustainable environmental economics and management. Principles and practice* (pp. 192-265). London: Belhaven.

Bateman, I. J., & Turner, R. K. (1993). Valuation of the environment, methods and techniques: The contingent valuation method. In R. K. Turner (Ed.), *Sustainable environmental economics and management. Principles and practice* (pp. 120-191). London: Belhaven.

Bed occupancy falls. (1998, May 15). *The Daily Nation,* p. 5.

Beinart, P. (1997). The new games in town. *New Republic, 216*(24), 23-26.

Beioley, S. (1995, May). Green tourism—soft or sustainable? *Insights,* B75-B89.

Bélisle, F. J., & Hoy, D. R. (1980). The perceived impact of tourism residents: A case study in Santa Marta, Colombia. *Annals of Tourism Research, 17,* 449-465.

Berger, D. J. (1996). The challenge of integrating Maasai tradition with tourism. In M. F. Price (Ed.), *People and tourism in fragile environments* (pp. 175-197). Chichester: Wiley.

Bienen, H. (1990). The politics of trade liberalization in Africa. *Economic Development and Cultural Change, 38,* 713-732.

Bird, C., & Metcalfe, S. (1995). *Two views from CAMPFIRE in Zimbabwe's Hurungwe district: Training and motivation. Who benefits and who doesn't?* (Wildlife and Development Series No. 5). London: International Institute for Environment and Development in association with the CAMPFIRE Collaborative Group.

Blunt, A. (1994). *Travel, gender, and imperialism: Mary Kingsley and West Africa.* London and New York: The Guildford Press.

Bond, I. (1994). The importance of sport-hunted African elephants to CAMPFIRE in Zimbabwe. *Traffic Bulletin, 14,* 117-119.

Boonzaier, E. (1996). Negotiating the development of tourism in the Richtersveld, South Africa. In M. F. Price (Ed.), *People and tourism in fragile environments* (pp. 123-137). Chichester: Wiley.

Borzello, A. (1994). Myth of Africa. *Tourism in Focus, 14*(12).

B & T. (1991). *A review of commerce and industry* (13th ed.). Gaborone: Rockhaven Press.

Bradford, H. (1994). A new framework for museum marketing. In K. Moore (Ed.), *Museum management* (pp. 41-51). New York: Routledge.

Bramwell, B., & Bernard, L. (1993). Sustainable tourism: An evolving global approach. *Journal of Sustainable Tourism, 1*(1), 1-5.

Brewer, T. L. (1981). Political risk assessment for foreign direct investment decisions: Better methods for better results. *Columbia Journal of World Business, 16,* 5-11.

Brigham, E. F., Nantel, T. J., Anbey, R. T., & Pettway, R. H. (1976). *Financial decision—management cases* (2nd ed.). Hinsdale, IL: The Dryden Press.

Britton, R. (1979). The image of the Third World in tourism marketing. *Annals of Tourism Research, 6*(3), 318-329.

Britton, S. G. (1982). The political economy of tourism in the third world. *Annals of Tourism Research, 9,* 331-358.

Brookshire, D., Eubanks, L., & Randall, A. (1983). Estimating option price and existence values for wildlife resources. *Land Economics, 59*(1), 1-15.

Brown, G., Jr., & Henry, W. (1989). *The economic value of elephants* (Environmental Economics Centre Paper 89-12). London: University College.

Brown, O. D. (1996). *The effects of channel power, destination attractiveness and political risk events on U.S tourism channel firms' performance: The case of African destinations.* Unpublished Ph.D. dissertation, Virginia Polytechnic Institute and State University.

Brown, O. D. (2000). Political risk and other barriers and threats to tourism promotion in Africa: Perceptions of U.S. travel intermediaries. *Journal of Vacation Marketing, 6*(3).

Brundtland, G. H. (1987). *The Brundtland report: Our common future.* Oxford: Oxford University Press for World Commission on Environment and Development.

Bruner, E. M. (1996). Tourism in Ghana: The representation of slavery and the return of the black diaspora. *American Anthropologist, 98*(2), 290-304.

Bryden, J. M. (1973). *Tourism and development: A case study of the Commonwealth Caribbean.* London: Cambridge University Press.

Bull, A. (1991). *The economics of travel and tourism.* Melbourne: Pitman Publishing.

Bunn, D. W., & Mustafaoglu, M. M. (1978). Forecasting political risk. *Management Science, 24*(15), 1557-1567.

Burns, P. (1995). Tourism training in Eastern Europe: The challenge for Romania's hotel sector. *Progress in Tourism and Hospitality Management, 1*(1), 53-62.

Burnes, P. (1999). Paradoxes in planning: Tourism elitism or brutalism? *Annals of Tourism Research, 26*(2), 329-348.

Burns, P., & Holden, A. (1995). *Tourism: A new perspective.* Englewood Cliffs, NJ: Prentice Hall.

Butler, R. (1980). The concept of a tourism area cycle of evolution: Implications for management of resources. *Canadian Geographer, 24*(1), 5-12.

Butler, V. (1995). Elephants by the truckload. *International Wildlife, 25*(4), 30-35.

Button, J. W. (1989). *Blacks and social change: Impact of the civil rights movements in southern communities* (2nd ed.). Princeton, NJ: Princeton University Press.

Carter, S. (1998). Tourists' and travellers' social construction of Africa and Asia as risky locations. *Tourism Management, 19*(4), 349-358.

Cater, E. (1987). Tourism in the least developed countries. *Annals of Tourism Research, 14*, 202-226.

Cater, E. (1994). Ecotourism in the third world—problems and prospects for sustainability. In E. Cater & G. Lowman (Eds.), *Ecotourism. A sustainable option?* (pp. 69-86). Chichester: John Wiley.

Central Intelligence Agency. (1997). *World factbook* [On-line]. www.odci.gov/cia/publications/factbook/country.html

Central Statistical Office. (1978-98). *Quarterly digest of statistics.* Harare: Author.

Chalker, L. (1999). *Public sector corruption from an international perspective.* Paper presented at the Stevenson Citizenship Lecture, University of Glasgow, UK, February 19.

Chaudhuri, A. (1988). Multinational corporations in less developing countries: What is in store? *The Columbia Journal of World Business, 23*, 57-63.

Cheru, F. (1992). Structural adjustment, primary resource trade and sustainable development in Sub-Saharan Africa. *World Development, 20*, 497-512.

Chilisa, A. D. (1990). *Tourism development from the perspective of the Botswana tourism industry.* Paper presented at the Botswana Tourism Symposium on Tourism Development: Future League of Growth, Gaborone, Botswana, October 15-19.

Chilisa, A. D. (1996a). *Smart partnership and economic growth and opportunities for the Southern African region.* Paper presented at the Southern Africa International Dialogue, Kasane, Botswana, May 19-22.

Chilisa, A. D. (1996b). *Tourism development in Botswana.* Paper presented at the World Economic Forum, Capetown, South Africa, July 22-24.

Chilisa, A. D. (1996c). *Creation of employment opportunities in the tourism industry of Botswana.* Paper presented at the Botswana Confederation of Commerce, Industry and Manpower (BOCCIM)

Conference on Employment Creation—Private Sector: The Engine of Growth, Francistown, Botswana, August 2-4.

Christ, C. (1994). Kenya makes revenue sharing top priority. Ecotourism Society Newsletter, 4 (1), 1-2, 5.

Clark, C. W. (1973). The economics of overexploitation. *Science, 181*, 630-634.

Clarke, J. (1997). A framework of approaches to sustainable tourism. *Journal of Sustainable Tourism, 5*(3), 224-231.

Clawson, M., & Knetsch, J. L. (1966). *Economics of outdoor recreation.* Baltimore: Johns Hopkins.

Cockroft, L., & Riddell, R. C. (1991). *Foreign direct investment in Sub-Saharan Africa* (Working Paper No. 619, pp. 35-37). Washington, DC: The World Bank.

Collier, P. (1988). *Women in development: Defining the issues* (World Bank Working Paper Series 129). Washington, DC: World Bank.

Commission of Land and the Environment. (1994). *Ecotourism and environmental conservation in Zanzibar.* Paper presented at the workshop jointly organised by the Commission of Land and Environment and the Commission for Tourism held at Inn by the Sea Zanzibar 21-24 March.

Conable, B. B. (1990). Africa's development crisis. *The Columbia Journal of World Business, 25*(1/2), 7-9.

Conable, B. B. (1991). *Africa's development and destiny.* Address to the 27th Session of the Organization of African Unity (OAU) Assembly of Heads of State and Government, Abuja, Nigeria.

Crush, J., & Wellings, P. (1987). Forbidden fruit and the export of vice. In S. G. Britton & W. Clarke (Eds.), *Ambiguous alternative: Tourism in small developing countries* (pp. 91-112). Suva: University of the South Pacific.

Cumming, D. H. M. (1990). *Wildlife projects and the marketplace: A view from Southern Africa* (WWF Multispecies Animal Production Systems Project, Project Paper 12, 1-25).

Curry, R. L., Jr. (1991). Regional economic co-operation in Southern Africa and Southeast Asia. *ASEAN Economic Bulletin, 1*(8), 15-28.

Curry, S. (1990). Tourism development in Tanzania. *Annals of Tourism Research, 17*, 130-149.

Curtin, P. D. (1971). The slave trade and the Atlantic basin: International perspectives. In N. I. Huggins, M. Kilson, & D. M. Fox (Eds.), *Key issues in the Afro-American experience* (pp. 74-93). New York: Harcourt Brace Jovanovich Inc.

Cypher, J. M., & Dietz, J. L. (1997). *The process of economic development.* London: Routledge.

Dann, G. (1996). *The language of tourism: A sociolinguistic perspective.* Wallingford: CAB International.

David, S. (1996). Scuba diving, coast tourism with a difference: Exploring the deeps. *The Jungle, 3*, 2.

Davidoff, P. (1965). Advocacy and pluralism in planning. *Journal of the American Institute of Planners, 7*(1), 56-68.

Davidson, R. (1993). *Tourism.* London: Pitman.

Dei, L. A. (1997a). Community participation in tourism. *Proceedings of First Central Region Tourism Development Conference,* October 10.

Dei, L. A. (1997b). *Agrotourism in Kakum national park: A new concept in participatory community development of a national park, in facing the storm: Five years of research in and around Kakum National Park* (pp. 160-166). Washington, DC: Conservation International.

de Kadt, E. (Ed.) (1979). *Tourism: Passport to development?* New York: Oxford University Press.

de Kadt, E. (1992). Making the alternative sustainable: Lessons from development for tourism. In V. Smith & W. Eadington (Eds.), *Tourism alternatives: Potentials and problems in the development of tourism.* Philadelphia: University of Pennsylvania.

Delupes, I. D. (1969). *The East African economic community and common market.* London: Longman.

Dembner, S. (1996). Forest peoples in the central African rain forest: Focus on the pygmies. *Unasylva, 47*, 3-7.

Development issues in Namibia. (1997, May 9). *The Namibian.*

Dhliwayo, D. (1997, July/August). SA-Zim trade relations nose-dive. *African Business, 223*, 24-25.

Dieke, P. U. C. (1988). *The development of tourism in Kenya and The Gambia—a comparative analysis.* Doctoral thesis, The Scottish Hotel School, University of Strathclyde, U.K.

Dieke, P. U. C. (1989). Fundamentals of tourism development: A third world perspective. *Hospitality Education and Research Journal, 13*(2), 7-22.

Dieke, P. U. C. (1991). Policies for tourism development in Kenya. *Annals of Tourism Research, 18*, 269-294.

Dieke, P. U. C. (1993a). Cross-national comparison of tourism development: Lessons from Kenya and The Gambia. *The Journal of Tourism Studies, 4*(1), 2-18.

Dieke, P. U. C. (1993b). Tourism and development policy in The Gambia. *Annals of Tourism Research, 20*(3), 423-449.

Dieke, P. U. C. (1995). Tourism and structural adjustment programmes in the African economy. *Tourism Economics, 1*(1), 71-93.

Dieke, P. U. C. (1998). Regional tourism in Africa: Scope and critical issues. In E. Laws, B. Faulkner, & G. Moscardo (Eds.), *Embracing and managing change in tourism: International case studies* (pp. 29-48). London and New York: Routledge.

Dixon, J. A., & Sherman, P. B. (1990). *Economics of protected areas: A new look at benefits and costs.* Washington, DC: Island Press.

Dossier: Tourism. (1990, July-August). *The Courier, 122*, 50-90.

Doswell, R. (1978). *Case studies in tourism.* London: Barrie and Jenkins.

Doswell, R. (1997). *Tourism—how effective management makes the difference.* Oxford: Butterworth Heinemann.

Duignan, P. (1990). Africa in the 1990s: What the West can do? *The World and I, 5*, 40-47.

Dunning, J. H., & McQueen, M. (1982a). *Transnational corporations in international tourism.* New York: United Nations Center on Transnational Corporations.

Dunning, J. H., & McQueen, M. (1982b). Multinational corporations in the international hotel industry. *Annals of Tourism Research, 9*, 69-90.

Easterly, W. (1996). Why is Africa marginal in the world economy? In G. Maasdorp (Ed.), *Can South and Southern Africa become globally competitive economies?* (pp. 19-30). Basingstoke: Macmillan.

Economic Commission for Africa. (1986). *Development of tourism in Africa: The intra-African tourism promotion of tourist products.* Addis Ababa, Ethiopia: Author.

Economic Commission for Africa. (1989). *African alternative framework to structural adjustment programmes for socio-economic recovery and transformation.* Addis Ababa, Ethiopia: Author.

Economic Commission for Africa. (1993). *Meeting the challenge of African development in the 1990s.* Addis Ababa, Ethiopia: Author.

Economic Commission for Africa. (1996a). *Africa in the 1990s and beyond: ECA-revised long-term development perspectives study.* Addis Ababa, Ethiopia: Author.

Economic Commission for Africa. (1996b). *Report of the conference of African ministers responsible for trade, regional cooperation, integration and tourism—first session (February 1-16).* Addis Ababa, Ethiopia: Author.

Economic Commission for Africa. (1999a). *Economic report on Africa 1999: The challenge of poverty reduction and sustainability.* Addis Ababa, Ethiopia: Author.

Economic Commission for Africa. (1999b). *The ECA and Africa: Accelerating a continent's development.* Addis Ababa, Ethiopia: Author.

Economist Intelligence Unit. (1990). *International tourism reports* (No. 1, pp. 32-46). London: Author.

Economist Intelligence Unit. (1991). *Kenya. International tourism reports* (No. 2). London: Author.

Economist Intelligence Unit. (1992). *Zimbabwe. International tourism reports* (No. 3, pp. 5-22). London: Author.

Edgell, D. L. (1990). *International tourism policy.* New York: Van Nostrand Reinhold.

Ehrenberg, R. G., & Smith, R. S. (1982). *Modern labour economics: Theory & public policy.* New York: Scott, Foresman & Company, Inc.

Eisenstadt, S. (1966). *Modernization: Protest and change.* Englewood Cliffs, NJ: Prentice-Hall.

Elkan, W. (1975). The relation between tourism and employment in Kenya and Tanzania. *Journal of Development Studies, 11*(2), 123-130.

Erbes, R. (1973). *International tourism and the economy of developing countries.* Paris: Organization of Economic Cooperation and Development.

Eritrea. (1994, July–August). *The Courier,* 146.

Eshel, I. (1993). *Eritrea: Its tourist industry and future development.* Asmara, Eritrea: Ministry of Trade, Industry and Tourism.

Eser, G. (1989). Air transport and tourism: Industry potential to be denied? *The Courier,* 122, 58–59.

European Union. (1993). *Directive on package travel.* Brussels: Author.

European Union. (1996). *National indicative programme for Namibia.* Windhoek: Author.

Fair, D. (1996). East African tourist trends. *African Insight, 26*(2), 156–161.

Farver, J. A. (1984). Tourism and employment in The Gambia. *Annals of Tourism Research, 11,* 249–265.

Federal Republic of Germany. (1979). *Facts about Germany.* Bonn: verlags gruppe, Bertelsmann, GmbH.

Filani, M. O. (1975). The role of national tourist associations in the preserving of the environment in Africa. *Journal of Travel Research, 13*(4), 183–192.

Firmin-Sellers, K. (1995). The politics of property rights. *American Political Science Review, 89,* 867–888.

Foottit, C. (1998, January). United we stand. *African Business, 228,* 38–40.

Forrester, V. (1989, April 17–23). Tourism boom to last. *West Africa, 3739,* 593.

Gann, L. H., & Duignan, P. (1962). *White settlers in tropical Africa.* Harmondsworth: Penguin.

Garrod, G., & Willis, K. (1991). The environmental impact of woodland: A two-stage hedonic price model of the amenity value of forestry in Britain. *Applied Economics, 24,* 715–728.

Garrod, G., Willis, K., & Saunders, C. M. (1994). The benefits and costs of the Somerset levels and moors ESA. *Journal of Rural Studies, 10*(2), 131–145.

George, S. (1989). *A fate worse than debt.* London: Penguin.

Geshekter, C. (1978). International tourism and African underdevelopment: Some reflections on Kenya. *Studies in Third World Societies, 6,* 57–88.

Getis, A., Getis, J., & Fellman, J. D. (1996). *Introduction to geography* (5th ed.). Dubuque, IA: WCB.

Getz, D. (1986). Models in tourism planning: Towards integration of theory and practice. *Tourism Management, 7*(1), 21–32.

Getz, D., & Jamal, T. B. (1994). The environment-community symbiosis: A case for collaborative tourism planning. *Journal of Sustainable Tourism, 2*(3), 152–173.

Ghana Ministry of Local Government. (1996). *New local government system.* Accra: Government Press.

Ghebrai, I. (1993). *Eritrea: Miracle land.* Washington, DC: Author.

Gibson, C. C., & Marks, S. A. (1995). Transforming rural hunters into conservationists: An assessment of community-based programs in Africa. *World Development, 2*(6), 941–957.

Gilroy, P. (1993). *The black Atlantic: Modernity and double consciousness.* New York: Verso.

Glassner, M. I. (1996). *Political geography* (2nd ed.). New York: Wiley.

Glasson, J. (1994). Oxford: A heritage city under pressure. *Tourism Management,* 137–144.

Global Environmental Management Initiative. (1992). *Environmental self-assessment based on the international chamber of commerce's business charter for sustainable development.* Washington, DC: Author.

Go, F. (1988). Key problems and prospects in the international hotel industry. *Travel and Tourism Analysis, 1,* 27–49.

Go, F., & Pine, R. (1995). *Globalization strategy in the hotel industry.* London and New York: Routledge.

Godfrey, M. (1986). *Kenya to 1990: Prospects for growth* (Special report 1052). London: EIU.

Good and bad at game. (1996). *The Economist, 340*(7973), 69–73.

Gore, R. (1977, September). Tracking the first of our kind. *National Geographer.*

Government of Botswana. (1965). *Report of the Ministry overseas development economic survey mission* (November 1965), Gaborone, Botswana. Margate, UK: The Thanet Press.

Government of Botswana. (1991). *National development plan, 1992/93–1997/98.* Gaborone: Government Printer.

Government of Botswana. (1997). *National development plan 8, 1997/98-2002/3.* Gaborone: Government Printer.

Government of Eritrea. (1993). *Eritrea: The birth of a nation.* Asmara: Author.

Government of Eritrea. (1994). *Threes seasons in two hours.* Asmara: Author.

Government of Ghana. (1996). *National tourism development plan.* Accra: Author.

Government of Indonesia. (1992). *Tourism sector policy & programming.* Jakarta: Author.

Government of Namibia. (1992). *Namibia tourism development plan.* Windhoek: Author.

Government of Namibia. (1993a). *Tourism development plan.* Windhoek: Author.

Government of Namibia. (1993b). *Transitional development plan.* Windhoek: Author.

Government of Namibia. (1994). *White paper on tourism.* Windhoek: Author.

Government of Namibia. (1995a). *National accounts 1980-95.* Windhoek: Author.

Government of Namibia. (1995b). *National development plan 1995/96-1999/2000.* Windhoek: Author.

Government of Namibia. (1996). *Estimates of revenues and expenditures for the financial year ended 31st March 1996.* Windhoek: Author.

Government of Namibia. (1997). *Project survey data.* Windhoek: Author.

Government of South Africa. (1996). *Development and promotion of tourism in South Africa—white paper.* Pretoria: Department of Environmental Affairs & Tourism.

Green, R. H. (1979). Toward planning tourism in African countries. In E. de Kadt (Ed.), *Tourism: Passport to development?* (pp. 79-100). New York: Oxford University Press.

Green, H., Hunter, C., & Moore, B. (1990). Application of the delphi technique in tourism. *Annals of Tourism Research, 17,* 270-279 .

Grenfell Price, A. (1939) White settlers in the tropics. *American Geographical Society, Special Publication,* 23.

Grimshaw, B. (1907). *In the strange south seas.* London: Hutchinson.

Gunn, C. (1988). *Tourism planning* (2nd ed.). New York: Taylor & Francis.

Grown, C., & Sebstad, J. (1989). Toward a wider perspective on women's employment. *World Development, 17,* 937-952.

Hackel, J. D. (1990). Conservation attitudes in Southern Africa: A comparison between KwaZulu and Swaziland. *Human Ecology, 18,* 203-209.

Hacker, A. (1992). *Two nations: Black and white, separate, hostile, unequal.* New York: Maxwell Macmillan International.

Hall, C. M. (1994). *Tourism and politics: Policy, power and place.* New York: John Wiley and Sons.

Hall, C. M., & Wouters, M. (1995). Issues in Antarctic tourism. In C. M. Hall & M. E. Johnston (Eds.), *Polar tourism: Tourism in the Arctic and Antarctic regions* (pp. 147-166). Chichester, UK: Wiley.

Hanley, N. (1988). Using contingent valuation to value environmental improvements. *Applied Economics, 20,* 541-549.

Hanley, N., & Spash, C. L. (1993). *Cost benefit analysis and the environment.* Aldershot: Edward Elgar.

Hannaford, S. (1997). *To establish the extent to which South African Tourism Board's consumer advertising campaigns in the Australian market have been successful in encouraging travel to South Africa.* Unpublished dissertation, Master of Tourism Management, Griffith University, Gold Coast, Australia.

Harden, B. (1990). *Africa: Dispatches from a fragile continent.* New York: Norton Press.

Harrison, A. J. M., & Stabler, M. J. (1981). An analysis of journeys for canal-based recreation. *Regional Studies, 15*(5), 345-358.

Harrison, D. (1988). *The sociology of modernization and development.* London: Routledge.

Harrison, D. (1992a). International tourism and the less developed countries: The background. In D. Harrison (Ed.), *Tourism and the less developed countries* (pp. 1-18). London: Belhaven Press.

Harrison, D. (1992b). Tourism to less developed countries: The social consequences. In D. Harrison (Ed.), *Tourism and the less developed countries* (pp. 19-34). London: Belhaven Press.

Harrison, D. (1992c). Tradition, modernity and tourism in Swaziland. In D. Harrison (Ed.), *Tourism and the less developed countries* (pp. 148-162). London: Belhaven Press.

Harrison, D. (1994). Tourism and prostitution: Sleeping with the enemy? *Tourism Management,*

1(6), 435-443.

Harrison, D. (1995). Development of tourism in Swaziland. *Annals of Tourism Research, 22*, 135-156.

Harrison, D. (1997a). Barbados or Luton? Which way to Paradise? *Tourism Management, 18*(6), 393-398.

Harrison, D. (1997b). Globalization and tourism: Some themes from Fiji. In M. Oppermann (Ed.), *Pacific Rim tourism* (pp. 167-183). Wallingford: CAB International.

Harrison, D., & Brandt, J. (1997). *Ecotourism in Fiji: Making sense of the muddle?* Paper presented at the Eighth Pacific Science Inter-Congress, Suva, Fiji, July 13-19.

Harrison, P. (1993). *Inside the third world* (3rd ed.). London: Penguin.

Hasler, R. (1995). *Political ecologies of scale: The multi-tiered co-management of Zimbabwean wildlife resources* (Wildlife and Development Series No. 7). London: International Institute for Environment and Development in association with the CAMPFIRE Collaborative Group.

Hazlewood, A. (1979). *The economy of Kenya: The Kenyatta era.* New York: Oxford University Press.

Hecht, M. L., Collier, M. J., & Ribeau, S. A. (1993). *African American communication: Ethnic identity and cultural interpretation. Language and language behaviour.* London: Sage.

Helle, V. G. (1970). *Tourism plan for Jozani forest reserve.* Zanzibar, Tanzania: Ministry of Agriculture, Livestock and Natural Resources.

Hemming, C. (1993). *Business success from seizing the environmental initiative.* London: Business and the Environment Practitioner Series, Technical Communications.

Henriques, F. (1974). *Children of Caliban: Miscegenation.* London: Secker and Warburg.

Herbst, J. (1990). The structural adjustment of politics in Africa. *World Development, 18*, 949-958.

Heritage & tourism (1996). *Annals of Tourism Research Special Issue, 23*(2).

Herliczek, J. (1996). Where is ecotourism going? *Amicus Journal, 18*(1), 31-35.

Hermans, H. C. L., & Stone, S. (1990). *Opportunities and problems of tourism in the economy of Botswana.* Paper presented at the Botswana Tourism Symposium, Gaborone, Botswana, October 15-19.

Hess, K., Jr. (1997). Wild success. *Reason, 29*(5), 32-44.

Hill, R. (1965). *Sudan transport: A history of railway, marine and river service in the Republic of the Sudan.* London: Oxford University Press.

Hitchcock, R. K. (1993). Africa and discovery: Human rights, environment, and development. *American Indian Culture and Research Journal, 17*, 129-152.

Hohnholz, J. H. (1994). Agrotourism—a new sector of rural integrated development, Malaysia and Germany as case studies. *Applied Geography & Development, 44*, 38-58.

Holloway, J. C., & Robinson, C. (1995). *Marketing for tourism.* London: Longman.

Hoof & Overgaar. (1995). *Motivational proposal for the establishment of the regional organization of Southern Africa—final draft.* Copenhagen: Author.

Hoogvelt, A. (1982). *The third world in global development.* Basingstoke: Macmillan.

Hooks, B. (1990). Postmodern blackness. *Postmodern Culture, 1*(1).

Hope, K. R. S. R. (1996). Growth, unemployment and poverty in Botswana. *Journal of Contemporary African Studies, 141*, 15.

Howarth, D. (1983). *Tahiti: A paradise lost.* New York: The Viking Press.

How corruption is killing Africa—Special report. (1999, June). *Business in Africa, 7*(3), 15-41.

Hughes, T. (1980). Development planning: Science or confidence trick? In B. Tupouniua, S. R. Crocombe, & C. Slater (Eds.), *The Pacific way: Social issues in national development* (pp. 18-26). Suva: South Pacific Social Sciences Association.

Husbands, W. (1989). Social status and perception of tourism in Zambia. *Annals of Tourism Research, 16*, 237-253.

Hutchinson, A. (1972, November). Tourism in Africa: Africa's tourism leaps ahead. *African Development*, 41-50.

Hyma, B., Ojo, A., & Wall, G. (1980). Tourism in tropical Africa: A review of literature in English and research agenda. *Annals of Tourism Research, 7*(4), 525-553.

Ichimura, S. (1983). *Institutional factors and government policies for appropriate technology: Survey findings in Indonesia, Thailand and the Philippines* (World Employment Program Working Paper, WEF 2-22/WP).

Inikori, J. E. (1982). Introduction. In J. E. Inikori (Ed.), *Forced migration: The impact of the export slave trade on African societies* (pp. 13-60). New York: Africana Publishing Company.

Inskeep, E. (1991). *Tourism planning: An integrated and sustainable development approach.* New York: Van Nostrand Reinhold.

International Bank for Reconstruction and Development. (1963). *The economic development of Kenya.* Baltimore: Johns Hopkins University.

International Bank for Reconstruction and Development. (1997). *1997 world development indicators.* Washington, DC: Author.

International Finance Corporation. (1980). *Measures to promote the role of the private sector in Caribbean development: A report to the Caribbean Group for Cooperation in Economic Development by the task force on private sector activities.* Washington, DC: Author.

International Labor Office. (1972). *Employment, incomes and equality: A strategy for increasing productive employment in Kenya.* Geneva: Author.

International Labour Organisation. (1976). *The organisation of hotel and tourism training in developing countries.* Report of a Regional Seminar on Human Resources Development and Tourism, Buenos Aires.

International Labour Organisation. (1994). *Foundations for sustainable employment in Eritrea.* Addis Ababa, Ethiopia: Author.

International Monetary Fund. (1979-1997a). *Balance of payments statistics.* Washington DC: Author.

International Monetary Fund. (1979-1997b). *International financial statistics.* Washington DC: Author.

Ioannides, D., & Debbage, K. G. (Eds.). (1998). *The economic geography of the tourist industry: A supply-side analysis.* London and New York: Routledge.

Isaacs, H. R. (1964). The new world of Negro Americans. In J. F. Szwed (Ed.), *Discovering Afro-Americans* (pp. 310-319). New York: Viking.

Jackson, R. T. (1973). Problems of tourist industry development on the Kenyan coast. *Geography, 58,* 62-65.

Jafari, J. (1986). Tourism for whom? Old questions still echoing. *Annals of Tourism Research, 13*(1), 129-137.

Japanese International Cooperation Agency & Republic of Kenya. (1995a). *The study on the national tourism master plan in the Republic of Kenya: National tourism development. Master plan draft final report vol. I.* Nairobi: Pacific Consultants International.

Japanese International Cooperation Agency & Republic of Kenya. (1995b). *The study on the national tourism master plan in the Republic of Kenya—supporting documents—draft final report volume 4.* Nairobi: Pacific Consultants International.

Japan International Cooperation Agency. (1994). *The study on the national tourism master plan in the Republic of Kenya* (interim report). Nairobi: Japan International Cooperation Agency.

Jarman, A. (1980) Planning or praxis: A false dichotomy? In S. Tupouniua, R. Crocombe, & C. Slater (Eds.), *The Pacific way: Social issues in national development* (pp. 42-52). Suva: South Pacific Social Sciences Association.

Jenkins, A. H. (1995). *Turning corners: The psychology of African-Americans.* New York: Allyn and Bacon.

Jenkins, C. L. (1982). The effects of scale in tourism projects in developing countries. *Annals of Tourism Research, 9*(2), 229-249.

Jenkins, C. L. (1990). *Sectoral support mission to the Republic of The Gambia,* 17-24 September. Unpublished manuscript

Jenkins, C.L. (1991). Tourism development strategies. In L. J. Lickorish, A. Jefferson, J. Bodlender, & C. L. Jenkins (Eds.), *Developing tourism destinations: Policies & perspectives* (pp. 61-77). Harlow, Essex: Longman.

Jenkins, C. L. (1994). Tourism in developing countries: The privatisation issue. In A. V. Seaton, C. L. Jenkins, R. C. Wood, P. U. C. Dieke, M. M. Bennett, L. R. MacLellan, & R. Smith (Eds.), *Tourism: The state of the art* (pp. 3-9). Chichester: John Wiley.

Jenkins, C. L. (1997a). Impacts of the development of international tourism in the Asia region. In F. M. Go & C. L. Jenkins (Eds.), *Tourism and economic development in Asia & Australasia* (pp. 48-64). London: Cassell.

Jenkins, C. L. (1997b). *Social impacts of tourism—background paper.* World Tourism Leaders' Meeting on Social Impacts of Tourism, Manila, Philippines, 22-23 May.

Jenkins, C. L., & Henry, B. N. (1982). Government involvement in tourism in developing countries. *Annals of Tourism Research, 9*(3), 499-521.

John, E. O. (1995). Ecotourism: The people friendly face of conservation. *SWALA: East African Wildlife Society, 18,* 6.

John, N. S. (1992). The challenge of ecotourism: A call for higher standard—Protected area specialist, 1828 Kilbourne Place, NW, Washington, DC 20010.

Jommo, R. (1987). *Indigenous enterprise in Kenya's tourism industry.* Geneva: Institut Universitaire d'Études due Développement.

Kaoneka, A. R., & Solberg, B. (1994). Forestry related land use in the west Usambara mountains, Tanzania. *Agriculture, Ecosystems and Environment, 49,* 207-215.

Kaufman, D. (1992). *Zimbabwe tourism development programme.* Bulawayo: K T & T Consulting, on behalf of EXA International, Paris.

Keefe, J. (1995). Disruption & displacement: Tourism and land alienation. In P. Burns (Ed.), *Tourism and minorities' heritage: Impacts and prospects* (pp. 41-57). London: University of North London Press.

Kennedy, P. M. (1988). *African capitalism: The struggle for ascendancy.* New York: Cambridge University Press.

Kenya Wildlife Service. (1990). *A policy framework and development programme 1991-96.* Nairobi: Author.

Keogh, B. (1990). Public participation in community tourism planning. *Annals of Tourism Research, 17,* 449-465.

Khatib, A. H. (1992). *Tourism development in the small island economy: The case of Zanzibar.* Unpublished Ph.D. thesis, Strathclyde University, UK.

Khatib, A. H. (1996). Ecotourism as a national strategy. *Karibu Zanzibar Magazine, 1,* 12-13.

Killick, T. (Ed.). (1995). *The flexible economy: Causes and consequences of the adaptability of national economies.* London: Routledge.

Koch, E. (1994). *Reality or rhetoric? Ecotourism and rural reconstruction in South Africa.* Geneva: United Nations Research Institute for Social Development.

Kotas, R. (1977). *Management accounting for hotels and restaurants: A revenue accounting approach.* Guildford, UK: Surrey University Press.

Krippendorf, J. (1989). *The holidaymakers.* Oxford: Butterworth-Heinmann.

Krippendorf, J. (1993). *Perspectives on tourism development in Eritrea* (conference paper). Asmara, Eritrea: Ministry of Trade, Industry and Tourism.

Kruer, O. (1996). The political foundations of economic development policies. *Journal of Development Studies, 32*(5), 645-668.

Kuper, H. (1947). *The uniform of colour: A study of white-black relationships in Swaziland.* Johannesburg: Witwatersrand University Press.

Laban, P. (1995). Accountability in integrated village land management in local resource management in Africa. In J. P. M. van den Breemer, C. A. Drijver, & E. B. Venema (Eds.), *Local resource management in Africa* (pp. 193-210). Chichester: John Wiley.

Lamb, D. (1982). *The Africans.* New York: Random House.

Lane, B. (1991). Sustainable tourism: A new concept for the interpreter. *Interpretation Journal, 49,* 1-4.

Lankford, S. V., & Howard, D. R. (1994). Developing a tourism impact attitude scale. *Annals of Tourism Research, 21,* 121-139.

Langhammer, R. J. (1993). Integrated "through market": High costs and risks of failure. *The Courier, 142,* 56-59.

Laws, E., Faulkner, B., & Moscardo, G. (Eds.). (1998). *Embracing and managing change in tourism: International case studies.* London: Routledge.

Lax, H. L. (1983). *Political risk in the international oil and gas industry.* Boston, MA: International Human Resources Development Corporation.

Lea, J. P. (1981). Changing approaches towards tourism in Africa: Planning and research perspectives. *Journal of Contemporary African Studies, 11*, 19-40.

Lea, J. P. (1993). *Tourism and development in the Third World.* London and New York: Routledge.

Lee, G. (1990). The tourism sector and Lomé IV. *The Courier, 122*, 61-63.

Legassick, M., & de Clerq, F. (1984). Capitalism and migrant labour in Southern Africa: The origins and nature of the system. In S. Marks & P. Richardson (Eds.), *Labour migration: Historical perspectives* (pp. 140-166). Hounslow: Maurice Temple Smith.

Lewis, W. A. (1966). *Development planning—the essentials of economic policy.* New York: Harper & Row.

Lickorish, L. J., & Jenkins, C. L. (1997). *An introduction to tourism.* Oxford: Butterworth-Heineman.

Lipsey, R. G. (1980). *An introduction to positive economics* (5th ed.). London: Weidenfeld & Nicolson.

Liu, J. C., Sheldon, P. J., & Var, T. (1987). Resident perception of the environmental impacts of tourism. *Annals of Tourism Research, 14*, 17-37.

Lockwood, M., Loomis, J. B., & DeLacy, T. (1993), A contingent valuation survey and benefit–cost analysis of forest preservation in East Gippsland, Australia. *Journal of Environmental Management, 38*, 233-243.

Lomé IV convention: Tourism–articles 121 & 122. (1996, January/February). *The Courier, 155*, 36.

Loomis, J. B., Creel, M., & Park, T. (1991). Comparing benefit estimates from travel cost and contingent valuation using confidence intervals from Hicksian welfare measures. *Applied Economics, 23*, 1725-1731.

Lovejoy, P. E. (1981). Slavery in the context of ideology. In P. E. Lovejoy (Ed.), *The ideology of slavery in Africa* (pp. 11-38). London: Sage.

Lundberg, D. E., & Lundberg, C. B. (1993). *International travel and tourism* (2nd ed.). New York and Chichester: Wiley.

Mabogunje, A. (1995). The environmental challenges in sub-Saharan Africa. *Environment, 37*(4), 4-9.

Maddison, A. (1982). *Phases of capitalist development.* Oxford: Oxford University Press.

Madrigal, R (1993). A tale of tourism in two cities. *Annals of Tourism Research, 20*, 336-353.

Making southern Africa work. (1998, August). *Africa Travel News.*

Mansfield, Y. (1992). Group perceptions of social impacts related to tourism development. *Professional Geographer, 44*, 377-392.

Martin, E. B. (1973). *The history of Malindi: A geographical analysis of an East African coastal town from the Portuguese period to the present.* Nairobi: East African Literature Bureau.

Martin, R. B. (1992). *CAMPFIRE—policy and current state.* Paper presented at a workshop at the University of Zimbabwe, September 28.

Mathieson, A., & Wall, G. (1982). *Tourism: Economic, physical and social impacts.* Harlow: Longman.

Matthews, H. (1978). *International tourism: A political and social analysis.* Cambridge: Schenkman.

Mazrui, A. A. (1990). *Cultural forces in world politics.* London: James Currey.

McIntosh, R. W. (1990). *Tourism: Principles, practices & philosophies.* New York: J.C. Foss, Elaine Caterbuck & Marie Clark.

McIvor, C. (1994). *Management of wildlife tourism and local communities in Zimbabwe.* Geneva: United Nations Research Institute for Social Development.

McKee, D. L., & Tisdell, C. (1990). *Developmental issues in small island economies.* New York: Praeger.

McNealy, J. A., Harrison, J., & Dingwall, X. (Eds.). (1994). *Protecting nature.* Washington, DC: IUCN.

Meier, G. M. (1996). *Leading issues in economic development* (6th ed.). New York: Oxford University Press.

Meldrum, A. (1995). The land scandal. *Africa Report, 40*, 28-31.

Memon, P. A., & Martin, E. B. (1976). The Kenya coast: An anomaly in the development of an "ideal type" colonial spatial system. *Kenya Historical Review, 4*(2), 187-206.

Middleton, J. (1992). *The world of the Swahili: An African mercantile civilization.* New Haven & London: Yale University Press.

Middleton, V. T. C. (1994). *Marketing in travel and tourism.* Oxford: Butterworth & Heinemann.

Ministry of Planning and Investment Zanzibar. (1997). *Zanzibar Free Economic Zone Authority.* Zanzibar, Tanzania: Author.

Mitchell, F. (1970). The value of tourism in East Africa. *Eastern Africa Economic Review, 2*(1), 1-21.

Mitchell, F. (1998). The economic value of wildlife viewing as a form of land use. *East African Agricultural and Forestry Journal, Special Issue, XXXIII,* 98-103.

Mitchell, R. C., & Carson, R. T. (1989). *Using surveys to value public goods: The contingent valuation method.* Washington, DC: Resources for the Future.

Mkhize, I. B. (1994). South African domestic tourism beyond apartheid. *Development Southern Africa, 11,* 249-252.

Mohamed, M. (1988). Moroccan tourism image in France. *Annals of Tourism Research, 15*(4), 558-561.

Moore, M. (1944). *Institution building as a development assistance method.* Sussex: Institute of Development Studies.

Muller, T. (1997). Environmental investment blueprint in Southern Africa. *Cost Engineering, 39,* 25-36.

Multinational Investment Guarantee Agency. (1997). *Working draft of PSD paper for tourism* (unpublished manuscript). Washington, DC: The World Bank.

Murphy, P. (1985). *Tourism: A community approach.* London: Routledge.

Musyoki, B. M. (1992). Marine national parks and reserves of Kenya. In C. J. Mayers & C. K. Rumisha (Eds.), *A proposal for the establishment of the Mafia Island marine park, Tanzania Part II,* Proceedings of the planning workshop 20th-24th October 1991. Dar es Salaam: World Wide Fund for Nature.

Muthee, L. W. (1992). Ecological impacts of tourists use on habitats and pressure point animal species. In C. G. Gakahu (Ed.), *Tourist attitudes and use impacts in Maasai Mara national reserve* (pp. 18-38). Nairobi: Wildlife Conservation International.

Nabane, N. (1995). *Lacking confidence? A gender-sensitive analysis of CAMPFIRE in Masoka village* (Wildlife and Development Series No. 3). London: International Institute for Environment and Development in association with the CAMPFIRE Collaborative Group.

National Election Monitoring Unit. (1993). *Courting disaster: A report on the continuing terror, violence and destruction in the Rift Valley, Nyanza and Western Provinces of Kenya.* Nairobi: Author.

Ndivanga, C. (1998). Namibia/Botswana-Maputo highway opens. *African Business, 232,* 36-37.

Neighbourhood watch in southern Africa. (1994). *The Economist, 333*(7892), 51-53.

Nettleford, R. M. (1970). *Mirror mirror—identity, race and protest in Jamaica.* Kingston, Jamaica: William Collins and Sangster Ltd.

Neuber, A. (1995). Adapting the economies of Eastern Europe. In T. Killick (Ed.), *The flexible economy: Causes and consequences of the adaptability of national economies* (pp. 111-148). London: Routledge.

Nevin, T. (1997). SA is business army on the march. *African Business, 222,* 7-11.

Newmark, W., Manyanza, D., Gamassa, D. G., & Sariko, H. (1994). The conflict between wildlife and local people living adjacent to protected areas in Tanzania: Human density as a predictor. *Conservation Biology, 8,* 249-255.

Nomvete, B. D. (1993). Regional integration of Africa; a path strewn with obstacles. *The Courier, 142,* 49-55.

Nowak, R. (1995). Uganda enlists locals in the battle to save the gorillas. *Science, 267,* 1761-1763.

Nyamwange, M. (1994). *Kenyan population growth and its impact on the environment* (pp. 143-147). Papers & Proceedings of Applied Geography, SUNY at Binghamton, Binghamton, NY.

Nyaruwata, S. (1986). European markets for African destinations. *Tourism Management, 7*(1), 56-60.

Obadina, T. (1998). The slave trade—A root of contemporary African crisis. *Africa Economic Analysis* [On-line]. http://www.afbis.com/analysis/slave.htm

O'Connor, A. M. (1983). *The African city.* London: Hutchinson.

Office National du Tourisme Tunisien. (1996). *Le tourisme Tunisien en chiffres.* Tunis: Author.

Ogot, B.A. (1974). Kenya under the British, 1895 to 1963. In B.A. Ogot (Ed.), *Zamani: A survey of East African history* (pp. 249-294). Nairobi: East African Publishing House & Longman.

Ogutu, Z.A. (1997). Conflicts over resources: Saiwa Swamp National Park (Kenya) and its environs. *GeoJournal, 41*, 25-31.

Olindo, P. (1991). The old man of nature tourism: Kenya. In T. Whelan (Ed.), *Nature tourism: Managing for the environment* (pp. 23-38). Washington, DC: Island Press.

Olsen, M. D., & Merna, K. M. (1993). The changing character of the multinational hospitality firm. In P. Jones & A. Pizam (Eds.), *The international hospitality industry: Organizational and operational issues* (pp. 89-103). New York: Wiley & Sons.

Organization of African Unity. (1979). *Monrovia declaration of commitment by Heads of State and Governments of the OAU on the guidelines and measures for national and collective self-reliance in economic and social development for the establishment of a new international economic order.* Monrovia, Liberia: Author.

Organization of African Unity. (1980). *Plan for action for the economic development of Africa.* Lagos, Nigeria: Author.

Organization of African Unity. (1991). *Treaty establishing the African Economic Community.* Abuja, Nigeria: Author.

Organization of African Unity. (1996). *Protocol on relations between the African Economic Community (AEC) and the Regional Economic Communities (RECs).* Addis Ababa, Ethiopia: Author.

Organization of African Unity. (1998). *Report on the review of the protocol on tourism of the African Economic Community (AEC).* Addis Ababa, Ethiopia: Author.

Osemeobo, G. (1993). Impact of land use on biodiversity preservation in Nigerian natural ecosystem: A review. *Natural Resources Journal, 33*(4), 1015-1025.

Othman, I. (1998). *Entrepreneurial opportunities for small and medium scale companies related to tourism development: The case of Langkawi, Malaysia.* Unpublished Ph.D. thesis, The Scottish Hotel School, University of Strathclyde, Glasgow.

Ouma, J. P. M. B. (1970). *Evolution of tourism in East Africa (1900-2000).* Nairobi: Kenya Literature Bureau.

Overholt, W. H. (1982). *Political risk.* London: Euromoney Publications.

Owusu, E. H. (1996). *Natural resource conservation in Ghana: The role of the Ghana Wildlife Society as an NGO, in facing the sun, five years of research in and around Kakum National Park, Ghana* (pp. 112-114). Washington, DC: Conservation International.

Pacione, M. (Ed.). (1985). *Progress in political geography.* Dover, NH: Croom Helm.

Payne, A. (1993). *The essence of services marketing.* London: Prentice Hall.

Pearce, D. (1989). *Tourist development* (2nd ed.). Harlow, UK: Longman.

Pearce, D. W., & Turner, R. K. (1990). *Economics of natural resources and the environment.* London and New York: Harvester Wheatsheaf.

Pearce, J.A. (1980). Host community acceptance of foreign tourism: Strategic consideration. *Annals of Tourism Research, 7*, 224-233.

Pearsall, J. (Ed.). (1998). *The new Oxford dictionary of English.* Oxford: Clarendon Press.

Perdue, R. R., Long, P. T., & Aller, L. (1987). Resident tourism perspectives and attitudes. *Annals of Tourism Research, 14*, 420-429.

Perham, M. (1974). *African apprenticeship: An autobiographical journey in Southern Africa, 1929.* London: Faber and Faber.

Pfafenberger, B. (1983). Serious pilgrims and frivolous tourists: The chimera tourism in the pilgrimages of Sri Lanka. *Annals of Tourism Research, 10*, 57-74.

Philipp, S. F. (1994). Race and tourism choice: A legacy of discrimination? *Annals of Tourism Research, 21*(3), 479-488.

Pizam, A. (1978). Tourist impacts: The social costs to the destination community as perceived by its residents. *Journal of Travel Research, 16*(1), 8-12

Pleumarom, A. (1994). The political economy of tourism. *The Ecologist, 24*(4), 142.

Podd, G., & Lesure, J. (1964). *Planning and operating hotels and motor hotels.* Columbus, OH: Ahrens Book Company, Inc.

Poirier, R.A. (1995). Tourism and development in Tunisia. *Annals of Tourism Research, 22*(1), 157-

171.

Poirier, R. (1997). Political risk analysis and tourism. *Annals of Tourism Research, 24*, 675–686.

Pons, S. (1998, March 28/29). Kruger gets back to nature. *The Weekend Australian*, p. 17.

Poon, A. (1993). *Tourism, technology and competitive strategies.* Wallingford: CAB International.

Poon, A. (1996). *Tourism cooperation in SADC—a time for action.* Johannesburg: Caribbean Futures Ltd.

Popovic, V. (1972). *Tourism in Eastern Africa.* Munich: Weltforum Verlag.

Potts, F. C., Goodwin, H., & Walpole, M. J. (1996). People, wildlife and tourism in and around Hwange national park, Zimbabwe. In M. Price (Ed.), *People and tourism in fragile environments* (pp. 199–229). Chichester: Wiley.

Pratt, C. B. (1991). Multinational corporations' social policy process for ethical responsibility in Sub Saharan Africa. *Journal of Business Ethics, 10*, 527–541.

Pratt, M. L. (1992). *Imperial eyes: Travel writing and transculturation.* London and New York: Routledge.

Prentice, R. (1993). *Tourism and heritage attractions.* London: Routledge.

Quaye, E. C. (1997). *Notes on forest conservation from perspective of the indigenous people in facing the storm, five years of research in and among Kakum National Park* (pp. 139–142). Washington, DC: Conservation International.

Rajotte, F. (1981). *The tourism industry in East Africa.* Aix-en-Provence: Centre des Hautes Etudes Touristiques.

Rajotte, F. (1983). The potential for further tourism development in Kenya's arid lands. *Kenyan Geographer, 5*(1 & 2), 133–144.

Rajotte, F. (1987). Safari and beach resort tourism Kenya. In S. G. Britton & W. C. Clarke, (Eds.), *Ambitious alternatives: Tourism in small developing countries* (pp. 78–90). Suva: University of the South.

Regional Tourism Organization of Southern Africa. (1996). *RETOSA charter.* Johannesburg: Author.

Regional Tourism Organization of Southern Africa. (1997). *Constructive cooperation in tourism.* Johannesburg: Lorton Publications.

Regional Tourism Organization of Southern Africa. (1998, April 24). *RETOSA business plan. Management paper presented to the Board of Directors.* Port Louis, Mauritius: Author.

Renninger, J. P. (1979). *Multinational co-operation in West Africa.* Oxford: Pergamon Press.

Republic of Botswana. (1990). *Tourism policy: Government paper No. 2 of 1990.* Gaborone: Government of Botswana.

Republic of Ghana National Planning Commission. (1995). *Ghana—Vision 2020.* Accra: Government Printing Office.

Republic of Ghana, United Nations Development Programme, World Tourism Organization. (1994a). *Project document for tourism development in Ghana.* Accra: UNDP.

Republic of Ghana, United Nations Development Programme, World Tourism Organization. (1994b). *Hotel and restaurant standards in Ghana—review, recommendations and training.* Accra: Ministry of Tourism.

Republic of Ghana, United Nations Development Programme, World Tourism Organization. (1995a). *Manpower development for the tourism industry in Ghana.* Accra: Ministry of Tourism.

Republic of Ghana, United Nations Development Programme, World Tourism Organization. (1995b). *Sociocultural impact of tourism in Ghana.* Accra: Ministry of Tourism.

Republic of Ghana, United Nations Development Programme, World Tourism Organization. (1995c). *Tourism public awareness programme and tourist behaviour code.* Accra: Ministry of Tourism.

Republic of Ghana, United Nations Development Programme, World Tourism Organization. (1995d). *Tourism marketing strategy and promotion programme for Ghana—1996-2000.* Accra: Ministry of Tourism.

Republic of Ghana, United Nations Development Programme, World Tourism Organization. (1996a). *Economic analysis of Ghana.* Accra: Ministry of Tourism.

Republic of Ghana, United Nations Development Programme, World Tourism Organization. (1996b). *National tourism development plan for Ghana— 1996-2010.* Accra: Ministry of Tourism.

Republic of Ghana, United Nations Development Programme, World Tourism Organization. (1996c).

Tourism development action programme for Ghana—1996-2000. Accra: Ministry of Tourism.

Republic of Ghana, United Nations Development Programme, World Tourism Organization. (1996d). *Tourism development financial plan for Ghana—1996-2000*. Accra: Ministry of Tourism.

Republic of Ghana, United Nations Development Programme, World Tourism Organization. (1996e). *Tourism project prefeasibility studies* (for ten projects throughout the country). Accra: Ministry of Tourism.

Republic of Kenya. (1966a). *Development plan for the period 1996-1970*. Nairobi: Government Printer.

Republic of Kenya. (1966b). *Economic survey 1966*. Nairobi: Government Printer.

Republic of Kenya. (1970). *Development plan for the period 1970-1974*. Nairobi: Government Printer.

Republic of Kenya. (1971a). *Proposed tourist resort on the Kenya coast: Report of the government working party*. Nairobi: Ministry of Lands and Settlement.

Republic of Kenya. (1971b). *Economic Survey 1971*. Nairobi: Government Printer.

Republic of Kenya. (1974). *Development plan for the period 1974-1978*. Nairobi: Government Printer.

Republic of Kenya. (1975). *Sessional paper No. 3 of 1975: Statement on future of wildlife management policy in Kenya*. Nairobi: Government Printer.

Republic of Kenya. (1980). *Economic survey 1980*. Nairobi: Government Printer.

Republic of Kenya. (1984). *Development plan for the period 1983-1988*. Nairobi: Government Printer.

Republic of Kenya. (1985a). *The wildlife (Conservation and Management) Act Chapter 376 Laws of Kenya*. Nairobi: Government Printer.

Republic of Kenya. (1985b). *The wildlife (Conservation and Management) Amendment Act 1989—Kenya Gazette Supplement No. 95(Acts. 9)*. Nairobi: Government Printer.

Republic of Kenya. (1989). *Development plan for the period 1989-1993*. Nairobi: Government Printer.

Republic of Kenya. (1991). *Development and employment in Kenya: A strategy for the transformation of the economy—report of the presidential committee on employment*. Nairobi: Government Printer.

Republic of Kenya. (1992). *Report of the parliamentary select committee to investigate ethnic clashes in western and other parts of Kenya 1992*. Nairobi: National Assembly.

Republic of Kenya. (1994a). *Development plan for 1994-1996*. Nairobi: Government Printer.

Republic of Kenya. (1994b). *Sessional paper No. 1 of 1994 on recovery and sustainable development to the year 2010*. Nairobi: Government Printer.

Republic of Kenya. (1994c). *Kenya forestry beyond 2000: An overview of the Kenya forestry master plan*. Nairobi: Ministry of Environment and Natural Resources.

Republic of Kenya. (1994d). *Statistical abstract 1994*. Nairobi: Government Printer.

Republic of Kenya. (1994e). *Economic survey 1994*. Nairobi: Government Printer.

Republic of Kenya. (1995). *Economic survey 1995*. Nairobi: Government Printer.

Republic of Kenya. (1996a). *Economic survey 1996*. Nairobi: Government Printer.

Republic of Kenya. (1996b). *Kenya economic reforms for 1996-1998: The policy framework paper*. Nairobi: Government of Kenya, International Monetary Fund & World Bank.

Republic of Kenya. (1997). *The eighth national development plan for the period 1997-2001*. Nairobi: Government Printer.

Republic of Kenya. (1998a). *Economic survey 1998*. Nairobi: Government Printer.

Republic of Kenya. (1998b). *Budget speech for the fiscal year 1998/99 (1st July - 30th June) by Simeon Nyachae, Minister for Finance*. Nairobi: Government Printer.

Republic of Kenya. (1998c, July 1). *Kenya Gazette*, C(36). Nairobi: Government Printer.

Republic of Lesotho. (1994). *Strategy for the development of the tourism sector*. Maseru: Government of Lesotho.

Republic of South Africa. (1995). *White paper: The development & promotion of tourism in South Africa*. Pretoria: Government of South Africa.

Republic of Swaziland. (1994). *Tourism development policy*. Mbabane, Swaziland: Government of

Swaziland.

Republic of Tanzania. (1991). *Tourism policy.* Dar-as-Salaam: Government of Tanzania.

Republic of Zambia. (1995). *Medium-term national tourism strategy & action plan for Zambia.* Harare, Zambia: Government of Zambia.

Republic of Zimbabwe. (1995). *Framework for tourism policy.* Harare, Zimbabwe: Government of Zimbabwe.

RETOSA ready for action. (1997, September 19). *Travel News Weekly.*

RETOSA recognises the operators. (1998, June). *Travel Trade Gazette South Africa.*

Rhoodie, N. (Ed.). (1972). *South African dialogue: Contrasts in South African thinking on basic race issues.* Johannesburg: McGraw-Hill.

Richards, G. (1980). Planning for the future development of the tourist sector in Kenya. In T. Pinfold & G. Norcliffe (Eds.), *Development planning in Kenya: Essays on the planning process and policy issues* (pp. 141-156, Geographical monographs 9). Ontario, Canada: York University.

Richter, L. (1980). The political use of tourism: A Philippine case study. *Journal of Developing Areas, 14,* 237-257.

Richter, L. (1989). *The politics of tourism in Asia.* Honolulu: University of Hawaii Press.

Robock, S. (1983). *International business and multinational enterprises.* Homewood, IL: Irwin Publishers.

Rodney, W. (1989). *How Europe underdeveloped Africa.* Nairobi, Kenya: Heinemann.

Roe, D., Leader-Williams, N., & Dalal-Clayton, B. (1997). *Take only photographs. Leave only footprints. The environmental impacts of wildlife tourism* (Wildlife and Development Series No. 10). London: International Institute for Environment and Development.

Rogerson, C. M. (1990). Sun international: The making of a South African tourism multinational. *GeoJournal, 22,* 345-354.

Root, F. (1987). *Entry strategies for international market.* Washington, DC: Heath and Company.

Rosen, S. (1974). Hedonic prices and implicit markets: Production differentiation in pure competition. *Journal of Political Economy, 82*(1), 34-55.

SADC leaders scrutinise RETOSA charter. (1997, September). *Africa Travel News.*

Said, E. (1978). *Orientalism: Western concepts of the Orient.* London: Routledge and Kegan Paul.

Sako, F. (1990). Tourism in Africa: An expanding industry. *The Courier, 122,* 69-72.

Salim, A. I. (1992). East Africa: The coast. In B. A. Ogot (Ed.), *General history of Africa volume V: Africa from the sixteenth to the eighteenth century* (pp. 750-775). Oxford, Berkeley, and Paris: Heinemann, California & UNESCO.

Sallie, S. S. (1994). The role of the Semitic peoples in the expansion of the world economy via the transatlantic slave trade. *Journal of Third World Studies, XI*(2), 166-201.

Schumpeter, J. A. (1965). *The theory of economic development: An enquiry into profits, credit, interest and the business cycle.* Oxford: Oxford University Press.

Shackley, M. (1993). Guest farms in Namibia: An emerging accommodation sector in Africa's hottest destination. *International Journal of Hospitality Management, 12,* 253-265.

Shackley, M. (1995). The future of gorilla tourism in Rwanda. *Journal of Sustainable Tourism, 3*(2), 61-72.

Shah, A. (1995). *The economics of Third World national parks: Issues of tourism and environmental management.* Aldershot: Edward Elgar.

Shipton, P. (1994). Land and culture in tropical Africa: Soils, symbols, and the metaphysics of the mundane. *Annual Review of Anthropology, 23,* 347-377.

Shivji, I. G. (Ed.). (1975). *Tourism and socialist development.* Dar es Salaam: Tanzania Publishing.

Sigelman, L., & Welch, S. (1991). *Black Americans' views of racial inequality: The dream deferred.* Cambridge: Cambridge University Press.

Sinclair, M. T. (1990). *Tourism development in Kenya.* Nairobi: World Bank.

Sinclair, M. T. (1992). Tour operators and policies in Kenya. *Annals of Tourism Research, 19,* 555-558.

Sinclair, M. T. (1998). Tourism and economic development: A survey. *The Journal of Development Studies, 34*(5), 1-51.

Sinclair, M. T., Alizadeh, P., & Onunga, E. A. A. (1992). The structure of international tourism development in Kenya. In D. Harrison (Ed.), *Tourism & less developed countries* (pp. 47-63). London: Belhaven Press.

Sinclair, M.T., Clewer, A., & Pack, A. (1990). Hedonic prices and the marketing of package tourism. In A. Ashworth & B. Goodall (Eds.), *Marketing tourism places* (pp. 85-103). London: Routledge.

Sinclair, M.T., & Stabler, M.J. (1997). *The economics of tourism.* London and New York: Routledge.

Sinclair, M.T., & Tsegaye, A. (1990). International tourism and export instability. *The Journal of Development Studies, 26,* 487-504.

Sindiga, I. (1994). Employment and training in tourism in Kenya. *Journal of Tourism Studies, 5*(2), 45-52.

Sindiga, I. (1995). Wildlife-based tourism in Kenya: Land use conflicts and government compensation policies over protected areas. *Journal of Tourism Studies, 6*(2), 45-55.

Sindiga, I. (1996a). Domestic tourism in Kenya. *Annals of Tourism Research, 23*(1), 19-31.

Sindiga, I. (1996b). Tourism education in Kenya. *Annals of Tourism Research, 23*(3), 698-701.

Sindiga, I., & Kanunah, M. (1998). Unplanned tourism in Sub-Saharan Africa with special reference to Kenya. *Journal of Tourism Studies, 10*(1), 25-39 .

Silvert, K. H. (1979). *Reason for democracy.* New York: The Vikings Press.

Smith, M.Y. (1998). *Commonwealth partnership for technology management.* Document distributed to participants at the Botswana National Smart Partnership Dialogue.

Smith, R.V. (1992). Tourism's role in the economy and landscape of Luxembourg. *Tourism Management, 13,* 423-428.

Smith, V. L. (1968). Economics of production from natural resources. *American Economic Review, 58*(3), 409-431.

Snepenger, D. J., & Johnson, J. D. (1991). Political self-identification and perceptions on tourism. *Annals of Tourism Research, 18,* 511-515.

Solbrig, O., & Young, M. (1992). Toward a sustainable and equitable future for savannas. *Environment, 34*(3), 3-17.

South Africa Department of Information. (1976). *South Africa 1977: Official yearbook of the Republic of South Africa.* Johannesburg: Author.

South African Tourism Update. (1997). Various articles [On-line]. http://rapidttp.com/tourism/97/97deck.html

South African Tourism Update. (1998). *The best of times and the worst of times* [On-line]. http://rapidttp.com/tourism/98/98jank.html

Southern Africa dreams of unity. (1995). *The Economist, 336*(7930), 35-36.

South Africans return to Mozambique. (1996). *The Economist 339*(7965), 44-46.

Southern African Development Community. (1992). *Declaration treaty of protocol of Southern African Development Community.* Windhoek, Namibia: Author.

Southern African Development Community. (1996). *Trade & investment: Tourism* [On-line]. http://www.sadc-usa.net/trade/tourism.html

Southern African Development Community. (1997). *Trade, industry and investment review.* Johannesburg: Author.

Southern African Development Community Secretariat. (1995). *Tourism sector.* Lilongwe, Malawi: SADC.

Southern African Development Coordination Conference Secretariat. (1981). *Lusaka declaration.* Lusaka: SADCC.

Spate, O. H. K. (1988). *The Pacific since Magellan, vol. III: Paradise found and lost.* London: Routledge.

Stamm, V. (1994). Non-commercial systems of land allocation and their economic implications: Evidence from Burkina Faso. *Journal of Modern African Studies, 32,* 713-717.

Stern, E. (1987). Competition and location in the gaming industry: The casino states of southern Africa. *Geography, 72,* 140-150.

Sugal, C. (1997). The price of habitat. *World Watch, 10*(3), 18-30.

Sugg, I., & Kreuter, U. (1994). *Elephants and ivory: Lessons from the trade ban.* London: Institute of Economic Affairs.

Summary, R. M. (1987). Tourism's contribution to the economy of Kenya. *Annals of Tourism Research, 14,* 531-540.

Survey: Eritrea. (1996, January 18). *The Financial Times*.

Swainson, N. (1980). *The development of corporate capitalism in Kenya, 1918-77*. London: Heinemann.

Swarbrooke, J. (1994). The future of the past: Heritage tourism in the 21st century. In A. V. Seaton, C. L. Jenkins, R. C. Wood, P. U. C. Dieke, M. M. Bennett, R. MacLellan, & R. Smith (Eds.), *Tourism: The state of the art* (pp. 222-229). Chichester: John Wiley.

Swiss Government. (1981). *The roles and responsibilities of Swiss tourist organisation*. Berne: Government Printer

Taylor, P. J. (1994). *Political geography: World-economy, nation-state and locality* (3rd ed.). New York: Wiley.

Taylor, R. (1995). *From liability to asset: Wildlife in the Omay communal land of Zimbabwe* (Wildlife and Development Series No. 8). London: International Institute for Environment and Development in association with the CAMPFIRE Collaborative Group.

Temperley, H. (1996). New world slavery, old world slavery. In M. L. Bush (Ed.), *Serfdom and slavery: Studies in legal bondage* (pp. 144-157). New York: Longman.

Tesfamichael, W. (1993). *Development of tourism in Eritrea*. Paper presented to First Conference for the Consideration of Different Policy Issues for the Development of Tourism in Eritrea. Asmara: Ministry of Trade, Industry and Tourism.

Teye, V. B. (1986). Liberation wars and tourism development in Africa: The case of Zambia. *Annals of Tourism Research, 13*(4), 589-608.

Teye, V. B. (1988). Coups d'etat and African tourism: A study of Ghana. *Annals of Tourism Research, 15*(3), 329-356.

Teye, V. B. (1991). Prospects for regional tourism cooperation in Africa. In S. Medlik (Ed.), *Managing tourism* (pp. 286-296). Oxford: Butterworth Heinemann.

The tourism industry on the mend. (1998, May 22). *The Weekly Review*, pp. 17-18.

Thomas, S. (1995). *Share and share alike? Equity in CAMPFIRE* (Wildlife and Development Series No. 2). London: International Institute for Environment and Development in association with the CAMPFIRE Collaborative Group.

Thomason, P., Crompton, J. L., & Kamp, D. B. (1979). A study of the attitude of impacted groups within host community toward prolonged stay tourist visitors. *Journal of Travel Research, 17*(3), 2-6.

Tibazarwa, C. M. (1988). The East African community—a tragedy in regional cooperation. *The Courier, 112*, 48-50.

Timewell, S. (1997). South Africa starts to roar. *The Banker, 147*(858), 48-50.

Todaro, M. P. (1986). *Economics for a developing world* (2nd ed.). Harlow, Essex: Longman.

Todaro, M. (1997). *Economic development* (6th ed.). London: Longman

Tosun, C. (1998). *Local community participation in the tourism development process: The case of Urgup in Turkey*. Unpublished Ph.D. dissertation, The Scottish Hotel School, University of Strathclyde, Glasgow.

Tosun, C., & Jenkins, C. L. (1998). The evolution of tourism planning in third world countries: A critique. *Progress in Tourism & Hospitality Research, 4*, 101-114.

Tourism earnings fall: Board blames coast violence. (1998, January 6). *East African Standard Business and Finance*, p. 7.

Travel and Tourism Intelligence. (1997). Zimbabwe. *International Tourism Reports, 3*, 75-89.

Truong, T-D. (1990). *Sex, money, & morality: Prostitution and tourism in South East Asia*. London: Zed Books.

Tse, E. C., & Olsen, M. D. (1991). Strategies of global hospitality firms. In R. Teare & A. Boer (Eds.), *Strategic hospitality management* (pp. 58-65). London: Cassell.

Tse, E. C. Y., & West, J. (1992). Development strategies for international hospitality markets. In R. Teare & A. Boer (Eds.), *Strategic hospitality management* (pp. 118-134). London: Cassell.

Tupouniua, S., Crocombe, R., & Slater, C. (Eds.). (1980). *The Pacific way: Social issues in national development*. Suva: South Pacific Social Sciences Association.

Turner, L. (1976). The international division of leisure: Tourism in the third world. *World Development, 4*, 253-260.

Turner, L., & Ash, J. (1975). *The golden hordes. International tourism and the pleasure periphery.* London: Constable.

United Nations. (1996). *World investment report 1995: Transnational corporations & competitiveness* (Ref. No. 95 II A.9). New York: United Nations.

United Nations Conference on Trade and Development. (1994). *Handbook of international trade and development statistics.* New York: United Nations.

United Nations Conference on Trade and Development. (1998a). *International trade in tourism-related services: Issues and options for developing countries* (TD/B/COM.1/EM.6/2). Geneva: Author.

United Nations Conference on Trade and Development. (1998b). *Report of the expert meeting on strengthening the capacity for expanding the tourism sector in developing countries, with particular focus on tour operators, travel agencies and other suppliers* (TD/B/COM.1/17-TD/B/COM.1/EM.EM.6/3). Geneva: Author.

United Nations Development Programme. (1993). *Guidelines for project formulation and the project document format.* New York: Author.

United States Agency for Internation Development & Shell Botswana. (1995). *Investment opportunities in the tourism industry and investment guide.* Gaborone: Shell Botswana.

Van den Breemer, J. P. M., Drijver, C. A., & Venema, L. B. (1995). *Local resource management in Africa.* Chichester: John Wiley.

van der Ploeg, F., & Tang, P. (1994). Growth, deficits, and research and development in the global economy. In F. van der Ploeg & P. Tang (Eds.), *The handbook of international macroeconomics* (pp. 535-579). Oxford: Basil Blackwell.

Vanderpost, C. (1995). Population change and environmental problems in the mid-Boteti region of Botswana. *GeoJournal, 35,* 521-529.

van de Walle, N., & Johnstone, T. J. (1966). *Improving aid to Africa—policy essay, 21.* Washington, DC: Overseas Development Council.

Walden Publishers (Ed.). (1996). *The world business and economic review 1996.* London: Kogan Page.

Wallerstein, I. (1979). *The capitalist world-economy.* Cambridge: Cambridge University Press.

Waters, M. (1995). *Globalization.* London: Routledge.

Weaver, D. (1998a). Peripheries of the periphery: Tourism in Tobago and Barbuda. *Annals of Tourism Research, 25*(2), 292-313.

Weaver, D. (1998b). *Ecotourism in the less developed world.* Wallingford: CAB International.

Weaver, D. B., & Elliott, K. (1996). Spatial patterns and problems in contemporary Namibian tourism. *Geographical Journal, 162*(2), 205-217.

Welford, R., & Gouldson, A. (1993). *Environmental management and business strategy.* London: Pitman.

Wellings, A., & Crush, J. (1983). Tourism and dependency in Southern Africa: The prospect and planning of tourism in Lesotho. *Applied Geography, 3,* 205-223.

Western, D., & Wright, R. M. (Eds.). (1994). *Natural connections—perspectives in community-based conservation.* Washington, DC: Shirley C. Strum.

Wheat, S. (Ed.). (1997). Wildlife tourism. *Tourism in Focus, 23.*

Wheatcroft, S. (1994). *Aviation & tourism policies: Balancing the benefits.* New York: Routledge.

White, O. C., & Bhatia, A. (1998). *Privatization in Africa.* Washington DC: The World Bank.

Wilkin, D. (1989). Spatial patterns of human ecosystem productivity in South West Africa (Namibia). *GeoForum, 20,* 329-337.

Wilkinson, P. F. (1997). *Tourism policy & planning: Case studies from the Commonwealth Caribbean.* New York: Cognizant Communication.

Willis, K. G. (1989). Option value and non-user benefits of wildlife conservation. *Journal of Rural Studies, 5*(3), 245-256.

World Bank. (1980-97). *World development report.* Oxford: Oxford University Press.

World Bank. (1989). *Sub-Saharan Africa: From crisis to sustainable growth—a long-term perspective study.* Washington, DC: Author.

World Bank. (1994). *Eritrea: Options for strategies and growth.* Washington, DC: Author.

World Bank. (1996). *World debt tables*. Washington, DC: Author.

World Bank. (1997). *World development report 1997: The state in a changing world*. New York: Oxford University Press.

World Bank. (1998a). *World development report, 1997. Summary*. Washington, DC: Author.

World Bank. (1998b). *The World Bank annual report 1997*. Washington, DC: Author.

World Commission on Environment and Development. (1987). *Our common future*. Oxford and New York: Oxford University Press.

World Investment Report. (1995). *Transnational corporations and competitiveness*. New York: United Nations Conference on Trade and Development, Division of Transnational Corporations and Investment.

World Resources Institute. (1994). *World resources 1994-95: A guide to the global environment*. New York: Oxford University Press.

World Tourism Organization. (1983). *Zanzibar. Tourism master plan. Research findings and recommendations*. Madrid: Author.

World Tourism Organization. (1990). *Tourism to the year 2000: Qualititative aspects affecting global growth*. Madrid: Author.

World Tourism Organization. (1991). *Integrated tourism resorts—an executive summary*. Madrid: Author.

World Tourism Organization. (1993). *Sustainable tourism development: Guide for local planners*. Madrid: Author.

World Tourism Organization. (1994). *National and regional tourism planning: Methodologies and case studies*. London and New York: Routledge.

World Tourism Organization. (1995). *Tourism market trends, Africa: 1985-1994*. Madrid: Author.

World Tourism Organization. (1996a). *Budgets of national tourism administrations: A special report*. Madrid: Author.

World Tourism Organization. (1996b). *Compendium of tourism statistics, 1990-1994: Sixteenth edition*. Madrid: Author.

World Tourism Organization. (1997a). *Yearbook of tourism statistics* (49th ed.). Madrid: Author.

World Tourism Organization. (1997b). *Tourism highlights*. Madrid: Author.

World Tourism Organization. (1997c). *Tourism market trends—Africa*. Madrid: Author.

World Tourism Organization. (1997d). UNESCO-WTO cultural and tourism project on "The Slave Route" Item 9 of the provisional agenda of the 30th meeting of WTO Commission for Africa (CAF) held in Addis Ababa, Ethiopia between 23 and 26 April (CAF/30/9).

World Tourism Organization. (1997e). *Tourism 2020 vision*. Madrid: Author.

World Tourism Organization. (1998a). *Tourism highlights 1997*. Madrid: Author.

World Tourism Organization. (1998b). *Tourism: 2020 vision*. Madrid: Author.

World Tourism Organization. (1998c). *Tourism market trends, 1998 edition— Africa*. Madrid: Author.

World Tourism Organization. (1998d). *Guide for local authorities on developing sustainable tourism*. Madrid: Author.

World Tourism Organization. (1999). *Tourism market trends, 1999 edition—Africa*. Madrid: Author.

World Tourism Organization, United Nations Environmental Program. (1982). *Joint declaration on tourism in the environment*. Madrid: World Tourism Organization.

World Tourism Organization, World Travel and Tourism Council, The Earth Council. (1995). *Agenda 21 for the travel and tourism industry: Towards environmentally sustainable development*. Madrid: World Tourism Organization.

Young, G. (1973). *Tourism: Blessing or blight?* Harmondsworth: Pengium.

Young, J. (1997). *Income generation for Jozani adjacent communities*. Zanzibar, Tanzania: Zanzibar Commission for Tourism.

Zanzibar Commission for Tourism. (1998). *International tourist arrivals by nationalities*. Zanzibar, Tanzania: Author.

Index

Tourism
Tourism
Tourism
Tourism
Tourism
Tourism
Tourism
Tourism
Tourism
Tourism
Tourism
Tourism
Tourism
Tourism
Tourism
Tourism
Tourism
Tourism
Tourism
Tourism
Tourism
Tourism
Tourism
Tourism

ANNOUNCING
"TOURISM DYNAMICS"
BOOK SERIES

TOURISM POLICY AND PLANNING:
Case Studies from the Commonwealth Caribbean
Paul Wilkinson, York University, Canada
(H) 1-882345-12-6 $38.00 (S) 1-882345-13-4 $30.00
Pub. Date July '97

CASINO GAMBLING IN AMERICA Origins,
Trends & Impacts
Klaus J. Meyer-Arendt, Rudi Hartmand,
Mississippi State University, USA
(H) 1-882345-16-9 $38.00 (S) 1-882345-17-7 $30.00
Pub. Date August '97

TOURISM DEVELOPMENT IN CRITICAL ENVIRONMENT
Tej Vir Singh & Shalini Singh,
Ctr. for Tourism Research & Development, India
(H) 1-882345-18-5 $38.00 (S) 1-882345-19-3 $30.00
Pub. Date November '97

TOURISM & GAMING ON AMERICAN INDIAN LANDS
Alan A. Lew, George A. Van Otten,
Northern Arizona University
(S) 1-882345-21-5 $30.00   Pub. Date December '98

SEX TOURISM AND PROSTITUTION
Martin Opperman, Griffith University, Gold Coast
(H) 1-882345-14-2 $38.00 (S) 1-882345-15-0$30.00
Pub. Date July '98

EVENT MANAGEMENT & EVENT TOURISM
Donald Getz, University of Calgary, Canada
(H) 1-882345-11-8 $74.50 (S) 1-882345-10-0$59.50
Pub. Date January '97

THE POLITICAL ECONOMY OF TOURISM DEVELOPMENT IN AFRICA
Peter U.C. Dieke, University of Strathclyde
(H) 1-882345-26-6 $74.50 (S) 1-882345-25-8$62.50
Pub. Date TBA

EVENT MANAGEMENT

An International Journal
Formerly
FESTIVAL MANAGEMENT & EVENT TOURISM

Editor-in-Chief:
Donald Getz, Ph.D.
Tourism Management
The Univ. of Calgary
2500 University Dr. N.W.
Calgary T2N 1N4, Canada
t: 403-220-7158 f:403-282-0095
e: getz@acs.ucalgary.ca

Aims & Scope:

Event Management, An International Journal intends to meet the research and analytic needs of a rapidly growing profession focused on events. This field has developed in size and impact globally to become a major business with numerous dedicated facilities, and a large-scale generator of tourism. The field encompasses meetings, conventions, festivals, expositions, sport and other special events. *Event Management* is also of considerable importance to government agencies and not-for-profit organizations in pursuit of a variety of goals including fund-raising, the fostering of causes and community development.

Event Management aims to be the leading source of research reports and analysis related to all forms of event management. This journal publishes refereed and invited articles, book reviews, and documentation of news and trends. It also invites opinion pieces, profiles or organizations, and management case studies.

Event Management is governed by an international board of editors consisting of experts in event management and related fields. This board conducts most of the article reviews and therefor plays a large role in setting the standards for research and publication in the field. The Editor-in-Chief receives and processes all manuscripts, from time to time, modifies and works to ensure a continuous improvement in quality.

Event Management is published quarterly, and sold by annual subscription only. The Editor-in-Chief, Editorial Board Members and the Publisher are not responsible for views expressed by the contributors.

EVENT MANAGEMENT: An International Journal
Beginning with Volume 6, 2000. Published quarterly (ISSN-1525-9951)

Subscription (*sold on a calendar years basis on volume numbers announced*)

	US & Canada	Rest of the World
Annual Library Rate, Vol. 6 (2000):	$150.00	$165.00
2 years, Vols. 6 & 7:	$270.00	$297.00.
Professional Subscription, Vol. 6:	$45.00	$60.00
IFEA Members, Vol. 6:	$40.00	$55.00.

FESTIVAL MANAGEMENT & EVENT TOURISM (1993-1999)
Volumes 1-5 w/index: $160.00 per volume.

Publisher: **Cognizant Communication Corp.** 3 Hartsdale Road, Elmsford, NY 10523
Phone: 914-592-7720, Fax 914-592-8981, Email: cogcomm@aol.com.
website: www.cognizantcommunication.com.